GETTING
AWAY
WITH
TORTURE

Related Titles from Potomac Books, Inc.

The Four Freedoms Under Siege: The Clear and Present Danger from Our National Security State—Marcus Raskin and Robert Spero

War and Destiny: How the Bush Revolution in Foreign and Military Affairs Redefined American Power—James Kitfield

———•••———

Also by Christopher H. Pyle

Extradition, Politics, and Human Rights

Military Surveillance of Civilian Politics, 1967–1970

The President, Congress, and the Constitution: Power and Legitimacy in American Politics, with Richard M. Pious

GETTING AWAY WITH TORTURE

Secret Government, War Crimes,
and the Rule of Law

CHRISTOPHER H. PYLE

POTOMAC BOOKS, INC.
WASHINGTON, D.C.

Published in the United States by Potomac Books, Inc. All rights reserved.

Library of Congress Cataloging-in-Publication Data
Pyle, Christopher H.
  Getting away with torture : secret government, war crimes, and the rule of law / Christopher H. Pyle. — 1st ed.
      p. cm.
  Includes bibliographical references and index.
  ISBN 978-1-59797-387-8 (hardcover : alk. paper)
  1. Torture—Government policy—United States. 2. Prisoners of war—Abuse of—United States. 3. Secrecy—Political aspects—United States. 4. War crimes—United States. 5. Rule of law—United States. 6. United States—Politics and government—2001– 7. War on Terrorism, 2001– I. Title.
  HV8599.U6P95 2009
  973.931—dc22

                                                                    2009003324

Printed in the United States of America on acid-free paper that meets the American National Standards Institute Z39-48 Standard.

Potomac Books, Inc.
22841 Quicksilver Drive
Dulles, Virginia 20166

First Edition

10 9 8 7 6 5 4 3 2 1

Rob Reiner's 1992 film *A Few Good Men*, written by Aaron Sorkin, ends with a courtroom confrontation between Col. Nathan Jessep (Jack Nicholson) and Lt. Daniel Kaffee (Tom Cruise). Kaffee is a U.S. Navy lawyer who wants to know what happened at Guantánamo Bay one night, when a young man under Jessep's command was beaten to death. Jessep is in the witness chair.

> JESSEP: You want answers?
> KAFFEE: I think I'm entitled to them.
> JESSEP: You want answers?
> KAFFEE: I want the truth!
> JESSEP: You can't handle the truth!

☞ **This book is dedicated to those who can.**

"All nationalists have the power of not seeing resemblances between similar sets of facts. . . . Actions are held to be good or bad, not on their own merits, but according to who does them, and there is almost no kind of outrage— torture, . . . imprisonment without trial, . . . assassination, . . .—which does not change its moral colour when it is committed by 'our' side. . . . The nationalist not only does not disapprove of atrocities committed by his own side, but he has a remarkable capacity for not even hearing about them."

—GEORGE ORWELL[1]

contents

preface

Writing this book was like chasing a moving target. When I began, the central question was whether the torture and abuse of suspected terrorists at Abu Ghraib, Guantánamo, and elsewhere by their American captors were the work of a few rotten apples or the predictable result of President George W. Bush's decision to suspend operation of the Geneva Conventions. I thought I might begin, as I had in the early 1970s when I investigated the U.S. Army's domestic intelligence operations, by interviewing former intelligence agents. But it quickly became apparent that the nation's best reporters were on the case, generating more information about the torture policy than all but a full-time observer could possibly digest.

So I undertook to place the crimes they uncovered in a larger bureaucratic, historical, and legal context. This approach led me to analyze the administration's legal arguments in light of what I knew, not just as a professor of constitutional law and civil liberties, but as a former military intelligence officer.

Extraordinary rendition had also caught my attention. In 2001 I had published a book entitled *Extradition, Politics, and Human Rights,* so I knew about Justice Department attempts to transform the United States from a nation of asylum into one that surrenders political fugitives to unjust regimes for reasons of state. I was acquainted with Supreme Court decisions that allow the executive branch to kidnap suspected drug lords and terrorists from foreign lands for trial in the United States. I also remembered how President George H. W. Bush invaded Panama, killing nearly a thousand people, in order to seize one criminal and deliver him for trial in Miami. Then that president's son went him one better. George W. Bush secretly authorized the Central Intelligence Agency (CIA) to kidnap suspected terrorists (some of whom turned out to be innocent) from European countries (often with the complicity of their secret agencies) and turn them over to the intelligence agencies of Egypt, Syria, Jordan, and Morocco, where they were interrogated under torture. That unprecedented development was strong evidence that the rule of law no longer mattered to American officials in power.

Then came the pictures from Abu Ghraib. Revealed to the world in an April 2004 episode of *60 Minutes II,* they proved what many generals and military lawyers predicted would happen once the commander in chief decreed that American soldiers were no longer bound by the Geneva Conventions. But a series of military inquiries, designed to protect the generals and their civilian superiors from legal scrutiny, made it increasingly clear that the highest officials in the Pentagon, the Justice Department, the CIA, and the White House not only knew about but had authorized, approved, and encouraged the torture and degradation of suspected terrorists. That revelation should not have come as a surprise. In November 2001, President Bush had authorized the use of military commissions to try alleged terrorists on the basis of information obtained by torture, but that signal had passed beneath most people's radar.

Also new was the illegal hiding of "ghost prisoners" from the International Committee of the Red Cross's inspections and the CIA's creation of secret prisons in Thailand, Afghanistan, Poland, Romania, and elsewhere. With snatch teams dressed like ninjas and employing a fleet of chartered aircraft, the CIA made suspected terrorists "disappear," as if the United States were little more than a Latin American dictatorship. Many of these prisoners still have not been found.

By the fall of 2004, the cumulative evidence was indisputable: the torture, cruelty, and degradation revealed in those Abu Ghraib pictures were not merely the work of a few "bad apples" but were the result of a conscious policy of the Bush administration—a policy imposed on a professional military that would have preferred, by and large, to follow the laws of war they had once championed. But as opinion polls and popular television programs like *24* demonstrated, a sizable minority of Americans, including a majority of Republicans, approved of torture in one form or another.[1] They wanted revenge for the atrocities of September 11, 2001. They did not know or care that more than 90 percent of the men and boys tormented at Guantánamo Bay had not been captured in combat but had been sold to the United States for large bounties. Further, most of the torture had not been conducted to obtain "actionable intelligence." The time for that had passed. The cruelties and degradations were meant to extract confessions, true or false, in order to justify continued detentions. Or the abuse was entertainment for guards, like those at Abu Ghraib, who lacked responsible supervision.

By the fall of 2004, the entire world knew of and condemned the Bush administration for its lies and hypocrisy about the torture policy. The condemnations were especially strong among people who once had faith in the United States as a leader in human rights. America's politicians and people might be flawed, as all leaders and people are, but its institutionalized commitment to liberty, justice, and the rule of law had once seemed indisputable.

Now that commitment is in doubt. To people in other lands who shared in the American dream, "Cowboy America" seems to have supplanted the founders' America. The Statue of Liberty, long the iconic image of America's promise, has been replaced by a hooded man standing on a box, with electrodes attached to his fingers.

In 2004 a coalition of Republicans, conservatives, and Southern evangelicals ignored widespread reports of torture to reelect George W. Bush for another four years. Why so many people should care so little about the administration's torture policy was deeply puzzling. For centuries American courts had refused to admit statements obtained by torture as evidence because they were unreliable, if not depraved.

Part of the explanation for the voters' indifference to the administration's policy may lie in the rationalizing force of the "ticking bomb" scenario, which is the most striking moral and practical hoax ever perpetrated on the American people. The widespread acceptance of that hoax, whose logic is contrary to what professional interrogators were saying at the time, suggests that the trauma of 9/11 may have stripped these voters of the capacity to think rationally. Not all voters suffered from this state, of course, but enough did to decide a closely fought election.[2] Many voters also seemed to believe that most covert operations succeed when, in fact, most fail. Whatever the explanation, the administration's policy of torturing prisoners and degrading their religious faith instilled deep hatred of the United States and generated more future terrorists than anything Osama bin Laden could possibly have done.

Congress and the courts are supposed to provide a brake on ill-advised and illegal presidential actions. This time, and progressively since World War II and the Cold War, legislators and judges have failed to exercise their oversight function, which has caused me to question why. It is not enough to expose the administration's wrongdoing or to explain why so many Bush administration officials were guilty of war crimes. We need to also ask why Congress would grant those officials amnesty, why federal judges would protect them from civil suits, and why congressional Democrats—and, perhaps, President Barack Obama— would let his predecessors get away with torture.

At the time of Watergate, Arthur M. Schlesinger, Jr., belatedly warned that "the American President ha[s] become on issues of war and peace the most absolute monarch (with the possible exception of Mao Tse-tung of China) among the great powers of the world."[3] In 1974, Richard M. Nixon was driven from office for using covert operatives to steal an election, a scandal he probably would have survived had he not kept tapes of his conversations. In the mid- to late 1980s, Ronald Reagan's administration got away with running a secret war against Nicaragua, in defiance of congressional opposition, and secretly funded it with profits it obtained by illegally selling arms to a terrorist nation. Now another Republican administration is getting away with torture.

In significant respects, it would appear that Nixon's successors have achieved his ambition. The United States is no longer a constitutional government under law. Thanks to helpful legislators and judges, its president is now an elected monarch who can, if he chooses, commit criminal acts with impunity. He need not think of himself as a constitutional officer pledged to uphold the Constitution and laws against all enemies, foreign and domestic. He can operate like an Afghan warlord with legions of kidnappers, covert paramilitary units, and clandestine prisons at his disposal.

At the moment, no one has any timely or effective legal protection against this warlord. Neither Congress nor the courts is disposed to confront this elected monarch until the terrorist threat, which the Republican Party has recklessly striven to make perpetual, has passed.

As a result, the United States is in the worst constitutional crisis in its history. Many of the wrongs for which the American colonists went to war in 1776 now pale in comparison to the crimes the Bush administration committed. Even during the bitter Civil War, neither side instituted a policy of torture.

The Bush administration is history; however, its legacy remains, not just in memory, but in legislation, legal doctrines, and clandestine agencies. President Obama has ordered the military to close Guantánamo and the CIA to shutter its secret prisons, but nothing in the law clearly bars their revival. Nothing short of criminal prosecution of the torture team will allow the U.S. government to reclaim its moral standing and reestablish the sacred principle that no one—not even a wartime president—is above the law. To do that, an amnesty will have to be repealed. New laws curbing secrecy must be passed. The word needs to go forth that the American people will not tolerate war crimes, no matter who commits them, and that no one has the authority to torture or degrade prisoners even if they are suspected or convicted terrorists.

Unfortunately, the new president and Congress have yet to demonstrate that they will defend the Constitution, bring the criminals to justice, curb secret government, and restore the rule of law before the elected monarchy that Schlesinger warned against becomes permanent.

CHRISTOPHER H. PYLE
SOUTH HADLEY, MASSACHUSETTS

1

A POLICY OF TORTURE

No president has ever done more for human rights than I have.
—George W. Bush[1]

On April 28, 2004, during oral arguments over the detention of alleged terrorists, Supreme Court justice Ruth Bader Ginsburg searched for a principle that might limit the Bush administration's claims to unlimited power in times of war. "Suppose," she mused, "the executive says, 'Mild torture, we think, will help get this information.' Some systems do that to get information."

"Well, our executive doesn't," Deputy Solicitor General Paul Clement replied.[2] Eight hours later the first photographs of prisoner abuse at the Abu Ghraib prison in Iraq appeared on national television.[3]

The idea that American soldiers would torture, humiliate, and degrade prisoners shocked viewers everywhere, but they shouldn't have been surprised. Maintaining self-restraint within an army of occupation while fighting an insurgency has always been difficult, and the My Lai massacre wasn't that long ago.

The day after the photographs were broadcast on CBS television, Gen. James Mattis noticed a group of Marines huddled around a television outside a mess tent in Al Asad, Iraq. "What's going on?" he asked the men. "Some assholes have just lost the war for us," a lance corporal replied.[4] Few Americans were as quick as the corporal to comprehend the pictures' significance, but General Mattis did. "When you lose the moral high ground," he explained later, "you lose it all."[5]

Secretary of Defense Donald Rumsfeld recognized that he had a public relations disaster on his hands. He had sat on the pictures for nearly four months, until CBS made them public. Then he tried to dismiss the abuse they revealed as "an exceptional, isolated . . . case."[6] President George W. Bush did the same, portraying the images as the "disgraceful conduct by a few" soldiers on the night shift.[7] But that was not what administration officials had been told before the pictures leaked. As the following pages will explain, the Red Cross had apprised them that prisoner abuse was widespread, happening not only in Iraq but in Afghanistan; at the U.S. Navy's base at Guantánamo Bay, Cuba; and at the CIA-run secret prisons. It had even occurred at federal detention centers to the immigrants Attorney General John Ashcroft rounded up after 9/11.[8]

In 2003, long before the military conducted its first torture investigation, the International Committee of the Red Cross (ICRC) reported more than 250 allegations of prisoner abuse to military commanders.[9] ICRC investigators warned the Defense Department's highest officials that the interrogation methods employed in Iraq constituted "an intentional system of cruel, unusual, and degrading treatment and a form of torture."[10]

Former secretary of defense James Schlesinger headed a blue-ribbon panel in 2004 that acknowledged approximately 300 allegations of prisoner abuse in Afghanistan, Iraq, and Guantánamo.[11] Since then, courts have ordered the release of more than 100,000 documents demonstrating direct torture and abuse by American authorities in Afghanistan, Iraq, Cuba, and the United States.[12] Meanwhile, journalists have reported that the CIA kidnapped as many as a hundred suspects for interrogation by brutal intelligence agencies in Egypt, Jordan, Syria, Morocco, Uzbekistan, Iraq, Afghanistan, and Pakistan.

By April 2006, Human Rights Watch was able to document more than 330 cases of prisoner abuse, involving approximately 460 prisoners and 600 military and civilian personnel.[13] Since April 2004, when the Abu Ghraib photographs were made public, about 800 military investigations have led to disciplinary action against more than 250 service personnel, including 89 who have been convicted at courts-martial.[14] The first of these investigations, conducted by Maj. Gen. Antonio Taguba, found "numerous incidents of sadistic, blatant, and wanton criminal abuses," which, contrary to the administration's spin, added up to the "systematic and illegal abuse of detainees."[15] Those investigations found that at least 98 prisoners died in U.S. custody between October 2001 and February 2006. Of those, 34 deaths were suspected or confirmed homicides.[16] At least 8 prisoners died from injuries sustained during interrogations.[17] The army's files on Abu Ghraib alone contain 1,325 photos and 93 videos, including 37 images of dogs being used to terrorize prisoners and 546 pictures of prisoners who died in custody.[18] Most of these, especially those involving the abuse of women, have never been made public.

Abuses this extensive cannot be attributed to a few "bad apples" in the enlisted ranks. Nor can responsibility be confined to those military officers who failed to adequately train and discipline their interrogators and guards. As we shall see, the highest officials in the Bush administration authorized, expected, encouraged, and protected the torture and abuse of prisoners.

A Metaphorical War

The hijackings and killings on September 11, 2001, were crimes that nineteen suicidal young men carried out on behalf of a loosely organized criminal syndicate. Motivated by a desire for revenge against military and economic policies that few Americans understood, their attacks were atrocious. To a furious and frightened American public, their scale made them appear to be an act of war, but they were, legally speaking, no more an act of war than Timothy McVeigh's 1995 bombing of a federal building in Oklahoma City. To point this fact out, even with the passage of time, seems cruelly insensitive, but it is central to an understanding of what went wrong afterward.

In the wake of al Qaeda's attacks, the United States was the beneficiary of enormous sympathy and support. Had the U.S. response stopped with the invasion of Afghanistan, much of that support would have remained, and al Qaeda and its copycats would have been the worse for it. But the Bush administration struck back with military fury and, in the end, strengthened its adversary and became the object of worldwide contempt.

The metaphor of war clearly expressed the vengeance that most Americans demanded after 9/11, but it also made a nuanced, calibrated, pragmatic response difficult, if not impossible. In a time of war, officials find it easy to assume that the end will justify almost any means, without reflecting on how a disgraceful means, like torture, can actually make the situation worse.

The rhetoric of war, which exaggerates the conflict's "us versus them" dimension, also creates the illusion that victory is possible. But victory is possible only if there are armies to defeat and leaders who can negotiate a surrender. In a guerrilla-style conflict, military victory is impossible. The best that can be achieved against an insurgency is a tolerable reduction in violence until a change in generations alters political realities.

Gen. David H. Petraeus, who in 2007 was put in charge of the multinational force in Iraq after all seemed lost, is one of those rare soldiers who understands the political nature of such conflicts. In the course of rewriting the army's field manual on counterinsurgency warfare, he came to realize that "war" was not an apt description of what his forces faced. War involves the overwhelming use of force. In counterterrorism operations, "soft" power, including diplomacy and foreign aid, is often more effective.[19] But in 2001, no one in a position of power was capable of subtlety or indirection. They were furious. Congress was enraged. The public wanted revenge.

"Kicking Ass": The Torture Policy Takes Shape

No one felt this rage more strongly than President George W. Bush. Richard Clarke, the White House's chief for counterterrorism at the time, recalled the meeting held the evening of September 11, when a furious President Bush declared, "Everything is available for the pursuit of this war. Any barriers in your way, they are gone." When Secretary of Defense Donald Rumsfeld noted that international law allowed the use of force only to prevent future attacks and not for retribution, Bush yelled, "No! I don't care what the international lawyers say, we are going to kick some ass!"[20]

Kick-ass thinking also dominated the meeting of the National Security Council (NSC) on September 12. When Federal Bureau of Investigation (FBI) director Robert S. Mueller warned that the government would have to avoid coercion in order to prosecute the attackers' accomplices, Attorney General John Ashcroft interrupted: "Let's stop the discussion right here. . . . The chief mission of U.S. law enforcement . . . is to stop another attack and apprehend any accomplices before they hit again. If we can't bring them to trial, so be it."[21] No one stopped to ask what would become of the accomplices after the use of coercion made their prosecution in ordinary courts impossible.

Bush remained furious five days later when he spoke to survivors at the still smoldering Pentagon: "I know an act of war was declared against America. . . .

[T]his is a different type of enemy. . . . There are no rules, . . . but we're going to smoke them out. And we are adjusting our thinking. . . . I want justice. . . . Dead or alive."[22]

Vice President Richard B. Cheney was no less adamant. "We also have to work through sort of the dark side, if you will," he told NBC's *Meet the Press.* "[I]t's going to be vital for us to use any means at our disposal, basically, to achieve our objective. . . . It is a mean, nasty, dangerous, dirty business out there, and we have to operate in that arena."[23]

The attacks of September 11 gave the vice president the opportunity he had long sought to expand executive power over clandestine operations, a power he believed Congress had curbed too radically in the 1970s. The Watergate investigation, Cheney believed, was just "a political ploy by [President Nixon's] enemies"[24] and not a legitimate inquiry into the burglaries Nixon's staff had ordered to find information with which to discredit the president's critics. The congressional investigations into the misuse of intelligence agencies to spy on the civil rights and anti–Vietnam War movements were attempts to exploit a weakened presidency and create an even stronger Congress. As a House member of the joint Iran-Contra Committee in the mid-1980s, Cheney considered Lt. Col. Oliver North a hero and not a criminal for illegally selling arms to Iran, then designated a terrorist state, and using the proceeds to support a secret war against the left-leaning Sandinista regime in Nicaragua—all in defiance of congressional prohibitions. That North had shredded documents and falsified records to obstruct a congressional inquiry into his crimes did not seem to bother the future vice president. The minority report that he and other conservative Republicans filed with the Iran-Contra Committee's report defended North's lawbreaking and blamed Congress for exceeding its constitutional authority and refusing to appropriate funds for the covert war.[25] He would make similar allegations of congressional overreaching after 9/11 to advance executive-centered government at the expense of constitutionally mandated checks and balances.

Secret Assertions of Unlimited Power

While President Bush was still deciding whether it was safe to return to Washington, Cheney and his legal aide, David S. Addington, were in the White House bunker deep below the East Wing, discussing what emergency powers the administration would need to deal with the crisis. Addington had joined the CIA's legal office right out of law school, moved to the House Intelligence Committee, and joined up with Cheney when, as the committee's ranking minority member, Cheney sought to protect President Reagan from the Iran-Contra Committee's investigations. Addington wrote the minority report.

Immediately after the attacks of 9/11, Addington contacted Timothy E. Flanigan, deputy White House counsel. He, in turn, contacted John C. Yoo, a young attorney in the Office of Legal Counsel (OLC), the Justice Department's legal brain trust. White House counsel Alberto Gonzales joined them later. According to Bradford A. Berenson, then an associate White House counsel, "Addington, Flanigan and Gonzales were really a triumvirate. Yoo was a supporting player."[26] Addington dominated the group, which would come to include William "Jim" Haynes II, Rumsfeld's general counsel.

The group, which met every few weeks to plot legal strategy, deliberately excluded Attorney General John Ashcroft; Jay S. Bybee, Yoo's superior at the OLC; the National Security Council legal staff; military lawyers; and William H. Taft IV, the State Department's legal adviser. The group's members called themselves the War Council.[27] Its work was done in great secrecy. The vice president's office was so secretive that it would not even disclose who worked there.[28]

For Cheney, and Ashcroft, the war on terrorism was about prevention, not prosecution.[29] The vice president would become an unrelenting advocate for detaining suspects on the merest suspicions, exaggerating terrorist capabilities, disregarding the evidentiary standards of American law, and encouraging brutal interrogations. With the largest vice presidential staff in history and access to all the e-mail traffic "in, out, and between" members of the NSC staff, he was in a perfect position to affect outcomes. Cheney could also work covertly within the White House because the president's staff was not allowed access to his staff's communications.[30]

The secretary of defense agreed with the vice president. In December 2001, Rumsfeld sent Gen. Tommy R. Franks an article, the conclusion of which he endorsed: "In the end, if we are going to lead, . . . we must be considered the madmen of the world, capable of any action. . . . If we are to achieve noble purposes we must be prepared to act in the most ignoble manner."[31]

The administration's focus was not on defeating terrorism by winning a contest for public opinion in the Middle East. Its objective was to "get" al Qaeda.

The only public opinion that seemed to matter to the president lay inside the United States, most especially within the base of the Republican Party.

The frightened and furious public wanted immediate action. Unfortunately, the administration did not supply deliberate, calculated, and informed action but an impulsive and unreflective reaction dominated by gut instincts, driven by fury, and wreathed in secrecy. Facts, reason, and evidence—like planning, diplomacy, and law—were of little concern to George W. Bush; instead, he expected American power to dictate the outcome.

One of Bush's senior advisers explained the president's thinking to journalist Ron Suskind. Deducing solutions from "the judicious study of discernable reality," he said, is

> not the way the world really works anymore. We're an empire now, and when we act, we create our own reality. And while you're studying that reality—judiciously, as you will—we'll act again, creating other new realities, which you can study too, and that's how things will sort out. We're history's actors . . . and you, all of you, will be left to just study what we do.[32]

Bush's faith in his capacity to shape reality derived, in no small part, from running political campaigns on television, where perception is nine-tenths of reality. "[I]n my line of work," he explained, "you've got to keep repeating things over and over and over again for the truth to sink in, to kind of catapult the propaganda."[33]

With a staff manufacturing propaganda for him, Bush felt liberated from the obligations of reasoned discourse that make the rule of law largely a matter of self-restraint. "I'm the commander," he explained to reporter Bob Woodward early in the war. "I don't need to explain . . . why I say things. That is the interesting thing about being president. Maybe somebody needs to explain to me why they say something, but I don't feel like I owe anybody an explanation."[34]

Cofer Black, the White House's chief of counterterrorism, would later tell Congress that "there was a 'before 9/11' and an 'after 9/11.' After 9/11, the gloves come [sic] off."[35] "The gloves are off" became a mantra for those who sought to use abusive detentions not just to obtain information but to punish this new and vicious enemy.[36]

The torture of suspected terrorists was entirely predictable. Anyone who has experienced basic training knows how easily the military can turn men and women of ordinary morality into brutal killers and how hard it can be for commanders to restrain their desire for personal vengeance. "If you are a military man," Secretary of State Colin Powell's chief of staff observed, "you know that . . . once you give the slightest bit of leeway there are those in the armed forces who will take advantage of that."[37] This situation will occur particularly if the soldiers are stressed out, don't understand the local language, and blame the local population for their casualties. Powell had experienced guerrilla warfare in Vietnam. To experienced military men like him, adherence to the Geneva Conventions is not just a moral imperative; it is a military necessity if commanders are going to avoid the kind of atrocities that lead civilians to take up arms against an occupying force.

But one does not have to have military experience to understand how total strangers wearing the mantel of apparent authority can turn ordinary people into torturers. Professor Stanley Milgram demonstrated this in a famous experiment at Yale in 1963, just a few years before George W. Bush arrived on campus. Milgram set up a mock control booth and hired people to question "subjects" (played by actors) and shock them with electricity whenever their answers were wrong. His purpose was

> to test how much pain an ordinary citizen would inflict on another person simply because he was ordered to by an experimental scientist. Stark authority was pitted against the subjects' strongest moral imperatives against hurting others, and, with the subjects' ears ringing with the screams of the victims, authority won more often than not. The extreme willingness of adults to go to almost any lengths on the command of an authority constitutes the chief finding of the study and the fact most urgently demanding explanation. Ordinary people, simply doing their jobs, and without any particular hostility on their part, can become agents in a terribly destructive process. Moreover, even when the destructive effects of their work become patently clear, and they are asked to carry out actions incompatible with fundamental standards of morality, relatively few people have the resources needed to resist authority.[38]

Milgram's experiment graphically demonstrated why there are laws of war.

On September 17, Bush issued a "memorandum of notification" secretly granting the CIA broad powers not only to assassinate al Qaeda's leaders anywhere in the world but also to kidnap their operatives and deliver them to regimes with the disposition to interrogate them under torture or to question them, under "enhanced techniques," in secret CIA prisons around the globe.[39] CIA director George Tenet prepared the memorandum.[40] Similar powers were later granted to the military, which often worked in conjunction with the CIA.[41]

This authorization was unprecedented. Never had an American president authorized the use of torture on or the cruel, inhumane, or degrading treatment of helpless captives. Anglo-American law had forbidden torture for centuries, and the State Department had denounced its use by other countries, most notably in its annual human rights reports. American military law banned torture; numerous treaties committed the armed forces to treat their wartime captives humanely. Following World War II, the United States had joined the Allies and prosecuted Nazi officials in Nuremberg and Japanese officials in Tokyo for the torture and abuse of captured soldiers and civilians. Now, that proud heritage was going to be secretly trashed.

On September 18, Congress authorized the president to use military force against "those responsible for the recent attacks."[42] By limiting the president's response to "those responsible," it rejected his demands for broader authority. But Bush and Cheney chose to disregard that limitation. They were eager to invade Afghanistan and Iraq, but just as their predecessors did during the Cold War, they also wanted to wage covert warfare against an "ism."

Terrorism, like communism, is one of those labels that politicians use to arouse fear while clouding judgment. Wars on terrorism have no beginning and no end. Fear of terrorism can be invoked to justify huge expansions of covert power to kill "enemies" secretly, without accountability, while suppressing dissent at home. Fear of terrorism has replaced fear of communism, but it would be a mistake to believe that the military and intelligence agencies that are trained to fight terrorism are truly interested in suppressing it everywhere. Most Americans would rather not notice, but presidents from both parties have for more than half a century supported terrorist governments and guerrillas of all stripes, including British state terrorists against Irish terrorists in Northern Ireland; French Army terrorists against Algerian terrorists in North Africa; Cuban exiles against Communist Cuba; the Pol Pot regime against North Vietnam; military terrorists in Argentina, Chile, Guatemala, and Venezuela against their leftist adversaries; *contra* guerrillas against the government of Nicaragua; Osama bin Laden and his Muslim fighters against the Russians; and the mujahideen of Afghanistan's Northern Alliance against the mujahideen of the Taliban.

Congress refused to give President Bush the blanket authority he sought to wage covert warfare against anything he chose to call terror, but he was not deterred. Addressing a joint session of Congress on September 20, he unilaterally declared his own global war on terrorism:

> Our war on terror begins with al Qaeda, but it does not end there. It will not end until every terrorist group of global reach has been found, stopped and defeated. . . . We will direct every resource at our command— . . . every tool of intelligence, every instrument of law enforcement, . . . and every necessary weapon of war—to the disruption and to the defeat of the global terror network. . . . Every nation, in every region, now has a decision to make. Either you are with us, or you are with the terrorists.[43]

On September 25, John Yoo issued a secret opinion assuring the president that he had far more power to retaliate against the attackers than Congress had authorized. Bush did not have to limit his counterattacks to al Qaeda and its Taliban hosts in Afghanistan, the thirty-four-year-old attorney wrote. He could strike "against any person, organization, or State suspected of involvement in terrorist attacks on the United States" and any "foreign States suspected of harboring or supporting such organizations." Yoo advised the president that on the basis of no more than a mere suspicion of terrorist activity and without further permission from Congress, he could attack any government or private organization, at any time, anywhere in the world.[44]

The impetus for this extraordinary assertion came from the vice president's office, but it carried extra weight because the OLC's legal opinions are normally deemed binding within the executive branch. Dick Cheney had first learned how useful the OLC's opinions could be in legalizing a president's agenda when he was Gerald Ford's chief of staff and future Supreme Court justice Antonin Scalia led the OLC. As vice president to George W. Bush, Cheney would come to rely as heavily on Yoo as he had on Scalia, even though Yoo was a junior attorney at the OLC and was not clearing his opinions with the attorney general. While Congress had limited the military's power to carrying out reprisals against al Qaeda and the Taliban, Yoo confidently ruled in response to a query from Cheney, that the president "may deploy military force preemptively against terrorist organizations or the States that harbor or support them, whether or not they can be linked to the specific terrorist incidents of September 11."[45]

Yoo was not discussing defensive warfare, or preemptive strikes against forces about to strike the United States. He was advocating a presidential power to conduct preventive warfare at will, a view that had no basis in either American or international law. President Bush did not need congressional authority, Yoo said, to attack any government that had been labeled a state sponsor of terrorism, presumably by the State Department's coordinator for counterterrorism. The department's list at that time included North Korea, Iran, Libya, Cuba, Sudan, and Syria.

By Yoo's reasoning, the president could send CIA or Special Forces units out to kill or capture members of alleged terrorist organizations even in Germany, Spain, the Philippines, or Russia, much as the CIA would later do in its program of extraordinary rendition. He could also go after "terrorist safe havens" in places like Guatemala, Yemen, Chechnya, or, for that matter, militia compounds in Idaho.

In a still secret memorandum dated October 17, 2001, Yoo claimed that the president could treat the United States as part of the worldwide "battlefield" against terrorists and conduct covert and paramilitary operations there, not just to collect intelligence, but to neutralize suspected al Qaeda cells. Yoo reasoned that the Posse Comitatus Act of 1878, which forbade the military to enforce civilian law in the United States, was no impediment because this was war, not law enforcement.[46] He went so far as to declare that the president could suspend the Fourth Amendment's protections against warrantless searches when necessary to prevent or deter terrorist attacks within the United States.[47] At the same time, the first draft of the Uniting and Strengthening America by Providing Appropriate Tools Required to Intercept and Obstruct Terrorism (USA PATRIOT) Act contained a provision that would have allowed the president to suspend within the United States the privilege of habeas corpus—the legal right to challenge the legality of one's detention or treatment while detained—making possible the indefinite detention of both aliens and citizens.[48]

In 2006, the Bush administration took Yoo's patently wrong advice and slipped a provision through Congress that authorized the president to decide, on his own, when a threat to public order within a state might require deploying federal troops without first obtaining permission from that state's governor, as had been the law for more than two hundred years.[49] In exercising this power over the opposition of state officials, the president could presumably detain American citizens indefinitely. He could even deny them access to the courts by unilaterally suspending the privilege of the writ of habeas corpus.

Along with these radical assertions of executive power was an appropriation of $385 million for KBR, then a subsidiary of Halliburton (which Cheney had headed before becoming vice president), to build a huge new detention facility somewhere in the United States to deal with an "emergency influx of immigrants . . . or to support the rapid development of new programs."[50] Neither the administration nor Republican leaders in Congress explained what those "new programs" might be.

In a separate memorandum, Yoo argued that Congress's authorization to use military force, passed on September 18, allowed the president to order warrantless wiretaps in violation of the Foreign Intelligence Surveillance Act (FISA) of 1978, which had been specifically passed to end such practices by the National Security Agency (NSA) and to make their resumption a felony punishable by up to five years in prison. Of course, Congress did not intend to repeal FISA. Repeal was never discussed, and it is well established in law that the implicit repeal of criminal statutes is not to be presumed. But Bush authorized the intercepts anyway. Yoo's memo and the president's order were both kept secret from anyone who might object, including John B. Bellinger III, who handled national security law for the White House.[51]

The president could do all this alone, Yoo argued, because "[t]he Framing generation well understood that declarations of war were obsolete." That assertion, too, was false. The founders had expressly given Congress, and Congress alone, the authority to declare war and issue letters of marque and reprisal to private warships—the way in which undeclared warfare was conducted in the eighteenth century. As James Madison wrote to Thomas Jefferson in 1794, the Constitution "supposes, what the History of all Govts demonstrates, that the Ex. is the branch of power most interested in war, & most prone to it. [The Constitution] has accordingly with studied care, vested the question of war in the Legisl."[52]

According to Yoo, the war powers belong to the president because Article II makes him commander in chief.[53] But the term "war powers" does not appear anywhere in the Constitution. Rather, it addresses specific powers "to declare War, grant Letters of Marque and Reprisal, and make Rules concerning Captures on land and Water; to raise and support Armies, to provide and maintain a Navy; to make rules for the Government and Regulation of the land and naval Forces; to provide for organizing, arming, and disciplining, the Militia"; and "to make all Laws which shall be necessary and proper for carrying into Execution the foregoing Powers." Article I grants all of these powers to Congress, not to the president.

Yoo went even further, declaring that no statute "can place any limits on the president's determinations as to any terrorist threat [including the] nature of the response. These decisions, under our Constitution, are for the president alone to make."[54] This claim flatly contradicted Article I, Section 8 of the Constitution, which gives Congress the authority not only "to make all laws necessary and proper for carrying into execution" its enumerated powers but "*all other Powers vested* by this Constitution in the Government of the United States, or *in any Department or Officer* thereof." (Emphasis added.)

Conspicuously absent from Yoo's memos was any mention of *Youngstown Sheet & Tube Co. v. Sawyer* (1952) in which the Supreme Court famously rejected President Harry S. Truman's equally broad assertion of presidential war powers. In that case, the justices ruled that the secretary of commerce could not seize the nation's steel mills, even at the height of the Korean War, to avert a strike and keep war-related production going, because Congress had already passed a law prescribing what the president could do in such an emergency. The "unarticulated assumption" behind the administration's claim of inherent wartime powers, Justice Robert H. Jackson wrote, is that "necessity knows no law. . . . Such power," he added, "has no beginning or . . . end."[55]

Yoo also neglected to mention the Supreme Court's decision in *Little v. Barreme* (1804) in which the justices ruled that President John Adams had unlawfully authorized the seizure of a ship during the undeclared war with France in 1799. Congress had authorized him to order the seizure of ships going to France, but Adams had directed the navy to seize ships coming to the United States from France as well. His order made logical sense, and had Congress refrained from instructing him, Adams might have gotten away with it. But Congress had spoken on the subject, the justices ruled, so additional powers could not be presumed.[56]

That early decision was consistent with the framers' intent to make Congress an integral part of the war-authorizing process. They rejected the monarchist view, prevalent in seventeenth-century Great Britain, that such decisions are the proper domain of the executive. Their Constitution created separate institutions sharing powers, not separate institutions with exclusive prerogatives.

At this point in his career, John Yoo was an obscure political appointee in the Justice Department's OLC, on leave from the University of California's law school at Berkeley. However, as a former clerk to Supreme Court justice Clarence Thomas and Judge Laurence H. Silberman of the Court of Appeals for the District of Columbia and as former general counsel on the Senate Judiciary Committee under Senator Orrin G. Hatch (R-UT), Yoo had powerful conservative connections. He had also championed a monarchist view of the presidency in his prolific writings.[57]

Cass Sunstein, then at the University of Chicago Law School, would later write that Yoo was a "good lawyer" only in the sense that he wrote one-sided opinions to "justify a particular set of predetermined conclusions."[58] In other words, he could be trusted to tell his bosses what they wanted to hear while neglecting to address the contrary views of most constitutional experts, past and present. Attorney General John Ashcroft, Yoo's nominal superior, would come to refer to him as "Dr. Yes."[59]

Yoo was the Justice Department's counterpart to Douglas Feith, the Pentagon undersecretary whose selective dissemination of erroneous intelligence about links between Iraq and al Qaeda helped manufacture the case for invading Iraq. Yoo's secret memos, which advanced dubious legal theories, were shielded from internal contradiction, much as Feith's assertions were protected from intelligence agency rebuttal. Indeed, Feith was an early advocate for evading the Geneva Conventions, and when he could not persuade military lawyers to endorse the idea, he turned to the Justice Department, where Yoo was more than eager to help.[60]

It was clear from the beginning that the vice president was in charge of the administration's response to the 9/11 attacks. When the chairmen and ranking minority members of the House and Senate intelligence committees were summoned to the White House for their first briefing on that response, they were ushered into the vice president's office. Bush had already told Senator Bob Graham (D-FL) that "the vice president should be your point of contact in the White House." He "has the portfolio for intelligence activities."[61]

Cheney was the logical choice. As chief of staff to President Ford in 1975, he had stonewalled investigations by both the House and the Senate intelligence committees into intelligence agency abuses.

Cheney Invents New Military Commissions

About the time that Yoo's secret memos were being welcomed in the White House, a "working group" of civilian political appointees, headed by Pierre-Richard Prosper, ambassador-at-large for war crimes issues, was trying to decide what to do with al Qaeda and Taliban fighters captured in Afghanistan. David Addington, the vice president's lawyer, was invited to participate in this group's discussions, but he refused. Instead, he worked with Tim Flanigan and Bradford Berenson of the White House counsel's office and Patrick Philbin of the OLC to hatch their own plan. They wanted to try alleged terrorists before military commissions, which would be free to make up their own rules of evidence, case by case.[62]

Legally there was no need for the administration to create special courts to prosecute persons seized on a battlefield while bearing arms; they could be detained indefinitely as prisoners of war (POWs) or tried for war crimes by the existing system of courts-martial. Courts without evidentiary standards could have only one purpose—to admit evidence that no constitutional court would consider reliable, including hearsay, secret evidence, and statements obtained by torture.

Cheney presented his plan to the president over lunch on November 13, 2001. By mid-afternoon, the order had been prepared and signed without the usual staff or agency review.[63] The new military commissions would not recognize rights normally granted to Americans, including homegrown terrorists like Timothy McVeigh, who had been convicted in June of bombing the Alfred P. Murrah Federal Building in Oklahoma City. Not only could the commissions receive evidence obtained by torture, they could withhold exculpatory evidence from the accused simply by allowing prosecutors to label it secret. Proof beyond a reasonable doubt was not required, a vote of 2-1 was sufficient to order a death sentence, and no appeal to a civilian court was permitted, as would be the case in an ordinary court-martial.

Cheney's plan was based on John Yoo's November 6 memorandum that claimed the president did not need congressional approval to create his own judicial system. The new commissions were not limited to trying persons captured pursuant to Congress's September Authorization for the Use of Military Force (AUMF) against the people responsible for 9/11; the president authorized them to try people captured anywhere on earth in his own global war on terrorism.

Articles I and III of the Constitution expressly allocate the power to create new tribunals to Congress. Article II does not grant the president any such power, but Yoo argued that the creation of a new judicial system was an *inherently* executive function. The State Department, the National Security Council, and the military's own lawyers were not consulted in the preparation of this novel opinion, even though the military would be tasked to run the commissions.

Attorney General John Ashcroft had been surprised to learn over the preceding weekend that the vice president's plan did not give the Justice Department any role in deciding which terrorists would be tried before the new military tribunals. He was also outraged to discover that John Yoo, without consulting him, had conspired to deny the jurisdiction of federal courts. Ashcroft sought to protest, but Cheney got to the president first.

No sooner had the order been announced than Cheney explained the reasoning behind it while speaking about tax cuts to a delegation from the U.S. Chamber of Commerce. Terrorists, he said,

> don't deserve to be treated as a prisoner of war [*sic*]. They don't deserve the same guarantees and safeguards that would be used for an American citizen going through the normal judicial process. This—they will have a fair trial, but it'll be under the procedures of a military tribunal. . . . We think it's—

guarantees that we'll have the kind of treatment of these individuals that we believe they deserve.[64]

Conservative columnist William Safire, who had been exposed to presidential hubris in the Nixon White House, quickly denounced the new commissions as "kangaroo courts." "On what legal meat," he asked, "does this our Caesar feed?"[65]

The Gloves Come Off

The shift to harsh interrogations began with the U.S. invasion of Afghanistan in October 2001. In November, Pakistani agents presented U.S. officials with their first "high value" prisoner, an al Qaeda training camp operator named Ibn al-Sheikh al-Libi. FBI agents began al-Libi's interrogation in Kabul by reading him his rights. Soon they had him talking about Richard Reid, the shoe bomber, and Zacarias Moussaoui, an aspiring hijacker.

But the CIA was impatient. With White House backing, the agency wrested al-Libi away from the FBI and tried for several weeks to force information out of him. When that failed, they shackled and gagged him and put him on a plane. "You're going to Cairo," a CIA agent whispered in his ear, but "before you get there I'm going to find your mother and I'm going to fuck her."[66]

In Egypt, al-Libi soon confessed to visiting Iraq and receiving training in chemical and biological weapons. In February 2002, human intelligence specialists from the Defense Intelligence Agency (DIA) warned the administration not to trust this statement, but Secretary of State Colin Powell did a year later while trying to justify the invasion of Iraq to the United Nations (UN). In March 2003, al-Libi recanted, insisting that his statements had been made under torture.[67]

FBI agent Dan Coleman was dismayed that anyone would have believed al-Libi's confession:

> It was ridiculous . . . to think that Libi would have known anything about Iraq. . . . He ran a training camp [in Afghanistan]. He wouldn't have had anything to do with Iraq. Administration officials were always pushing us to come up with links, but there weren't any. The reason they got bad information is that they beat it out of him. You never get good information that way.[68]

Because al-Libi's statement had been coerced, nothing in it could be used against him or any anyone else in a regular civilian or military court. Only Bush's military commissions could admit evidence obtained by torture, if they survived judicial review.

Punishing a Surrogate for Bin Laden

One of the first captives to be subjected to the administration's torture policy was an American citizen, John Walker Lindh. A twenty-year-old Californian, he had joined the Taliban hoping to fight against Northern Alliance warlords for a stricter government that would enforce a version of his Islamic faith. However, when al Qaeda attacked the United States, Lindh suddenly found himself at war with his own country.

Lindh had not joined the Taliban to fight the United States. About the time he joined the Taliban in 2000 it had received a $43 million grant from the United States to eradicate opium poppies.[69] Lindh did not commit any hostile acts against American forces and was in very bad physical shape when he was turned over to them. He had been shot during a prison revolt and nearly burned alive when Northern Alliance soldiers poured flaming oil into the basement where he and other captives had taken refuge.[70] Crippled by a bullet wound in his thigh and delirious from having gone without food and water for nearly a week, Lindh posed no threat to anyone. But U.S. soldiers stripped him naked, taped him to a stretcher, and kept him blindfolded in a cold, windowless metal shipping container for eight days. During this time, according to his lawyers, they threatened him with torture and death.[71] Not until after December 14, when he was transferred to the USS *Peleliu,* did military doctors address his festering wound.

Rogue agents operating on their own did not carry out this treatment. Lindh was a prize catch. Pentagon officials monitored his interrogation several times a day. Jim Haynes, the Defense Department's general counsel, reportedly authorized military interrogators to "take the gloves off."[72] So Lindh was questioned naked, in the freezing cold, while taped to a stretcher.

Harsh treatment was not necessary to get Lindh to talk; he had spoken on camera with a CNN reporter (and, apparently, also with a medic) following his capture.[73] At least part of the abuse was gratuitous; his captors amused themselves by writing "shithead" on his blindfold and taking souvenir photographs with him. One told Lindh that he would be hanged and that they would sell their photographs to raise money for a Christian organization.[74]

According to an army order issued in October 2001, all prisoners were entitled to the protections of the Geneva Conventions. White House press secretary Ari Fleischer announced that Lindh was being held as a prisoner of war under the Geneva Conventions.[75] But that was not true.

While the military was abusing Lindh, the Justice Department was planning a show trial, something it could not do if he was a prisoner of war. If he was to be treated as a criminal, interrogators would have to warn him of his rights to remain silent and to consult with an attorney, which the military and CIA failed to do. This well-known constitutional requirement was ignored until the ninth day of Lindh's captivity, when an FBI agent finally arrived in Kabul to build the case against him.

Even then, the FBI, the CIA, and the army did not grant Lindh's requests for a lawyer. According to his attorneys, the FBI agent falsely insisted that no attorneys were available while military commanders prevented the Red Cross from telling Lindh that a lawyer hired by his family was trying to get in touch with him. For fifty-four days, he was not even told that there were military lawyers in the area who could have represented him.[76]

These actions were deliberate violations of Lindh's constitutional rights as an American citizen. They were not inadvertent transgressions by ignorant soldiers in the heat of battle; they were decisions by high-level Defense Department officials who disregarded the express advice of the Justice Department's Office of Professional Responsibility (OPR). The OPR attorney who gave this legal advice was not just ignored; her e-mails transmitting the advice were purged from the prosecution's legal file and not revealed to the court, as required by law.[77] When she protested this breach of legal ethics, her superiors threatened to give her a negative employment review and then forced her to resign. Later, when she gave copies of the e-mails to *Newsweek,* the department threatened a criminal investigation, which effectively ended her post-government employment with a private firm.[78]

Administration officials knew both that Lindh had been abused and humiliated and that his admissions had been obtained without a valid warning of his legal rights. Readers of the *New York Times* did too,[79] but there was little public protest. Former president George H. W. Bush observed that Lindh was a "poor fellow" who hadn't done much. Kenneth Starr, the former special prosecutor, saw Lindh as "a young kid with misplaced idealism" who "doesn't seem like a Benedict Arnold."[80] Even the sitting president Bush seemed sympathetic: "Obviously, he has been misled."[81]

But Attorney General John Ashcroft saw Lindh differently—as a political surrogate for Osama bin Laden, who had escaped capture. Ashcroft accused the young man of treason, terrorism, and conspiracy to kill a CIA agent who had died in the prison revolt—all charges that could not possibly stand up in court. To lead the show trial, Ashcroft appointed a high-profile legal team that included future Homeland Security secretary Michael Chertoff and Paul McNulty, a future deputy attorney general. They saw to it that the defendant would be tried in Northern Virginia, the site of a 9/11 attack and a judicial district packed with conservative judges who were more than likely to overlook violations of his rights.[82] Judge T. S. Ellis III cooperated with the prosecutors by scheduling Lindh's trial for late August, so that the case might go to the jury near the first anniversary of the September 11 attacks.

However, Pentagon officials did not want to advertise how their forces had mistreated Lindh, so they pressured the prosecutors, after their media blitz had influenced potential jurors, to settle the case out of court.[83] Knowing that their client could not possibly get a fair trial under the circumstances, Lindh's lawyers recommended that he accept the prosecution's offer of a deal. The terrorism-related charges would be dropped (Lindh had never been a terrorist) in return for his admission that he had violated an obscure law from President Bill Clinton's era that imposed economic sanctions on the Taliban.[84] He agreed, and Judge Ellis promptly sentenced him to twenty years in prison.

Chertoff and McNulty insisted on two other conditions. Lindh had to sign a paper claiming that neither his person nor his rights had been "intentionally mistreated," and he had to agree not to reveal how he had been treated for the duration of his sentence. In return, the government promised to do its best to see that Lindh served his sentence in a medium security facility close to his family in California. After a few months, however, the Bureau of Prisons transferred him to a maximum security prison in Florence, Colorado, and from there to a prison in Terra Haute, Indiana, where family visits would be infrequent at best. As late as April 2005, Attorney General Alberto Gonzales would claim, disingenuously, that Lindh had pled guilty to "terrorism-related charges."[85]

Legal Black Holes

According to the Bush administration, the United States was at war with terrorists, and because it was at war, the president enjoyed unlimited war powers, including the authority to detain terrorists for eventual trial before military commissions as war criminals. However, its lawyers insisted, the laws of war, including the Geneva Conventions, did not apply to this conflict because al Qaeda's operatives did not wear uniforms and fight in military units. They also claimed the power to label civilians who have never served in military units as enemy combatants, to deny them prisoner of war status, and to hide them away in military brigs and secret prisons, where U.S. interrogators could torture and abuse them for years.

In short, the administration demanded the powers of a wartime dictatorship for a war arguably without end. They sought to create legal "black holes" within which neither the laws of war nor the criminal law would apply to their interrogators and guards. Within these black sites, they insisted, military and CIA interrogators were legally free to detain and torture prisoners with impunity because the prisoners had no legal rights. In addition, they argued that the use of torture by the United States was itself a state secret, which made American torturers immune from all forms of accountability. Not since *Dred Scott v. Sandford* (1856), when the Supreme Court ruled that blacks had no rights that white people needed respect, had Americans heard such an argument.[86]

The best known of all legal black holes, of course, was the U.S. naval base at Guantánamo Bay, Cuba, or "GTMO" in navy-speak. The idea of using the base to evade the application of American law, interestingly, had already been developed by the administration of George W. Bush's father and continued under the Clinton administration so that the United States could detain Haitian boat people there without having to obey American immigration law.[87]

The idea that prisoners in time of war have no rights was anathema to most military lawyers. Starting with the Lieber Code of 1863,[88] the U.S. Army had championed the rule of law in times of conflict. The Defense Department's manual for officers bore this declaration, endorsed by the legendary World War II general George C. Marshall:

The United States abides by the laws of war. Its Armed Forces, in dealing with all other peoples, are expected to comply with the laws of war, in the spirit and the letter. In waging war, we do not terrorize helpless non-combatants, if it is within our power to avoid so doing. Wanton killing, torture, cruelty, or the working of unusual hardship on enemy prisoners or populations is not justified under any circumstance. Likewise, respect for the reign of law, as that term is understood in the United States, is expected to follow the flag wherever it goes.[89]

Marshall's message echoed article 31 of the Fourth Geneva Convention, which states, "No physical or moral coercion shall be exercised against protected persons [e.g. civilians], in particular to obtain information from them *or from third parties.*"[90] It was reaffirmed in 1994 when the United States agreed, when ratifying the United Nations Convention Against Torture, that "no exceptional circumstances whatsoever, whether a state of war or a threat of war, internal political instability or any other public emergency, may be invoked as a justification for torture."[91]

Until the Bush administration, wartime powers were thought to be exceptions to peacetime rules, lasting no longer than the emergency that justified their exercise. But Bush's global war on terrorism was to be perpetual and know no geographical bounds. Like the war between Oceana and Eurasia or East Asia in George Orwell's *1984,* it would never end because there would always be some threat to address, if only to bolster political support for the politicians in power or for appropriations for defense contractors.[92] In the pursuit of new enemies, the nature and scale of which he kept secret, President Bush claimed the authority to send CIA and Special Forces commando teams into any country on earth, with secret orders to capture and kill terrorists without regard to international legal prohibitions or UN approval.

War, Not Law became the Bush administration's mantra, as if Americans faced an either-or choice between safety and justice. Implicit was the unexamined assumption that torture would produce accurate and timely information whose value would outweigh the long-term hatred such actions would generate among the next generation of enemy sympathizers.

When critics questioned the "war, not law" premise, John Yoo claimed to be baffled. "Why is it so hard for people to understand that there is a category of behavior not covered by the legal system?" he asked. "Historically, there were people so bad that they were not given protection of the laws."[93] David Frum and Richard Perle, two early advocates of invading Iraq, made the same point in their book on *An End to Evil: How to Win the War on Terror*: "[A] nation of laws must understand the limits of legalism. . . . War has its rules, of course—but by those very rules our enemies in this war on terror are outlaws."[94]

Frum, Perle, and Yoo hearkened back to the Middle Ages, when a person could be declared an outlaw in Anglo-Saxon England. Outlaws had no legal rights and could be killed with impunity.[95] This practice made little sense, except to vengeful nobles. Stripping people of all rights created brigands and pirates and encouraged murder by vigilantes and mobs.

The nobility was particularly opposed to outlawry when it was practiced on them. In 1215, on the plains of Runnymede, noblemen forced King John to sign the Magna Carta. Clause 39 solemnly promised, "No free man shall be taken or imprisoned or stripped of his rights or possessions, or outlawed or exiled, or deprived of his standing in any other way, nor will we proceed with force against him, or send others to do so, except by the lawful judgment of his equals or by the law of the land." Gradually, the writ of habeas corpus became the procedure by which the Magna Carta's prohibitions against outlawry and arbitrary detention came to be enforced.[96]

By the seventeenth century, when the American colonies were settled, the prevailing assumption of the criminal justice system was that white persons, at least, were rights holders no matter what they were accused of doing. Fugitive slaves, meanwhile, were treated as outlaws by the United States and many state governments until slavery was abolished in 1866.[97] After that, outlawry was little more than a rhetorical justification for vigilante justice on the western frontier.[98]

But the temptation to create legal pariahs did not die out. During World War II, Chancellor John Allsebrook Simon of Great Britain proposed reviving the law of outlawry so that Nazi war criminals could be shot without trials. Winston Churchill, Clement Attlee, and Anthony Eden also favored summary executions while Joseph Stalin preferred that the Nazis be given show trials and then shot. The new American president, Harry S. Truman, did not wish to be remembered as a vengeful man, however. He not only rejected a plan Secretary of the Treasury Henry Morgenthau, Jr., proposed for a punitive peace (which had been such a disaster after World War I), he demanded genuine trials for alleged Nazis. The other leaders ultimately agreed once they realized there was no neat way to separate those who deserved to be shot outright from those who deserved a trial and possibly a lesser sentence.[99]

Suspending the Geneva Conventions

When the United States invaded Afghanistan in October 2001, General Franks of Central Command issued the customary order directing his troops to obey the Geneva Conventions.[100] Some of his interrogators were attempting to do so when the first detainees were deposited at Guantánamo Bay on January 11, 2002.[101]

That same day a delegation from the Central Intelligence Agency met in the White House situation room with White House counsel Alberto Gonzales; the vice president's attorney, David Addington; and OLC attorney John Yoo. According to Yoo, "The CIA guys said, 'We're going to have some real difficulties getting actionable intelligence from detainees if the Geneva Conventions apply.'"[102] Yoo would later claim that this assertion was "the first time that the issue of interrogations [came] up" among top-ranking White House officials,[103] but he had anticipated the request in a memorandum completed two days earlier.[104]

Vice President Cheney and Secretary Rumsfeld were the chief advocates for coercive interrogations. Having worked in the Ford administration at the height of the House and Senate investigations into intelligence agency abuses, both strongly opposed post-Watergate restraints on executive power. Each had sought to revive the powerful presidency that Richard M. Nixon had envisioned. Although Rumsfeld had done his senior thesis at Princeton on the famous *Youngstown* decision that had rejected unlimited presidential power in times of war, he was determined to establish the opposite—that wartime presidents are above the law even if the war is largely metaphorical.

Opposing them were career lawyers from the military's Judge Advocate General (JAG) Corps. Cheney and Rumsfeld had spent much of their careers trying to subordinate these professionals to politically appointed lawyers of their own choosing, but their efforts had failed. This time the JAGs would have to be circumvented or overridden. The person to do this work was David Addington, or Cheney's "Cheney," one of the most aggressive bureaucratic infighters ever to darken White House doors.

The JAGs favored the Geneva Conventions. Like most military professionals, the military lawyers thought further ahead than the civilians they worked for and did not wish to give any enemy in this conflict or any other an excuse for mistreating captured Americans. Addington, however, wanted immediate results. On January 25, 2002, he complained vehemently that the "strict limits on questioning of enemy prisoners" imposed by the Geneva Conventions had impeded efforts "to quickly obtain information from captured terrorists."[105] In this sentiment, he was not alone. He could count on the support of two key Rumsfeld aides: Stephen Cambone, who became deputy secretary of defense for intelligence, and Jim Haynes, Rumsfeld's general counsel (and an Addington protégé). Together they would force the military to abandon the laws of war, at least where the interrogation of suspected terrorists was concerned.

Part of the strategy was to find a place to imprison suspects that would be outside the rule of law. In late 2001, Jim Haynes asked Rear Adm. Donald J. Guter, then the navy's judge advocate general, whether hundreds of terrorists could be held on navy warships. "It became apparent pretty quickly," Guter recalled, that Rumsfeld's lawyer wanted a prison "outside the courts."[106]

Maj. Gen. Thomas Romig, who was the army's JAG in 2001, recalled tense meetings in November and December with administration lawyers. "John Yoo wanted to use military commissions in the manner they were used in the Indian wars. I looked at him and said, 'You know, that was 100-and-something years ago. You're out of your mind; we're talking about the law.'"

"As they viewed it," Romig added, "due process is legal mumbo jumbo. . . . If you're caught as a terrorist, you're presumed guilty and you have to prove you're innocent. It was crazy."[107]

On December 28, OLC lawyers John Yoo and Patrick F. Philbin sent Jim Haynes a secret memorandum formally advising him that the federal courts had no authority to hear habeas petitions from any prisoners held at the U.S. Naval Base at Guantánamo.[108] This assertion, too, was a questionable claim, but it was all the military needed. On January 11, 2002, the first detainees, drugged and in chains, were flown to the base from Afghanistan.

John Yoo was there to witness their arrival but not before he had drafted yet another memo. On January 9, he and Special Counsel Robert J. Delahunty advised Haynes that the Geneva Conventions did not protect members of al

Qaeda or the Taliban.[109] Al Qaeda was not a country, they said, so its members were not entitled to any rights under the Geneva Conventions, including a review of their status by "competent tribunals," as required by article 5. The simple expedient of decreeing all prisoners were enemy combatants rather than prisoners of war would place their detentions beyond question.

Yoo and Delahunty did not bother to mention that army regulations had rejected this view for more than fifty years. According to military doctrine, every captive was entitled to the protection of the Geneva Convention's Common Article 3, which banned cruel, inhumane, and degrading treatment.[110] There was no such thing, the army said, as a person without rights. This traditional legal view was not to prevail, however, in part because Rumsfeld and Cheney did everything they could to privilege Yoo's advice and to exclude military lawyers from the policy-making process.

William Howard Taft IV, the State Department's legal adviser, immediately took issue with Yoo's advice. On January 11, Taft sent Justice Department lawyers a forty-page memorandum declaring that their analysis of the Geneva Conventions was "untenable," "incorrect," and "confused." Their claim that Afghanistan was a "failed state" and therefore not covered by the conventions was also contrary to "[t]he official United States position before, during, and after the emergence of the Taliban." The legal adviser also warned the president that if he chose to disregard the Geneva Conventions in this conflict, he could himself be prosecuted for war crimes.[111]

Taft sent a copy of his memo to Gonzales. Yoo fired back a rebuttal, but their exchanges did not matter. President Bush had already decided on January 8, without the benefit of legal counsel, to declare the Geneva Conventions inapplicable to his war on terrorism.[112]

Yoo's January 9 memo was not written to protect captives; instead, he wanted to explain how U.S. interrogators and their superiors could escape prosecution under the War Crimes Act of 1996. That law, which a conservative Republican had proposed after meeting a survivor of the "Hanoi Hilton," the North Vietnamese prison for American POWs, enjoyed the Defense Department's support and was passed without a dissenting vote. It made "grave breaches" of the Geneva Conventions federal war crimes punishable in civilian, as well as military, courts.[113]

On January 22, Jay Bybee, head of the Office of Legal Counsel, circulated another memo insisting that the president has "the plenary constitutional power to suspend our treaty obligations toward Afghanistan during the period of the conflict."[114] This extraordinary assertion became the linchpin of the torture strategy. The president, Bybee advised, "has unrestricted discretion, as a matter of domestic law, in suspending treaties" simply by deciding that "the conditions essential to [the treaty's] continued effectiveness no longer pertain."[115] In other words, treaties are not the "supreme law of the land," as Article IV of the Constitution clearly says; they are mere political agreements that the president can honor or disregard, in whole or in part, publicly or secretly.[116]

On January 25, 2002, Gonzales amplified Bybee's memo. In a memorandum drafted largely by David Addington,[117] the White House counsel advised the president that the war on terrorism "is a new kind of war, . . . which places a high premium on . . . the ability to quickly obtain information from captured terrorists and their sponsors in order to avoid further atrocities against American civilians. . . . In my judgment, this new paradigm renders obsolete Geneva's strict limitations on questioning of enemy prisoners."[118]

Gonzales's advice echoed the reasoning of Field Marshal Wilhelm Keitel, Hitler's de facto minister of war, when he refused to grant POW status to Russian soldiers captured on the Eastern Front. The Hague and Geneva conventions, Keitel said, were the "outmoded relic of a chivalrous notion of warfare" and inappropriate to the "struggle to the death for the destruction of Bolshevik terrorism."[119] Keitel was convicted at Nuremberg and hanged as a war criminal.

Gonzales's advice was ill founded for at least three reasons. First, his recommendation ignored the settled wisdom of the military, the FBI, and even the CIA that physical torture rarely produces quick, reliable intelligence. Second, his advice and that of the Justice Department attorneys did not mention that the harsh interrogation practices they were contemplating violated the UN Convention Against Torture and Other Cruel, Inhuman, or Degrading Treatment or Punishment (CAT)[120] and its implementing statute.[121] Nor did any of them mention the Supreme Court's rejection in 1952 of their theory of unlimited executive power, which again was the subject of Rumsfeld's college thesis.[122] Third, by dismissing the conventions without public discussion, Gonzales rejected more than fifty years of American law as well as the settled judgment of most foreign nations.

Gonzales's purpose was clear:[123] "By concluding that the GPW [Geneva prisoner of war convention] does not apply to al Qaeda and the Taliban," the president "substantially reduces the threat [to his officials] of domestic criminal prosecution under the War Crimes Act of 1996."[124]

Given what had been done to John Walker Lindh, it is not difficult to understand why Gonzales would seek to shield top administration officials from being charged with war crimes either by U.S. prosecutors or by "independent counsels who may in the future decide to pursue unwarranted charges" under the Geneva Conventions and the War Crimes Act.[125] But Gonzales wasn't just trying to protect those who had conducted and supervised Lindh's torment, which might come out at trial. He also sought to create a pseudo-legal framework that would permit brutal interrogations in the future.

Gonzales conceded that a "determination that the GPW does not apply to al Qaeda and the Taliban could undermine U.S. military culture . . . and could introduce an element of uncertainty in the status of adversaries."[126] However, neither he nor Secretary Rumsfeld took any steps to reduce this uncertainty. For example, they never explained what would constitute the inhumane treatment of prisoners. Nor did they set up a system of oversight.

The policy's civilian architects displayed no appreciation of how much a well-ordered military depends on clear-cut guidelines for maintaining discipline among soldiers who are trained to hate their enemies and who are ill disposed, after taking casualties, to treat hostile civilians kindly. They saw a need for coerced information and had no patience for military lawyers, whose idea of "military necessity" was to obey the Geneva Conventions if only to encourage decent treatment of captured Americans and to avoid provoking civilians in occupied areas.

Like most military men, Secretary of State Colin Powell supported the laws of war, but he did not offer his opinion until January 25. By that time, and possibly without his knowledge, the decision had already been made. Ignoring the conventions, the former general wrote, would

reverse over a century of U.S. policy and practice . . . and undermine the protection of the law of war for our troops, both in the specific conflict and in general. . . . It will undermine public support among critical allies, making military cooperation more difficult to sustain. . . . It may provoke some . . . foreign prosecutors to investigate and prosecute our officials and troops.[127]

Powell's legal adviser, William Taft, followed with a memorandum of his own, reminding the torture advocates that "the United States has dealt with tens of thousands of detainees without repudiating its obligations under the Geneva Conventions."[128]

In their rush to action, the hard-liners did not stop to think about what suspending the conventions would do to the way American soldiers conducted themselves at war and in an occupation. They knew that terrorists were not likely to follow the conventions and saw no particular value in holding the moral high ground. Convinced that they could achieve a swift military victory in what was really a long-term contest for public opinion, the hard-liners were willing to squander the enormous sympathy that had flowed to the United States following the 9/11 attacks.

Like Gonzales, Attorney General John Ashcroft admitted that "the War Crimes Act of 1996 makes violation of parts of the Geneva Convention a crime in the United States," but he too recommended evasion, not compliance. Judicial review of "the facts [alleging] that detainees were unlawful combatants could involve substantial criminal liability for involved U.S. officials," Ashcroft advised the president on February 1. A "determination against treaty applicability," he wrote, "would provide the highest assurance that no court would subsequently entertain charges that American military officers, intelligence officials, or law enforcement officials violated Geneva Convention rules relating to field conduct, detention conduct or interrogation of detainees."[129] Like Gonzales and Yoo, Ashcroft understood that his job was not to enforce the law protecting foreigners from American abuse and captured Americans from foreign torture but instead to shield American torturers and their superiors from legal liability by stripping their victims of all legal rights.

In one respect, the attorney general went beyond the White House counsel's assertions. He not only sought to protect military and intelligence officers from prosecution, he also tried to shield "law enforcement officials" as well, thus signaling his expectation that his FBI agents would also violate the War Crimes Act of 1996, when necessary, to obtain information.

On February 7, 2002, President Bush announced publicly what he had secretly ordered weeks earlier:[130] no one suspected of al Qaeda connections would be entitled to any of the convention's protections, either as prisoners of war or as civilians under Common Article 3 of the Fourth Geneva Convention. Bush also declared that Taliban soldiers were not entitled to legal protections, not because theirs was a "failed state," but because they did not fight according to the laws of war. In so ruling, he contradicted the position that the United States had taken when North Vietnam offered the same excuse for abusing American and South Vietnamese prisoners during the 1960s and 1970s.[131] Indeed, he adopted the same reasoning that Nazi officials had used to deny prisoner of war status to American and British commandos captured behind their lines.[132] No president or military commander in American history had ever gone that far.

To obscure the enormity of what he was ordering within a fog of ambiguity, Bush recited a script that Addington had prepared for him.[133] "As a matter of policy," the president said, "the U.S. Armed Forces shall continue to treat detainees humanely" and in "a manner consistent with the principles of Geneva" but only "to the extent appropriate and consistent with military necessity."[134]

What had once been law was now reduced by a presidential assertion to mere policy. The military could torture and degrade people if "necessary." The order did not mention the CIA, so the agency could torture and degrade people without demonstrating any necessity at all.

Tim Flanigan, a deputy White House counsel and member of the so-called War Council when this double-talk was issued, was asked at a Senate hearing in 2005 to define "humane treatment." He could not, and later he wrote to the committee that he was "not aware of any guidance provided by the White House specifically relating to the meaning of humane treatment." Alberto Gonzales subsequently confirmed that "the term 'humanely' had no precise legal definition."[135]

The president's statement and the legal memorandums he had received were deeply flawed. Al Qaeda and Taliban fighters might not be *soldiers* under the Third Geneva Convention, because they did not wear uniforms and carry weapons openly, but they were still *civilians* protected from inhumane treatment by the Fourth Geneva Convention. State Department and military lawyers tried repeatedly to explain that there was no such thing as a person without some rights to humane treatment under the Geneva Conventions. The international legal community was also unanimous on that point, but the OLC and the War Council refused to listen.

The American public might have been confused, but the guards at Guantánamo Bay were not. "You are in a place where there is no law," they told their prisoners. "We are the law."[136]

Lt. Gen. Ricardo S. Sanchez, who authorized harsh interrogation techniques as the commander of Coalition forces in Iraq in 2003, would later describe Bush's order as

> a watershed event in U.S. military history. Essentially, it set aside all of the legal constraints, training guidelines, and rules for interrogation that formed the U.S. Army's foundation for the treatment of prisoners on the battlefield since the Geneva Conventions were revised and ratified in 1949. . . . According to the president, it was now okay to go beyond those standards with regard to al Qaeda terrorists. And that guidance set America on a path toward torture.[137]

Hyping the Threat

Administration officials, like Americans generally, were outraged and frightened by the attacks of 9/11. Rumsfeld was in the Pentagon when the plane struck, and the Capitol was a possible target of a fourth airliner, which passengers forced the hijackers to crash in a Pennsylvania field. On Capitol Hill, members of Congress were doubly alarmed when, during the week following the attack, someone mailed envelopes containing anthrax to two Democratic senators and several East Coast media outlets. The attacks ended up killing five people and infecting twenty-two others. The targeted senators, Tom Daschle of South Dakota and Patrick Leahy of Vermont, were remarkably calm about the anthrax, which was more likely linked to the U.S. Army's laboratory at Fort Detrick, Maryland, than to al Qaeda. Vice President Cheney, however, was anything but calm, declaring that even "a one percent chance of catastrophe must be treated 'as a certainty'" in the war against terrorism.[138]

In January 2002, as the first orange-suited prisoners were being dragged to their cages at Guantánamo, Secretary Rumsfeld proclaimed them "the most dangerous, best trained, vicious killers on the face of the earth."[139] They were so vicious, Joint Chiefs chairman Gen. Richard B. Myers claimed, that they "would gnaw hydraulic lines in the back of a C-17 to bring it down."[140]

But when Alberto Gonzales asked the Pentagon to prepare a one-page charge sheet on each new prisoner, the military quickly admitted that it did not have enough information about most prisoners to charge them, even before a military commission with lax rules of evidence.[141] Evidence to justify most of the detentions would have to be obtained from the prisoners themselves. When Maj. Gen. Michael Dunlavey arrived at GTMO in February to supervise interrogations, he discovered that as many as half of the prisoners were of little or no intelligence value.[142]

In the early days of 2002, most fighters captured in Afghanistan were presumed to be terrorists and were sent to Cuba, including one who was so brain damaged that he could not talk.[143] In March, the deputy camp commander, Lt. Col. Bill Cline, complained that an unknown number of detainees were innocent "victims of circumstance" who just happened to be in the wrong place at the wrong time.[144] A month later, Dunlavey flew to Afghanistan to protest the shipment of "Mickey Mouse" prisoners to Cuba.[145] Guantánamo had become a dumping ground for prisoners whom senior officials at Camp Doha in Kuwait did not wish to keep in Afghanistan but dared not release.[146]

As late as July 2005, after 180 captives had been released, Rumsfeld continued to insist that "they're terrorists, trainers, bomb makers, recruiters, financiers, [bin Laden's] bodyguards, would-be suicide bombers, probably the 20th 9/11 hijacker."[147] But according to Michael F. Scheuer, who ran counterterrorism activities for the CIA until 2004, it was common knowledge by the fall of 2002 that fewer than 10 percent of Guantánamo's prisoners were high-value operatives. "Most of the men," he said, "were probably foot soldiers at best who were going to know absolutely nothing about terrorism."[148]

One source for Scheuer's estimate was an Arabic-speaking CIA analyst who interviewed at least thirty prisoners during the summer of 2002 and "came back convinced that we were committing war crimes in Guantánamo." "Based on [the analyst's] sample," a CIA official told reporter Seymour Hersh, "more than half of the people . . . didn't belong there. He found people lying in their own feces," including "two prisoners in their eighties who were clearly suffering from dementia."[149]

According to Sami al-Haj, an Al Jazeera journalist, forty-five of his fellow prisoners were juveniles. His attorney, Clive Stafford Smith, compared al-Haj's list to the military's, which was released under a court order. He identified sixty-four juveniles, but the military would acknowledge only twenty-seven. Three were ages ten, twelve, and thirteen at the time of their capture.[150] A Saudi youth, captured at age seventeen, committed suicide at twenty-two.[151]

Other prisoners were old and infirm. Haji Nusrat, an eighty-year-old stroke victim, shuffled around GTMO with a walker for four years, talking in riddles.[152] Mohamed Sadiq was ninety-three when he was released.[153]

Gen. John A. Gordon, deputy national security adviser for combating terrorism, was shocked by the CIA report, which he received in the summer of 2002. He and John Bellinger III, an NSC lawyer, warned both Addington and Gonzales that "this is a violation of basic notions of American fairness." Addington's response, according to persons familiar with the meetings, was that "these are 'enemy combatants.' Please use that term. They've all been through a screening process. We don't have anything to talk about."[154]

In fact, the prisoners had not been screened by competent tribunals, as required by the Geneva Conventions.[155] The evidence against each prisoner would not be formally reviewed by Combat Status Review Tribunals (CSRTs) until the summer of 2004 and then only because the Supreme Court required the reviews.[156] Another lengthy court battle would be needed to pry the findings of these tribunals out of the Defense Department, but in 2006, Seton Hall law professor Mark Denbeaux was finally able to study the evidence against 517 of the more than 750 Guantánamo prisoners.

The evidence he found was very thin. Contrary to Rumsfeld's claims, most of Guantánamo's prisoners were not "the worst of the worst." Nor were "all of them captured on a battlefield."[157] Quite the contrary, only 7 percent, or 21 of the 517 prisoners examined by CSRTs, had been captured on a battlefield, and American forces had apprehended only one of them.[158] Most (66 percent) had been turned over by Pakistani authorities or the Northern Alliance (11 percent), typically for generous bounties. According to then-president Pervez Musharraf of Pakistan, his government "captured 672 [al Qaeda members] and handed over 369 to the United States" and, in the process, "earned bounties totaling millions of dollars."[159]

Between January 11, 2002, and December 22, 2006, more than 775 prisoners were held without trial at Guantánamo Bay. CSRTs eventually decided that 520 men (67 percent) were "enemy combatants," but only 8 percent of the 517 prisoners whose files Denbeaux reviewed were alleged to be al Qaeda fighters. Forty percent, he found, had no definitive connection to al Qaeda, and 18 percent had no connection to either al Qaeda or the Taliban. Sixty percent had never spoken to an al Qaeda member. The military believed that more than half had not committed hostile acts against the United States or its allies.

The CSRT files revealed that much of the evidence against the prisoners had come from warlords and Pakistani intelligence officers and could not later be verified by military prosecutors. Information obtained during U.S. interrogations was often tainted by coercion. One prisoner improbably accused more than sixty fellow inmates.[160] Some of the detainees were classified as enemy combatants not because they had engaged in combat but because they worked for charities suspected of ties to the Taliban, al Qaeda, or its affiliates.[161] Of the seventy-two organizations that the CSRTs used to establish guilt by association, the Department of Homeland Security considered only sixteen dangerous enough to have their members barred from the United States.[162]

After six years of coercive interrogations, the military was able to charge less than two dozen prisoners with some sort of conspiracy to aid a terrorist organization. But that was not enough to support a prosecution because, as Justice John Paul Stevens observed in *Hamdan v. Rumsfeld* (2006), Congress has yet to make conspiracy a crime against the law of nations.[163] The evidence has to show that the defendant went further and attempted, alone or in concert with others, to commit a war crime, whether the defendant succeeded or failed. In the summer of 2008, the Bush administration managed to convict one GTMO prisoner— Salim Ahmed Hamdan, bin Laden's driver—of giving material assistance to al Qaeda, but the commission acquitted him of five other, more serious charges.[164] By the end of November 2008, only 250 of GTMO's original 775 prisoners remained in custody.[165] The rest had been quietly released.

Even so, the frightening rhetoric and falsehoods about Guantánamo's detainees served their political purposes: to stampede Congress and the public into accepting unlimited executive power and to justify the abuse of prisoners.

2

UNLEASHING THE DOGS OF WAR

I always knew the Americans would bring electricity back to Baghdad.
I just never thought they'd be shooting it up my ass.
—IRAQI TRANSLATOR[1]

To the founders of the American republic, the basic rights of man were God-given, self-evident, or "natural." They were not dispensations from the executive or legislative branches; they would exist, if only as morally legitimate assertions, even in the absence of government. The founders did not subscribe to the idea of "the state" as some sort of overarching, metaphysical, collective entity that wields sovereignty over all persons within its territory.

In the early seventeenth century, King James I of Great Britain claimed to possess absolute "sovereignty"—that legal authority above and beyond which there is no authority. His royal prerogatives could not be questioned in any other place, he insisted. Whatever legitimate authority soldiers, sheriffs, or secret agents might have, by commission, came from him. Whatever countervailing rights his "subjects" possessed also came from him, even if those rights had been reluctantly acknowledged by a predecessor on the plains of Runnymede or enacted into law repeatedly by Parliament during the previous three hundred years.

The American colonists had a different creed. Starting with the Mayflower Compact of 1620, they preferred a republican form of government that, as Jefferson would later put it, derived its "just powers from the consent of the governed." They were Protestants, in no small part, because they detested the Catholic Inquisition, which extracted confessions of heresy through secret interrogations and torture. In reaction to such practices, the common-law courts of Britain had refused to admit evidence obtained by torture even before Henry VIII broke with Rome in the sixteenth century.

That refusal did not stop all torture, but it did force Tudor and Stuart monarchs to confine its use to irregular courts until the early seventeenth century, when the Puritans revolted.[2] The Puritan revolt was not just about theology; it was a rebellion against the abuses of unlimited executive power, including military commissions, secret legal proceedings, and the infamous Court of the Star Chamber, which, like Bush's commissions, accepted evidence obtained by torture.

The great hero of the day was a young Puritan named John Lilburne, who defied virtually everyone in authority to advance the basic principles of due process that Americans now take for granted. Lilburne was just twenty-four years old in 1637 when the king's agents arrested him for illegally importing and distributing unregistered religious tracts. The king's council, sitting as the Court of the Star Chamber, demanded that he answer questions without knowing the charges against him. Just as American intelligence agents have in the war against terrorism, the council sought to conduct a fishing expedition and build its case against him out of his own mouth. Lilburne refused, saying that no person should be required to answer any questions except in response to specific charges presented to him in his own language. His well-publicized protest would eventually inspire both the constitutional right to be informed of the charges justifying arrest and trial and the privilege against self-incrimination.[3]

The Court of the Star Chamber convicted Lilburne without his help and sentenced him to be tied to the back of a cart and flogged for two miles through the streets of London. Although he received more than two hundred lashes from a three-tail whip, Lilburne had enough stamina left, while bent over in a pillory, to denounce his tormenters to a huge crowd of admirers. The Star Chamber then increased his punishment. It directed his jailer to shackle him hand and foot and deny him all visitors, books, and writing materials. It even tried to cut off his food and water, but other prisoners kept him alive. Lilburne not only managed to survive four months of solitary confinement, he published a sensational account of his ordeal and became an almost instant legend.

Lilburne's defiance helped the Puritans overthrow the monarchy and establish a republic in its place. But when the Puritans began to suppress freedom of speech and religion, he denounced them with equal fervor. When Parliament launched an inquisition, he again refused to testify and was again sent to prison, from which he continued to issue tracts that advocated religious liberty, freedom of the press, and the right to remain silent at interrogations. His defiance helped persuade Englishmen on both sides of the Atlantic that no man should be forced to be an instrument of his own doom.

When the monarchy was restored in 1660, the idea that the king could stand above the law was gone. Sovereignty no longer belonged to the king; the monarch had been euphemized into "the Crown," for which the king's ministers, chosen by Parliament, now spoke. The Star Chamber was abolished, and secret legal proceedings were banned. Military commissions fell into disuse. Ordinary civilian courts determined the rights of ordinary individuals, and acts of Parliament guaranteed the privilege of the writ of habeas corpus, or the right to challenge the legality of detentions without trial.

The largely self-governing American colonies followed suit. As early as 1641, Massachusetts legislators passed a "Body of Liberties" that declared, among other things, that "[n]o man shall be forced by Torture to confess any Crime against himself nor any other."[4]

So far as most colonists were concerned, authority came from free men. Elected officials were viewed less as stand-ins for the king (or Crown) and more as public servants of the people who elected them. During the American Revolution, the concept of legislative sovereignty was dominant, but that idea lasted only until the 1780s. Americans then invented constitutions ratified by the people meeting in conventions so that the powers of government could be said, with some force, to derive from "we, the people."

That was the founding theory, even as important rights were denied to nonvoters, including blacks, Native Americans, women, and children. The theory became enshrined in the Ninth Amendment to the federal Constitution, which instructs judges not to read that document's enumerations so restrictively as to deny other rights, not expressly mentioned, that belong—or should belong—to free people.

The Bush administration defied this theory, and the country's heritage, from the start. Its lawyers claimed that the Constitution grants no rights that "sovereign" officials may not take away, up to and including the right to be free from arbitrary detentions, torture, and military commissions. According to the

Justice Department, anyone—citizen or alien—can be stripped of his or her most basic rights by a mere act of executive labeling, just as the Imperial Japanese Army during World War II permitted itself to torture American POWs at its Ofuma Interrogation Center after relabeling them "belligerents."[5]

To facilitate unlimited detention and torture, Bush's lawyers invented new labels for prisoners in the war against terrorism and asserted an indisputable right to attach these exclusionary labels to whomever they wished. Persons who would be entitled to extensive rights if labeled criminals or prisoners of war were denied those rights by the mere act of labeling them unlawful combatants, enemy combatants, unprivileged belligerents, or security detainees. For example, the Justice Department argued in court that "a little old lady in Switzerland who writes checks to what she thinks is a charity that helps orphans in Afghanistan but really is a front to finance al-Qaeda" would, by that act alone, qualify as an enemy combatant and could be imprisoned at Guantánamo.[6]

"Fucking the PUCs"

Under the new regime, enemy captives were not to be called prisoners of war because that term implied equal dignity and reciprocal obligations, as the black flags with bowed heads still remind us. Nor were civilians deemed to be protected persons, as required by the Fourth Geneva Convention.[7] One new label for captives was persons under control (PUCs). The term was invented at the Bagram Air Base in Afghanistan to characterize prisoners of such uncertain intelligence value that they might be let go before they were entered into an official database. "We were pretty much told that [our prisoners] were nobodies," a military policeman (MP) later explained. "I think that giving them the distinction of soldier would have changed our attitudes toward them."[8]

According to three soldiers from the 82nd Airborne Division, brutalizing PUCs was a daily practice at Camp Mercury, a forward operating base close to Fallujah and west of Baghdad. "The 'Murderous Maniacs' was what [the Iraqis] called us," a sergeant recalled, "because they knew if they got . . . detained by us before they went to Abu Ghraib then it would be hell to pay."[9]

"It was like a game," he said. "To 'Fuck a PUC' means to beat them up. We would give them blows to the head, chest, legs, and stomach, pull them down, kick dirt on them. This happened every day."

To "smoke" a PUC, the sergeant explained, was "to put them in stress positions until they get muscle fatigue and pass out. That happened every day. Some days we would just get bored so we would . . . make them get in a pyramid. This was before Abu Ghraib but just like it. We did that for amusement."

"Leadership failed to provide clear guidance so we just developed it," he continued.

> They wanted intel. As long as no PUCs came up dead it happened. We heard rumors of PUCs dying so we were careful. We kept it to broken arms and legs and shit.
>
> On their days off people would show up all the time. Everyone in camp knew if you wanted to work out your frustration you show up at the PUC tent. In a way it was sport. The cooks were all U.S. soldiers. One day a sergeant shows up and tells a PUC to grab a pole. He told him to bend over and broke the guy's leg with a mini Louisville Slugger. . . . We had guys from all over the base just come to guard PUCs so they could fuck them up. . . . One night a guy came and broke chem. lights and beat the PUCs with it. That made them glow in the dark which was real funny but it burned their eyes and their skin was irritated real bad.[10]

Abusing prisoners for fun was not limited to the 82nd Airborne Division or to camera-toting guards at Abu Ghraib in Iraq. It also occurred in 2003 under the highly restrictive conditions at Guantánamo Bay. A Marine guard told a reporter that members of his squad were instructed to "give the prisoners a visit" once or twice a month, when there were no witnesses around. "We tried to fuck with them as much as we could—inflict a little bit of pain. We couldn't do much," he added, because "there were always news people there. That's why you couldn't send them back with a broken leg or something. . . . I wasn't trying to get information. I was just having a little fun—playing mind control."[11]

The CIA's Gulags

During the 1970s, Americans criticized Argentina's generals for making suspects disappear in their "dirty war" against alleged terrorists. On September 17, 2001, President Bush not only authorized the CIA to kill or capture suspected al Qaeda members anywhere and render them to foreign torturers, he also directed the agency to detain suspects in its own prisons, where they could be subjected to "enhanced interrogation techniques" and made to disappear from view, unseen by inspectors of the International Committee of the Red Cross. These prisons were to be the blackest legal holes of all.

The CIA created an archipelago of secret prisons in at least eight foreign countries, including Thailand, Afghanistan, Poland, and Romania.[12] It also delivered prisoners to Morocco, Egypt, Jordan, Syria, and Uzbekistan. Threatening to turn prisoners over to these notoriously brutal regimes was, according to Bagram interrogator Chris Mackey (a pseudonym), an effective way to force prisoners to cooperate.[13]

Together with the military, the CIA operated at least five prisons in Afghanistan. Several were located near Kabul: Bagram Air Base, "the Salt Pit," and the "Prison of Darkness" (also known as the "Discotheque" for blaring music around the clock). A fourth was in Kandahar and a fifth outside Asadabad. The military ran the Bagram and Kandahar facilities, but the CIA kept prisoners there in shipping containers. The CIA exclusively ran the Salt Pit, which was located in a former brick factory. Other government agencies (OGAs), including the CIA and British intelligence, used military facilities as holding pens. They would take prisoners off to their own offices for interrogation and then return them to the military police for safekeeping.[14]

The public has yet to see any photographs of how CIA interrogators treated their prisoners, but eight detainees have recounted what it was like to be held at the agency's underground Prison of Darkness near Kabul International Airport between 2002 and 2004. According to their attorneys, each was kept in isolation and in total darkness, chained to walls, often deprived of food and drink, and subjected to loud rap or heavy metal music for weeks on end. One recalled being interrogated in a room with a strobe light while shackled to a ring in the floor and threatened with rape.[15]

Sanad al-Kazimi spent some time at the Prison of Darkness before being moved to Guantánamo and was so traumatized by the treatment, his lawyer says, that "he can barely speak of it. He breaks down in tears." Al-Kazimi alleges that he was suspended by his arms for long periods of time, which caused his legs to swell painfully. He also said that he was beaten with electric cables.[16]

The hanging position was developed, in part, to prevent prisoners from sleeping. According to a former CIA officer interviewed by the *New Yorker*'s Jane Mayer, "Sleep deprivation works. Your electrolyte balance changes. You lose all balance and ability to think rationally. Stuff comes out."[17]

In July 2002, an eighteen-year-old Afghan held near Asadabad died after he was handcuffed and left unattended, without water, for four days during a heat wave.[18] Between October 2001 and December 2004, according to the Pentagon, at least eight Afghans died in U.S. custody.[19]

In November 2002, a CIA case officer at the Salt Pit ordered Afghan guards to strip a prisoner of his clothing and chain him outdoors for the night, where he froze to death. The CIA referred the matter to the Justice Department, but it decided not to prosecute on the grounds that the prison was not a U.S. facility. The department came to this conclusion because the prison's guards were not Americans. The case officer was later promoted.[20]

According to Chris Mackey, the military interrogators with whom he served at Bagram in late 2001 and early 2002 tried to follow the Geneva Conventions. That behavior changed as military interrogators became more frustrated and came under the influence of the more freewheeling CIA. By late 2002, around-the-clock lighting in the giant Soviet-era hangar at Bagram was used to drive prisoners to exhaustion. Outside their pens, captives were required to stand or kneel in painful positions for hours with stifling hoods over their heads or spray-painted goggles covering their eyes. A female interrogator stepped on the neck of one prisoner and kicked another in the genitals. A shackled prisoner was forced to roll across the floor and kiss the boots of his interrogators. Another was forced to remove plastic bottle caps from a drum filled with excrement.[21]

From July 2002 until August 2003, Lt. Carolyn Wood, a military intelligence (MI) officer, was in command of about twenty interrogators and analysts at Bagram. Sometime that summer, before Guantánamo's interrogators received permission to "enhance" their techniques, she authorized her guards to shackle prisoners in painful positions, humiliate them through nakedness, isolate them for up to thirty days, subject them to sensory deprivation, and threaten them with snarling dogs. The army's interrogation manual did not authorize any of these techniques. Wood apparently borrowed them from the CIA and used them, just as the agency did, to "soften up" the prisoners before they were interrogated.

In December 2002, two Afghan PUCs died at Bagram. One was a frail, twenty-two-year-old taxi cab driver named Dilawar who had been seized, along with three passengers, for possible involvement in a rocket attack. The passengers were sent to Guantánamo, only to be freed a year later without charges. Dilawar was not so fortunate. A subsequent court-martial determined that he had been trussed to the ceiling of his cell, off and on, for four days. When he was hauled from his cell at 2:00 a.m. for what was to be his last interrogation, his legs bounced uncontrollably. He pleaded for water, which Specialist Joshua Claus squirted in his face. An MP tried to push Dilawar to his knees, but they would not bend. By then most of the interrogators had decided that he wasn't involved in the attack, but guards still chained him to the ceiling of his cell. A few hours later a physician noticed rigor mortis setting in.

Pentagon officials claimed that Dilawar died from natural causes, but an autopsy determined that he had died from being kicked in the sides of his legs some one hundred times in the course of twenty-four hours. An army doctor testified that Dilawar's legs "had basically been pulpified." Had he survived, she testified, both of his legs would have had to have been amputated.[22]

A soldier later admitted at trial to kicking Dilawar's legs thirty-seven times. Three other soldiers admitted to applying "kicks to the groin and leg, . . . slamming [the prisoner] into wall/table, forcing [him] to maintain painful, contorted body positions, . . . and forcing water into his mouth until he could not breathe."[23] They kicked him, they told the court, because he repeatedly called for "God's help."[24]

The kicking technique actually has a name. Called a peroneal strike, it was brought to Afghanistan by soldiers who had worked as civilian guards in American prisons.

On December 3, two days before Dilawar's death, a mullah named Habibullah died at the same facility, also from blunt force injuries to his legs. The autopsy declared his death a homicide, but the Defense Department attributed it to natural causes.[25]

Savagery of this sort does not normally occur where the jailers have respect for the humanity of their prisoners. But humane treatment was not expected. Quite the contrary. Sgt. James Leahy told army investigators that "we sometimes developed rapport with detainees," but "Sergeant Loring [Leahy's superior] would sit us down and remind us these were evil people and talk about 9/11." Loring made it clear that his soldiers should hate and fear their captives, whom he said, echoing Rumsfeld, were "the worst of the worst."[26]

When the *Washington Post* first disclosed the existence of the CIA's secret prisons in November 2005, the agency refused to comment,[27] but on September 6, 2006, President Bush not only admitted that the prisons existed but defended the "alternative interrogation procedures" used at them. On February 5, 2008, CIA director Michael V. Hayden finally admitted that in 2002 and 2003 at least three al Qaeda operatives were "waterboarded"—that is, strapped to a board and nearly drowned with water.[28]

Virtually all the CIA's prisoners were "ghost" detainees. Their imprisonment was not known to anyone outside the agency, the military, or cooperating foreign governments, and it was hidden from the ICRC. The prisoners were disappeared from all who knew them as completely as any of the victims of the state-sponsored violence in Argentina and Chile during the 1970s. According to U.S. Army Gen. Paul Kern, who headed one of the Abu Ghraib investigations, the United States held as many as a hundred ghost detainees in Iraq alone, including three dozen at Abu Ghraib.[29] Between April 2003 and March 2004, a dozen or so non-Iraqis were removed from Iraq to CIA prisons in other countries in violation of the Geneva Conventions. On March 19, 2004, Jack L. Goldsmith, then head of the OLC, produced a secret memorandum (which the Bush administration refused to release) declaring that these transfers were legal.[30] Before that memo was issued, however, Maj. Gen. Antonio Taguba, in his report on the Abu Ghraib scandal, condemned the practice as "deceptive, contrary to Army Doctrine, and in violation of international law."[31]

Special Forces

During the early days of the war in Afghanistan, the press had celebrated covert agents from the CIA's Special Activities Division for riding about on horses, in tribal dress, and waging irregular warfare alongside the Northern Alliance. Not to be outdone, Secretary Rumsfeld dispatched army and navy commandos to do similar work. They operated out of uniform and, at times like the CIA, without regard for the laws of war. Task Force 5, the first of these covert units, was sent to Afghanistan in the fall of 2001 to capture or kill Osama bin Laden. In 2003,

Task Force 20—comprised of army Green Berets, Delta Force commandos, air force Pararescue operators, and navy SEALs (Sea, Air, Land)—infiltrated Iraq in advance of the main invasion force. Its orders were to capture or kill "high-value targets" (HVTs), including Ba'ath Party members. Together with soldiers from the 101st Airborne Division, they managed to kill Saddam Hussein's two sons, Uday and Qusay, in a fourteen-hour firefight. Elements of Task Forces 5 and 20 merged into Task Force 121, which worked with the CIA and friendly Iraqis to capture Saddam Hussein.[32] Task Force 134 supervised detainee operations after the scandal at Abu Ghraib.[33]

To prevent military lawyers from second-guessing these covert operations, Secretary Rumsfeld took the military task forces out of the regular chain of command and ordered them to report directly to his deputy, Stephen Cambone, through a Special Operations Command.[34] Cambone was given this responsibility even though he lacked military experience.[35]

The "enhanced interrogation techniques" that the task forces used on their prisoners were sometimes lethal. For example, in November 2003, navy SEALs attached to Task Force 121 pummeled Manadel al-Jamadi, a suspected insurgent, with rifle butts before delivering him, naked from the waist down, to the prison at Abu Ghraib as an unrecorded ghost detainee. On November 4, 2003, the same night that guards took the iconic photograph of the hooded prisoner on the box, with wires on his fingers, CIA interrogators decided to subject al-Jamadi to what Israeli interrogators called a Palestinian hanging,[36] not knowing that the SEALs had already broken several of his ribs. The agents shackled al-Jamadi's wrists behind him and trussed him up to the bars of a window. His agony was so great, a nearby prisoner recalled, that "we listened as his soul cracked."[37]

A half hour later, when the interrogators tried to reposition al-Jamadi, they discovered he was dead. CIA agent Mark Swanner told the guards to cut him down. When they did, "blood came gushing out of his nose and mouth, as if a faucet had been turned on," according to Walter A. Diaz, one of the MPs on duty that night. Panicked, the interrogators, including Col. Thomas M. Pappas of military intelligence, wrapped al-Jamadi's body in plastic, packed it in ice, and locked it in a shower room overnight while they debated what to do. The next day army medics inserted an IV needle into his arm and carried his body out of the prison on a stretcher so as not to alarm the other prisoners. The medics delivered the corpse to a military pathologist, who ruled that his death was a homicide. However, al-Jamadi's death was not acknowledged until April 2004, when CBS broadcast a photograph of his corpse, which guards had discovered and photographed themselves with, they said, for souvenirs.[38] They called him "the Iceman" and "Mr. Frosty."[39]

GTMO

Most of Rumsfeld's interrogation techniques were ill defined; soldiers were expected to be creative, and they were. FBI agents were aghast at what they witnessed and filed reports that caused the bureau to document more than two dozen cases of abuse.[40] They included wrapping a prisoner's head in duct tape for chanting the Koran, dressing a soldier as a Catholic priest and pretending to "baptize" a Muslim prisoner, and draping an Israeli flag over an Arab prisoner. FBI agents reported seeing a female soldier handle a prisoner's genitals and wipe what she said was menstrual blood in his face, acts that would be would be especially offensive to observant Muslims.[41]

An FBI agent wrote to headquarters,

> On a couple of occasions I entered interview rooms to find a detainee chained hand and foot in a fetal position on the floor, with no chair, food or water. Most times they urinated or defecated on themselves, and had been left there for 18–24 hours or more. On one occasion, the air conditioning had been turned down so far . . . that the barefooted detainee was shaking with cold. . . . On another occasion [the air conditioner] had been turned off, making the temperature in the unventilated room well over 100 degrees. The detainee was almost unconscious on the floor, with a pile of hair next to him. He had apparently been literally pulling his hair out throughout the night.

Such tactics, FBI agents complained, were not just cruel; they constituted "torture."[42] They also failed to produce useful intelligence and "destroyed any chance of prosecuting" the detainees.[43]

But Rumsfeld wanted harsh interrogations. In October 2002, he was happy to replace Brig. Gen. Rick Baccus, head of the detention facility at Guantánamo, with Gen. Geoffrey Miller. Baccus allegedly coddled prisoners and disciplined guards who harmed them.[44] Miller, a hard-charging artillery officer with no experience in corrections, intelligence, or law enforcement, shared the secretary's antipathy toward suspected terrorists. The general had lost friends on 9/11 and encouraged GTMO's guards to hate their captives.[45] Like Rumsfeld, and despite the FBI's objections, Miller was convinced that harsh treatment could work and that useful intelligence could be extracted from a prisoner long after his capture. Nor was the general deterred by the fact there was still not enough evidence to prosecute most of GTMO's detainees, even before military commissions rigged to favor convictions.

When Rumsfeld and his staff continued to ignore the bureau's protests, FBI director Robert Mueller withdrew his agents from Guantánamo. He did not wish to read of prisoners accusing FBI agents of war crimes, which was possible when military interrogators switched to civilian clothes and pretended to be G-men.[46] But while FBI agents witnessed what they considered to be "grave breaches" of article 3 of the Geneva Conventions in both Cuba and Iraq, Mueller did not initiate any prosecutions or order follow-up interviews. This inaction continued even after the director received an urgent report in June 2004 from an FBI agent who had "observed numerous physical abuse incidents of Iraqi civilian detainees" in Iraq, including "strangulation, beatings, [and] placement of lit cigarettes into the detainees' ear openings."[47] The signal remained clear: Mueller and Ashcroft were not eager to prosecute Americans for war crimes.

Harsh treatment was necessary to produce information, Pentagon officials claimed, but much of the abuse in Afghanistan, Iraq, and Cuba was just cruel. At GTMO, prisoners were supposed to receive at least three hours of recreation a week, but during the hot summer of 2002, recreation for prisoners consisted of being trussed up in pseudo-straightjackets, with their arms lashed in back, their legs strapped together, their eyes blinded by black goggles, and their heads encased in stifling hoods. Thus bound, prisoners were taken out into a narrow dog run at midday and allowed to move about, as best they could, on their knees. Most just baked in the tropical sun.[48]

At night, some prisoners were subjected to the "frequent flier" program—awakened, chained, and dragged from one cell to another to deny them sleep. For example, during one fourteen-day period, Mohammed Jawad was moved an average of eight times a night—or about once an hour—between cells L40 and L48.

In 2004 an International Committee of the Red Cross report was leaked to the press. It documented many of these abuses and concluded that how prisoners were handled at Guantánamo "cannot be considered other than an intentional system of cruel, unusual, and degrading treatment and a form of torture."[49] Meanwhile, General Miller required his soldiers to chant the camp slogan each time they saluted a superior officer: "Honor bound to defend freedom."[50]

Abu Ghraib

Rumsfeld was so pleased by Miller's aggressive methods, and so frustrated at how little the military knew about its adversaries in Iraq, that he dispatched the general to Baghdad in late August 2003 to intensify interrogation methods at fifteen American-run detention centers in Iraq, including the newly rehabilitated Abu Ghraib facility outside of Baghdad.[51]

Turning Abu Ghraib into an American prison was an extraordinary decision. An officer with the Coalition Provisional Authority protested at the time it was "no different than going into Dachau and saying, 'We're going to use this as a prison facility.'" Thousands of Iraqis had been tortured and killed within its walls; the hanging ropes and death chamber were still there when American troops arrived.[52] But the symbolic impact of reopening Saddam's torture center as an American facility did not deter Ambassador L. Paul Bremer, head of the Coalition Provisional Authority, or Deputy Secretary of Defense Paul Wolfowitz, even after they toured the facility, including its death house, in July 2003. Nor did it bother Secretary Rumsfeld, who visited a month later. Perhaps they thought it sufficient that the prison's staff had replaced Saddam's portrait with a large new sign that declared, in both English and Arabic, "America is a friend of all Iraqi people."[53]

General Miller arrived on August 31, bringing with him a team of his most experienced interrogators, including a woman who specialized in sexually taunting Muslim men. Although most of Abu Ghraib's prisoners at that time were civilians, legally entitled to humane treatment under the Fourth Geneva Convention,[54] the general announced his intention to "Gitmo-ize" their interrogations.[55]

Again, the guards and interrogators were not told what was forbidden, but they got an idea what was wanted when Miller introduced three "Tiger Teams" of interrogators and insisted, as Lieutenant Wood had at Bagram, that military police guards "set the conditions for interrogations."[56] This instruction was a euphemism for so exhausting and humiliating prisoners that they would be unable to resist their interrogators.[57]

"When I got to Abu G," interrogator Tim Dugan recalled,

> they had . . . these tiger teams that were classified as breaker teams, and they worked from 8 P.M. to 8 A.M. when the vast majority of us worked from 8 A.M. to 8 P.M. The breaker teams did their interrogations in the hard site and, dang, then all the abuse happened at the hard site at nights. The breaker teams weren't allowed to talk about anything they were doing. So you tell me what the hell was going on in the hard site at nights. I don't think those kids came up with that BS by themselves.[58]

Miller also persuaded the commander of Combined Joint Task Force 7, Lt. Gen. Ricardo S. Sanchez, to issue memorandums specifying which interrogation techniques were approved and, to this end, gave him the list of interrogation techniques that Rumsfeld had approved for GTMO in April. On September 14, Sanchez approved twenty-nine specific techniques, some of which were harsher than Rumsfeld's twenty-four, including the use of dogs.[59] The animals were used not only to frighten prisoners but to offend them, because many Muslims have a strong religious aversion to dogs as unclean. Five teams of dog handlers were dispatched to Iraq from Guantánamo after Miller's visit. Per Sanchez's guidelines, the dogs were supposed to be muzzled, but according to Col. Thomas M. Pappas, the military intelligence commander at Abu Ghraib, Miller told him that the dogs could be used "with or without a muzzle."[60] The straps came off. In one instance, which guards photographed,[61] a prisoner was so severely bitten that twelve stitches were required to close the wound.[62]

Dogs were not just used in interrogations. One army specialist recalled watching a dog team terrorize two cowering prisoners: "When I asked what was going on . . . the handler stated that . . . he and another of the handlers [were] having a contest to see how many detainees they could get to urinate on themselves."[63] Staff Sgt. Ivan "Chip" Frederick, later convicted for abuses at Abu Ghraib, called this the doggie dance.[64]

General Miller wanted prisoners to be humiliated. In August 2003, he told Abu Ghraib's commanding officer, Brig. Gen. Janis L. Karpinski, "You're too nice. They don't know you are in charge." To gain control of the prisoners, "you have to treat them like dogs. If . . . they believe they're any different than dogs, you have effectively lost control of your interrogation from the start. . . . And it works. This is what we do down at Guantánamo Bay."[65] Miller later denied saying it, but the message got through. A few months later guards photographed PFC Lynndie England, a prison clerk, holding a naked prisoner by a leash. Treating prisoners like dogs was also used to humiliate Muhammed al-Qahtani, a high-value al Qaeda detainee, when Miller was in command at Guantánamo.[66]

An investigation headed by Maj. Gen. George R. Fay would conclude—in a classified section of his report—that the "manner in which [dogs] were used on some occasions [at Abu Ghraib] clearly violated the Geneva Conventions."[67] In January 2006, Miller invoked his constitutional privilege against self-incrimination rather than testify at the trial of one of Abu Ghraib's dog handlers.[68]

Miller was not the only officer who brought harsh techniques to Abu Ghraib. Carolyn Wood, who had been promoted to captain and awarded a Bronze Star despite the fact that her unit killed several prisoners at Bagram, was put in charge of interrogations. She also helped draft General Sanchez's guidelines, drawing upon her experience in Afghanistan and borrowing some "rules of engagement" from Task Force 20, the joint Special Forces–CIA unit that had killed Saddam's sons.

While Wood was making her recommendations and setting up the "hard site" at Abu Ghraib, Capt. William Ponce, who worked in the Human Intelligence Effects Coordination Cell within Sanchez's command, sent an e-mail to all military intelligence units in Iraq asking them to submit wish lists of any interrogation techniques they wanted authority to use, adding that "the gloves are coming off, gentlemen, regarding these detainees." He also suggested, erroneously, that the Geneva Conventions' protections did not apply to any enemy combatants within their custody.[69]

Even if the president said that the conventions did not apply to suspected terrorists in Afghanistan, the Geneva Conventions applied to both military and civilian prisoners in Iraq. But even that principle became blurry as the war slid into an occupation and Coalition troops faced an insurgency, elements of which were alleged to be the work of al Qaeda outsiders.

The first civilian interrogators arrived at Abu Ghraib in September and October 2003. Some were former soldiers who had served with the army in Bosnia, Afghanistan, and GTMO. All were hired for military intelligence by CACI International, a private American firm, and were assisted by translators from Titan Corporation, another American company.

One of the civilians was "Big Steve" Stefanowicz, a former U.S. Navy petty officer with a commanding presence, a six-figure salary, and no experience conducting interrogations.[70] When Specialist Charles A. Graner, Jr., asked the deputy commander of his military police company whether he should obey Stefanowitz, the reply was, "Our mission is to support MI."[71]

The civilians shared advantages that their military employers lacked: they were not bound by the Uniform Code of Military Justice (UCMJ), which governed American soldiers, and the governing Coalition Provisional Authority had decreed that they were not bound by Iraqi law. Army interrogators who had worked with the CIA in Afghanistan appeared during the summer and fall, along with CIA agents, but it wasn't until November—after the base had been shelled almost nightly with mortars—that what Maj. Gen. Antonio Taguba called the "sadistic, blatant, and wanton criminal abuses" photographed on the night shift occurred. According to his investigation, which focused only on military policemen, these abuses included

> breaking chemical lights and pouring the phosphoric liquid on the detainees; pouring cold water on naked detainees; beating detainees with a broom handle and a chair; threatening male detainees with rape; allowing a military police guard to stitch the wound of a detainee who was injured after being slammed against the wall of his cell; sodomizing a detainee with a chemical light and perhaps a broom stick; and using military working dogs to frighten and intimidate detainees with threats of attack, and in one instance actually biting a detainee.[72]

The pictures, first broadcast on April 28, 2004, showed guards taunting naked prisoners. One was on a leash; others were forced to masturbate, pile themselves in a pyramid, or simulate oral sex.[73] The MPs had learned during their cultural awareness training at Fort Lee, Virginia, that Muslim men would find such humiliations especially degrading, but no one appears to have told the MPs to respect the Muslim faith. On the contrary, they learned to single out the most devout prisoners for the most demeaning forms of sexual humiliation.[74]

The most infamous photograph showed a prisoner in a blanket with a bag over his head, looking, to Americans, very much like a witch or a Klansman in a pointed hood and robe. He was in a "stress position," balanced on a narrow cardboard box, with wires attached to his extremities. Guards told him that if he fell off the box he would be electrocuted.

The blue-ribbon panel headed by former defense secretary James R. Schlesinger tried to minimize what happened at Abu Ghraib by comparing it to the movie *Animal House* and its fraternity pranks, but there was nothing fraternal about threatening a prisoner with electrocution. The practice could have been brought to Abu Ghraib by the CIA, which aided Brazilian intelligence during its dirty war against terrorists in the 1980s. Brazilian interrogators called this technique "the Vietnam."[75]

The photographs also showed the battered bodies of two prisoners who had died from their beatings at Abu Ghraib and an empty room smeared with blood. One of the pictures showed smiling guards posing with one of the corpses and flashing thumbs-up signs. But many of the most distressing pictures were never disclosed. According to NBC News, unpublished photographs showed army guards "severely beating an Iraqi prisoner nearly to death, having sex with a female Iraqi prisoner, and 'acting inappropriately with a dead body.' [T]here also was a videotape, apparently shot by U.S. personnel, showing Iraqi guards raping young boys."[76] General Taguba, who conducted the first investigation, recalled seeing "a video of a male American soldier in uniform sodomizing a female detainee."[77]

Sgt. Javal Davis, one of the guards, would later call Abu Ghraib "a city of lost souls."[78] He also came to understand Friedrich Nietzsche's warning: "Whoever fights monsters should see to it that he does not become a monster in the process."[79] "That place turned me into a monster," Davis said.[80]

Ameen Sa'eed al-Sheikh, a Syrian, described what happened to him in October 2003 after military policemen at Abu Ghraib shot him in the legs while trying to confiscate a pistol that had been smuggled into him by an Iraqi guard:

Every hour or two, soldiers came, threatening . . . they were going to kill me and torture me and I'm going to be in prison forever. . . . "We will make you wish to die and it will not happen." The night guard came over, his name is GRANER, open[ed] the cell door, [and] came in with a number of soldiers. They forced me to eat pork and put liquor in my mouth. . . . One of them told me he would rape me. . . . Someone else asked me: "Do you believe in anything?" I said to him, "I believe in Allah." So he said, "But I believe in torture and I will torture you." They ordered me to curse Islam and because they started to hit my broken leg, I cursed my religion. They ordered me to thank Jesus I'm alive, and I did what they ordered me. This is against my belief. They left me hang[ing] from the bed and after a while I lost consciousness.[81]

In time, Abu Ghraib became one of the largest military intelligence operations since World War II, but its interrogators regularly deferred to representatives of OGAs. This euphemism not only covered the CIA but the FBI, the Defense Intelligence Agency, and secret CIA–Special Forces units such as Task Force 121. OGA personnel often wore civilian clothes and ski masks, revealing only their eyes. They rarely disclosed their true names.

Sometimes, when army interrogators did not get the information they wanted, they would hand prisoners over to the OGAs. What they did in the shower rooms and beneath the stairs is not known, but other prisoners could hear screams. When these OGAs were not successful, they sometimes turned prisoners over to collaborating Iraqis known as "Scorpions," who went by such nicknames as "Alligator" and "Cobra."[82]

One might think that American soldiers would have some interest in following the Geneva Conventions because they, too, might be captured. But abstract lectures in the military schools mean little without command reinforcement, and that leadership did not exist, in part because soldiers were encouraged to think of the war in Iraq as part of the war in Afghanistan—where, the president continued to insist, the Geneva Conventions did not apply. As a member of the 377th Military Police Company explained, persons unprotected by the conventions were not fellow soldiers; "they were nobodies."[83]

The Schlesinger panel concluded that General Sanchez had been derelict in overseeing the Iraqi prisoners' detention. A classified portion of the panel's report found that Sanchez had approved some of the more severe interrogation techniques originally authorized for use in Afghanistan and at Guantánamo Bay. The panel concluded that his orders illegally suspended the Geneva Convention by misclassifying all prisoners in Iraq as unlawful combatants.[84] It also found that Sanchez and his legal advisers contributed to the confusion by changing the rules governing interrogations three times in thirty days.[85] But the Schlesinger panel failed to mention that both Donald Rumsfeld and his deputy, Paul Wolfowitz, personally called interrogators at Abu Ghraib and on some occasions received nightly briefings on what the interrogations were producing.[86]

General Karpinski's power over Abu Ghraib's MPs had been transferred to military intelligence officer Col. Thomas Pappas following Miller's August 2003 visit. When Karpinski arrived to inspect the cell blocks in January 2004, the cover-up was nearly complete, but the army's Criminal Investigative Division had missed one piece of paper taped to a pole outside an interrogator's office. It was Secretary Rumsfeld's memo of December 2, 2002, authorizing the use of loud music, nighttime lights, dogs, and stress positions. To one side was Rumsfeld's handwritten notation: "Make sure this happens!"[87] A separate DIA report, dated May 19, 2004, quoted an officer in charge of interrogators as saying that Sanchez's command had issued a thirty-five-page order spelling out the rules interrogators were supposed to follow. He added that interrogators were encouraged "by people who wanted information [to] go to the outer limits to get [it]"[88] from detainees.

Like the occupation itself, Abu Ghraib was plagued by inadequate preparation, training, management, and staff. The prison was the place where the army dumped Iraqi males seized during neighborhood sweeps. Fewer than three hundred guards were expected to secure more than five thousand prisoners. The base was subject to mortar attacks nearly every night, and the temperature in the summer could reach 120 degrees Fahrenheit. There were never enough officers to supervise the guards and interrogators, especially at night. But when General Karpinski, the nominal commander, complained to Sanchez's second in command, Maj. Gen. Walter Wojdakowski, about the lack of staff to run the overcrowded prisons, he exploded: "I don't care if we're holding 15,000 innocent civilians! We're winning the war!"[89]

The abuses were not limited to Abu Ghraib. For example, when fifty-seven-year-old Iraqi Maj. Gen. Abed Hamed Mowhoush surrendered in Qa'im on November 10, 2003, seeking leniency for his sons, he was beaten almost senseless by Iraqis working for the CIA. Two days later CWO Lewis E. Welshofer, Jr., and a military guard from the 3rd Armored Cavalry stuffed the general into a green sleeping bag, tied it up with twenty feet of electrical wire, and laid him out on the floor. Welshofer sat on the prisoner's chest until he died of asphyxiation caused, in part, by six or seven broken ribs. This technique was not authorized by the army's field manual, but as one of the two men later testified at trial, they thought such measures were permitted because their commanders had told them that "the gloves were coming off."[90]

According to Dr. Steven H. Miles, who has studied the role of doctors in the war on terrorism, at least nineteen prisoners are known to have died of beatings, asphyxiation, or suspension by American soldiers or intelligence personnel in at least ten different facilities in Afghanistan and Iraq. Many more died under suspicious circumstances or from medical neglect. The dead are listed in Dr. Miles's book, *Oath Betrayed: Torture, Medical Complicity, and the War on Terror.*[91]

According to guards who were later court-martialed, interrogators from military intelligence, the CIA, or civilian contractors ordered the initial abuse. The interrogators would come to the guards and say, "This guy needs to have a bad night." The guards on the night shift were expected to use their imaginations. Some of the abuse was anticipated in written interrogation plans, but much of it appears to have been casual, or the foreseeable consequence of deliberately suspending the laws of war.

When Specialist Graner arrived at Abu Ghraib in October 2003, he complained about the orders he was receiving from the intelligence officers. "I'm having to do things to detainees that I feel are morally and ethically wrong," he told a fellow policeman.[92] But soon, the same MP recalled, Graner "got addicted to power" and began tormenting prisoners "as if it were a party."[93] He even admitted to the pleasure, telling another guard that "the Christian in me says it's wrong. But the corrections officer in me says I love to make a grown man piss himself."[94] His work resulted in a glowing commendation from Lt. Col. Steve Jordan, who commanded one of the intelligence units at Abu Ghraib when the abuses were photographed.[95]

None of the military police at Abu Ghraib had received any training in how to guard prisoners. Among Army intelligence agents, only enlisted men were taught how to conduct interrogations. Some of them had little more than a high school diploma.[96] Most could not speak Arabic. In the heat and stench of Abu Ghraib under nightly mortar attacks, they were allowed to take out their frustrations on the prisoners.

The most potent training in how to abuse prisoners came not from army classrooms but from the survival, evasion, resistance, and escape (SERE) exercises run by combat training units. To persuade their soldiers and airmen not to surrender, American forces for decades have sent recruits out into the woods at night, armed only with a compass, and directed them to make their way through to the other side without being captured by aggressor troops. Those who fail are taken to a mock interrogation center, where interrogators and guards torment them. The abuse is supposed to make them better able to resist such mistreatment should an enemy capture them. What most soldiers take away from this experience, of course, is that the best way to break a prisoner is to hurt and humiliate him and, if he takes refuge in his religion, to try to destroy his faith.

The SERE program was based on a study of how Communist soldiers extorted *false* confessions from American prisoners in Korea. On December 10, 2002, a secret memorandum "reverse engineered" those procedures into the SERE Interrogation Standard Operating Procedure for extorting *true* confessions from alleged terrorists.[97] "In addition to degradation of the detainee," the memo said, "stripping can be used to demonstrate the omnipotence of the captor." For best effect, clothing should be torn "from detainees by firmly pulling downward against buttons and seams. Tearing motions shall be downward to prevent pulling the detainee off balance." The memo also recommended slapping, hooding, and several stress positions, including one called Worship-the-Gods.[98]

The murder of General Mowhoush is a case in point. One of his interrogators, a former SERE instructor, recalled that the "sleeping bag technique," including the use of wire "to limit movement . . . and help bring on claustrophobic conditions," had proved very effective in SERE training.[99] The use of SERE techniques to abuse prisoners was so widespread by 2004 that the army finally ordered SERE graduates to pledge, in writing, not to use them on captives.[100]

Of course, an army that uses humiliation and brutality as central elements of basic training can hardly expect its recruits not to use the same techniques on people under their control. Army doctrine is based on the assumption that the only way to control soldiers and train them to plunge obediently into almost certain death is to break them down and make them wholly dependent on their officers. Only then can they be turned into amoral killing machines. Given this ethos, it is not difficult to understand how guards and interrogators at Abu Ghraib and elsewhere could not only soften up prisoners on command but enjoy doing it, even though their vestigial moral training or briefings about the laws of war told them it was wrong.

The scandal at Abu Ghraib did not end the torture. Specialist Tony Lagouranis worked there after the photos were published and later served with a Marine reconnaissance unit south of Baghdad between August and October 2004. The Marines, he said,

> would go out and do a raid and stay in the detainees' homes, and torture them there. They were far worse than anything that I ever saw in a prison. They were breaking bones. They were smashing people's feet with the back of an axe head. They burned people. . . . One guy was forced to sit on an exhaust pipe of a humvee . . . he had a giant blister, third-degree burn on the back of his leg.[101]

This abuse continued more discreetly at various bases throughout Iraq even after the Americans turned Abu Ghraib over to the Iraqis in August 2006, because an atmosphere of permissiveness continued to emanate from the highest echelons, including the White House.

Scarless Torture

It would be reassuring to view the abuse of suspected terrorists since 9/11 as aberrations attributable to poor training, staffing, or discipline or to the excessive zeal of one administration. But torture did not begin with the Bush administration; it had been part of the CIA's repertoire for decades. Between 1950 and 1962, scientists working for the CIA spent more than a billion dollars on secret research into electric shocks, hallucinogenic drugs, and sensory deprivation. The ostensible purpose was to develop ways of resisting Communist interrogations, as through SERE training, but it was also associated with research into mind control.

Worse followed. Between 1968 and 1972, the agency, together with U.S. Army Special Forces units, assassinated thousands of suspected Viet Cong, some after brutal interrogations.[102] When the congressional investigations of the 1970s rendered assassination unacceptable, CIA interrogators turned to hooding, sleep deprivation, blaring noise, stress positions, sexual humiliation, and waterboarding. These techniques did not leave incriminating scars and helped persuade some victims that their stubbornness was the cause of their pain.

Between 1963 and 1975, the CIA recommended the "no scars" approach to Asian and Latin American police through its infamous *KUBARK Counterintelligence Interrogation* manual. That publication was suspended in the 1970s, but it resurfaced in Central America in 1983 as the *Human Resource Exploitation Training Manual* and was distributed by U.S. Army Mobile Training Teams. When this manual was issued, David Addington was assistant general counsel at the CIA.[103]

Scarless torture, including sexual humiliation and waterboarding, was revived in 2001 in part because it was easy to deny or cover up. Practitioners could persuade themselves that they really hadn't tortured anyone because no marks were visible.[104] John Yoo's memo, which OLC head Jay Bybee issued on August 1, 2002, encouraged this self-deception by defining torture as physical but not mental cruelty. Thus, when three young prisoners hanged themselves in June 2006, GTMO's commander denied that mental anguish inflicted by guards, interrogators, and the sheer hopelessness of indefinite detention might be contributing causes. Rear Adm. Harry B. Davis insisted that the suicides were "not an act of desperation, but an act of asymmetric warfare aimed at us here at Guantánamo,"[105] while a spokeswoman for the State Department dismissed the deaths as a mere "public relations" gesture.[106]

The Bush administration insisted that stress positions, sensory deprivation, incessant noise, sleep deprivation, sexual humiliation, and waterboarding do not rise to the level of torture because they leave no lasting scars.[107] In documents like the Bybee memo, officials tried to claim that cruel, inhumane, and degrading treatment cannot rise to the level of torture, ignoring substantial evidence that psychological harm can do more lasting damage than physical pain. Memories of physical pain fade. Wounds heal, but the psychological pain caused by being helpless in the face of cruelty may never go away. Like the experience of battle, it can permanently disfigure its victim's character and personality.[108]

The Supreme Court recognized this obvious fact in 1960. It wrote,

[C]oercion can be mental as well as physical. . . . [T]he blood of the accused is not the only hallmark of an unconstitutional inquisition. A number of cases have demonstrated, if demonstration were needed, that the efficiency of the rack and the thumbscrew can be matched, given the proper subject, by more sophisticated modes of "persuasion."[109]

The psychological harm done by U.S. detention practices has been extensive. More than forty of GTMO's prisoners have attempted suicide.[110] Three succeeded in hanging themselves in 2006, another killed himself in 2007.[111] Still others have tried to starve themselves to death.

By July 2003, 120 of approximately 625 prisoners at Guantánamo were on antidepressant drugs. According to the base's only Muslim chaplain, an entire cell block within the section known as Camp Delta was set aside for prisoners who babbled "in a childlike voice, talking complete nonsense." Some of these prisoners had regressed to the point where they spent their time drawing pictures with crayons, which nurses allowed them to display on walls of their cells.[112]

Another form of scarless torture involved the force-feeding of hunger strikers at Guantánamo Bay. The strike, which began in June 2005, grew to involve at least 131 detainees by mid-September, when the military responded with force-feeding. Special "restraint chairs" were brought in to make insertion of forty-three-inch plastic tubes down the prisoner's nose easier.[113] Gen. John Craddock, commander of the Southern Command (SOUTHCOM), which oversees Guantánamo Bay, insisted that the chairs were "pretty comfortable; it's not abusive,"[114] although they had been linked to dozens of deaths in U.S. prisons and institutions.[115] The prisoners were given a choice of colors of feeding tubes. Craddock added, "They like the yellow."[116]

Prisoners called the chairs, which resemble an electric chair, the torture chair,[117] but the forced feeding worked. By August 2007, the number of hunger strikers was down to about twenty. Both the American Medical Association and the World Medical Association condemned the practice,[118] which Alexander Solzhenitsyn had compared to rape.[119]

Dr. William Winkenwerder, Jr., assistant secretary of defense for health affairs, disagreed. "There is a moral question," he declared. "Do you allow a person to commit suicide?"[120] As a matter of law and medical ethics, the answer happens to be yes. Under the American legal system, as well as the World Medical Association's 1975 Declaration of Tokyo, all competent patients have a right to refuse medical treatment. Force-feeding constitutes an assault upon the patient unless the patient, or someone empowered to act on his or her behalf, gives voluntary, informed consent.[121]

For the military, however, the issue had nothing to do with the well-being of its prisoners. It didn't want suicides to dramatize just how desperately many prisoners felt about their situation. Solzhenitsyn understood the politics of this type of situation: "[T]he hunger strike is a purely moral weapon. It presupposes that the jailer has not entirely lost his conscience. Or that the jailer is afraid of public opinion. Only in such circumstances can it be effective."[122]

Overview

Seven years into the so-called war on terrorism, much remains to be learned about the mistreatment of suspected terrorists, but some conclusions are indisputable. First, the abuses photographed at Abu Ghraib cannot be blamed on a few bad apples on the night shift. Torture was intended from the start. That is why the president authorized the secret prisons and military commissions that could admit evidence based on torture, and that is why he suspended the Geneva Conventions.

Of course, not all of the abuses, including fucking the PUCs, were intended by Bush and his torture team. The abuse was just the foreseeable consequence of a series of signals that legitimated the prisoners' harsh treatment. The president made it perfectly clear: this war was different. Previously established norms of humanity no longer applied.

So far, not one instance of torture can be directly traced to credible reports of a "ticking bomb" or its equivalent. Most of the harsh interrogations took place long after such a weapon would have exploded. Some first-round interrogations sought information about the suspects' associates, information that could be useful in capturing other terrorists and insurgents. But most late-term interrogations, conducted years after the prisoners were captured, had nothing to do with the search for usable intelligence. Their purpose was to justify the detentions that were based on the unsubstantiated allegations of bounty hunters or on the vague suspicions of U.S. soldiers who conducted indiscriminate sweeps of hostile neighborhoods. Interrogators and guards tried to force prisoners to incriminate themselves because they had no good reason to hold them and because no one in the chain of command dared release a prisoner who might latter attack Coalition forces, if for no other reason than that he had been humiliated while in custody.

The architects of the torture policy never thought ahead to the day when they would have to decide what to do with their prisoners. The driving force behind their war on terrorism was an understandable, and disastrous, lust for revenge.

3

TORTURE BY PROXY

We don't kick the shit out of them. We send them to other countries
so that they can kick the shit out of them.
—A U.S. INTELLIGENCE OFFICER[1]

There is more to this story than the abuse of prisoners in Afghanistan, Guantánamo, and Iraq. As mentioned earlier, President Bush also authorized a separate, highly secret program of extraordinary rendition, by which suspected terrorists were kidnapped from the United States or other countries and delivered for questioning to countries that routinely practice torture.

The purpose of this program was to obtain information through torture. President Bush made this clear to the Saudi ambassador, Prince Bandar, on September 13, 2001, when he said, "If we get somebody and we can't get them to cooperate, we'll hand them over to you."[2]

When the president signed a memorandum of notification secretly authorizing the program on September 17, 2001,[3] he empowered the CIA to select its own candidates for abduction.[4] This move gave him the option of denying knowledge of the kidnappings, in case any of them went bad. He also authorized the creation of secret CIA prisons in various countries around the world.[5]

Origins of the Program

Where the president got the authority to have anyone abducted for torture has never been explained. The practice runs counter to more than two hundred years of international and American law, which sought to substitute judicially approved extradition for what used to be called self-help.[6] Torture by proxy also violates the UN Convention Against Torture, which the United States ratified in 1994.[7]

Although it is hard to imagine now, the United States was founded as a nation of asylum for failed revolutionaries whom European monarchs considered terrorists in their day. For its first half century, the United States was reluctant to extradite any alleged criminal back to his country of origin even to stand trial. Americans knew how unjust most foreign legal systems were. When extradition treaties were finally negotiated in the mid-nineteenth century, U.S. courts had to determine not only that the foreign regime had probable cause to believe that the accused had committed a serious crime but that his or her crime was not an offense of a political nature. Political offenders, including revolutionary terrorists and state terrorists, were exempt from extradition. In addition, the United States refused to negotiate extradition treaties with Communist and Muslim regimes for the obvious reason that they did not meet Western standards of justice.

The government's revulsion with foreign injustice began to wane with the Reagan administration, which had no use for foreign revolutionaries and was eager to swap suspected criminals without judicial interference. It renegotiated extradition treaties to eliminate the political offense exception, which was a kind of judicially granted asylum. It also sought ways to substitute deportation—an executive practice with few safeguards—for extradition, a judicial procedure with some safeguards. Historically, when people were deported from the United States, they were free to go to any country that would have them. Starting in the 1980s, the Justice Department began to arrange targeted deportations. For example, it deported Provisional Irish Republican Army (IRA) suspects to Northern Ireland, where they could be prosecuted as "terrorists" before Crown judges who had no sympathy for the IRA's revolt against British imperialism and Protestant persecution. The United States had a legal obligation not to deport persons to regimes that were likely to persecute them,[8] but Reagan's Office of Legal Counsel skirted this requirement by claiming to have obtained assurances from the foreign regime that the deportees would not be abused. The assurances were pro forma, unspecific, and rarely, if ever, followed up by State Department monitoring.[9]

Reagan-Bush Abductions

The Reagan administration did not content itself with targeted deportations; it also began the modern practice of kidnapping. The inspiration grew out of a much-celebrated, daring, and illegal operation masterminded by Lt. Col. Oliver North in 1985. On October 8, 1985, four members of the Palestine Liberation Front (PLF) seized the Italian cruise ship *Achille Lauro* and demanded that Israel release Palestinian prisoners. In the process, they shot Leon Klinghoffer, a wheelchair-bound American, and threw him overboard. The Egyptian government agreed to give the hijackers safe passage to the headquarters of the Palestine Liberation Organization (PLO) in Tunis if they wouldn't kill anyone else. However, Israeli intelligence was listening to the Egyptian president's phone calls and was able to inform the United States not only of the plan but also of the tail numbers of the plane that would fly the hijackers to Tunis. With this information, Colonel North alerted the aircraft carrier USS *Saratoga,* and four of its fighter jets intercepted the Egyptian airliner and forced it to land at the North Atlantic Treaty Organization (NATO) base in Sigonella, Sicily. There, a team of Delta Force commandos, with orders from the White House, prepared to storm the plane but were stopped by Italian soldiers who had orders from their own government not to allow the Americans to kidnap the hijackers. A tense standoff ensued, but cooler heads prevailed. The hijackers were turned over to Italy, which promised to entertain an extradition request. Before that could happen, however, Italy, under pressure from Egypt, allowed the hijackers to escape.

The Reagan administration was furious with its NATO ally but also elated at the public support it received for its daring interception. That winter and spring, hawkish members of Congress and the administration pushed hard to make abduction a central strategy in their "war" against Middle Eastern terrorists.

In Congress, the most aggressive leadership came from freshman Senator Arlen Specter (R-PA). Even before the 1985 interception, he had introduced a bill to authorize the attorney general to permit the CIA, the FBI, or the armed forces to conduct snatches of alleged terrorists on their own authority.[10]

Two former federal judges opposed Specter's bill—FBI director William Webster and State Department legal adviser Abraham Sofaer. Both recognized the illegalities. Webster worried that abductions would sour cooperation with foreign police departments,[11] and Sofaer feared that exercising such power would harm the State Department's ability to manage foreign relations.[12]

The bill was also opposed by two deputy directors of the CIA, John McMahon and Clair George, who distrusted "cowboys" like Colonel North and CIA director William Casey, even as they worked with them to resupply the

Nicaraguan rebels known as contras. In 1984, agency professionals had been ordered, against their better judgment, to assemble a counterterrorism force of Lebanese, Palestinians, and other non-Americans, only to be embarrassed in 1985 when renegade members of the group hired other Lebanese to plant a car bomb at the Beirut home of Hezbollah leader Mohammed Hussein Fadlallah. The cleric had survived, but more than eight other people had been killed.[13]

In the public arena, the opponents of abduction appeared to win. Congress did not enact Specter's bill.[14] In the secret precincts of the Reagan White House, however, the cowboys prevailed. While Congress and the press thought that abduction was still an option to be explored, the president secretly authorized the CIA to kidnap *criminal* suspects.[15] This finding, which violated the CIA's statutory mandate,[16] was signed in January 1986 at about the same time that President Reagan was authorizing illegal arms sales to Iran. The finding allowed the agency not only to abduct alleged terrorists but also to sabotage their supplies, finances, travel, recruiting, and operations in foreign countries. A month later, Colonel North won approval to create a secret interagency committee called the Operations Sub-Group (OSG) to oversee kidnappings and other covert operations.[17]

In 1987 the CIA used this secret authority for the first time to lure a suspected terrorist (and hijacker of a Jordanian airliner) to Cyprus and onto a yacht, where FBI agents captured him for prosecution in the United States. Because the seizure of Fawaz Younis (misspelled "Yunis" by the court) took place in international waters, the Justice Department claimed that no national sovereignty had been violated. The claim was dubious—under customary international law, the law of the yacht's registry should have governed—but Cyprus did not protest. A federal judge would later rule that Younis, whose wrists were broken by the FBI, had no standing to challenge the kidnapping.[18]

Buoyed by this victory, the George H. W. Bush administration turned to kidnapping suspected drug lords, including Panama's dictator, Manuel Noriega, again for prosecution in the United States.

Clinton-Gore Abductions

The Clinton administration went beyond extradition, deportation, and kidnapping for purposes of prosecution in American courts and authorized the CIA to abduct terrorists for delivery to foreign regimes. According to counterterrorism expert Richard Clarke, White House counsel Lloyd Cutler objected to the abductions because they violated international law.[19] The president seemed to agree until Vice President Al Gore laughed and said, "Of course it's a violation of international law; that's why it is a covert operation."[20]

The agency entered into its first rendition agreement with Egypt in 1995, despite the State Department's condemnation of Egypt for its inhumane treatment of prisoners. The first person to be secretly delivered to Egypt without benefit of law was Talaat Fouad Qassem, who was under an Egyptian sentence of death, *in absentia,* for his involvement in President Anwar Sadat's assassination in 1981. In 1995 Croatian police seized Qassem in Zagreb and turned him over to American agents. They in turn questioned him on board a ship in the Adriatic before delivering him to Egypt, where he was probably executed on the basis of a previous conviction, in absentia, by a military tribunal.[21]

In 1997 FBI agents kidnapped Mir Aimal Kasi from a hotel in Pakistan and returned him to the United States to stand trial for gunning down five CIA employees and killing two in 1993 while they were waiting for a traffic light outside the CIA's main gate in Langley, Virginia. A federal district court found him guilty and sentenced him to death.[22]

In 1998 the CIA captured five Islamic fundamentalists, including Shawki Salama Attiya, in Tirana, Albania, and flew them to Cairo for interrogation. There, Attiya claims, he was hung by his limbs, subjected to electric shocks to his genitals, and kept in a cell with filthy water up to his knees.[23] Two of the other men, who had already been condemned to death in absentia before the CIA abducted them, were hanged. According to Michael Scheuer, who ran the rendition program, the CIA could give Egyptian interrogators a list of questions for the suspects in the morning and receive answers in the evening. CIA agents were eager to join in the interrogations, but the Egyptians refused.[24]

The program's underlying assumption seems to have been that abductions have no consequences for anyone other than the abductees. But that may not have been the case with the five fundamentalists. On August 5, 1998, an Arab-language newspaper in London published a letter from the International Islamic Front for Jihad threatening retaliation for their abduction. Two days later al Qaeda operatives bombed two U.S. embassies in Africa, killing 224 people.[25]

Scheuer assured Jane Mayer of the *New Yorker* that all the suspects rendered during the Clinton years had been convicted in absentia by a foreign regime and that their kidnapping had been approved by CIA lawyers.[26] Whether President Clinton personally approved the kidnappings is not known, but it does seem clear that kidnapping suspects for delivery to foreign regimes likely to use torture began under a Democratic administration.

Bush-Cheney Abductions

To implement its rendition program, the Bush-Cheney administration authorized the navy to rent at least thirty-three civilian aircraft, including a Boeing 737.[27] Since September 2001, CIA security teams have secretly transported more than a hundred suspects in these "torture taxis."[28]

Some of the victims of extraordinary rendition were high-ranking members of al Qaeda, against whom the U.S. government had amassed credible evidence of terrorist training and actions. Others were blameless victims. One was a college professor who was falsely accused by a disgruntled student, an al Qaeda member, to whom he had given a low grade.[29] Whatever their culpability, all appear to have been terrorized, tortured, or abused by the CIA or foreign agents working with the CIA or U.S. Special Forces.

FROM SWEDEN TO EGYPT

On December 18, 2001, a special removal unit from the CIA abducted two Egyptian asylum seekers from Stockholm and flew them to Egypt for interrogation. According to an eyewitness interviewed on Swedish television in 2003, eight hooded Americans accompanied by two men in suits who said they were from the U.S. embassy carried out the operation. The suspects, Ahmed Agiza and Muhammed al-Zery, had been arrested earlier in the evening by the Swedish security police, strongly suggesting a joint operation. Once the men were in CIA custody, their clothes were cut from their bodies. Sedatives were inserted in their anuses, after which they were fitted with diapers, dressed in overalls, blindfolded, chained, and hooded. A Gulfstream jet delivered them to the Masra Tora prison in Cairo. When the Swedish ambassador visited the men five weeks later, both said they had been tortured, but neither could be linked to al Qaeda. The Egyptians released al-Zery without charges but sentenced Agiza to twenty-five years in prison on the basis of a previous conviction, in absentia, for belonging to a radical Islamic organization.[30]

FROM THE UNITED STATES TO SYRIA

On September 26, 2002, Maher Arar, a Syrian-born Canadian, was about to change flights at Kennedy International Airport in New York when he was pulled aside for questioning—not ordinary, polite questioning but abusive, insulting, degrading interrogations by the Immigration and Naturalization Service, the FBI, New York City policemen, and CIA agents. His name had come up on the watch list.

Arar requested a lawyer and was told, wrongly, that he could not have one because he wasn't an American citizen. He asked to call his family but was refused. Instead, he was chained, shackled, and made to disappear, first at Kennedy Airport and then inside the Metropolitan Detention Center in New York, to the great distress of his wife and young daughters who did not know what had happened to him. Finally, he was permitted to call his mother-in-law in Canada. The Canadian consul visited but could not persuade the FBI to release him. Instead, Deputy Attorney General Larry Thompson secretly authorized Arar's deportation to Syria, despite Arar's protests that he would be tortured there for evading military service.[31]

Historically, deportees have been allowed to choose the country to which they would be sent because deportation is an executive process for getting rid of illegal aliens, not an aid to foreign law enforcement. If a foreign country wants the United States to return a fugitive for prosecution, it is supposed to seek extradition through a U.S. court because the liberty of a person is at stake. Starting in the 1980s, however, the Justice Department undermined this safeguard so that alleged terrorists could be exchanged administratively so long as the requesting country promised not to torture them.[32] According to the department, it can deliver a suspected terrorist to any regime on earth, provided its lawyers are willing to claim that it is probable that the regime will not torture him. The department does not need a written promise not to torture; it doesn't need any promise at all. A mere subjective claim by someone in the department will do. The Bush administration even argued, unsuccessfully, that a court cannot review the secret diplomatic assurances from the receiving country that it will refrain from torturing a deportee.[33]

Had the Bush administration wanted Arar to be questioned by lawful techniques, it could have charged him with a crime. Or it could have sent him home to Canada, where his accusers could have questioned him. If it had probable cause to believe that he had violated the criminal law of some other country, it could have arranged his extradition, but it did not have such evidence. It had only the vaguest suspicions, which is why it sent him to the Syrian government's military intelligence arm, an agency well known for brutal interrogations.[34] The Canadian government was not informed of the decision.[35]

At 3:00 a.m. on October 8, 2002, the FBI put Arar on an unmarked Gulfstream V corporate jet at Newark International Airport and flew him to Washington, D.C. There a CIA team took over and flew him to Jordan, which delivered him to Syria's military intelligence agency. The Syrians did not ask to question Arar. They had no wish to prosecute him, not even for evading military service. As an officer of the Canadian Security Intelligence Service (CSIS) noted at the time, "I think the U.S. would like to get Arar to Jordan where they can have their way with him."[36]

Syrian agents questioned Arar, beat him for two weeks, and kept him in a foul, underground cell, where he could hear other torture victims scream. Eventually he falsely confessed to having attended an al Qaeda training camp, and after ten months the Syrians turned him over to Canadian authorities. He returned home forty pounds lighter, with a pronounced limp and chronic nightmares.[37]

Why was Arar's name on the American watch list? According to a Canadian commission that investigated his kidnapping, the Royal Canadian Mounted Police had informed the FBI in a PowerPoint presentation that Arar was "an Islamic extremist individual" who had been in the Washington, D.C., area on September 11. The issue was debated among CIA, Justice Department, and White House officials for more than two years.[38] In fact, Arar had been in San Diego at the time, working as a computer engineer. The Mounties had become suspicious of Arar because the lease to his apartment contained the name of a Syrian-born Canadian whose brother had been mentioned in an al Qaeda document. Tortured by the Syrians into giving up the names of their associates, the two brothers mentioned Arar, although they barely knew him.[39] The commission concluded that "categorically there is no evidence" he had done anything wrong,[40] but Attorney General Ashcroft insisted that this information was more than enough to justify delivering him to Syria.[41]

Arar was not an enemy combatant at war with the United States. He was a Canadian citizen lawfully on U.S. soil and legally entitled to the protection of the U.S. Constitution and laws, including those against incommunicado interrogations and kidnapping for purposes of torture. The Canadian commission cleared him of all suspicion. The Canadian government apologized for its mistake, accepted the police commissioner's resignation for putting out false information, and granted Arar the largest legal settlement in Canadian history—C$10.5 million.[42]

But the Bush administration continued to deny all responsibility for his suffering. When Attorney General Gonzales was asked whether Arar deserved an apology, he replied, "Well, we were not responsible for his removal to Syria" (even though the deportation order was signed by his deputy, Larry Thompson). Asked whether Arar had been subjected to extraordinary rendition, Gonzales declared, "That's not what happened here. It was a deportation."[43]

The Canadian minister for public safety eventually asked the Justice Department to remove Arar's name from its no-entry list, but it refused. Indeed, the American ambassador to Canada went so far as to declare that it was "a little presumptuous" for the Canadian minister "to say who the United States can and cannot allow into our country."[44]

FROM TANZANIA TO YEMEN

In December 2003, two months after Arar was released, American agents seized Muhammad al-Assad in Dar es Salaam, Tanzania, while he was having dinner with his wife. The agents hooded and shackled him and flew him away in the night, probably to Djibouti, where he was interrogated by a man and a woman who said they were FBI agents. The questioners wanted to know why, six years earlier, al-Assad had leased office space to the Al-Haramain Islamic Foundation, a charity that the bureau suspected of funding terrorists. After two weeks, his captors flew him to a cold climate—probably Afghanistan—and held him for about three months in two dark, filthy jails. Then they moved him to a new prison, where the guards, dressed entirely in black, communicated only by hand signals. He languished there for another thirteen months before the CIA flew him to Yemen. Yemeni authorities held him for nine more months and then offered him a plea bargain he could not refuse. In return for pleading guilty to obtaining forged travel documents, he was sentenced to time served.[45]

FROM MACEDONIA TO AFGHANISTAN

On December 31, 2003, an out-of-work car salesman from Germany named Khaled el-Masri was pulled off a bus in Macedonia because his name was essentially the same as that of Khalid al-Masri, an associate of a 9/11 highjacker. The head of the CIA's al Qaeda unit "didn't really know" much about the German el-Masri, a former agency official recalled; "she just had a hunch." But that was enough for her to order a team of masked agents to fly el-Masri to Afghanistan. They used the same brutality that had attended the earlier abduction of two men from Sweden to Egypt.[46] The CIA did not just move prisoners; it terrorized and humiliated them in the process.

El-Masri was delivered to the Salt Pit, the squalid CIA prison on the outskirts of Kabul. There he was kicked and beaten and thrown into a cell with no bed, one dirty blanket, and a bottle of putrid water. He was questioned by six or seven men in black clothing and ski masks who were aided by a masked American doctor and a translator. They told him, "You are here in a place where there is no law. We can bury you here or forget you for twenty years. No one will ever know."[47]

Over the next five months, el-Masri was interrogated only three or four times more because it soon became clear he was not the person they were looking for. The problem was how to fix what Secretary Condoleezza Rice would later call a "mistake" and whether to apologize.[48] The CIA officer who had ordered him shipped to Afghanistan was reluctant to admit that her hunch had been wrong. As John Radsan, who worked in the general counsel's office at the CIA until 2004, observed, "I don't think anyone's thought through what we do with these people."[49]

In March 2004, el-Masri began a thirty-seven-day hunger strike, which ended when a doctor shoved a feeding tube down his throat. The pain was excruciating, and the force-feeding made him extremely ill. Finally, in May 2004, the CIA and State Department stopped dithering. El-Masri was flown to Albania and released on a remote hilltop without an explanation or apology.[50] On January 31, 2007, a German court issued warrants for the arrest of the thirteen persons involved in his abduction[51] while the CIA officer who had kept him wrongly imprisoned was promoted to a top intelligence post in the Middle East.[52]

FROM ZAMBIA TO GTMO

Martin Mubanga, a dual citizen of Great Britain and Zambia, had gone to Pakistan in October 2000 to study Islam and Arabic. After spending some time in Peshawar, he attended two madrasas (schools) in Afghanistan and decided to leave when the Americans began bombing in 2001. At that time he discovered his British passport had disappeared. Crossing into Pakistan, he had his Zambian passport mailed to him and flew to Africa to stay with relatives. There, an agent of MI6, Britain's external secret intelligence service, tracked him down. His British passport had been found in an al Qaeda cave, which led MI6 to believe that he had flown to Zambia on false documents and therefore must be a terrorist. Three weeks later a CIA snatch team flew him to Guantánamo Bay, where he was held for nearly three years.

Mubanga described his treatment as a prisoner:

> I needed the toilet and I asked the interrogator to let me go. But he just said, "You'll go when I say so." I told him he had five minutes to get me to the toilet or I was going on the floor. He left the room. Finally, I squirmed across the floor and did it in the corner, trying to minimize the mess. . . . He comes back with a mop and dips it in the pool of urine. Then he starts covering me with my own waste, like he's using a big paintbrush, working methodically, beginning with my feet and ankles, and working his way up my legs. All the while, he's racially abusing me, cussing me: "Oh, the poor little negro, the poor little ######." He seemed to think it was funny.[53]

In June 2004, the Supreme Court ruled that the military had to appoint competent tribunals to review the grounds for holding prisoners.[54] In October, a GTMO-based Combat Status Review Tribunal refused Mubanga's request that it call his sister, aunt, and brother to testify in his defense. He insisted that they could prove he had not traveled to Zambia on false documents. But the tribunal decided that these witnesses were not "reasonably available" and that, in any case, their testimony would be irrelevant. A reviewing officer rejected that decision, and when the prisoner' family was consulted, the government's case for holding Mubanga collapsed.[55]

FROM ITALY TO EGYPT

On February 17, 2003, a forty-two-year-old Muslim cleric named Osama Hassan Moustafa Nasr (also known as Abu Omar) was abducted in Milan, Italy, by a team of masked CIA agents. He later said they wrapped his head in tape, injected him with drugs, and flew him to Egypt (by way of Germany), where an American agent offered him money if he would become an informant. When he refused, Egyptian jailors beat him so severely that he lost his hearing in one ear. They also administered electric shocks through a wet mattress, he said, and burned him with stun guns while strapped to an iron rack called the Bride.[56] On May 10, 2004, the Egyptians suddenly released Nasr. He immediately called his wife in Italy, who until that moment had not known why he had disappeared. During that call, which was taped by Italian agents, Nasr urged her to destroy the contents of a computer. Two days later the Egyptians arrested him again, suggesting a three-way abduction plot.[57] When Nasr was next released in February 2007, he showed reporters dark, circular scars around his wrists and ankles that he said had been caused by electrical shocks. "I have scars of torture all over my body," he added.[58]

On February 15, 2007, an Italian court indicted twenty-five CIA agents, one U.S. Air Force lieutenant colonel, and seven Italian agents involved with the kidnapping. The Italian government has been persuaded not to demand extradition of the Americans, but the court began, and then postponed, trying them in absentia.[59]

FROM PAKISTAN TO MOROCCO

Binyam Mohamed is an Englishman. He was arrested in Pakistan on April 10, 2002, and turned over to the CIA, which moved him from Afghanistan to Morocco, back to Afghanistan, and finally to Guantánamo, seeking to get him to admit that he conspired with an American, José Padilla, to make a radioactive "dirty bomb" for use inside the United States. The original accusations came from two al Qaeda operatives, who said that they had been forced to make them under torture.

Parts of Mohamed's account are unexceptional: his arrest, his delivery to American agents, and an FBI agent's statement that "the rules have changed. You don't get a lawyer."[60] The prisoner's description of being held at the CIA's

Prison of Darkness outside of Kabul during the early months of 2004 resembles the accounts of other detainees. He was held in total darkness, Mohamed said; subjected to deafening music; and hung up for days at a time, until his legs were swollen and his wrists and hands became numb. He recalled hearing other prisoners "knocking their heads against the walls and doors, screaming their heads off."[61]

What is unusual is Mohamed's account of what allegedly happened between July 2002 and January 2004 when he was being interrogated by Moroccan agents, at the CIA's behest, outside Rabat. The Moroccans, he said, cut his chest and penis with a scalpel while asking questions about Khalid Sheikh Mohammed (KSM), Abu Zubaydah, José Padilla, and the bomb plot that appeared to have come from British and American intelligence.[62]

In a letter to the British government in July 2008, the United States denied Mohamed's account, but on August 28, 2008, the British high court found that denial "untenable," and ordered the release of potentially exculpatory material to Mohamed's lawyers in advance of his trial at GTMO.[63] Among other things, the documents were said to reveal that Mohamed had admitted seeing plans on the Internet for making a dirty bomb, but called them "a joke" because they recommended "adding bleach to uranium-238 in a bucket and rotating it about one's head for 45 minutes."[64]

On October 22, 2008, the Bush administration dropped all charges against Mohamed.[65] A few days later Jacqui Smith, the British home secretary, asked the British attorney general, Baroness Patricia Scotland, to investigate both MI5, which is Britain's domestic intelligence service, and the CIA for possible "criminal wrongdoing."[66]

FROM PAKISTAN TO EGYPT

Mamdouh Habib, an Australian citizen of Egyptian birth, claims that he was seized by Pakistani authorities in October 2001, beaten, and then turned over to two Americans in black short-sleeved shirts. One of the Americans had a tattoo of an American flag attached to a finger-like pole, he recalled; the other a tattoo of a large cross. They took him to an airfield, cut his clothes away, put him in a jumpsuit, strapped blackened goggles over his eyes, and flew him to Egypt in a private jet. There, he says, the Egyptians beat him with blunt instruments, including one that looked like a cattle prod. He was also forced to stand on his tiptoes in water up to his neck and then in a room with a ceiling so low that he had to stoop painfully for hours. Finally, he was put in a room with water up to his ankles, within view of a generator and its switch, and told that he would be electrocuted if he didn't confess. Eventually, he signed multiple confessions, all of which, he insisted, were false.

After six months in Egyptian custody, Habib was flow to Bagram Air Base in Afghanistan and from there to GTMO. He was detained there until January 2005, when the administration released him for lack of evidence that would stand up in court. The U.S. government has refused to admit or deny that it rendered Habib to Egypt for interrogation.[67]

FROM MALAWI TO AFGHANISTAN

Laid Saidi, an Algerian, had run a branch of the international Al-Haramain Islamic Foundation in Tanga, Tanzania. The Saudi Arabian government has since shut the group down on suspicion of funding terrorists. On May 10, 2003, Tanzanian authorities delivered Saidi to Malawian police, who held him, apparently at the behest of some Americans, in a mountain prison for a week before turning him over to a gray-haired Caucasian woman and five masked men in black. Following the CIA's standard procedure, they taped his eyes shut and inserted a plug in his anus before diapering and dressing him. Then they covered his ears, shackled his hands and feet, and put him on the floor of an airplane for a long flight to Kabul. There other men in black took Saidi to a dark prison that played very loud Western music. Over the din, one of the men shouted something in English, and the translator said, "You are in a place that is out of the world. No one knows where you are; no one is going to defend you."

Saidi was held at the Prison of Darkness for a week, chained by one wrist to the wall of a windowless cell. Then he was transferred to the Salt Pit, where the CIA often shackled him to both the ceiling and the floor. That practice, which in Saidi's case caused his wrists, legs, and feet to swell painfully, was not discontinued until two Afghan prisoners later died from it. Then the CIA transferred Saidi to a third prison outside Kabul, where he was held for many months in a filthy cell with a zinc-clad door. There he and Khaled el-Masri, who had been kidnapped in Macedonia, exchanged phone numbers. Interrogators questioned Saidi daily for weeks and eventually played for him the tape of a phone conversation in which, they said, he talked with his brother in Kenya about airplanes. But the translator had made a mistake. The brothers did not discuss airplanes (*tayarat* in Arabic); they had talked about the sale of some tires (*tirat*) in a mixture of Arabic and English.[68]

In the late spring or early summer of 2004, the Americans flew Saidi to Tunisia, where the local authorities held him for seventy-five days for having a fake passport. He admitted he was not a Tunisian but an Algerian. The Americans then flew him to Algiers, where Algerian agents held him for a few days and then dropped him off at a bus stop. For all his troubles over the previous sixteen months, they gave him some clothes, a small sum of money, and a pair of white shoes.[69]

Disputing Responsibility

According to Michael Scheuer, the practice of extraordinary rendition, a program he ran between 2001 and 2004, had the approval of the Department of Justice, the National Security Council, the congressional intelligence committees, and President George W. Bush.[70] Indeed, he wrote, he had never seen "a set of operations that was more closely scrutinized by the Director of Central Intelligence [George Tenet], the National Security Council, and the Congressional intelligence committees. [W]e told them—again and again and again"—that the detainees shipped to other countries might be mistreated.[71] Each individual operation, he added, "went to either the Director of Central Intelligence or to the Assistant Director. . . . So, basically, the number one and two men in the intelligence community are the ones who signed off."[72]

The CIA has not officially admitted that this program exists, but its director, George Tenet, informed the Senate Select Committee on Intelligence in February 2000 that the agency had "helped render more than two dozen terrorists to justice" by "working with foreign governments worldwide."[73] Four years later he told the 9/11 Commission that the agency had brought about "the rendition of many dozens of terrorists prior to September 11, 2001," but he remained silent about post-9/11 operations, except for a passing reference in his memoir to "transferring" al-Libi to "a third country for further debriefing."[74]

Attorney General Ashcroft expressly acknowledged the rendition program on November 19, 2003, when he defended the delivery of Maher Arar to Syria.[75] Attorney General Gonzales affirmed the program's existence in January 2005 and again the following March.[76] In December 2005, Secretary of State Condoleezza Rice admitted to German chancellor Angela Merkel that the kidnapping of Khaled el-Masri had been a "mistake."[77] President Bush conceded the program's existence, too, even as he declared, "We do not render to countries that torture."[78]

Craig Murray, the former British ambassador to Uzbekistan, disagreed with the president. "We receive intelligence obtained under torture from Uzbek intelligence services . . . showing what the Uzbek government wants the U.S. and U.K. to believe."[79] Murray told *New Yorker* writer Jane Mayer that he knew of at least three instances in which the United States had rendered suspected militants from Afghanistan to Uzbekistan. He did not know what happened to the men, but "[t]hey almost certainly would have been tortured." In Uzbekistan, he added, "partial boiling of a hand or an arm is quite common." He knew of two instances in which prisoners were boiled to death.[80] By collaborating with the Uzbek government, he concluded, "we are selling our souls for dross."[81]

Extensive disclosures did not stop Bush administration officials from trying to minimize their responsibility for extraordinary rendition. For example, Attorney General Ashcroft insisted that Maher Arar was not sent to Syria to be tortured because the Syrians (whom the U.S. State Department has routinely denounced for torturing prisoners) promised they wouldn't torture him.[82] Ashcroft did not explain where the administration got the authority to kidnap anyone. He did not explain why it was necessary to ship Arar to Syria in total secrecy or why no one checked to see if he was being treated humanely.[83] Nor did he clarify how the administration's trust in Syrian assurances could be squared with President Bush's statement on November 7, 2003, that Syria has left its people "a legacy of torture, oppression, misery, and ruin."[84]

In November 2005, Secretary Rice insisted, "The United States has not transported anyone, and will not transport anyone, to a country when we believe he will be tortured." She added, "Where appropriate, the United States seeks assurances that transferred persons will not be tortured."[85] This assertion, too, was false. Michael Scheuer had already admitted to *60 Minutes* that his program's purpose was "finding someone else to do your dirty work."[86] Former CIA agent

Robert Baer had also explained, "If you want a serious interrogation, you send a prisoner to Jordan. If you want them tortured, you send them to Syria. If you want someone to disappear—never to see them again—you send them to Egypt."[87] Vincent Cannistraro, who used to head the CIA's counterterrorism division, was equally candid: "You would have to be deaf, dumb, and blind to believe that the Syrians were not going to use torture, even if they were making claims to the contrary."[88]

According to Rice, rendition involved the cooperation of the host countries from which prisoners were taken. However, the cooperation to which she referred was not the open cooperation of the host country's courts but the covert assistance of its intelligence agencies. The prisoners were flown elsewhere, she said, for "legal reasons,"[89] a claim she would not have made if the suspects were Americans kidnapped off the streets of the United States. Indeed, Rice has even admitted that rendition is an alternative to law. "We must track down terrorists who seek refuge in areas where governments cannot take effective action," she explained, "including where the terrorist *cannot in practice be reached by the ordinary processes of law*."[90] (Emphasis added.)

Perhaps abduction is the best a government can do when the suspect is located in the wilds of Afghanistan or Yemen, where the rule of law as we know it does not exist. In the United States, however, the ordinary processes of law should have protected Maher Arar. As a person physically in the United States, he was entitled to the Fourth Amendment's protection against unlawful seizure and the Fifth Amendment's guarantee of due process. The ordinary processes of law should also have protected the suspects whom the CIA agents in ski masks secretly abducted from Sweden, Italy, and Macedonia.

The scale of the torture-by-proxy program remains unknown. Using the reports of various human rights organizations, Peter Bergen of the New America Foundation was able to document fifty-three cases of extraordinary rendition by the CIA between September 11, 2001, and March 2008.[91] Scott Horton, who helped prepare a report on rendition for the Brennan Center at New York University's School of Law, estimates the number to be at least 150 renditions between 2001 and 2005.[92] Given that the CIA made use of a fleet of thirty-three aircraft and abducted suspects to its own prisons in at least eight countries, the number could be higher.

Whatever the numbers, Condoleezza Rice was right when she said, "Torture and conspiracy to commit torture are crimes under U.S. law, wherever they may occur in the world."[93] Even so, the Justice Department has yet to prosecute a single person for participating in these crimes.

4

SIGNALING PERMISSION

What is lacking among all . . . moralists . . . is an understanding of the brutal character of . . . all human collectives, and the power of self-interest and collective egoism in all intergroup relations. . . . They do not see that the limitations of the human imagination, the easy subservience of reason to prejudice and passion, and the consequent persistence of irrational egoism, . . . make social conflict an inevitability in human history, probably to its very end.

—Reinhold Niebuhr[1]

According to *New York Times* reporter James Risen, the CIA's own inspector general has been unable to find any documentary evidence that President Bush authorized the torture policy.[2] This pronouncement is not surprising. No president would consciously sign anything that would destroy his ability to deny knowledge of or responsibility for war crimes.

Nor would most subordinates implicate a president in such a policy. To save George W. Bush from having to inform members of Congress about the secret prisons, kidnappings, and torture, CIA director George Tenet appears to have treated those measures as normal intelligence collection rather than covert operations. That way he did not have to draft a formal memorandum of notification for the president to send to House and Senate leaders.

Suspending the Rule of Law

Meanwhile, the president signaled what he wanted through a series of decisions. The first and most obvious signal was his decision to treat the attacks of September

11 as acts of war and not as crimes. As a result, responsibility for interrogating suspected terrorists was taken from the FBI and assigned to intelligence agencies. The FBI had become too law abiding, administration officials said, following the congressional investigations of the 1970s. It would investigate only after an attack occurred and then only to prosecute the attackers. While this observation was a misconception of how modern law enforcement works, the bureau was seen, more or less accurately, as an unimaginative, rule-bound bureaucracy, and the new administration hated bureaucracies that played by constitutional rules. The president wanted agents who would fight al Qaeda as ruthlessly as al Qaeda fought the United States and without feeling constrained by law or custom.

There was nothing unusual about this preference. Americans have always admired action heroes who disregard the law, from the cowboy novels of the nineteenth century, through the renegade cops of the twentieth, to the latest superheroes of comic book origin. Just as Presidents Kennedy and Reagan did, George W. Bush romanticized hard-charging, can-do characters like James Bond or Jack Bauer, who dare to cast the rules aside and do what has to be done. He signaled what he expected (because it was already being done) in his 2003 State of the Union message:

> To date, we've arrested or otherwise dealt with many key commanders of al Qaeda. . . . All told, more than 3,000 suspected terrorists have been arrested in many different countries. Many others have met a different fate. Let's put it this way—they are no longer a problem to the United States.[3]

What happened to the many others who "met a different fate" is not known for certain, but the most obvious implication is that they were killed.

Second, the president signaled the kind of interrogation he wanted by declaring that the Geneva Conventions did not apply to prisoners seized in Afghanistan. By so doing, Bush essentially released both military and CIA interrogators from having to follow the laws of war, even as they were allegedly fighting a "war" against al Qaeda. No president in American history had ever gone that far.

Admitting Evidence Obtained by Torture

Third, by creating military commissions, the president signaled that he did not want interrogators to feel bound by the Constitution, legal precedents, or established rules of evidence. The chief feature of these new courts was that they could admit evidence obtained by torture. They could also hide evidence of the interrogators' own crimes by trying the suspects in secret or by classifying as secret the evidence obtained by torturing accusers and then withholding it from the accused. To forestall legal challenges, Bush decreed that the commissions' decisions could not be reviewed by any civilian court either by appeal, as would have been the case with convictions by military courts-martial, or by petitions for habeas corpus review.[4] In so doing, the president usurped for himself the power to suspend the chief guarantee against detention without trial—namely, the privilege of the writ of habeas corpus, which is an emergency power granted by the Constitution to Congress and not to the president.

Bush attempted to downplay the usurpation by saying that he *intended* only to deny that right to foreign terrorists, but in fact he stripped at least two citizens—José Padilla and Yaser Esem Hamdi—of the right as well. His authority to do so would be the subject of extensive litigation for the next seven years. (See chapter 9.)

Bush's order was cribbed from one that President Franklin D. Roosevelt used to create the commission that tried the eight German saboteurs captured in the United States during World War II. A strong argument could be made that the World War II commissions were constitutionally defective; they certainly violated due process. It could also be argued that the summary justice traditionally accorded alleged spies and saboteurs had been rendered obsolete by the Geneva Conventions of 1949, the Uniform Code of Military Justice in 1951, and the War Crimes Act of 1996. But no one was given the opportunity to raise these objections.

Bush's order also violated Articles I and III of the Constitution, which clearly assign the creation of new courts to Congress. Nothing in the Constitution gives the president the power to create his own court system, for the obvious reason that legislative and judicial powers were supposed to be separate from, not concentrated in, the executive.

The administration claimed that history was on its side because military commissions had been used in the past. But most commissions, including those during the Mexican War, the Civil War, and Reconstruction and those following World War II, were temporary expedients meant to facilitate a military occupation. They were not intended, as Bush's were, to replace regular American military or civilian courts.[5]

Less frequently, military commissions have been used to deliver summary justice to alleged spies, saboteurs, assassins, and war criminals captured during a time of war. Most of these hasty proceedings resulted in what may be fairly characterized as legalized lynchings, including the trial and execution of Maj. John André during the Revolution, the drumhead trial of Dakota Indians in 1862 (resulting in the largest mass execution in American history), the unnecessary use of a military commission to try and convict persons alleged to have conspired in President Abraham Lincoln's assassination in 1865, the trial and execution of six German saboteurs in 1942, and the conviction and execution of Japanese Gen. Tomoyuki Yamashita in 1946. But summary justice was precisely what President Bush and his lawyers wanted.

Evading Accountability Abroad

The administration also signaled its support for torture by attacking the new International Criminal Court (ICC), which had been created to prosecute the very sort of war crimes that the invasion of Iraq was supposed to end.[6] Although more than ninety nations joined this court, the United States refused to do so because, as Gonzales candidly admitted in his memorandum of January 25, 2002, the administration did not want its officials prosecuted anywhere for crimes they might commit in the global war on terrorism.[7]

They had reason to worry. Human rights groups had persuaded a number of countries to assert universal jurisdiction over both criminal and civil cases against war criminals and torturers who harmed their citizens abroad. In 1980, the U.S. Court of Appeals for the Second Circuit had allowed Dolly Filártiga to sue a former member of the Paraguayan secret police in New York for torturing her brother to death in Paraguay because of their father's politics.[8] The $10.4 million judgment she won encouraged similar suits, not only in the United States, but also in other countries.

In 1998 Great Britain's House of Lords invoked universal jurisdiction and rejected sovereign immunity to authorize the extradition of Gen. Augusto Pinochet, the former Chilean dictator, from London to Spain so he could stand trial for torturing and murdering Spaniards as well as Chileans during the dirty war in the 1970s.[9] In 2001, while lecturing in France, former secretary of state Henry Kissinger received his first summons regarding his contributions to that clandestine war. In 2002, he canceled a speech in Brazil rather than risk interrogation there about his support for dirty war operations in South America. Furious, he complained to Donald Rumsfeld about what administration officials were beginning to call "lawfare," or the judicialization of politics both at home and abroad.[10]

Rumsfeld did not just worry about foreign courts; he also feared the new International Criminal Court, which might prosecute him for violations of the laws of war, including torture. As a matter of law, the secretary of defense had no reason to fear that the International Criminal Court just getting under way at the Hague might prosecute American soldiers and CIA agents for *random misconduct* in the course of war. To avoid such prosecutions before the ICC, the United States could simply try its war criminals in its own courts. But that was the problem, because the Bush administration had no intention of prosecuting its people for their war crimes.

To assume jurisdiction, the ICC's judges would also have to find that the alleged war crimes were "part of a plan or policy."[11] That, too, posed a problem. The abuses inflicted on prisoners held by the United States were part of a conscious policy. Knowing that more kidnappings and torture were planned, the administration instructed Undersecretary of State John R. Bolton (later, interim ambassador to the United Nations) to pressure more than a hundred governments to sign "Article 98 agreements," pledging not to extradite any Americans accused of war crimes to the new international court. If a government refused, its foreign aid would be cut off. A Republican Congress made that threat a matter of law.[12]

One of the architects of the administration's response was Jack L. Goldsmith, who first worked for Defense Department general counsel Jim Haynes before heading the Justice Department's Office of Legal Counsel. The ICC should be resisted, Goldsmith warned, because U.S. soldiers (and presumably intelligence agents) are involved all over the globe and are "thus easy to grab and bring to The Hague—especially in a world of rampant anti-Americanism." The ICC, he advised Rumsfeld, "is at bottom an attempt by militarily weak nations that dominated ICC negotiations to restrain militarily powerful nations." He cautioned, "Even if no defendant is brought before the ICC, the ICC can still cause lawfare mischief by being a public forum for official criticism and judgment of U.S. military action."[13]

On March 19, 2004, in a still secret memo, Goldsmith advised that the CIA could take Iraqi prisoners out of their country for interrogation, provided they were treated humanely.[14] When news of that opinion leaked the following December, some international lawyers argued that the OLC had again misread the Geneva Conventions.[15]

Evading the Military's Chain of Command

Military officers were a potential obstacle to implementation of the torture policy. Some did not like it when Secretary Rumsfeld ordered American Special Forces units to operate largely on their own—covertly and out of uniform—not just inside Afghanistan but in other countries around the world.[16] Nor did they all agree when the president declared that al Qaeda and Taliban soldiers did not deserve any protection from the laws of war because they operated clandestinely and out of uniform. But the administration plunged ahead, heedless of the risks. President Bush signaled his support for this sort of irregular warfare by issuing a secret presidential finding. It authorized the commandos to capture or kill suspected terrorists and to interrogate them at forward bases and black site prisons without the usual restraints, much as the CIA's cowboys were already doing.[17]

To prevent regular officers from challenging these commandos and their methods, Rumsfeld removed them from the regular chain of command and put them under his civilian intelligence chief, Deputy Secretary of Defense Stephen Cambone.[18] To restrict knowledge of their operations, he labeled them Special Access Programs (SAPs) and code-named them "Gray Fox." The president's finding was communicated to the House and Senate intelligence committees, but their members were unable to question the wisdom or legality of these operations or even to discuss them with colleagues or staff because they were highly classified.[19] At least one of these SAPs involved torturing and sexually humiliating suspected insurgents in Iraq in August 2003.[20]

Rumsfeld and Haynes did not seek the advice of senior JAG officers when developing the torture policy, but they uncritically embraced novel interpretations of military law by politically appointed civilian attorneys such as John Yoo in the Office of Legal Counsel. They also prevented military lawyers from interfering with these harsh interrogations by hiring civilian contractors to question the suspects and then placing those civilians outside the military's normal chain of command.[21] In October 2004, Senator Lindsey Graham (R-SC) persuaded Congress to pass a law forbidding Pentagon officials to interfere with the capacity of JAG lawyers to "give independent advice," but when President Bush signed the law, he also issued a signing statement insisting that the legal opinions of his political appointees would still "bind all . . . military attorneys."[22]

Evading Legal Challenges

Administration lawyers also sought to evade accountability by placing alleged terrorists in what Johan Steyn, a member of Britain's House of Lords, has called "a legal black hole"[23]—a hole so deep and inaccessible that no lawyer would be able to challenge the incarceration or abuse of prisoners in court.

The original location of this hole was slated to be the island of Guam, a remote outpost in the western Pacific.[24] But when Rumsfeld learned that the island contained a federal district court and an independent federal prosecutor, he nixed that plan. A large American base in Germany was rejected for a similar reason. As Pierre-Richard Prosper, the U.S. ambassador-at-large for war crimes, admitted, "We'd have to deal with the European Court of Human Rights."[25] John Yoo and Patrick Philbin advised Jim Haynes that the naval base at Guantánamo was beyond the jurisdiction of federal courts, and that station became Rumsfeld's choice.[26] GTMO was offshore, out of sight, and, through exaggerated claims of military security, largely inaccessible to lawyers, the press, human rights groups, and the United Nations. For more than two years, the administration was able to use the absence of a federal court as an excuse for barring all legal challenges to its detention and mistreatment of prisoners. Government lawyers at the base celebrated this lawless state by issuing joke certificates that proclaimed their membership in the Guantánamo Bay Bar Association, an organization "dedicated to justice . . . on a Caribbean island outside the venue of any Cuban or U.S. federal court."[27]

When the U.S. Supreme Court rejected that idea of a "law-free zone" in 2004,[28] Alberto Gonzales offered another ploy. At his confirmation hearing for attorney general, he insisted that the prohibition against cruel, inhumane, or degrading treatment, which the United States accepted in 1994 when it ratified the UN Convention Against Torture,[29] was meant only to protect foreigners held *inside* the United States.[30] Foreigners held by U.S. agents *outside* the United States could be subjected to cruel, inhumane, or degrading treatment at will.

Of course, it was unnecessary for the United States to sign a treaty promising to protect foreigners from torture inside the United States. Plenty of laws forbade that already.[31] Nor was it conceivable that the United Nations, or any other international organization or country, would intentionally make a treaty that would allow Americans to torture foreigners, so long as they did so outside the United States. Gonzales's bizarre claim was quickly rejected by Abraham Sofaer, who, as the State Department's legal adviser, had negotiated the treaty for the Reagan administration. The convention's purpose, he informed Congress, was to create uniform legal standards regardless of where the interrogations or detentions took place.[32]

The Torture Memos

Nothing signaled the administration's desire for harsh interrogations more strongly than its numerous secret legal memorandums offering strained legal arguments to shield torturers and their superiors from prosecution.

In April 2002, U.S. forces obtained custody of Abu Zubaydah, supposedly one of Osama bin Laden's top deputies. The debate over how to make him talk would shape the administration's torture policy.

When Zubaydah was captured in Pakistan, he was thought to be a military strategist, a recruiter, a training camp operator, and a crucial link to terrorists in other countries. That assessment was soon downgraded to a logistics chief and operator of safe houses in Afghanistan and Pakistan. It would be downgraded further when investigators read his diary and discovered that he had not one but three different personalities. FBI agent Dan Coleman, a member of the interrogation team, reported, "This guy is insane, certifiable, split personality." But that discovery came too late to save Zubaydah from torture. The president had inflated the significance of Zubaydah's capture in speeches and did not want to back down. "I said he was important," Bush remarked to CIA director George Tenet at a daily briefing. "You're not going to let me lose face on this, are you?" Tenet replied, "No, sir, Mr. President."[33]

At the CIA prison in Kandahar, FBI agents began Zubaydah's interrogation by speaking in both Arabic and English. They urged medical treatment for bullet wounds to his abdomen and groin, but the CIA balked and asked the White House for permission to take over. According to former CIA officer John Kiriakou, a member of the team that interrogated Zubaydah, the decision to torture him—and Kiriakou considered it torture—"was made at the White House with concurrence from the National Security Council and Justice Department." Blanket authority was not issued; each technique was the subject of a separate, special request.[34] Alberto Gonzales convened a meeting of lawyers from the Justice and Defense departments and, after considering "five or six pressure techniques" proposed by the CIA, gave the agency an informal go-ahead without first obtaining legal clearance from the Office of Legal Counsel.[35]

In Zubaydah's case, the lawyers gave the CIA permission to beat the prisoner, waterboard him, and threaten to render him to countries that would do even worse. According to Kiriakou, waterboarding worked, and Zubaydah gave the CIA "detailed information on planned al-Qaeda attacks" and, later, "information on al-Qaeda's leaders."[36] Waterboarding would later be used on at least two other high-value detainees: Khalid Sheikh Mohammed, the alleged mastermind of the 9/11 attacks, and Abd al-Rahim al-Nashiri, a suspect in the bombing of the USS *Cole.*[37]

"We knew that Zubaydah had more information that could save innocent lives," President Bush later explained, "but he stopped talking."[38] So they put him in a cell without a cot or blankets and turned up the air-conditioning until, one official said, he seemed to turn blue. They also tormented him with harsh lighting and ear-splitting noise.[39] Zubaydah's wounds were not addressed until after the agency flew him to Thailand. As a result, he nearly died. Even then, CIA doctors administered a short-acting pain medicine intravenously so that the interrogators could inflict pain whenever they wished simply by turning off the drip.[40]

According to President Bush, these "procedures were tough and they were safe and lawful and necessary," and had been approved by the Department of Justice.[41] But by the time the CIA was done with Zubaydah, according to FBI agents, he was mentally unhinged.[42]

The use of waterboarding created a controversy within the administration. Waterboarding, or *tormenta de toca,* had been deemed torture when the Spanish Inquisition used it in the fifteenth century. U.S. soldiers had been court-martialed for using it in the Philippines in the early 1900s,[43] and as recently as 1983, the U.S. Department of Justice had successfully prosecuted a Texas sheriff and his deputies for waterboarding prisoners.[44] Because it is a form of mock execution, waterboarding also violates both the Convention Against Torture and the statute implementing it.[45] John Yoo did not mention any of this background in his January 2002 memos. When the CIA's lawyers still had doubts, White House counsel Gonzales commissioned yet another legal opinion.

On August 1, 2002, Assistant Attorney General Jay Bybee replied.[46] His fifty-page memorandum, which Yoo drafted with contributions from David Addington, Timothy Flanigan, and former Texas judge Alberto Gonzales, sought to assuage the CIA's fear that its agents would be held criminally liable for what they had done to Zubaydah. The memo did not mention the Texas sheriff's conviction, which occurred in the U.S. district court in Houston while Gonzales was practicing law in that city. Instead, it purported to narrow the definition of torture radically.[47]

For more than a half century virtually all governments, including that of the United States, had defined torture to include psychological as well as physical harm. Like the Geneva Conventions, the UN Convention Against Torture said it explicitly.[48] In case anyone wanted to quibble, the convention didn't just ban torture but cruel, inhumane, and degrading treatment as well. But Bybee's memo chose to quibble.

Torture, its authors said, was physical harm "equivalent in intensity to the pain accompanying serious physical injury, such as organ failure, impairment of bodily functions, or even death."[49] The CIA's repertoire of scarless abuse, including waterboarding, hypothermia, brutally loud music, sleep deprivation, strobe lights, and perpetual darkness, for years on end, would not qualify, no matter how much psychological damage those techniques caused.

According to the quibblers, interrogators could threaten prisoners with death so long as they didn't promise "imminent death." They could inject prisoners with mind-altering drugs so long as the drugs were not likely to "penetrate the core of an individual's ability to perceive the world around him."[50] They could inflict mental harm so long as it was not "prolonged."[51] To qualify as torture, the harm had to be traceable to some intentional act, a linkage that, in nearly all cases, would be impossible to prove in court.[52]

The memo did concede that some practices might constitute torture, including mock executions, Russian roulette, threats of imminent death, electric shocks to genitals, and sexual assaults.[53] But it left the door open for practices that the military had banned for years, including the infliction of pain through drugs or bondage; forcing prisoners to stand, sit, or kneel in stress positions for long periods of time; withholding food; depriving prisoners of sleep; or subjecting them to chemical hypnosis.[54] The memo's definition of torture was so narrow that nothing North Vietnamese interrogators did to Senator John McCain (R-AZ) during his captivity would qualify. Indeed, as the dean of the Yale Law School, Harold H. Koh, later told Congress, Bybee's definition "would have exculpated Saddam Hussein."[55]

Because the law against torture requires proof that the interrogator specifically intended to cause severe harm, Bybee suggested that a torturer could escape punishment by claiming that "he had acted in good faith" not to hurt the prisoner but to protect American lives.[56] The memo also claimed that interrogators could assert a right of self-defense not on behalf of themselves but for the U.S. government. If that didn't work, they could plead "necessity," or in the tradition of Nazi Holocaust administrator Adolf Eichmann, obedience to "superior orders."[57] (A similar memo meant to reassure military interrogators was issued in March 2003 but remains classified.) Of course, all of this advice directly contradicted both the federal and international law on torture, which provides that torture is never justified or excused under any circumstances.[58] The Eichmann (or public authority) defense would later be rejected by the U.S. district court that convicted CIA contractor David Passaro of beating a prisoner who later died.[59]

Bybee's memo also insisted that the president's authority to manage a military campaign must take precedence over any legal prohibitions against torture, including the Convention Against Torture and its implementing statute: "Any effort by Congress to regulate the interrogation of battlefield combatants would violate the Constitution's sole vesting of the Commander-in-Chief authority in the President."[60] Thus, "the Department of Justice could not enforce [the law against torture][61] against federal officials acting pursuant to the President's constitutional authority to wage a military campaign."[62] In short, the laws of war were not binding on the United States—just on other countries.

This assertion, too, was extraordinary. The OLC was essentially denying the constitutionality of the War Crimes Act of 1996, which punishes grave breaches of the Geneva Conventions; the Uniform Code of Military Justice, which prohibits cruel and inhumane treatment of prisoners; and federal laws against murder and assault.[63]

"It is true . . . of journeys in the law," Justice Felix Frankfurter once wrote, "that the place you reach depends on the direction you are taking. And, so, where one comes out on a case depends on where one goes in."[64] Logically, the torture memos proceed from two assumptions. First, contrary to the Declaration of Independence and the Constitution, there is nothing wrong with the president declaring certain persons as utterly without rights, so that his interrogators can do anything to them that he does not personally forbid. Second, nothing in the Constitution or the law prevents the president from wielding unlimited power over a suspected enemy and then concealing that cruelty behind claims of national security. In other words, when fighting terrorism, the president's authority equals that of an Afghan warlord.

Bybee's memo, journalist Anthony Lewis observed, "read like the advice of a mob lawyer to a mafia don on how to skirt the law and stay out of prison."[65] Jack L. Goldsmith, the conservative Republican (and later Harvard law professor) who replaced Bybee as head of the OLC in October 2003, observed that the memo "seemed more an exercise in sheer power than a reasoned analysis."[66] Worse, it was "an advance pardon," or "get-out-of-jail-free card," because prosecutors would find it almost impossible to convict anyone who chose to claim that he relied in good faith on an OLC opinion.[67] Dean Harold Koh of the Yale Law School, who had been Yoo's professor and mentor, considered his former student's torture memo "perhaps the most clearly erroneous legal opinion I have ever read" and "a stain upon our law and our national reputation."[68]

But the memo was not Yoo's work alone. It received advance approval from many officials, including lawyers at the National Security Council, the White House Counsel's Office, and the vice president's office.[69] A CIA attorney would later praise it as his agency's "golden shield."[70] CIA officials would have preferred to receive their legal cover in the form of a presidential finding, but they were sufficiently reassured by both the Bybee and Yoo memos to issue secret guidelines permitting waterboarding and the denial of pain medication, among other things, although such practices violated the UN Convention Against Torture, the Geneva Conventions, and the War Crimes Act.

Neither National Security Adviser Condoleezza Rice nor Secretary of State Colin Powell had been consulted. When they learned of the torture memos on June 8, 2004, they confronted Gonzales in his office. According to the *Washington Post,* quoting a former White House official with firsthand knowledge, Rice "very angrily said that there would be no more secret opinions on international and national security law" and threatened to take the matter to the president if Gonzales kept them in the dark again. But neither official protested to Bush or Cheney.[71]

It would be reassuring to think of the torture memorandums as the aberrant work of a single administration, but that is not the case. Bybee's memorandum drew heavily on efforts by Presidents Ronald Reagan and George Herbert Walker Bush to condition U.S. ratification of the UN Convention Against Torture on nineteen "understandings" that would protect the CIA's use of stress positions, sensory deprivation, and sexual humiliation.[72] According to its final formulation, cruel and inhumane treatment would not rise to the level of torture unless it was "specifically intended to inflict excruciating and agonizing physical or mental pain or suffering." Mental pain would not qualify unless it was prolonged or intentionally inflicted, involved "mind-altering substances or other procedures calculated to disrupt profoundly the senses or the personality," threatened imminent death, or threatened these actions against some other person.[73] In 1994 the Clinton administration ratified the Convention Against Torture with all of the previous two administrations' understandings intact.

On August 1, 2002, John Yoo issued another OLC memorandum that has yet to be made public. It approved a list of specific interrogation techniques that the CIA wanted, including waterboarding, even though the United States had declared that practice a war crime in 1947. According to the *New York Times,* this memo actually spelled out how long and how often particular techniques could be used.[74] Yoo did reject one proposal. It would be illegal, he advised, for interrogators to threaten to bury a captive alive.[75]

Evading Opposition within the Government

To ensure Bush's torture policy would prevail within his administration, a group of political lawyers deliberately excluded potential dissenters from the process. For example, the order creating military commissions was secretly drafted by a few conservative attorneys, including the vice president's lawyer, David Addington, and Bradford Berenson and Timothy Flanigan of the White House counsel's office. It caught many officials by surprise, including Secretary of State Colin Powell and his legal advisers, National Security Adviser Condoleezza Rice, legal adviser to the National Security Council John Bellinger III, the Justice Department's criminal division, the Joint Chiefs of Staff (JCS), and the judge advocates of the armed services. When the JAGs got wind of the commission's order, a few days before it was issued, they demanded revisions, but Jim Haynes, Rumsfeld's general counsel, brushed them aside.[76]

Similar end runs produced the notorious torture memos. According to a former CIA attorney, the administration "could have separated the big question from classified details . . . and had an open debate. Instead, an inner circle of lawyers and advisers worked around likely dissenters and one-upped each other with extreme arguments."[77]

To reduce the risk of congressional opposition, the administration limited its briefings to the chairmen and ranking Democratic members of the House and Senate intelligence panels and bound them to complete secrecy. The CIA also refused to give Senator John "Jay" D. Rockefeller IV (D-WV), vice chair of the Senate Intelligence Committee, backup material supporting the CIA inspector general's 2004 report, which questioned the legal basis for extraordinary renditions.[78]

Enhancing the Techniques

The driving force behind the military's harsh interrogation practices was Secretary of Defense Donald Rumsfeld. Often through teleconferences, he and his deputy for intelligence, Stephen Cambone, put intense pressure on commanders in the field to come up with actionable intelligence. Rumsfeld's appetite for instant intelligence was insatiable. When it could not be satisfied, his staff and members of the vice president's War Council pushed the military to try more aggressive techniques.

The effort appears to have begun as early as July 25, 2002, when a member of Jim Haynes's staff asked the Joint Personnel Recovery Agency (JPRA) at Fort Bragg, North Carolina, for information about its SERE training program.[79] The next day, the JPRA's chief of staff, Air Force Lt. Col. Daniel Baumgartner, sent Haynes a long explanation of how the program worked.

SERE training, of course, was about resisting torturers, not emulating them, but that distinction did not give the administration pause. Dave Becker, chief of the Defense Intelligence Agency's Interrogation Control Element at GTMO, told an army investigator that his unit's subsequent requests for enhanced authority were "a direct result of the pressure we felt from Washington to obtain intelligence and the lack of policy guidance being issued by Washington."[80] At the same time, of course, the interrogators wanted the protection of explicitly authorized procedures before they gave in to Pentagon demands.[81]

In preparing their wish list, GTMO's leadership appears to have relied on at least four sources of inspiration. One was the abusive interrogations American soldiers experienced in SERE training, and to that end a delegation from GTMO visited Fort Bragg in September 2002 to witness the abuses firsthand.

A second source was Jonathan Fredman, chief counsel of the CIA's Counterterrorism Center, who visited the naval base in October. When asked where the line should be drawn between legitimate and illegitimate interrogations, Fredman offered a simple rule: "If the detainee dies, you're doing it wrong."[82]

A third source was what the military and CIA were actually doing to prisoners in Afghanistan. At the meeting with Fredman on October 2, Lt. Col. Diane Beaver, General Dunlavey's judge advocate, acknowledged that sleep deprivation was already being used on prisoners at Bagram Air Base, but "officially it is not happening." She then added, "We may need to curb the harsher operations while the ICRC is around." Fredman concurred: "In the past, when the ICRC has made a big deal about certain detainees, the [Defense Department] has moved them away from the attention of the ICRC."[83]

Finally, the GTMO staff took inspiration from the television series *24*, in which fictional terrorists were tortured almost every week into revealing the location of ticking bombs before they exploded. "We saw it on cable," Beaver explained. "People had already seen the first series; it was hugely popular."[84]

She also recalled brainstorming sessions in which thirty or more soldiers discussed what they might do to coerce confessions: "You could almost see their dicks getting hard as they got new ideas." General Dunlavey was particularly partial to waterboarding, she remembered. He had served in Vietnam and was convinced that it worked.[85]

Dunlavey and his staff did not come up with these new "counter-resistance" techniques entirely on their own. They were visited on September 25 by a number of political lawyers, including Jim Haynes, Alberto Gonzales, David Addington, CIA Counsel John Rizzo, and Michael Chertoff, then head of the Justice Department's Criminal Division and later secretary of the Department of Homeland Security. The visitors watched interrogations, received briefings, and discussed techniques. The message Lieutenant Colonel Beaver received was clear enough: interrogators should do "whatever needed to be done."[86]

On October 11, GTMO's brass formally requested authority for at least three categories (or levels) of coercion. Category 1 and 2 techniques included humiliating Muslim men with "forced nudity" and "forced grooming" (shaving off their hair and beards). The interrogators also proposed putting prisoners in solitary confinement for up to thirty days at a time, disorienting them as to night and day, subjecting them to strobe lights and loud music, and terrorizing them with snarling dogs. Inflicting physical pain was permissible so long as it was not "severe," and mental harm could be done so long as it wasn't "prolonged." What was severe or prolonged was left to the interrogators to decide for themselves.

Under category 3, Dunlavey's crew sought permission for practices they had already employed for nearly two years, including "exposure to cold weather" (hypothermia) or "water" (i.e., waterboarding) and threats to harm the prisoners' families. The use of "mild, non-injurious physical contact"—e.g., pushing, poking, and open-handed slapping—was also recommended.

Attached to the proposal was a legal memorandum from Lieutenant Colonel Beaver claiming that all the requested methods were legal. General Dunlavey, a judge in civilian life, had tried to persuade Beaver to approve the techniques orally, but she wanted them in writing and signed by everyone in the chain of command so that there would be, as she put it in her memo, "immunity in advance."

SOUTHCOM passed the proposal on to the chairman of the Joint Chiefs of Staff, Gen. Richard Myers. His JAG officer, U.S. Navy Capt. Jane Dalton, promptly solicited opinions from the military services. Their initial reactions were negative. They believed many of the proposed techniques would expose servicemen to criminal prosecution under federal law, the Uniform Code of Military Justice, or international law. They would also violate the president's directive that prisoners were to be treated humanely. But before a full review could be conducted, Dalton was ordered to stand down. Jim Haynes "does not want this [review] to proceed," Myers told her.[87]

As a result, the only attorney to endorse the proposal was GTMO's Diane Beaver, but that backing was enough for Haynes. On November 27, 2002, he advised Rumsfeld to approve all of the category 1 and 2 techniques, as well as mild, non-injurious physical contact from category 3. The general counsel also endorsed two other category 3 techniques: hypothermia, managed with a rectal thermometer, and waterboarding. However, he proposed that they be held in reserve, to be authorized by the secretary's office on a case-by-case basis. Thus Haynes anticipated that the secretary would directly and personally authorize some forms of scarless torture.

Category 3, of course, involved what Americans used to call the "third degree," the highest level of brutality commonly practiced by police interrogators in the nineteenth and early twentieth centuries. Nazis who subjected captured resistance fighters in France and Norway to the third degree were later convicted of war crimes.[88]

The interrogation techniques that Haynes proposed went beyond those prescribed in the U.S. Army's Field Manual 34-52, *Intelligence Interrogation.* They also violated Common Article 3 of the Geneva Conventions, which prohibited cruel, inhumane, or degrading treatment, and the Uniform Code of Military Justice, which barred assaults. But on December 2, 2002, Rumsfeld authorized them anyway, adding in a handwritten note next to his signature, "I stand for 8–10 hours a day. Why is standing limited to 4 hours?"[89]

The secretary apparently saw no difference between forcing a prisoner to stand in a stress position, which can be excruciating within minutes and damage joints permanently, and his working at a stand-up desk, where he was able to relax and walk about. When a prisoner is forced to stand for long periods, the CIA (and the former Soviet Union's intelligence and internal security agency, the KGB) discovered, his or her legs begin to swell. Lesions form and erupt. The prisoner begins to hallucinate and the kidneys start to shut down.[90] Most of the procedures Rumsfeld authorized had been banned by the U.S. military, in no small part because they had been inflicted on American POWs during World War II and the Korean War.[91]

When Rumsfeld's memo reached Guantánamo on December 2, Col. Brittain Mallow, commander of the Defense Department's Criminal Investigation Task Force (CITF), immediately prohibited his agents from "participat[ing] in the use of any questionable techniques" and ordered them to report "all discussions of interrogation strategies and approaches" to his office.[92] FBI agents remonstrated with Maj. Gen. Geoffrey Miller to no avail; Rumsfeld's expectations were controlling.[93] Agents of the Naval Criminal Investigative Service (NCIS), like the FBI agents, also complained to their Pentagon superiors that prisoners at GTMO were being subjected to "physical abuse and degrading treatment."

Alberto J. Mora, the navy's general counsel, could have ignored NCIS's report. Navy personnel had no direct responsibility for interrogations; they just ran the base. But Mora chose to investigate and, with the support of Navy Secretary Gordon England, informed Haynes that the new interrogation policy violated the law, verged on torture, and could ultimately expose "the entire . . . chain of command" to prosecution.[94] When that advice was ignored, Mora did what the FBI did: he ordered navy investigators "to disengage, stand clear, and report any questionable interrogation practices."

Mora was particularly opposed to the administration's effort to separate torture from abuse:

> If cruelty is no longer declared unlawful, but instead is applied as a matter of policy, it alters the fundamental relationship of man to government. It destroys the whole notion of individual rights. The Constitution recognizes that man has an inherent right, not bestowed by the state or laws, to personal dignity, including the right to be free of cruelty. It applies to all human beings, not just in America—even those designated as "unlawful enemy combatants." If you make this exception, the whole Constitution crumbles. It's a transformative issue.[95]

On January 15, after Haynes had ignored his advice for more than a month, Mora sent him a draft memorandum declaring that the category 2 and 3 techniques constituted cruel and unusual treatment, if not torture, in violation of both American and international law. Then he warned Haynes's staff that he planned to sign the memo later that afternoon.

Mora's memo was a ticking time bomb. The navy's top lawyer was an administration appointee and a staunch conservative who had been inside the Pentagon when it was attacked on September 11. If his memo were leaked, the Defense Department—indeed, the entire administration—would be deeply embarrassed. Before the afternoon was over, Haynes called Mora to say, "I'm pleased to tell you the secretary has rescinded the authorization. We'll set up an interrogation group and do this proper."[96]

The new working group, however, was a scam. Haynes packed it with politically appointed lawyers and put U.S. Air Force general counsel Mary Walker, one of Rumsfeld's most reliable loyalists, in charge. Even before the group met, Haynes asked the OLC for yet another memorandum, and on March

14, 2003, John Yoo produced an eighty-one-page secret memo declaring that the infliction of cruel, inhumane, degrading treatment at Guantánamo Bay would not violate the anti-torture statute because it was only meant to ban mistreatment of prisoners *within* the United States or at an arguably non-U.S. base abroad.[97] Specifically, the statute was not meant to apply within the "special maritime or territorial jurisdiction of the United States,"[98] which included GTMO and U.S. ships at sea. They remained legal black holes.

Yoo also argued that the president is not bound by federal laws of general applicability. If such statutes were "misconstrued to apply to the interrogation of enemy combatants," they would conflict with the Constitution's grant of the power of the commander in chief solely to the president.[99]

Under our Constitution, he added, "the sovereign right of the United States on the treatment of enemy combatants is reserved to the President as Commander-in-Chief."[100] So much for the power of Congress to make laws defining "Offences against the Law of Nations" and "rules for the Regulation of the land and naval forces."[101] So much, too, for Congress's power, under Article I, clause 18, "to make all Laws which shall be necessary and proper to . . . carrying into execution . . . Powers vested by this Constitution in the Government of the United States, or in any Department or Officer thereof."[102] Neither power can restrict the sovereign in his wars against alleged enemies.

Yoo also claimed that "the sovereign retains the discretion to treat unlawful combatants as it sees fit."[103] In other words, the president is not just a public servant. He is the sovereign, despite what the preamble says about sovereignty (i.e., the ultimate legal authority) residing with we, the people.

In addition, Yoo argued that the laws forbidding torture, assault, maiming, and war crimes were never meant to limit what the president's agents could do to alleged enemy combatants, especially if they did it within the special maritime or territorial jurisdiction of the United States.[104] One way or another, he implied, successive Congresses always meant for the president and his secret agents to be above the law.

Although Attorney General Ashcroft approved Yoo's advice, Mora was not persuaded.[105] At one meeting, he criticized the Justice Department's theory of "extreme and virtually unlimited [presidential] authority" and asked Yoo flat out "whether the president could order the application of torture." Yoo's answer was yes.[106]

Should his theories of presidential power not prevail, Yoo parsed the criminal laws that might apply at Guantánamo. He concluded that a variety of scarless tortures, including "alterations to the detainee's cell environment"[107] (i.e., hypothermia monitored with a rectal thermometer), did not constitute criminal acts.

In late March 2003, Jim Haynes directed the working group to accept Yoo's memorandum as controlling authority, and it dutifully gave Rumsfeld the legal cover he sought. Following the OLC's lead, the group's April report went beyond the army's field manual and endorsed a number of scarless cruelties that the State Department had routinely condemned when practiced by other countries.[108] The military panel did not expressly endorse waterboarding or other forms of mock (or near) execution, but it did not forbid them either. Rather, it rubber-stamped most forms of scarless torture and recommended that the secretary continue to authorize "exceptional techniques" on a case-by-case basis.[109] The lawyers also endorsed the Eichmann defense of following superiors' orders. Then, as if they were unsure of their advice, they urged the secretary to obtain a "presidential directive or other writing" designating, among other things, "the strategic interrogation facilities that are authorized to use 'exceptional techniques.'"[110]

On April 16, 2003, Rumsfeld accepted twenty-four techniques—the harshest ever allowed in armed forces history—recommended by the working group and forwarded them to General Miller's interrogators at GTMO.[111] Members of the working group who disagreed with Yoo's opinion were not informed of the report's existence. Indeed, they were led to believe that the project had been abandoned.[112] Mora would not learn that the policy he considered criminal had been reinstated until the Abu Ghraib scandal broke a year later.[113]

Torturing al-Qahtani

Nor was Mora told that Secretary Rumsfeld had personally approved "special interrogation plans" for Muhammed al-Qahtani, one of several persons suspected of being a twentieth hijacker, while the December 2 order was in effect.[114] Al-Qahtani had been captured the previous spring but had revealed so little in early interrogations that the new interrogation techniques were developed over the summer and fall with him in mind.

Administration officials would later try to blame military officers for the new interrogation techniques, but Addington, Gonzales, Haynes, Rizzo, and Chertoff had visited GTMO in late September to discuss al-Qahtani's resistance. "They wanted to know what we were doing to get this guy," General Dunlavey recalled. "Addington, in particular, was interested in how we were managing it." Rumsfeld, too, "was directly and regularly involved" in those discussions.[115]

From August 8, 2002, until January 15, 2003, al-Qahtani was held in solitary confinement in a continually lighted cell. By November, FBI agents complained, he was exhibiting extreme symptoms of psychological trauma: hearing voices, talking to imaginary people, and crouching in his cell, covered by a sheet, for hours. But these complaints were not enough to prevent Rumsfeld from verbally authorizing a special interrogation plan for al-Qahtani that included isolation for up to thirty days, "20-hour interrogations for every 24-hour cycle," and intimidation by military dogs.[116] From November 23, 2002, until January 15, 2003, al-Qahtani was subjected to virtually nonstop interrogation and abuse, eventually involving every technique that Secretary Rumsfeld had approved on December 2.[117]

The interrogators apparently believed that they could force reliable information out of the prisoner by questioning him while he was exhausted. According to Lt. Gen. Randall M. Schmidt, "This guy was [interrogated] for 20 hours a day for at least 54 days . . . in the white cell." Even when he was taken to another white room to rest, the lights were left on and "stuff [was] going on."[118]

General Miller's men subjected him to hooding, ear-splitting music, and extreme temperatures. They also shaved his head and his beard, which denigrated his faith. At one point he was given an enema; on another occasion a medic injected him with three and a half bags of intravenous solution, which forced him to urinate on himself. A dog was brought in to growl, bark, and bare his teeth at the prisoner while he was chained to the floor, both before Haynes's memo was adopted and afterward. They subjected him to hypothermia until his heart rate dropped to thirty-five beats per minute, and he had to be temporarily hospitalized twice. Interrogators ordered him to draw up a will, implying that he would not survive the ordeal, and then tore it up in front of him.[119]

Although the military's interrogation plan had been discussed for six months before the secretary of defense approved it, it was remarkably juvenile in its execution. For example, interrogators made the prisoner wear a woman's bra, draped a thong over his head, led him around on a leash, and forced him to perform dog tricks. They made him dance with a male interrogator while wearing a towel on his head "like a burka," and they forced him to wear a smiley face mask cut from a box. Interrogators also stripped him naked in front of female interrogators, sexually insulted his female relatives, poured water on his head, and hung pictures of swimsuit models around his neck.

While al-Qahtani was being tortured, two SERE instructors gave GTMO's interrogators a short course on "the theory and application of the physical pressures utilized during our training." The list of coercive techniques that the instructors recommended had been copied verbatim from a 1957 report describing what Chinese interrogators had done to American POWs during the Korean War. Only the title, "Communist Attempts to Elicit False Confessions from Air Force Prisoners of War," had been removed, thereby concealing the report's key point: these techniques, which included isolation, long periods of forced standing in the cold, sensory deprivation, and exhaustion, had been used by Chinese Communists, whom the United States considered war criminals, in order to elicit *false* confessions.[120] Why anyone thought that using them on al-Qahtani—and his interrogators tried them all—would produce a *true* confession has never been explained.

General Schmidt, who saw al-Qahtani as he was "coming out of this thing," said that he "looks like hell. He has got black coals for eyes." But nothing the interrogators did amounted to torture, the general concluded. It was not even cruel, inhumane, or degrading.[121]

The U.S. Army, U.S. Navy, and Marine Corps JAGs would later disagree. Testifying before the Senate Armed Services Committee in 2005, they all agreed that what was inflicted on al-Qahtani would have been illegal if another country had imposed it on Americans.[122] The procedures Rumsfeld approved, they said, constituted "outrages upon personal dignity" and "humiliating and degrading treatment" in violation of the army's field manual and Common Article 3 of the Geneva Conventions.

Schmidt, too, would have second thoughts when interviewed by the Defense Department's inspector general. "Here's this guy manacled, chained down, dogs brought in, put [in] his face, told to growl, show teeth, and that kind of stuff. And you can imagine the fear. . . . You know . . . if you had a camera and snapped that picture, you'd be back to Abu Ghraib."[123]

Al-Qahtani's torture ended on January 15, 2003. Its termination coincided with a rising tide of objections from the FBI, NCIS, and the navy's general counsel to the abuse of GTMO's prisoners. But President Bush, in his State of the Union address two weeks later, boasted, "One by one, the terrorists are learning the meaning of American justice."[124]

"Somewhere there had to be a throttle [i.e., a control] on this," Schmidt later wrote, especially from the secretary of defense, who was "personally involved in the interrogation of this person" and who was "personally being briefed on this" in the course of weekly telephone conversations with General Miller.[125] But there wasn't. Nothing in the secret log of al-Qahtani's interrogation indicates that any new information was obtained.[126]

Assassination Next?

During the 1960s and 1970s, the CIA undertook a series of assassination plots against foreign heads of state, including Fidel Castro. So far as we know, all were unsuccessful, but when they became known, members of Congress were appalled. They could easily imagine foreign reprisals on the streets of Washington. A legislative ban was proposed but interdicted by President Gerald Ford, who issued a 1976 executive order declaring that "no person employed by or acting on behalf of the United States government shall engage in or conspire to engage in assassination."[127] However, this very public and unqualified prohibition did not deter the Clinton administration's OLC from approving attempts to kill military targets, such as Osama bin Laden and the staffs of his training camps, with cruise missiles.[128]

Then, on September 17, 2001, George W. Bush secretly countermanded Ford's executive order and authorized the CIA and, later, Special Forces to kill, capture, or detain suspected al Qaeda operatives anywhere in the world.[129] According to John Yoo, Bush's order—along with a list of targets, including Osama bin Laden and his partner in crime, Dr. Ayman al-Zawahiri—was committed to writing and was shared with the House and Senate intelligence committees.[130] That, too, constituted a powerful signal that the legal gloves were to come off.

It was also a signal that the law was to be ignored. But then George W. Bush was not the first president to claim the power to kill enemies without first obtaining some sort of congressional authorization. In 1986, President Reagan launched an attack on the home of Libyan dictator Muammar Qadhafi in reprisal for the bombing of a discotheque in Germany. Reagan did so in disregard of the marque and reprisal clause of the Constitution, which assigns the reprisal power, like the power to declare war, to Congress and not to the president.

President Clinton claimed the same power when he tried to kill Osama bin Laden and his associates with missile attacks on al Qaeda training camps in Afghanistan and when he bombed a factory in the Sudan. Clinton's Office of Legal Counsel agreed that bin Laden could be assassinated on the president's authority alone because he was a legitimate military target who posed an imminent threat to the United States.[131] As commander in chief, the president presumably has some authority to direct the armed forces to target enemy leaders in time of war, but is the United States engaged in that kind of conflict now? If the Cold War did not justify assassinations, what justifies them now?

Following September 11, a CIA-operated drone flying over Yemen launched a Hellfire missile that killed six al Qaeda suspects, one of whom was an American citizen.[132] Congress's Authorization for the Use of Military Force of September 18, 2001, against those responsible for the 9/11 attacks might have authorized this killing, had it been carried out in Afghanistan. But the attack took place in Yemen and was carried out by a civilian agency. If the CIA is to wage clandestine warfare with its missile-carrying planes in nonbelligerent countries, shouldn't Congress have to authorize it first?

Most wars have relatively clear geographical boundaries within which most of our enemies can be found. But if the president can declare a worldwide quasi-war against an organized crime syndicate like al Qaeda and kidnap suspects in New York for delivery to Syrian torturers, then what is to prevent him from secretly authorizing the CIA—or any other agency or private corporation—to assassinate suspects within the United States? And if the president of the United States is legally free to delegate to CIA officials the power to detain, kidnap, torture, or assassinate suspected terrorists anywhere on earth, then what is to prevent foreign intelligence agencies from doing the same to American citizens here or abroad? In 1976, Chile's secret police killed Orlando Letelier, a former Chilean diplomat, and Ronni Moffitt, his American aide, by blowing up the car in which they were traveling in downtown Washington, D.C.

Such are the signals that authorized, encouraged, and helped conceal the Bush administration's policy of torture.

5

COVERING UP

Let me make very clear the position of my government and our country.
We do not condone torture. I have never ordered torture. I will
never order torture. The values of this country are such that
torture is not part of our soul or our being.
—PRESIDENT GEORGE W. BUSH[1]

"When those horrible pictures began to be published," Office of Legal
Counsel attorney Jack L. Goldsmith recalled, "everyone in the government
scrambled for cover."[2] In fact, the concealment began a year earlier, when Lt.
Gen. Ricardo Sanchez, head of the Multi-National Force in Iraq (MNF-I), and
his staff ignored disturbing reports of prisoner abuse from the International
Committee of the Red Cross. The first report, early in 2003, documented some
two hundred incidents at numerous detention centers. More reports followed in
May, July, and November.

Called before Congress in May 2004, General Sanchez swore that the Red
Cross reports did not cross his desk until January 2004, after the incriminating
photos had been turned in. Technically, that may have been true, but his staff met
with representatives of the ICRC during the previous year. His staff members must
have read the reports they received because they denied Red Cross investigators
further access to prisoners.[3]

In the late summer and early fall of 2003, Sanchez took Maj. Gen. Geoffrey
Miller's advice and authorized three protocols for interrogating prisoners, each
harsher than those prescribed by the U.S. Army's interrogations manual. At one

point Sanchez exploded, "Why are we detaining these people? We should be killing them."[4]

Gen. John P. Abizaid, who was responsible for military operations in both Iraq and Afghanistan, also swore that the Red Cross reports had not come to his attention. He assured the Senate committee that no "culture of abuse existed in my command."[5]

Months after the Criminal Investigations Division (CID) began its investigation and weeks after Maj. Gen. Antonio Taguba's report reached the Pentagon, Secretary Rumsfeld claimed ignorance of the wrongdoing. The claim is difficult to square with his practice of reaching down past the chain of command to obtain information directly from interrogators in the field. His denials of any knowledge of the cover-up is also difficult to reconcile with his admission that he "ordered an Iraqi national held at Camp Cropper, a high security detention center in Iraq, to be kept off the prison's roles and not presented to the International Red Cross," even though hiding prisoners in Iraq clearly violated the Geneva Conventions.[6]

The secretary must have had considerable confidence in the capacity of his military commanders to keep embarrassing information from leaking; otherwise, he would not have approved the torture and abuse of prisoners personally. Despite this confidence, he was surprised during a press conference in November 2005 when Gen. Peter Pace, chairman of the Joint Chiefs of Staff, declared—consistent with military law—that it is "absolutely the responsibility of every U.S. service member, if they see inhumane treatment being conducted, to intervene to stop it." Rumsfeld immediately moved to correct him: "But I don't think you mean they have an obligation to physically stop it; it's to report it." No, the general replied, "if they are physically present when inhumane treatment is taking place, sir, they have an obligation to try to stop it." A few minutes later the general joked, "I'm not trainable, today!"[7]

Rumsfeld would later claim that learning about the abuses at Abu Ghraib was his worst day in office,[8] implying disappointment at the misbehavior of a few bad apples. However, when he first learned that the torture pictures existed, he did not express concern for the victims, the breakdown of discipline, the inflaming of insurgents, or the disgrace of it all. He simply exclaimed, "I didn't know you were allowed to bring cameras into a prison."[9]

Damage Control

Contrary to all the talk of military honor, the most important lesson any young officer learns from the so-called West Point Protective Association is "cover your ass" (CYA). Like corporate bureaucracies, the military is geared to drive credit up and blame down.[10] No commander has to tell his subordinates to make him look good and refrain from reporting any information that will set him up to be scapegoated by his own blame-avoiding superiors. That duty goes without saying and is reinforced each time a career (usually that of a reservist or national guardsman) is destroyed for failure to protect a commanding officer (usually a West Point graduate). General Taguba underscored this fact of military life when he observed, "From the moment a soldier enlists, we inculcate loyalty, duty, honor, integrity and selfless service. And yet, when we get to the senior officer level, we forget those values."[11]

At Abu Ghraib the cover-up began in January 2004. Shortly after Specialist Joseph Darby slipped a computer disk containing Specialist Charles Graner's photographs under their door, the CID agents realized they had a public relations bomb on their hands. Whoever generated the disk must have copies of the photos on his or her computer. Copies could have been e-mailed anywhere, including to the press. CID went straight to General Sanchez's staff, which just as quickly initiated damage control measures.

The highest-ranking intelligence officer at Abu Ghraib, Col. Thomas M. Pappas, who was personally involved in the death of Manadel al-Jamadi, responded to Darby's disclosures by issuing a memorandum that granted guards and interrogators a forty-eight-hour period of amnesty during which "without penalty or legal consequence" they could get rid of photographs, tapes, or computer files "containing images of any criminal or security detainee currently or formerly interned" at the prison.[12] Amnesty boxes were set up so that soldiers could discard these potentially incriminating materials without identifying themselves. When Brig. Gen. Janis L. Karpinski visited the prison after the scandal broke and asked, "What's this about photographs?" a sergeant replied, "Ma'am, I've heard of the photographs, but I don't know what they're photographs of. Maybe somebody took pictures of prisoners, but we don't know anything. None of us do." When she asked to see prison logbooks, the sergeant informed her that CID had taken them away.[13]

Karpinski's public affairs officer, Lt. Col. Vic Harris, witnessed the cover-up firsthand.

> I heard the discussions of the staff and our commanders, and there was no intention of doing anything other than to try to contain [the situation]. There was no intention of trying to bring the people to justice that were obviously committing crimes, in some cases war crimes, in those images. . . . The only intent was to hide it and try to prevent the images from getting out to the media. . . . I was very disappointed.

Harris was disappointed enough to tip off a producer at CBS News, and the photos were broadcast on April 28, 2004, during an episode of *60 Minutes II*.[14] The ensuing scandal was enormous. Overnight, respect for America and the Bush administration plummeted.

Before the controversy ran its course, the Pentagon was forced to order a dozen investigations. Consistent with the CYA doctrine, each focused on low-ranking personnel so as to shield superior officers and the CIA from embarrassment. This "modified, limited hangout," to use John Dean's memorable term, was accomplished by assigning relatively low-ranking generals to conduct each inquiry, knowing that army regulations did not permit these generals to investigate officers of higher rank. As one general told the *New Yorker's* Seymour Hersh in 2007, "I was legally prevented from further investigation into higher authority."[15] No military investigation examined the conduct of anyone higher in the chain of command than General Sanchez.[16]

The first inquiry, conducted by General Taguba, was confined to the activities of just one unit—General Karpinski's 800th Military Police Brigade. Taguba was forbidden to question interrogators who worked for Pappas's military intelligence unit or any OGA personnel. He was also prohibited from examining events prior to November 1, 2003, including the torture of three alleged rapists on October 25, during which MI soldiers had been photographed.

Despite these restrictions, which General Sanchez proposed and General Abizaid of Central Command approved,[17] Taguba did what he could and produced a report that revealed far more than his superiors wanted. This fact became painfully clear when he appeared at the Pentagon to brief the secretary of defense on the eve of congressional hearings. Rumsfeld signaled his disapproval with mocking sarcasm: "Here . . . comes . . . that *famous* General Taguba—of the Taguba report!" The secretary's first question to the general was not "What happened at Abu Ghraib?" but "How did your report get leaked to the press?"[18]

Rumsfeld's displeasure ended Taguba's career. Military superiors accused him of "being overzealous and disloyal," Taguba later revealed. "They ostracized me for doing what I was asked to do." Eventually Thomas F. Hall, the assistant secretary of defense for reserve affairs, informed him, "I have to let you go" for not being a loyal "member of the team."[19]

What happened to the conscientious general was not lost on subsequent investigators. Vice Adm. Albert T. Church's report, for example, implausibly concluded that "none of the pictures of abuse at Abu Ghraib bear any resemblance to approved policies at any level, in any theater."[20] Lt. Gen. Randall Schmidt and Brig. Gen. John Furlow's investigation of FBI complaints found that prisoners at Guantánamo had been short shackled, threatened with dogs, denied sleep, and exposed to extreme temperatures, but they concluded that the "degrading and abusive treatment . . . did not rise to the level of being inhumane treatment."[21]

Maj. Gen. George R. Fay affirmed that torture had occurred at Abu Ghraib and that "twenty-seven MI . . . personnel allegedly requested, encouraged, condoned, or solicited . . . MP personnel to abuse detainees and/or participated in detainee abuse."[22] He might have learned more, however, had he not discouraged candor by beginning his interviews with a warning: "Now, if anyone saw anything and did not intervene, they can be charged with a crime. Did anyone see anything and fail to intervene?"[23] Not one of the twenty-seven MI agents was ever prosecuted.

When the military's limited investigations were derided in the press, Rumsfeld appointed what he called an independent body of investigators. It was anything but. The secretary handpicked each of its members. He put his old friend James R. Schlesinger in charge and then made it clear that resolving "issues of personal accountability" was not part of the panel's job.[24] The resulting report was a masterpiece of Washington double-talk. The executive summary concluded that there was no official policy mandating torture while the body of the report detailed how decisions by the president, vice president, and secretary of defense led directly to abuses under investigation.[25]

Destroying Evidence

On May 24, 2005, the army's surgeon general revealed that all interrogations at Guantánamo since 2002—more than twenty-four thousand—had been videotaped. In February 2008, GTMO's commander, Rear Adm. Mark H. Buzby, claimed that videos of the interrogations no longer existed. The tapes had been recorded over, he said.[26]

According to State Department cables, foreign agents were warned that their interrogations of prisoners at GTMO would be taped and that copies of their final reports would have to be shared with the U.S. government. Among the countries that sent interrogators to the prison were the United Kingdom (MI5), Canada, Belgium, France, Bahrain, Egypt, Jordan, Libya, Saudi Arabia, Tunisia, Yemen, China, and Russia. According to a former interrogator, however, U.S. agents indexed the foreign interrogations, which suggests, contrary to Admiral Buzby's claim, that they would not have been routinely taped over.[27]

In June 2008, prosecutors admitted that interrogators at GTMO had been urged to destroy their notes in case they were called to testify. These instructions were not verbal; they came from a secret interrogations manual published in January 2003, about the time that al-Qahtani's ordeal ended.[28] Destroying evidence of torture and cruelty was thus a standard operating procedure under General Miller's command.

The tapes and notes were, of course, the best possible evidence to support or discredit the findings of Combat Status Review Tribunals. They would have confirmed or debunked allegations of abuse by prisoners, FBI agents, and agents of the Naval Criminal Investigative Service. Tapes and notes would also have revealed how interrogators from various branches of military intelligence, the FBI, the CIA, and foreign governments treated or threatened the prisoners they interrogated at GTMO.

Their destruction also violated a basic principle of constitutional law: the prosecution must give criminal defendants all evidence favorable to them.[29] The duty extends not just to the prosecutors but to all government agencies involved in prisoner interrogations.[30]

The army was not the only organization to destroy tapes. In 2002 the CIA taped its interrogations of at least three high-value prisoners: Khalid Sheikh Mohammed, the alleged mastermind of 9/11; Abd al-Rahim al-Nashiri, who allegedly coordinated the attack on the USS *Cole*; and Abu Zubaydah, once thought to be a close aide to Osama bin Laden.[31] What to do with this evidence, which comprised hundreds of hours of video and audio recordings and showed the prisoners being waterboarded, became a serious political as well as legal problem when lawyers for Zacarias Moussaoui, José Padilla, and the 9/11 Commission requested information that the tapes contained—information that might show that allegations against them had been made under duress.[32] The tapes not only showed prisoners being tortured—prisoners the government planned to prosecute before military commissions—they identified the agents and private contractors who carried out the torture and who might well be able to implicate their superiors. What to do about this incriminating evidence was a frequent topic of discussion among White House lawyers, including Harriet E. Miers, then deputy chief of staff; John B. Bellinger III, senior lawyer at the NSC; Alberto R. Gonzales, then White House counsel; and David S. Addington, Vice President Cheney's counsel.

According to a former senior intelligence official with direct knowledge of the matter, there had been vigorous sentiment among some White House aides to destroy the tapes, but no one appears to have told the CIA that destroying the film would be illegal. Nor, apparently, did any of these aides order the tapes' preservation. However, in July 2005, John D. Negroponte, director of national intelligence, sent CIA director Porter Goss a formal memorandum advising against their destruction.[33] Representative Jane Harman (D-CA), the ranking Democrat on the House Intelligence Committee, claims to have sent Goss a similar letter.[34]

The Senate Intelligence Committee asked the CIA twice in 2005 to see a report about the tapes written by the agency's general counsel but was twice refused, according to the then-ranking minority member, Senator Jay Rockefeller (D-WV).[35] Meanwhile, court orders directing the preservation of information relating to interrogations multiplied. At least nine were issued before November 2005 and eight afterward.[36] In June 2005, Judge Henry H. Kennedy, Jr., of the U.S. District Court in Washington, D.C., specifically directed the government "to preserve and maintain all evidence and information regarding the torture, mistreatment and abuse of detainees" at Guantánamo.[37] In July, Judge Gladys Kessler issued a nearly identical order.[38] None of the three CIA prisoners had been tortured at Guantánamo, but it was only a matter of time before someone would think to widen the request.

On November 3, 2005, Judge Leonie Brinkema specifically asked the government whether it had video or audio tapes that might show that Moussaoui had no role in the attacks of 9/11.[39] Four days later the Supreme Court agreed to hear the *Hamdan v. Rumsfeld* case, and suddenly it became clear that the justices might rule that the Geneva Conventions did apply at the time the waterboarding took place. If so, the tapes would constitute evidence of war crimes not just by CIA interrogators but by their superiors. Then, on November 9, the *New York Times* revealed that John L. Helgerson, the CIA's inspector general, had warned in 2004 that ten of the agency's interrogation techniques, including waterboarding, may have violated the UN Convention Against Torture.[40] Helgerson, who personally viewed the videotapes of waterboarding, also issued reports describing prisoner abuse by CIA personnel and forwarded them to the Department of Justice for possible prosecution.[41]

The CIA's clandestine service could wait no longer. Its chief, José A. Rodriguez, Jr., cabled the CIA station in Bangkok and ordered the tapes destroyed.[42] In so doing, he fulfilled a vow he had made regarding the tapes to his former deputy, Robert Richer: "I'm not going to let my people get nailed for something they were ordered to do."[43] According to anonymous sources, Rodriguez did not consult with any of his superiors at the CIA, White House, or Justice Department but acted on the basis of a still secret legal memorandum written by two CIA lawyers, Steven Hermes and Robert Eatinger. Whether that assertion is true remains to be seen, but neither Porter Goss nor his successor, Michael V. Hayden, reprimanded Rodriguez. He had not just protected his own people, he had shielded his superiors too. Instead of punishing Rodriguez, Hayden ordered a review of former inspector general Helgerson's investigations into prisoner abuse.[44] Meanwhile, Rodriguez found the resources to hire Robert S. Bennett, one of the most expensive and influential lawyers in Washington, to defend him.

On November 29, 2005, when government lawyers finally presented summaries of Zubaydah's interrogation to Judge Brinkema, they did not bother to tell her that the CIA had just destroyed the best evidence of their content.[45] In February 2008, CIA director Hayden claimed, despite the existence of seventeen court orders, that the tapes had been destroyed because they were no longer relevant to any court proceeding, including the Moussaoui trial.[46] When Congress threatened to investigate the tapes' destruction, Rodriguez then let it be known that, like Col. Oliver North during the Iran-contra affair, he would not testify unless he was granted immunity from prosecution."[47]

Thomas H. Kean and Lee H. Hamilton, cochairs of the 9/11 Commission, had no patience for the cover-up. "Those who knew about those videotapes— and did not tell us about them," they wrote for the *New York Times,* "obstructed our investigation."[48]

Attorney General Michael B. Mukasey agreed to investigate the tapes' destruction, presumably to delay congressional hearings, but he refused to investigate whether waterboarding might be a crime. It would be wrong, he told the House Judiciary Committee, for him to prosecute officials who had relied in good faith on legal advice from the Justice Department's Office of Legal Counsel.[49]

That stance was not Mukasey's idea. John Yoo had advanced this defense strategy based on the "good faith reliance on the advice of counsel" for torturers in his secret memorandums, and Senator John McCain accepted it as part of his Detainee Treatment Act of 2005. (See chapter 8.) Mukasey simply accepted this variant of the Eichmann defense of following orders on the assumption that if an OLC lawyer decrees that it is legal to torture prisoners, then his decree is conclusive for the entire government. Simply by issuing a secret legal opinion, a Justice Department lawyer can suspend the entire criminal law passed by Congress, preempt the role of prosecutors and courts, and, in effect, issue secret pardons in advance of anticipated crimes. Private citizens cannot avoid prosecution by swearing that their lawyers said they could break the law, but government officials may. And this came from a former judge.

More Torture Memos

In December 2004, the Justice Department announced that it was revoking Jay Bybee's torture memorandum. Torture, the Office of Legal Counsel declared in a new memo, was "abhorrent." For a moment it looked as if the torture policy itself and, with it, the cover-up might end.

Bybee's torture memo had actually been withdrawn the previous June by then-OLC chief Jack Goldsmith, but his decision was not disclosed until

December and then only because the administration needed to mollify senators who were disposed to oppose the nomination of White House counsel Alberto Gonzales as attorney general.[50] A new memorandum, issued by Daniel Levin, Goldsmith's successor, boldly proclaimed that "torture is abhorrent," but it did not repudiate any of the twenty-four interrogation techniques that Rumsfeld had approved.[51] The OLC's newfound objections to the torture memos (and to the wiretapping memos Goldsmith also revoked) were simply to their overbroad and unnecessarily provocative assertions of unlimited executive power. Buried in the unclassified portion of Levin's memo was a footnote decreeing that all previously approved techniques remained legal, and a secret appendix expressly authorized the CIA to continue a number of coercive techniques, including waterboarding.[52] John Yoo, now a law professor at the University of California at Berkeley, acknowledged the deception when he declared that in "the real world of interrogation policy, nothing had changed."[53]

But this wasn't the end of the scam. In March 2006, after Gonzales was confirmed, Levin's successor, Stephen G. Bradbury, secretly authorized interrogators to employ the harshest techniques yet. Bradbury, a former law clerk to Supreme Court justice Clarence Thomas, did not revoke Levin's "torture is abhorrent" memo and reinstate Bybee's. Rather, he ruled that a variety of techniques, including slapping prisoners in the head, bombarding them with deafening noise, or subjecting them to isolation, extreme temperatures, and mock drowning (waterboarding), would not violate the Geneva Conventions *if the need for obtaining information from them were dire enough.* Under dire circumstances, Bradbury reasoned, none of those techniques—alone or in conjunction with others—would shock the conscience of a reasonable person.[54]

As the acting head of the OLC, Bradbury was in a difficult spot. He would not advance beyond acting head of the office unless he gave the White House what it wanted. One lawyer who was not so easily intimidated was Deputy Attorney General James Comey, who defied both Bush's and Cheney's staffs in 2005 by refusing to approve warrantless wiretapping. Speaking at the National Security Agency on Law Day 2007, Comey remarked, "It takes far more than a sharp legal mind to say 'no' when it matters most. It takes an understanding that in the long run, intelligence under law is the only sustainable intelligence in this country."[55]

In July 2006 another shell game was initiated. While the Pentagon was reinstating the Geneva Conventions after the Supreme Court's decision in *Hamdan v. Rumsfeld* overturned their suspension, President Bush secretly authorized the CIA to use a variety of as yet undisclosed "enhanced interrogation techniques."[56] In August the president led reporters to believe that the transfer of fourteen high-value prisoners to Guantánamo meant that the CIA had emptied its secret prisons. Scores of prisoners remained unaccounted for, but their apparent disappearance—possibly into the custody of other regimes—did not make headlines. Rumors of prisons in Africa persisted,[57] but the kidnapping program was not cancelled. In February 2007, the president refused to ratify a UN treaty promising not to make prisoners disappear.[58] In March the administration refused to say that secret prisons were not being used, and in July 2007 it issued yet another secret order governing the interrogation of prisoners held by the CIA.[59]

Thus, while proclaiming his opposition to torture, President Bush never issued a specific order forbidding a single practice. On the contrary, he repeatedly fought every effort to restrain interrogators or hold them accountable. The military and CIA destroyed records of the torture while the Justice Department issued secret legal opinions authorizing torture, and then fought every effort to grant the victims their day in court.

Combat Status Review Tribunals: Another Hoax

On June 29, 2004, the Supreme Court decided two important cases against the Bush administration. In *Rasul v. Bush* the justices ruled that Guantánamo was under the dominion and control of the United States. Therefore, prisoners had a statutory right to challenge the legality of their detention by habeas petitions in federal court. In *Hamdi v. Rumsfeld* the justices ruled that the Geneva Conventions gave prisoners the right to have a neutral tribunal determine if the evidence their captors and interrogators collected warranted their continued detention.[60] Vague affidavits by Pentagon officials with no direct knowledge of the facts were not sufficient, Justice John Paul Stevens wrote for the majority.

The Supreme Court's decision vindicated the advice that William Taft, the State Department's legal adviser, had given the administration in January 2002. The use of military panels to screen prisoners was standard practice under the Geneva Conventions. The United States had done it in previous wars, most recently in the Gulf War of 1991, when two thousand Iraqi prisoners had been examined in short order. But the Bush administration did not want lawyers second-guessing intelligence agencies and depriving them of prisoners who might give up useful information in the course of extended questioning.

During the summer and fall of 2004, the military created Combat Status Review Tribunals to review the evidence against each of the GTMO detainees. If the military tribunals were kangaroo courts because of their ability to leap from accusations to conclusions without questioning the evidence, the CSRTs were, in attorney Clive Stafford Smith's inspired image, "wallaby" courts.[61] Prisoners were not allowed to have the assistance of counsel, to examine all the evidence against them, or to call other prisoners to testify on their behalf. Like the big kangaroo commissions, the little wallaby tribunals could admit evidence obtained by torture, keep that evidence secret, and use it to justify imprisoning an innocent person for the rest of his life.

Attorneys for the prisoners quickly exposed the tribunals' many failings, but the most searing indictment came from Lt. Col. Stephen E. Abraham, a decorated intelligence officer with twenty-two years of service in the U.S. Army Reserves. A lawyer in civilian life (and a political conservative who said he cried when President Nixon resigned), Abraham was called to active duty in 2004 following the *Hamdi* decision and assigned to the Office for the Administrative Review of the Detention of Enemy Combatants.[62] It was a chaotic period. More than two hundred people from multiple agencies had finally been assigned to gather enough evidence against each detainee to justify the detentions to Combat Status Review Tribunals at Guantánamo. As a liaison officer, one of the colonel's duties was to work with other intelligence agencies and review many of the documents submitted in hundreds of the CSRTs' 558 cases.

Abraham was shocked by what he found. The unclassified evidence lacked the corroboration he would have expected while "the classified information was stripped down, watered down, removed of context, incomplete, and missing essential information."[63] "There were too many assumptions," the colonel said. "Too many presumptions." But his complaints went unheeded, even when he asked to be released from the assignment because it "may be in conflict with my obligations as an attorney."

Abraham returned to civilian life in March 2005. Two years later, an attorney for some detainees asked him to review an affidavit in which Rear Adm. James

McGarrah, head of the screening program, extolled its hearing process. That was too much for the colonel to stomach.[64] In an affidavit filed with the Supreme Court in June 2007, in a case challenging the adequacy of the CSRTs, Abraham offered a blistering indictment of the tribunals.

"What purported to be specific statements of fact" presented to the CSRTs, he wrote, often "lacked even the most fundamental earmarks of objectively credible evidence."[65] Like the affidavit that the Supreme Court rejected in *Hamdi,* most submissions were generalized statements devoid of proof. "In very few instances," Abraham told a reporter, "would you find very specific information from which you could conclude that [the prisoner] was an enemy combatant." When he asked intelligence agencies to "provide a written statement that there was no exculpatory evidence" in their files, Abraham said, they refused.[66] The CSRT hearings "amounted to a superficial summary of information, the quality of which would not have withstood scrutiny in a serious law-enforcement or intelligence investigation."[67]

Members of the tribunals, he added, sometimes lacked the training to understand intelligence reports and were expected to presume that the prisoners were guilty. When a panel on which Abraham served ruled 3-0 that the evidence against a Libyan prisoner was inadequate, it was ordered to examine the case again. The members did and came to the same conclusion, but that did not satisfy their superiors. Another panel was convened and came to the opposite conclusion. Colonel Abraham was not asked to serve on any more CSRTs,[68] but his affidavit would eventually persuade the Supreme Court, in *Boumediene v. Bush* (see chapter 9), to consider whether the panels met its requirement of impartiality.

The Bush administration claimed that the CSRTs accorded prisoners at GTMO more due process than prisoners in any war. The tribunals' rulings, however, had little influence on who was actually released. In 2005, the tribunals cleared 133 prisoners, but two years later 40 of them remained locked up.[69] Fifteen of the 55 prisoners cleared by CSRTs in 2006 remained at GTMO two years later, in some cases because their own governments might abuse them but more often because our military could not guarantee that the prisoners, once released, would not attack the United States. Meanwhile, dozens of detainees were released without impartial hearings and on orders from the Pentagon, usually in response to diplomatic demands.[70]

The military has repeatedly said that it plans to prosecute about eighty prisoners before military commissions. In February 2008, after six years of detention and interrogation, it finally charged six with complicity in the September 11 attacks. One of those was Muhammed al-Qahtani, the so-called twentieth highjacker. Three months later, Defense Department attorney Susan Crawford, the convening authority (and Cheney protégée), decided to drop the charges against him because there was no way to hide how brutally he had been tortured.[71]

Obstructing Justice

Bush's lawyers worked overtime to prevent both military and civilian attorneys from challenging the detention and torture of suspected terrorists. They began by decreeing that the prisoners had no rights under the Geneva Conventions and therefore no right to be represented by counsel. Once that argument was struck down in *Hamdi,* they found ways to prevent defense counsel in habeas cases from seeing their clients; for example, they told the Muslim prisoners that their attorneys were Jews and told the lawyers that their clients did not wish to see them. The military delayed issuing security clearances to the lawyers and censored their notes of privileged conversations.[72]

This obstructionism had little to do with security and everything to do with the cover-up. During the summer of 2004, after the Abu Ghraib scandal and the Supreme Court's decisions granting habeas rights to prisoners, military lawyers at Guantánamo were instructed to come up with reasons why conversations between defense counsel and prisoners would have to be monitored. "Why are we doing this?" GTMO's chief of staff, Col. Tim Lynch, asked his superiors in Miami. "My guys have told me that they don't need it. The boots-on-the-ground guys, they don't need it."[73] The answer, according to Lt. Cmdr. Matthew Diaz, a Navy lawyer at GTMO, was that the Department of Justice "wanted this, so we had to make up some reasons why we needed it." Justice Department lawyers, who prepared rules for federal courts to impose on the prisoners' lawyers, drafted an affidavit for the base commander to sign declaring that some of the prisoners had been trained to pass "coded messages in furtherance of terrorist operations" to fellow terrorists on the outside. Defense counsel asked Diaz and intelligence officers to explain how twelve prisoners from Kuwait might carry out such a plot, but they couldn't. "It was a reach," Diaz admitted later. "We were just throwing up these obstacles in [the] way of implementing the *Rasul* decision."[74]

How low the administration would stoop to impede defense counsel became clear in January 2007, when Charles "Cully" Stimson, the Pentagon's attorney in charge of detainee affairs, used a radio interview to call upon the corporate clients of civilian defense counsel to force those attorneys to "choose between representing terrorists or representing reputable firms. Some will maintain that they are [defending the prisoners] out of the goodness of their hearts," Stimson said, "and I suspect they are; others are receiving monies from who knows where, and I'd be curious to have them explain that." The insinuation, as insulting as it was unfounded, was that the lawyers were on the payroll of terrorist groups.

Stimson went on to name a number of "major law firms" that, he said, "are representing the very terrorists who hit their [corporations'] bottom line in 2001." The next morning, Robert L. Pollock, a member of the *Wall Street Journal's* editorial team, cited Stimson's fourteen-page list and quoted an unnamed "senior U.S. official" as saying that "corporate C.E.O.'s seeing this should ask firms to choose between lucrative retainers and representing terrorists."[75]

Calling on corporations to blacklist law firms was something that not even Senator Joseph McCarthy attempted during the height of his anti-Communist crusade. It was also extraordinarily ambitious; by then, 500 lawyers from 120 law firms were representing GTMO prisoners without charge.

Not surprisingly, the tactic backfired. Conservative as well as liberal lawyers denounced the proposal.[76] The Pentagon disowned it,[77] and Stimson retreated to the Heritage Foundation, a right-wing Washington think tank.[78]

"Wrongdoers Will Be Brought to Justice"

When the abuses at Abu Ghraib became public, President Bush immediately promised that the "wrongdoers will be brought to justice."[79] But the investigations were compromised by unexplained delays and the transfer of potential witnesses. Officers who might have implicated high-ranking military and civilian leaders received immunity. Interrogators largely escaped prosecution while the charges or sentences levied against the few enlisted personnel who were prosecuted were substantially reduced from what they would have been had their victims been Americans. CIA agents escaped prosecution entirely.

For example, the U.S. Army took longer than a year to charge twenty-seven soldiers in connection with cab driver Dilawar's death in Afghanistan. None was charged with murder, although investigators identified the kicker.[80] Fifteen were prosecuted. Five pleaded guilty to lesser crimes, and the most severe sentence totaled five months. One soldier was convicted of assault, maiming, maltreatment, and lying. The court reduced him in rank, but his commander granted him an honorable discharge.[81]

In January 2004, Abdul Jaleel, a Sunni tribal leader, was kicked and beaten during four days of interrogation at a Forward Operating Rifles Base in Al Asad, Iraq. He died from being "lifted to his feet by a baton held to his throat." Army investigators recommended prosecution of the soldiers who killed him, but the local commander refused, insisting that Jaleel's death had resulted from "a series of lawful applications of force in response to repeated aggression and misconduct by the detainee."[82]

Only twelve men and women were convicted of abusing prisoners at Abu Ghraib on January 16, 2005. Specialist Charles Graner, the ringleader and chief photographer at Abu Ghraib, received the stiffest sentence of ten years. PFC Lynndie England, who held one prisoner on a leash and grinned ghoulishly over the corpse of another, got three years; she was released in March 2007 after serving half her sentence.[83] The guards who photographed themselves grinning over al-Jamadi's corpse were sent to prison, but the interrogators who ordered him strung up, including Mark Swanner of the CIA and Col. Thomas M. Pappas of military intelligence, escaped prosecution. Colonel Pappas and his subordinate, Lt. Col. Steven L. Jordan, both lied to military investigators but were not prosecuted for their deceptions, ostensibly because investigating generals failed to warn them of their legal rights.

A military police captain, Donald J. Reese, testified at a previous trial that he had heard Pappas exclaim, as he stood over al-Jamadi's body, "I'm not going down for this alone."[84] To make sure that he didn't, Pappas gave guards and interrogators time in which to destroy evidence of their crimes. But the chief reason he escaped prosecution may be that he could have implicated the secretary of defense. In December 2003, Pappas told his subordinates that he had just gotten off a conference call with General Sanchez and Secretary Rumsfeld. According to Tim Dugan, an interrogator who worked for the private firm CACI International, Pappas explained,

"We're starting a special projects team, and we're going to break the back of the resistance. Anybody who does not want to volunteer for this has to leave the room. And if you volunteer, you can't talk about this to anybody." We all volunteered and he said that all approach techniques were authorized. Someone asked, "Even dogs?" "Yep, even dogs." He's like, "We got a chance to break this unlawful insurgency, and the people in an unlawful insurgency have no protection under the Geneva Conventions."[85]

Instead of prosecuting Pappas, the army granted him immunity in return for testifying against Lieutenant Colonel Jordan.[86] This decision was made with knowledge that Jordan was unlikely to be convicted. Pappas, meanwhile, had been mentioned 125 times in General Fay's report, which found numerous derelictions of duty. Witnesses could testify that Pappas had been present during al-Jamadi's fatal interrogation and personally directed the effort to conceal how the prisoner had died. The army also had the colonel's memorandum encouraging destruction of incriminating photos and tapes. In the end, however, Maj. Gen. Bennie E. Williams let Pappas off with two administrative reprimands: one for failing to train his troops properly and another for allowing dogs to be present during interrogations. The general also fined Pappas two months' pay.[87]

As expected, Jordan was acquitted on all charges, except one—disobeying an order not to talk about the investigations with anyone but his attorney. For that and that alone, he was sentenced to a reprimand.[88]

The only other officer to be chastised was Brig. Gen. Janis Karpinski. She had not authorized the illegal actions at Abu Ghraib; tactical responsibility had been taken from her in the fall of 2003 by General Sanchez's staff and transferred to Colonel Pappas. Karpinski first learned of Rumsfeld's order after the scandal broke, when she saw a copy attached to a cell block's post.[89] Nonetheless, she was demoted to colonel and forced out of the service, ostensibly on a shoplifting charge.

If a foreign soldier had killed an American in the course of an interrogation, the U.S. Army would have sentenced him to death. But CWO Lewis Welshofer, Jr., who wired Iraqi general Mowhoush into a sleeping bag and sat on him until he died, was given sixty days' confinement to barracks, ordered to forfeit $6,000 in pay, and granted an honorable discharge.[90]

Rewarding Wrongdoers

Like the army's brass, the architects of the torture policy also went free. John Yoo returned to his tenured professorship at the University of California's law school in Berkeley. Jay Bybee was made a judge on the U.S. Court of Appeals for the Ninth Circuit. David Addington became Vice President Cheney's chief of staff. White House counsel Alberto Gonzales replaced John Ashcroft as attorney general, and the president bestowed the Medal of Freedom on CIA director George Tenet. When Maj. Gen. Geoffrey Miller retired in March 2006, he was awarded the Distinguished Service Medal in a ceremony in the Pentagon's Hall of Heroes.[91] And when Donald Rumsfeld was finally fired in 2007, the Hoover Institution at Stanford University appointed him a distinguished fellow.[92]

6

THE WAR CRIMINALS

Should any American soldier be so base and infamous as to injure
[any prisoner], I do most earnestly enjoin you to bring him to such severe
and exemplary punishment, as the enormity of the crime may require.
Should it extend to death itself, it will not be disproportioned to its
guilt, . . . for by such conduct they bring shame, disgrace and
ruin to themselves and their country.
—GEN. GEORGE WASHINGTON, 1775[1]

So far, Bush administration officials have escaped prosecution for authorizing, encouraging, and concealing the torture and abuse of prisoners. They
concealed facts, undermined investigations, tried to eviscerate the legal definition
of torture, and invented novel legal defenses. The various legal memorandums
and cover-ups were not the actions of innocent men. They were tacit admissions
of guilt.[2] Here is how they could and should be prosecuted—first in broad
outline, then in greater detail.

Conspiracy

The core of any prosecution of Bush administration officials for torture or
cruelty in the interrogation of prisoners would be the law of conspiracy—that
is, conspiracy to cause others to commit crimes.[3] Prosecutors would not need to
prove that the conspirators knew who would carry out the crimes; it would be
sufficient that they intended for the crimes to proceed. Nor would the government have to prove that the officials knew the identity of specific victims. It
would be enough that they intended the harm to occur and that they committed
acts, including otherwise lawful acts, to advance the criminal purpose.

121

Members of the torture team can be prosecuted not only for persuading others down the chain of command to commit crimes but for plotting among themselves to violate federal laws, including the treaties and statutes that make torture and cruelty war crimes. Prosecutors need not prove a formal agreement among the principals; agreement can be inferred from the totality of their actions, including creating kangaroo courts, suspending the Geneva Conventions, and circulating bogus assurances of legality. Members of the conspiracy can also be held liable for the reasonably foreseeable acts of other conspirators—for example, the actions of CIA kidnapping teams and the torture that foreign intelligence agencies did afterward.

Cheney and Rumsfeld

Vice President Dick Cheney and his former mentor, Secretary of Defense Donald Rumsfeld, were the driving forces behind the torture policy. Inexperienced lawyers did not mislead them. On the contrary, they chose such sycophants as David Addington, Jim Haynes, and John Yoo because they would produce whatever legal advice their superiors wanted. Cheney and Rumsfeld deliberately excluded potential naysayers, including JAG lawyers, from the policy-making process. Alberto Gonzales and John Ashcroft had expressly warned, in their January 2002 memorandums, that what Cheney and Rumsfeld wanted interrogtors to do would violate the Geneva Conventions and the War Crimes Act of 1996. That is why they urged the president to declare the conventions inapplicable and put John Yoo and others to work inventing ways to shield interrogators from prosecution.

Cheney and Rumsfeld knew that suspending the Geneva Conventions would violate military policies of long standing, but they insisted that they knew more about military necessity, diplomatic consequences, and relevant law than the professionals did. They also knew from the International Committee of the Red Cross, the FBI, the Naval Criminal Investigative Service, human rights groups, and the media that military interrogators, CIA operatives, and civilian interrogators employed by the CIA and the military were violating the Geneva Conventions, the Uniform Code of Military Justice, the Convention Against Torture, and the War Crimes Act, but they did not move to stop those crimes. On the contrary, they encouraged their commission while trying to evade disclosure and accountability.

No cabinet-level official of the U.S. government has ever been tried for war crimes. However, as we have seen, the United States and its World War II allies did prosecute German and Japanese officials of comparable rank for similar crimes. Federal criminal law makes no exception for status or position: "Whoever . . . aids, counsels, commands, induces, or procures [an offense against the United States] is punishable as a principal."[4] Rank and nationality are supposed to be irrelevant. What binds our enemies should bind us.

The Doctrine of Command Responsibility

In the course of explaining why he had no regrets about the Abu Ghraib scandal, Rumsfeld told an interviewer that "what was going on in the midnight shift in Abu Ghraib prison halfway across the world is something that clearly someone in Washington, D.C., can't manage or deal with."[5] Under the doctrine of command responsibility, distance should not matter.

Like anyone in the chain of command, the secretary of defense has a legal duty under both international and domestic law to ensure that war crimes do not occur and to stop them if they do. The U.S. Army's field manual on *The Law of Land Warfare* expresses this doctrine in no uncertain terms:

> The commander is . . . responsible if he has actual knowledge, or should have knowledge, through reports received by him or through other means, that troops or other persons subject to his control are about to or have committed a war crime and he fails to take the necessary and reasonable steps to insure compliance with the law of war or to punish violators thereof.[6]

Even the Military Commissions Act of 2006 adopted the doctrine of command responsibility to hold enemy combatants responsible for war crimes.[7]

This "should-have-known" standard was applied by the military commission that sentenced Japanese general Tomoyuki Yamashita to death following World War II for atrocities that soldiers under his command committed. He did not order the crimes and may not have known, except circumstantially, of their commission,[8] but he was still held criminally responsible. As a commander in wartime, he had an affirmative obligation not just to make policy but to know and manage how his subordinates were responding to orders and signals received through the chain of command. This is what command responsibility entails, and it is well established in American and international law.

If the torture and abuse American interrogators and guards inflicted had been mere aberrations, a finding of command responsibility might be unjust. But those offenses were the foreseeable consequences of a deliberate policy, as State Department and military lawyers warned at the time.

Once officials unleash the "dogs of war," it is their duty to lead, restrain, inquire, and correct them. Not knowing what one's subordinates are doing in response to one's orders, legal advice, and signals of various kinds is no excuse. When criminal activity becomes widespread within a military command, the commander's failure to know, and then take corrective action, can constitute criminal negligence because soldiers cannot be trusted to restrain themselves in the passions and confusion of war.

Two of Rumsfeld's generals would later claim that ICRC reports documenting the abuse in 2003 had been "lost," but that assertion is no more believable than the old excuse of "the dog ate my homework." As with all countries at war, the United States has a legal obligation under the Geneva Conventions to permit Red Cross inspections and heed the resulting reports. Any general holding prisoners who does not receive Red Cross reports should know enough to request them. The same goes for their civilian superiors. The Geneva Conventions do not require ICRC inspections just so that commanders can ignore them.

The secretary of defense also received complaints of prisoner abuse from the government of Afghan president Hamid Karzai,[9] Secretary of State Colin Powell,[10] and Ambassador L. Paul Bremer.[11] No fewer than fourteen reports of prisoner abuse were published prior to the Abu Ghraib disclosures of April 2004.[12] The Schlesinger Committee, whose members Rumsfeld handpicked, found approximately three thousand allegations of prisoner maltreatment in Afghanistan, at Guantánamo, and in Iraq between the fall of 2001 and the summer of 2004.[13] Rumsfeld had to have known of the Red Cross's concerns and its legal duty and authority to inspect detention centers because in at least one instance he personally ordered the military to hide a prisoner from that organization's inspectors in direct violation of the Geneva Conventions.[14]

At a Senate hearing in May 2004, the secretary of defense claimed that he had only become aware of the extent of the abuses at Abu Ghraib and had seen the photographs the day before his testimony. That he did not see the report earlier is extremely unlikely. Maj. Gen. Antonio Taguba began his investigation in January 2004 and circulated his report, together with photos and videos, to Pentagon managers weeks before the Senate hearing. Rumsfeld's testimony that the pictures were "not yet in the Pentagon" also seems unlikely, unless someone ordered them kept in Iraq in order to grant him deniability. According to General Taguba, "The photographs were available to him, if he wanted to see them. Rumsfeld is very perceptive and has a mind like a steel trap. There's no way he's suffering from CRS—Can't Remember Shit—He's trying to acquit himself."[15]

Direct Responsibility

The principle of command responsibility is not necessary to establish Rumsfeld's guilt under Common Article 3 or the War Crimes Act of 1996. Unlike General Yamashita, the secretary of defense was directly involved in making the policy and approving lists of illegal techniques. His order of December 2, 2002, authorizing harsh interrogation techniques at Guantánamo, eventually migrated to Iraq, probably with General Miller's team. A copy bearing the secretary's handwritten notes was posted at Abu Ghraib and became the basis of Lt. Gen. Ricardo Sanchez's own list of approved techniques, including the use of dogs to intimidate prisoners. Rumsfeld also talked with Colonel Pappas at Abu Ghraib by telephone or videoconference, seeking updates on specific interrogations and authorizing harsh interrogation methods.[16]

The secretary personally monitored the interrogation of Muhammed al-Qahtani at GTMO in 2002. When it did not produce actionable intelligence fast enough, Rumsfeld approved rougher tactics and personally authorized the interrogation plan that led to al-Qahtani's marathon torture at GTMO between November 2002 and January 2003.

It is difficult to imagine how Rumsfeld could plausibly plead ignorance of what was going on in the detention centers pursuant to his orders. The International Committee of the Red Cross first reported abuses to administration officials in 2002. More were reported by the FBI, the NCIS in 2003, and official military investigations starting in 2004, before the Abu Ghraib scandal broke that April. By June 2004, the facts about the torture, cruelty, and degradation, and the use of torture by proxy were well known throughout the world. Foreign nations protested them too, but still the secretary refused to change course. He not only permitted the abuses to continue, he designed a succession of military investigations to conceal evidence of his own involvement and, after the Abu Ghraib photos came out, issued an order barring personal cameras and camera phones from the prisons. For all these machinations the former secretary of defense should be held criminally responsible as a principal and as an accessory after the fact.

Responsibility of Military Commanders

Soldiers can be court-martialed, while on active duty, for carrying out the conspirators' plan.[17] After their military service is over, they can be prosecuted in federal courts for violating specific laws, including the War Crimes Act[18] and the Anti-Torture Statute.[19]

All military personnel still on active duty who relayed or implemented Rumsfeld's illegal orders arguably violated article 93 of the UCMJ, which makes cruel treatment of anyone subject to their orders, including captives, a crime.[20] Like General Yamashita, U.S. commanders from the Joint Chiefs of Staff down to General Sanchez knew enough about the abuse of prisoners that they had a duty to make inquiries and impose limitations. They had an obligation to the law that trumped obedience to their political superiors or at least obliged them to demand that the orders to torture prisoners be transmitted in writing, as Lt. Col. Diane Beaver did. But they went along with Rumsfeld, Cambone, and Haynes.

The Uniform Code of Military Justice punishes many torture-related crimes worldwide, including homicide, assault, cruelty, and maiming.[21] In addition, any soldier who fails to stop cruelty toward or fails to report the mistreatment of prisoners is guilty of dereliction of duty.[22] For example, in December 2003 Col. Stuart A. Herrington (Ret.) properly warned General Sanchez that some detention practices could be technically illegal and were likely to make "gratuitous enemies." In particular, Herrington told the general that Task Force 121 had abused prisoners throughout Iraq and used a secret interrogation facility to hide its actions, but there is no evidence that Sanchez acted on that information.[23]

Similarly, Col. Marc Warren, Sanchez's senior legal adviser, could be prosecuted for failing to pass ICRC reports of prisoner abuse on to his superiors and then for restricting that organization's access to prisoners after receiving its November 2003 report.[24]

General Miller could also be a candidate for prosecution under article 93, which bans cruelty, in part because the ICRC found that the practices he authorized at Guantánamo were "tantamount to torture" and "an intentional system of cruel, unusual, and degrading treatment," which, in the aggregate, also constituted "a form of torture."[25] Former detainees and FBI agents can testify to abuses inflicted on prisoners by General Miller's men that violated both the Geneva Conventions and the UCMJ. As a retired officer, Miller is no longer subject to prosecution under military law, but he could be prosecuted for violating the War Crimes Act and the Anti-Torture Statute. He could also be docked retirement benefits.

CIA Culpability

CIA directors George Tenet, Porter Goss, and Michael Hayden, as well as clandestine services chief José Rodriguez, Jr., exposed themselves to criminal liability both in the United States and abroad by authorizing or failing to prevent the torture and abuse of prisoners,[26] running their program of extraordinary rendition,[27] operating a network of secret prisons,[28] and causing the disappearance of as many as a hundred prisoners into that network in violation of the Geneva Conventions. According to the UN Commission on Human Rights, "prolonged incommunicado detention . . . can, in itself, constitute a form of cruel, inhumane, and degrading treatment."[29]

CIA officials could be prosecuted in a number of foreign countries and in the International Criminal Court, as Italian prosecutors were trying to do in March 2009, for a variety of international and domestic crimes, including homicide, kidnapping, assault, sexual abuse, torture, and forced disappearances.[30] Obtaining witnesses for and against them and getting those witnesses past John Bolton's non-extradition agreements would be difficult. Once on trial, though, no one would be allowed to claim, as the Nazis at Nuremberg could not claim, that "my lawyer said I could do it."

CIA agents could even be prosecuted under the criminal conspiracy laws of several American states for plotting to kidnap and assault persons as part of their program of extraordinary rendition.[31]

Officials involved in waterboarding prisoners are also guilty of war crimes. That was the finding of a U.S. military commission that in 1947 sentenced a

Japanese officer, Yukio Asano, to fifteen years in prison at hard labor for water-boarding an American civilian during World War II.[32] The CIA's own inspector general has concluded that techniques used on Khalid Sheikh Mohammed, including waterboarding, were excessive,[33] while the Department of State has condemned Tunisia's use of waterboarding as torture.[34]

Lawyers as War Criminals

What of the political lawyers: Alberto Gonzales, John Ashcroft, Jim Haynes, David Addington, John Yoo, and others? Technically speaking, they were not in the chain of command, but they were responsible for making the policy, imposing it on a reluctant military, and giving interrogators legal cover. As craftsmen of the policy, they plotted to violate the Geneva Conventions. Four of the eight justices who decided *Hamdan* in 2006 believed that the conventions themselves do not independently punish conspiracies to commit war crimes,[35] but the lawyers could arguably be charged under the main federal conspiracy statute as accomplices in the creation of the administration's torture policy and the rendition program.[36]

Whether the "invisibles" at the OLC who wrote the torture memos are also guilty of grave breaches of the Geneva Conventions is a closer question. According to Yoo, neither he nor the White House counsel are to blame because "the administration never ordered the torture of any prisoner . . . and these incidents did not result from any official orders." That claim may be technically true; the lawyers, like the politicians, did not directly order the torture of prisoners. They were too clever to put such a command in writing and, in any case, were not part of the chain of command. But these lawyers and their bosses clearly authorized, facilitated, urged, concealed, and protected the use of cruel, inhumane, and degrading treatment in violation of Common Article 3. Without their legal blessing, the crimes might not have occurred. Under federal conspiracy law, that responsibility is enough.

After the Abu Ghraib scandal broke, both Gonzales and Haynes claimed that the interrogation policy they promulgated did not cause the abuses that occurred at Abu Ghraib. Nor, they contended, did the fun and games on the night shift at Abu Ghraib have anything to do with the president's order of February 7, 2002, which released the armed forces from their obligations under the Geneva Conventions. But as the Schlesinger Report found, Lieutenant General Sanchez relied on the president's memorandum in deciding that some of the Coalition's prisoners in Iraq qualified as enemy combatants and were thus not entitled to the protections of the Geneva Conventions. The president's statement of February 7, 2002, the commission observed, was itself "based on the OLC opinions."[37]

"We did not take a policy position," John Yoo has said. "All we did was give advice, as lawyers do, on what would be a defense if you got into trouble."[38] Were that true, however, their memorandums would have been more informative, more balanced, and less "tendentious," to use Jack Goldsmith's characterization.[39] They would have told their superiors that the Supreme Court had rejected their claim to unlimited wartime power in 1952.[40] They would have discussed the Convention Against Torture and its implementing statute in their early memos. Instead, they ignored the established law because they had not been hired to provide dispassionate, evenhanded, comprehensive legal advice that was based on fair readings of precedent. Like house counsel in many corporations or the OLC when it was headed by William H. Rehnquist in the early 1970s and Antonin Scalia in the 1980s, they were expected to be enablers and not internal watchdogs. As White House attorney Bradford Berenson explained, "Legally, the watchword became 'forward-leaning,' by which everybody meant: 'We want to be aggressive. We want to take risks.'"[41] Or, as Yoo later put it, the objective of their secret memos was to "advance the law."[42]

Oliver Wendell Holmes, Jr., once called this approach "the bad man's theory of the law."[43] To bad people, law is nothing more than what they cannot get away with. The substantive rules, the morality behind them, or the concept of legitimacy are of no consequence to such people so long as accountability can be avoided by manipulating technicalities—for example, denying the jurisdiction of independent courts, stripping plaintiffs of standing to sue, hiding evidence of official crimes behind walls of secrecy (including the state secrets privilege), and asserting dubious defenses and immunities.

To the "bad men" who devised the torture policy, law is about power, not morality. It is not a higher calling but a contest to see who can manipulate the system most by denigrating judges, attacking judicial review, and packing the courts, the Justice Department, and the U.S. attorneys' offices with authoritarian conservatives while keeping their war crimes secret.

The memo writers and their political superiors sought to circumvent the rule of law by creating legal black holes—places like Guantánamo and the CIA's chain of black site prisons—in which torture could occur unrestrained. The interrogations they sought to facilitate in the January 2002 memorandums were not lawful; they were *lawless*. These attorneys did not seek to preserve a government under law. They sought to facilitate, encourage, and defend criminal activity by separating their definition of law from three centuries of legal development, during which due process replaced torture, extradition replaced state-sponsored kidnapping, and checks and balances supplanted monarchy.

Their job, as they saw it, was to help their political superiors erect a legal facade for lawless action. In so doing, they did not report settled law or rebut it; they sought to create doubt where none existed. They knew that they did not need to win the legal debate to keep detainees behind bars; instead, they needed only to buy time. This dissembling is not what advice-giving lawyers employed by the U.S. government should do. Their overriding responsibility is to provide honest, evenhanded advice as to what the law is and not provide a legal-sounding cover for criminal activity.

The inward face of the legal facade they constructed was meant to persuade skeptical interrogators that they would be protected from prosecution. The January 2002 memorandums and others that followed were not written in response to hypothetical questions. They were prepared to answer explicit demands for legal cover, demands that CIA and military officials would make repeatedly.

Had Bush's lawyers simply rendered erroneous judgments as to what the law was, they might be excused from criminal liability. It is not a crime to be mistaken about a point of law. But when lawyers use their legal skills to authorize, justify, encourage, or conceal a program of torture and cruelty, then they exceed the canon of legal ethics for advice-giving attorneys.[44] Like Mafia lawyers, they become liable to prosecution as principals.[45] The same would be true of the CIA's attorneys.

Interestingly, the August 2002 torture memos were prepared *after* the CIA repeatedly waterboarded Abu Zubaydah, not before. This timing may be why John Yoo and Jay Bybee devoted so much of their torture memos to imagining improbable defenses should the torturers be caught (like the bizarre "self-defense of the nation" claim). If it can be shown that the lawyers knew of the waterboarding and then offered untested legal defenses in order to assure the interrogators that they were not in legal jeopardy, then the lawyers are guilty of encouraging the commission of similar crimes in the future. That situation would make them participants in an ongoing criminal enterprise,[46] in violation of the Torture Convention's implementing statute.[47]

Together with their superiors, the lawyers may also be prosecuted as principals under the War Crimes Act of 1996.[48] That law makes it a federal war crime to inflict cruel, inhumane, or degrading treatment on prisoners in violation of Common Article 3 of the Geneva Conventions. Ironically, this law was passed with Republican sponsorship.

The lawyers are also vulnerable to prosecution in the International Criminal Court and in foreign nations' courts for violations of international law. Actions similar to theirs led a tribunal at Nuremberg, in a series of trials made famous by the film *Judgment at Nuremberg*, to convict a number of German lawyers for war crimes. For example, two attorneys in the Nazi Ministry of Justice were prosecuted for issuing the so-called Night and Fog Decree that permitted German soldiers to abduct suspected resistance fighters from occupied countries and disappear them in secret detention facilities, where they could be summarily convicted and shot. American prosecutors successfully argued that the German attorneys were guilty of war crimes because they had to have known that the decree violated the Hague and Geneva conventions and "would probably cause the death of human beings."[49] The same, of course, could be said of Bush's lawyers, who knew about the administration's program to torture and degrade prisoners; to render them to foreign torturers; to hide them away in CIA, military, and foreign prisons; and to conceal their imprisonment and torture from the ICRC.

Franz Schlegelberger, the Nazi lawyer who led the Third Reich's Ministry of Justice, was charged with "prostituting [the] judicial system for the accomplishment of criminal ends."[50] Just as Bush's administration created military commissions in order to evade the judicial standards of federal courts and regular military courts-martial, Schlegelberger's ministry created secret tribunals to prosecute foreign resistance leaders pursuant to the Night and Fog Decree. They did so after regular army officers argued against holding secret trials so that foreigners brought into Germany could be made to disappear without a trace.[51]

Joseph Altstoetter, another German lawyer, was convicted, among other things, for participating in a cover-up. He "helped to cloak the shameful deeds of [the SS] from the eyes of the German people."[52]

These parallels have led University of Houston law professor Jordan J. Paust to conclude that "Not since the Nazi era have so many lawyers been so clearly involved in international crimes concerning the treatment and interrogation of persons detained during war."[53]

Whether they are prosecuted or not, the lawyers deserve to be disbarred for violating Rule 1.13 (b) of the American Bar Association's *Model Rules of Professional Conduct.* This rule provides that when a government lawyer knows that the officials he is advising intend to violate federal law, he is obliged not only to advise against the lawbreaking but to report that knowledge to his superiors.[54] Political lawyers often forget this duty when they join an administration after months of campaigning, but the United States, not their immediate boss, is the client to whom they owe a duty of due diligence. Violation of this duty is, or should be, grounds for disbarment.

The President as War Criminal

Finally, as commander in chief, President Bush had a similar duty to stop the torture and abuse after learning about them from many sources, including the press. Part of his obligation was a matter of command responsibility; part of it was direct responsibility for the crime.

Bush was directly responsible for unleashing the military and the CIA from all legal restraints and for ordering the CIA to kidnap suspects for the purpose of torture. As he explained to reporter Bob Woodward,

> I had to show the American people the resolve of a commander in chief that was going to do whatever it took to win. No yielding. No equivocation. No—you know—lawyering this thing to death, that we're after them. And that was not only for domestic, for the people at home to see. It was vitally important for the rest of the world to watch.[55]

Bush also bears responsibility for not doing everything in his power to stop the abuse once he learned of it, and he was responsible for the cover-ups that followed. He was not just a passive witness to his subordinates' crimes; he fought legislatively to shield them from prosecution, even as he had a legal obligation to stop the crimes and prosecute those involved.

About his knowledge of the torture policy, there can be no doubt. According to Colin Powell, Secretary Rumsfeld kept the president "fully informed of the [ICRC's] concerns."[56] In 2002, then-national security adviser Condoleezza Rice chaired the National Security Council's Principals Committee, which included Cheney, Rumsfeld, Powell, and Tenet. The members repeatedly discussed and approved a number of harsh interrogation techniques, including slapping, pushing, sleep deprivation, and waterboarding.[57] When asked about the group's work by ABC News, President Bush admitted, "I'm aware our national security team met on this issue. I approved."[58]

More specifically, the president defended the use of waterboarding on Khalid Sheikh Mohammed. "We had legal opinions that enabled us to do it," he said, "and, no, I didn't have any problem at all trying to find out what Khalid Sheikh Mohammed knew."[59] If this ABC News account is accurate, then Bush may be guilty, by his own admission, of aiding and abetting the CIA and his NSC staff in violating the federal torture statute and Common Article 3 of the Geneva Conventions.

On January 30, 2008, Attorney General Mukasey told the Senate Judiciary Committee that the president was then, and had been in the past, part of a three-step process for approving harsh interrogation techniques. The first step involved a finding of need by the CIA director. The second involved a finding of legality, under the proposed circumstances, by the attorney general. Then the president could give his approval.[60] On September 6, 2006, the president personally acknowledged his involvement in the interrogation of Abu Zubaydah, which, Director Hayden later revealed, involved waterboarding.[61] During Zubaydah's interrogation, which occurred in April 2002, Bush let CIA director George Tenet know that withholding pain medication was an acceptable interrogation technique.[62] By that statement, if no other, President Bush directly authorized a grave breach of Common Article 3 of the Geneva Conventions.

7

TORTURE RECONSIDERED

> For every complex problem there is a well-known solution:
> neat, plausible, and wrong.
> —Attributed to H. L. Mencken

Central to the Bush administration's defense of torture was the assertion that these terrorists today are unlike any the United States has ever faced. But that is not true. For two and a half centuries, the frontiers of the English colonies and their successor states were riven by terrorism on both sides. The shortsighted attitudes of bravado, vengeance, and vigilantism that found expression in the Bush administration can be traced, in no small part, to the Indian wars that accompanied the westward expansion of European settlements in North America. They also fueled the fear of slave uprisings and inspired the terrorism that led to more than two thousand lynchings of black Americans during the century that followed the Civil War.

Terrorism, no matter who practices it, is based on the very simple idea of "us versus them." "They" are, by definition, less moral than we, no matter what we have done to them. This Manichean view, so dominant in the Bush administration, permits us to assume our "manifest destiny" is to conquer them and to make the world safe for us at their expense.[1]

A second doubtful assumption is the belief that they reject our values so that we have nothing in common with them except mutual hostility, which can only end in their defeat. A corollary to this assumption is the view that we can do no wrong and they intend no right. Accordingly, if they torture some of us, they are depraved, but if we torture some of them, we are justified, because we can do no wrong. Morality, according to a George W. Bush or an Osama bin Laden, simply describes the obligations that the practitioner of terrorism owes his group and his group only.

The Ticking-Bomb Scenario

The administration's case for answering depravity with depravity was made with characteristic clarity by conservative columnist Charles Krauthammer:

> Ethics 101: A terrorist has planted a nuclear bomb in New York City. It will go off in one hour. A million people will die. You capture the terrorist. He knows where it is. He's not talking.
>
> Question: If you have the slightest belief that hanging this man by his thumbs will get you the information, are you permitted to do it? . . . On this issue, there can be no uncertainty. Not only is it permissible to hang this miscreant by his thumbs. It is a moral duty.[2]

Variants of this scenario have been raised by many people, including Jeremy Bentham,[3] Jean-Paul Sartre,[4] Michael Walzer,[5] and Alan Dershowitz.[6] They are especially favored by professors who like to humiliate students by demanding immediate answers to complicated questions that require multilayered thought.

The most obvious flaw in the hypothetical is that it stampedes reasonably moral people into endorsing measures that they would not allow American police departments to use when questioning persons suspected of the most heinous crimes. They would denounce these measures as war crimes if foreign intelligence agencies used them on captured Americans.

It also presents the question of torture as a matter of individual choice, unconnected to any institutional context. It insists that we think existentially, like vigilantes or outlaws, and disregard the habits and cultures of armies and clandestine services. It asks that we forget that for an institutional policy to have moral consequences, it must be designed for flawed people to carry out under less than ideal circumstances.[7] The authors of the laws of war understood this problem, which is why they issued a flat prohibition against torture. So, too, did Sir William S. Holdsworth, the historian of English law, when he warned,

"Once torture becomes acclimatized in a legal system, it spreads like an infectious disease."[8]

Because the hypothetical poses the problem in strictly personal terms, it also assumes that the law against torture can be brushed aside. It doesn't just reject specific laws and treaties; it rejects the idea of law itself. Contrary to what its proponents claim, the hypothetical does not ask us to acknowledge a rare exception to a well-established moral rule. Its purpose is to sweep away all objections, moral or practical, to "taking off the gloves." For example, Krauthammer says that he would limit the use of torture to finding ticking bombs and extracting "slow-fuse information" from al Qaeda masterminds like Khalid Sheikh Mohammed. But neither situation is rare. Nor is it reasonable to expect that interrogators will use torture to find a nuclear weapon but not an AK-47. It is also unrealistic to assume that the details of an enemy plot will be known only to its masterminds. Tony Lagouranis, who served in Iraq as an Arabic-speaking interrogator in 2004, wrote about his experience, "Once torture is introduced in war, torture will inevitably spread because the ticking bombs are everywhere." In his case, they came in the form of roadside bombs and mortar attacks that threatened to kill him and his fellow interrogators almost every day. "[I]f you accept the logic that we have to perform torture to prevent deaths," he warned, "each and every prisoner [suspected of involvement in the insurgency] is deserving of torture."[9]

The hypothetical also asks us to assume the interrogators will *know with great certainty* that there is a ticking bomb, the prisoner knows where it is, the interrogators know that he knows its location, he will tell where it is if only they have the courage to torture him, and he will disgorge the truth in time for the bomb to be found and defused. In this respect, the scenario recalls the film *Minority Report,* in which psychics with supernatural powers can predict with certainty who will commit crimes if not stopped. In real life, however, *nothing is that certain*. To claim that it is or could be is profoundly dishonest.

But the proponents of the ticking-bomb example do not really demand certainty. For example, Krauthammer insists that torture is morally acceptable "if you have the *slightest belief* that [torture] will get you the information to save a million people." (Emphasis added.) According to Vice President Cheney, a 1 percent chance of catastrophic risk is enough to risk torturing innocent prisoners. What this statement means, of course, is that we are being asked not only to abandon the presumption of innocence that has lain at the heart of our jurisprudence for centuries but also to embrace its opposite.

Secretary Rumsfeld took a different tack to achieve the same end. He insisted that all the government's prisoners were hardened terrorists when, in fact, he knew that evidence to support that claim was, in nearly all instances, extremely weak. Prisoners were pressured to sign false statements precisely because almost nothing in their intelligence files was certain.

According to the Bush administration, people about whom little is known may be tortured when interrogators have "the slightest belief" that doing so will save many lives. This is war, they reminded us, and war presupposes that innocent people will occasionally suffer. But that is not what the ticking-bomb hypothetical assumes. It insists that our interrogators will never torture an innocent person. Only the guilty will be tortured, and when pressured, they will swiftly abandon the cause for which they were prepared to martyr themselves.

The better question to ask in a hypothetical is whether it would be permissible to torture a clearly innocent child in order to make his possibly guilty parent talk. So confronted, even the most cold-blooded people are likely to admit some empathic limits to their practicality. Still it is difficult to persuade people who want vengeance that not all suspects are guilty. Most proponents of torture are reluctant to admit the now proven fact that most of the prisoners at Abu Ghraib and Guantánamo were not terrorists but innocent people who were caught in street sweeps or falsely accused by bounty hunters.

Torture advocates ask us to believe that an alleged terrorist will, if tortured, quickly reveal *reliable* information *in time* to find and defuse the bomb. That scenario is not something any professional investigator would assume. To put the issue starkly, would you willingly risk your life, and the lives of men under your command, on the basis of intelligence obtained by torture?

Dan Coleman was an FBI agent who worked closely with CIA agents for ten years, investigating such terrorist operations as the 1998 embassy bombings in Kenya and Tanzania. His patient cultivation of suspects—in return for plea bargains—broke major cases prior to 9/11 and helped convict four al Qaeda operatives on 302 counts. His work also generated extensive information about that organization's funding, structure, and operations. Coleman expressed contempt for the CIA's legal staff, which allowed almost any interrogation practice so long as it was used overseas. "Have any of these guys ever tried to talk to someone who's been deprived of his clothes?" he asked a reporter. "He's going to be ashamed, and humiliated, and cold. He'll tell you anything you want to hear to get his clothes back. There's no value in it."[10]

Due process, Coleman argued, makes detainees more cooperative, not less. Cooperative prisoners may tell lies too, but they have less reason to. Even meeting with lawyers, or receiving a warning of legal rights, does not stop all suspects from talking. Some enjoy telling their story, and lawyers sometimes persuade reluctant clients to trade information for plea agreements. "People don't cooperate with you unless they have some reason to," Coleman observed. "Brutalization doesn't work. We know that. Besides, you lose your soul."[11]

At some level, most people understand that not all suspects are guilty, not all people tell the truth, and information obtained by torture cannot be trusted. When judges in nearly all countries refuse to accept evidence based on torture, they do so only partly out of empathy for the accused, who might be innocent. Mainly they do so because coerced statements cannot be trusted. Relying on such statements wastes valuable investigative resources, punishes the innocent, and lets the guilty go free.

Can Anyone Calibrate Torture?

Of course, it is not unreasonable to assume that torture will occasionally produce reliable information in time to save lives. But how many innocent people may our government torture in order to save how many innocent lives? Is there a moral way of calculating the relative costs and benefits of torture?

Similarly, how shall we determine the degree of torture to be administered? According to Krauthammer, "The level of the inhumanity . . . would be proportional to the need and value of the information. Interrogators would be constrained to use the least inhumane treatment necessary to the magnitude and imminence of the evil being prevented and the importance of the knowledge being obtained." Stuart Taylor, a legal columnist for the *National Journal,* claims that the ban on cruel, inhumane, and degrading treatment already envisions "the commonsense principle that the toughness of interrogation techniques should be calibrated to the importance and urgency of the information likely to be obtained."[12]

How would these conservatives calibrate the degree of torture that may be applied in each instance? Would a smaller bomb or more time on the clock mean that interrogators would recognize that the situation calls for a lesser degree of torture? (Would anyone really know how much time is left on the clock?) Would more severe torture be appropriate if the potential victims are Americans? Should the number of potentially innocent suspects who might have to be tortured be included in the hypothetical? If the number of potential victims or the value of the property to be bombed is great, and the clock is running out, may the government increase the torture in order to get the suspect to talk? For example, may interrogators, acting with our authority, extract a suspect's fingernails, slice his penis, or torture his child before his eyes? Again, are there empathetic limits to what even a cold-blooded utilitarian will permit in the hope of saving thousands of lives? If so, how do they get factored into the analysis?

Who would make these calculations—interrogators in the field or high-level officials at the Pentagon or in the CIA? According to Krauthammer, the torture would be carried out by "highly specialized agents who are experts and experienced in interrogation, and who are known not to abuse it for the satisfaction of a kind of sick sadomasochism." But how would the government qualify these experts? Is there a Harvard College of Torture from which the CIA can recruit them? How would the college or the agency ascertain that its experts are not sadists? How long might a specialized agent torture suspects before he or she becomes a sadist? And what do we do with the sadists once they have been found unfit to torture suspects any longer?

Like Professor Dershowitz, Krauthammer would require torturers to obtain "written permission from the highest political authorities in the country or from a quasi-judicial authority," unless time is short (i.e., the bomb is ticking). In that case they could "act on their own." Rumsfeld took this view too, when he specified that interrogators would have to get his permission to use the most severe category 3 techniques. Even former president Bill Clinton endorsed torture warrants, but they had to be issued by presidents, pursuant to a narrowly drawn statute, and subject to judicial review, if only after the fact, by the secret Foreign Intelligence Surveillance Court.[13]

But what qualifies politicians or judges to make these moral (or practical) judgments? How informed, specific, and calibrated must these written authorizations be? And wouldn't the interrogators, like wiretappers, almost always claim that there wasn't time to request permission from Washington?

A policy of torture necessarily hurts innocent people, just as the firebombing of Japanese cities during World War II killed innocent people. Those bombings were morally acceptable, American officials reasoned at the time, because incinerating "their" innocent people would protect "our" innocent people by bringing the war to a swifter end. The officers who chose which cities to incinerate may also have assumed that the enemy's population wasn't really innocent, that they assumed the risk of getting bombed when they allowed their military to bomb our Pearl Harbor.

But if that kind reasoning is valid, then we must concede that the American victims of 9/11 were not innocent either. They assumed the risk of retaliation when they allowed the U.S. government to build bases in Saudi Arabia and to embargo trade with Iraq, which the 9/11 terrorists believed contributed to the deaths of hundreds of thousands of children. In truth, most people assume no such risk for the obvious reason that they have little or no influence over their nation's war makers, not even in the United States.

Does Torture Work?

The ticking-bomb discussion, like so many conundrums of its sort, is highly speculative. For example, it assumes that torture produces reliable intelligence when, according to a study released by the Pentagon in May 2007, there is little evidence that it does.[14]

The Pentagon's researchers found that the noncoercive techniques American interrogators used on German prisoners during World War II were more effective than the coercive tactics used by the Bush administration, possibly because the World War II questioners were well educated and spoke their prisoners' language flawlessly. By comparison, our more recent interrogators were poorly trained, mostly ignorant of their prisoners' religion and culture, juvenile in their understanding of human nature, and heavily dependent on translators with their own agendas. When FBI agents tried to build rapport with suspected terrorists, they were pushed aside by intelligence agents with little experience in interrogations but great faith in the efficacy of fear, pain, exhaustion, and humiliation. Those agents also appear to have assumed that if something works well in small doses, it will work even better in large doses.

According to the Pentagon's report, the interrogation effort failed to consult extensive research on the efficacy of different interrogation techniques. During the 1950s and 1960s, the CIA spent billions of dollars on research that confirmed that physical torture is not as effective as psychological manipulation. Similarly, the Pentagon's own post-9/11 researchers found that "most professionals believe that pain, coercion, and threats are counterproductive to the elicitation of good information."[15] However, these opinions were swept aside in the days following 9/11.

Law enforcement agencies had extensive experience in noncoercive methods, but the president and his staff made it clear from the start that they preferred coercion to persuasion. At their direction, "the gloves came off," so interrogators had no choice but to improvise.[16] To the extent that they felt the need for advice, the report found, interrogators consulted partners in the rendition program like Saudi Arabia, Egypt, Jordan, Israel, and Morocco. They also learned coercion from the Arabic-speaking Israelis whom CACI International recruited for Abu Ghraib. Then they reverse engineered the torments inflicted during their own SERE training, which was modeled on the abuses that Communists had inflicted on their captives in the Korean and Vietnam wars.[17]

The Pentagon study also raises questions about the competence of the intelligence effort. Less vengeful or arrogant officials might have considered whether it is ever wise to alienate by coercion a population that might, if courted, volunteer important information about insurgents in their midst. Historically, the best sources of information have always been walk-ins from the local population, especially where American agents cannot operate effectively undercover. In Vietnam, ignorance of the local language confined American intelligence agents to relatively secure compounds, where the best they could do was question local residents through bilingual collaborators. Outside those compounds, frustration and fear led American soldiers to treat their Vietnamese prisoners harshly, which engendered even more support for the Viet Cong.[18]

Interrogator Chris Mackey has written that "our experience in Afghanistan showed that the harsher the methods we used, . . . the better the information we got and the sooner we got it."[19] "If a prisoner will say anything to stop the pain," he declared, "my guess is that he will start with the truth."[20] But that is just a guess, since Mackey claims that he never tortured anyone. He exhausted prisoners but could not recall an instance in which exhaustion led anyone to reveal useful intelligence. He did find, however, that threatening to deliver prisoners to a brutal regime would persuade some of them to talk. But whether their statements were accurate or complete he could not say for certain.

Mackey also recalled instances in which resentful prisoners dissembled and described an al Qaeda manual that told them how to do it.[21] These prisoners were like John McCain, who, when the Vietnamese tortured him to disclose the names of fellow fliers, revealed instead the starting lineup of the Green Bay Packers football team.[22] Deceiving interrogators may be one of the few amusements that prisoners have left.

Those who claim that torture works typically have no experience interrogating hostile prisoners. They also assume ideal conditions, including the competence of those who will wield the power. But war is chaotic, as Tim Dugan, a civilian interrogator, discovered when he arrived at Abu Ghraib in November 2003:

> It was Charlie Foxtrot [a vulgar slang for a mess] without a doubt. . . . I've never seen anything like that, [a] bunch of unprofessional schmucks that didn't know their damned jobs, all thrown together, mixed up with a big-ass stick. . . .
>
> Most of our interrogators were eighteen-year-old kids that were reservists. Think about it. You got a forty-five- to sixty-year-old one-, two-, or four-star general you're going to be talking to, and you're eighteen years old, just out of high school, joined the Army, and went to interrogator school. These kids are intimidated as hell, and the generals and the colonels and these older guys know it. And it's like they laugh at them.

These soldiers, not knowing the language or culture of their prisoners, had no choice but to rely on interpreters with agendas of their own. Not surprisingly, Dugan concluded, "nobody really got any intelligence there, very few of us."[23]

But given the circumstances, the issue is not simply, does torture work? Instead, we should ask, "Does it work better, faster, or more accurately than lawful modes of interrogation?" As proof that it does, administration officials typically cite the confession of Khalid Sheikh Mohammed, the self-proclaimed mastermind of 9/11. Waterboarding, they say, persuaded him to disgorge valuable information, including how United Flight 93 was supposed to crash into the Capitol Building and how the hijackers communicated in code with Osama bin Laden and 9/11 team leader Mohammad Atta. But there is a problem with their claim. Both Khalid Sheikh Mohammed and Ramzi bin al-Shibh volunteered essentially the same information to Al Jazeera correspondent Yosri Fouda before they were captured.[24] CIA agents did not have to torture either prisoner to learn these details; they just had to log on to the Internet. Had the interrogators used lawful methods of interrogation and research first, coercion would not have been necessary, and the Justice Department would have been able to prosecute both men.

Escalation

One of the assumptions of the ticking-bomb scenario is that the necessary torture will occur immediately upon capture and will not last long before the suspect confesses. In most instances from the war on terrorism, coercive interrogations quickly escalated and lasted for long periods as the objective switched from obtaining actionable intelligence to justifying indefinite detentions and proving domination.

Tony Lagouranis believes that torture will work, to the extent that it can, only if the prisoner knows that pressure can be increased. Once a prisoner discovers the limits of what the interrogators can do to him, usually within twenty-four hours, and realizes that he can endure their worst, then he is not likely to talk or be honest and complete in what he says. When interrogators realized that a prisoner had found them out, Lagouranis observed, they had to hurt him more or lose their dominion over him and over all other prisoners who heard from him on the cellblock.

> I learned in Mosul, while trying a set of techniques on prisoners, that torture cannot be effective, even for the limited goal of domination over a prisoner, unless there is escalation and the continued threat of escalation. . . . I could cause fear, but it would plateau, and I found myself wanting to go further, push harder, and cause more pain. . . . Once I got started, it seemed pointless to stop, and each escalation appeared seamless, natural, and justified.[25]

Lagouranis recalled the same temptation at work among his superiors. Frustrated by the lack of usable intelligence, they would demand more from interrogators and signal a willingness to look the other way if questionable techniques produced results. When Lagouranis was pressured into escalating, he would describe his use of harsh techniques in his interrogation reports, which infuriated his superiors, who wanted to maintain deniability. Not surprising, those incriminating reports were "lost."

Once the abuse of prisoners started, it became habitual. Lagouranis recalls

> how one interrogator would prepare for each and every interrogation by putting the detainee in a stress position for 45 minutes before he asked a single question. This seemed logical. If he assumed these techniques worked and were legal (and because of the written rules we saw, we all certainly thought they were), why not use them every chance he got?[26]

In understaffed prisons like Abu Ghraib, the temptation to escalate was substantial and could have been restrained, if at all, only by unambiguous rules of engagement or a swift turnover of the prisoner population. Once interrogators give in to the temptation to escalate, Lagouranis observed, "torture cannot be contained. It is not something you can do once and then go back to your regular routine, hoping you won't have to do it again, but keeping it in reserve just in case." For this reason, he concluded, "we can't let short-term gain or practical considerations decide this [torture] question for us. We have to look at a much larger picture before we decide."[27]

Alfred W. McCoy, the historian of CIA torture, agrees with Lagouranis. "There is no such thing as a little torture," he has observed. "Torture is contagious," he warned, echoing Holdsworth. It "spreads like wildfire."[28] Israel learned this lesson, or should have, in the closing decades of the twentieth century. In 1987, an Israeli government commission charged with investigating interrogation methods concluded that "moderate coercion" by interrogators could be lawful so long as the payoff in Israeli lives saved was likely to be greater than the suffering inflicted on Palestinian suspects. The government then allowed exceptions to the rules against torture, only to discover that once the rules were waived, Israeli interrogators routinely tortured and abused up to 85 percent of all prisoners.[29]

In Iraq, Lagouranis reported,

> We moved from seeking intelligence . . . to seeking confessions. It was as
> if the domination we exercised over our prisoners was not complete until
> they admitted what they had done. This was the most frightening change
> that came over us, because it signaled a shift from torture for an intelligence
> purpose to torture for the sole purpose of controlling another.[30]

All of this behavior could have been anticipated by anyone who knew what
American prison guards do when unsupervised. Judge Richard Posner, who favors
enhanced interrogation techniques under supposedly controlled circumstances,
admits that the danger of escalation is great enough to justify a flat-out legal ban
on torture.[31] But what neither Posner nor the Bush administration appreciates
is how the cruelty of guards also escalates and why, therefore, a ban on cruel,
inhumane, and degrading treatment was attached to a ban on torture.

The natural tendency of guards to degrade prisoners in order to dominate
them and to escalate the degradation over time unless restrained was demonstrated
most graphically in 1971 by the well-known Stanford Prison Experiment. Professor
Philip Zimbardo built a mock prison and hired college students to inhabit it,
night and day, for two weeks. Half of the students were designated prisoners; half
were guards. None of the guards had any reason to hate the prisoners because
they were students like themselves. Zimbardo and his colleagues went to great
lengths to select "good apples" for his experiment and were shocked at how
quickly they went bad.[32] Their student guards quickly felt a need to distrust and
fear their prisoners and then came to enjoy dominating them absolutely. The
experiment was scheduled to last two weeks but had to be shut down after just
five days, because guards on the night shift were forcing prisoners to strip naked
and simulate sex acts. The researchers found that

> [t]he use of power was self-aggrandizing and self-perpetuating. The guard
> power, derived initially from an arbitrary label, was intensified whenever there
> was any perceived threat by the prisoners and this new level subsequently
> became the baseline from which further hostility and harassment would

begin. . . . The absolute level of aggression as well as the more subtle and "creative" forms of aggression . . . increased in a spiraling function.[33]

They also concluded that the torture of innocent captives has more to do with institutional contexts, including the lack of moral supervision, than it does with individual moral choice.[34]

The Bush administration's torture policy was grounded in the belief that intelligence agents are better than law enforcement personnel are at getting "actionable intelligence." However, intelligence agencies may well be less "intelligent" than law enforcement because they separate collection from analysis. Detectives analyze information as they proceed, knowing that they must produce an account that can overcome all reasonable doubts. Intelligence agents are much less rigorous. Cloaked in secrecy, they are rarely held accountable for getting their facts wrong. An excessive devotion to secrecy also leads intelligence services to compartmentalize their operations, which prevents interrogators and analysts from learning relevant information in a timely manner.

In a memoir about his imprisonment at Guantánamo, Bagram, and Kandahar, British bookseller Moazzam Begg documented the ignorant and unimaginative questions that American interrogators repeated in the course of some three hundred interviews. For the most part, he found, they did not think much about what he had to say. They just wanted a confession. Anything would do; they did not bother to correct errors in statements he might be willing to sign. Nor were they interested in producing a coherent narrative that would help others understand who he was and why he had gone to Afghanistan. They just wanted to extract a statement, survive an unpleasant tour of duty, and go home.[35]

This kind of behavior is understandable. It is also incompetent and raises the question: Why weren't the agents' superiors more professional and make sure that the system was designed to produce *reliable* information? Perhaps they didn't because obtaining reliable information takes time, and their political superiors were impatient.

Knowing all this, one would expect that the strongest opponents of torture would be intelligence agents themselves, but they were no more likely than the Bush administration to view their actions in a larger context. Most of the military's interrogators were too young to have remembered the failures of Vietnam. The Pentagon's brass did not bother to train interrogators in the languages or tactics that they would need in order to sustain a successful occupation. Then the administration demanded victory in what was not a conventional war. As a result, abusive interrogators and guards fueled an insurgency and became, as the lance corporal told the general, the "assholes who just lost the war for us."[36]

Torture's Downside

Another assumption of the ticking-bomb scenario is that torture does no lasting harm to the nation that uses it. That theory, too, is contradicted by the record.

Just how much the abuse of prisoners in Iraq, as opposed to killing civilians generally, contributed to the insurgency against the American occupation cannot be measured with certainty, but between 2003 and 2004, *terrorist attacks worldwide* increased 300 percent. In 2005, there were 360 suicide bombings, compared to 472 for all the five preceding years.[37] According to one opinion poll, Osama bin Laden commanded the respect of more Pakistanis than did the United States.[38] Before the photographs from Abu Ghraib were broadcast in April 2004, the Coalition Provisional Authority claimed that 63 percent of Iraqis polled supported the occupation. One month later, only 9 percent did.[39]

In 1999, the State Department's Office of Research found that large majorities in Germany (78 percent), Indonesia (75 percent), and France (62 percent) held favorable views of the United States. That approval skyrocketed following the atrocities of 9/11, only to plummet after the crimes at Abu Ghraib were revealed. In January 2007, the British Broadcasting Company found that 52 percent of people polled in eighteen countries had a "mainly negative" view of the United States, and only 29 percent had a "mainly positive" view. In France only 39 percent were mainly positive; in Germany it was 37 percent. In Indonesia, the world's largest Muslim country, the approval rate was a mere 30 percent.

According to a survey done by the Pew Research Center in 2006, the opinion of people in the Middle East was profoundly negative toward the United States. Egyptians were 70 percent negative, Pakistanis 73 percent, and Turks a staggering 88 percent. In April 2007, the Chicago Council on Global Affairs found that a majority of people in thirteen out of fifteen foreign countries, including Argentina,

France, Indonesia, India, and Australia, believed that "the U.S. cannot be trusted to act responsibly in the world."[40]

Do Larger Consequences Matter?

Proponents of the ticking-bomb justification for torture insist that time is too short to consider anything but the immediate situation. But if the decision to torture is to be made by individual soldiers, interrogators, or guards and based on their assessment of the immediate circumstances, what is to prevent the desire for revenge from transforming questionable suspicions into false certainties, as happened after Guantánamo detainees were labeled the "worst of the worst"? What is to prevent torture and cruelty from becoming habitual and routine as interrogators and guards struggle to maintain domination of their captives?

Our forefathers wrestled with these questions during the American Revolution. As a member of the Continental Congress, John Adams insisted on what he called the policy of humanity. Gen. George Washington abided by it. Although he had personally watched from New Jersey as British and Hessian troops put surrendering Americans to the sword in New York, he refused to retaliate. "Treat them with humanity," he said of captured soldiers, "and Let them have no reason to Complain of our Copying the Brutal example of the British army."[41]

The same policy was adopted during World War II, with great success in Europe. Expecting decent treatment at the hands of Western troops led hundreds of thousands of German soldiers to surrender rather than go on fighting or risk capture by the Soviets. There were reciprocal benefits as well. According to the American Red Cross, 99 percent of all American soldiers captured by the Germans survived because of Germany's reciprocal compliance with the Geneva Convention of 1929.[42] By contrast, the failure of Germany and the Soviet Union to apply the convention on the Eastern Front led to the death of 55 percent of all German-held Soviet prisoners and 38 percent of all Soviet-held Germans.[43]

According to the Bush administration, times have changed and rendered the policies of Adams, Washington, and Dwight Eisenhower quaint and obsolete. The enemies we face today are different, apparently because some of them are— how shall we say it?—kamikazes. But if one of the objectives of a war is not to provoke the conquered population into supporting resistance groups during the occupation, then shouldn't we, like our forebears, enforce rules against torture and cruelty—even if it costs us some useful intelligence? Or has a desire for vengeance blinded contemporary Americans to the larger picture?

We are told that torture is permissible because the other side cannot be expected to follow the Geneva Conventions, and it is true that terrorists and insurgents lack the capacity to incarcerate many prisoners. It is incontrovertible that al Qaeda and the Iraqi insurgents tortured and murdered captured Americans in Iraq, as the Japanese did during World War II. But does an enemy's depravity absolve the United States of its moral obligation not to torture its captives or to subject them to cruel, inhumane, or degrading treatment? Those who demand revenge say yes, American forces must be ruthless in order to deter the enemy. Besides, some argue, "they started it."

The Japanese started World War II. Their army treated its captives with great savagery, and yet the Americans had no equivalent to Abu Ghraib during that war or afterward during the occupations of Japan or Germany, which were remarkably successful. Can torture and cruelty now be considered wise policies, when the most important objective of any war should be to prevent the conquered population from turning against its conquerors?

Given the many interests that the United States has throughout the world, was it smart for the Bush administration to torture prisoners, establish military commissions, and deny alleged terrorists the rudiments of due process of law? Was it prudent to believe that such actions could be kept secret, especially when digital cameras are everywhere, or to assume that none of the prisoners would eventually be released to tell the world of their mistreatment? Was it wise to lie, deceive, and dissemble about what was being done to alleged terrorists, especially when some of them were citizens of friendly countries like Canada, Great Britain, Australia, Spain, Germany, and Saudi Arabia?

Early in the war on terrorism, several foreign governments refused to extradite alleged terrorists to the United States so long as they were likely to face the death penalty.[44] Later, several European countries pulled their forces out of Iraq. Others refused to support the U.S. occupation by sending troops. The Bush administration did not just discount world opinion regarding the war and torture; it expressed disdain for foreign critics and for international law. Is it unreasonable to suppose that its lack of respect had something to do with these countries' refusal to join the war in Iraq and the withdrawal of troops by Spain, Italy, and the United Kingdom?

Confronted with the argument that torture undermines America's standing with foreign nations and their people, David Addington had a stock reply: "They don't vote."[45]

Early in the conflict, Vice President Cheney insisted that al Qaeda's terrorists did not deserve the level of due process accorded criminals in the United States. Even John Ashcroft disputed that claim. Why, Ashcroft asked, shouldn't the United States give foreign suspects the same kind of justice it extended to Timothy McVeigh when he was charged with the Oklahoma City bombing? By Cheney's reasoning, McVeigh didn't deserve justice either.[46]

No matter how strenuously officials deny it, torture is a form of terrorism. So how can a nation that needs the moral high ground to fight a successful war against terrorism deliberately torture its prisoners? How can former president Bush claim to have liberated Iraq from tyranny when his administration tortured and humiliated Iraqis in the very prison where thousands of Saddam Hussein's victims were tortured and killed?

In March 2008, a deputy to Gen. David Petraeus, then the American commander in Iraq, briefed reporters on what the military had learned about al Qaeda in Iraq. In many instances, he said, new recruits joined al Qaeda after being shown photographs of the abuses at Abu Ghraib.[47]

The Impact at Home

Finally, can the short-term tactical benefits of torture, whatever they are, possibly outweigh the damage that a policy of torture does to our moral standards as a nation or our self-respect as individuals? George Kennan's warning about the moral pitfalls of excessive anticommunism may be relevant here. "[S]omething may occur in our own minds and souls," he warned,

> which will make us no longer like the persons by whose efforts this republic was founded and held together, but rather like representatives of that very power we are trying to combat: intolerant, secretive, suspicious, [and] cruel. . . . The worst thing that our Communists could do to us, and the thing we have the most to fear from their activities, is that we should become like them.[48]

Our nation traces its legal roots to the English common law and its moral sensibility to the humanism of the Enlightenment. The common law taught us that coerced confessions were not to be trusted; the Enlightenment insisted that even suspected criminals have a right to be treated with dignity and respect. As we've noted, the humane treatment of prisoners has been accepted military doctrine since the earliest days of the American Revolution. As General Petraeus put it in a letter to his troops, "Some argue that we would be more effective if we sanctioned torture. . . . They would be wrong. . . . While we are warriors, we are also all human beings."[49]

So what does it say about the current state of our republic that these understandings, forged over many centuries, could be cast aside so easily? What does it say about our society when a transient administration can institutionalize torture in the military or the CIA? Do we really believe that individual interrogators and guards can engage in torture without suffering long-term moral and psychological consequences?

The short answer to these questions may be that substantial portions of the American electorate have already abandoned our legal and moral heritage (if they ever learned it) in favor of coercive interrogations of suspected terrorists abroad. A romance with raw power seems to drive many voters, especially within the Republican Party. For example, on May 15, 2007, during a debate in South Carolina, all but one of that party's presidential hopefuls responded to a ticking-bomb question by endorsing the use of enhanced interrogation techniques, including waterboarding, to uncover the proverbial ticking bomb. Each received strong audience applause.

Sen. John McCain, who eventually won the Republican Party's nomination, was the lone exception. "When I was in Vietnam," he explained, "one of the things that sustained us as we . . . underwent torture [was] the knowledge that if we had our positions reversed and we were the captors, we would not have imposed that kind of treatment on them. It's not about the terrorists; it's about us. It's about what kind of country we are."[50] His remarks were met with silence.

Banal or Evil?

In 1964, Hannah Arendt attempted to explain how a seemingly ordinary German bureaucrat could efficiently arrange to transport millions of Jews to the gas chambers. She later said of her account, *Eichmann in Jerusalem: A Report on the Banality of Evil,* that the subtitle did not describe a

> theory or doctrine but something quite factual, the phenomenon of evil deeds, committed on a gigantic scale, which could not be traced to any particularity of wickedness, pathology, or ideological conviction in the doer, whose only personal distinction was perhaps an extraordinary shallowness. However monstrous the deeds were, the doer was neither monstrous nor demonic, and the only specific characteristic one could detect in his past as well as in his behavior during the trial and the preceding police examination was something entirely negative: it was not stupidity but a curious, quite authentic inability to think.[51]

Can we say that the people who organized, encouraged, enabled, or covered up the torture of prisoners in the U.S. war against terrorism were unable to think? George W. Bush may be considered a "stupid" man, if arrogance, impulsiveness, and a lack of curiosity indicate stupidity. But the same cannot be said for those below him in the chain of command or for lawyers such as John Yoo. They were well educated and clever.

To Arendt, however, thinking requires more than knowledge or cleverness. It must be imbued with moral judgment and the courage to resist the demands of those in power. To exercise moral judgment within a bureaucratic structure, one must also think through the consequences of any line of action and not be stampeded by a public that wants revenge. It may be too much to expect that politicians will have the wit or courage to resist the baser instincts of the electorate, but is it too much to expect of cabinet secretaries, generals, or government lawyers?

In times of righteous indignation, people are prone to make hasty decisions, but at some point cooler heads must prevail. The Bush administration, unfortunately, never developed a sense of moral balance. Its torture policy lasted longer than World War II. The policy survived the Abu Ghraib scandal and continued in the secret prisons of the CIA. This policy raises the following questions: What should we conclude about officials who initiate a program of torture, scorn their critics, fail to monitor the policy's implementation, and classify the use of torture as a state secret so that they cannot be sued by the victims—the innocent victims—of their crimes? What shall we say about officials who continue the policy, even though it fails to produce much useful intelligence, fuels an insurgency, disgraces the nation, and undermines the constitutional foundations of our republic? And what should we think of the Obama administration, if it allows war crimes to go unpunished? Should we think of these officials as banal, evil, or both?

No man is above the law? Although Secretary of Defense Donald Rumsfeld, President George W. Bush, and Vice President Dick Cheney committed war crimes when they authorized the torture of prisoners, a Republican Congress granted them amnesty from prosecution. The Democrats who succeeded them, including President Barack Obama, have shown no interest in repealing that amnesty or prosecuting these criminals, thereby signaling that future presidents and their secret agents can, as a practical matter, commit the most brutal crimes and get away with them. —AP/STF

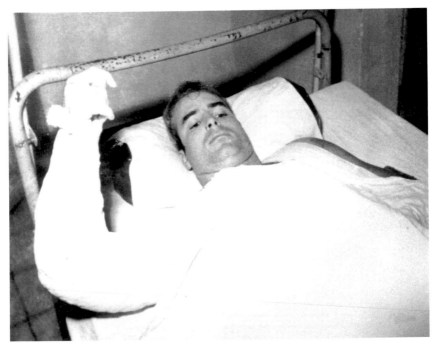

McCain not tortured. John McCain's North Vietnamese captors beat him repeatedly, denied him prompt and adequate medical treatment, and isolated him for so long that he attempted suicide. According to Bush administration lawyers, however, such actions (as well as "Palestinian hangings" and waterboarding) do not rise to the level of torture, or even cruelty, when done to suspected terrorists by American interrogators acting "in good faith." —AP

Vice president for torture. The most powerful and secretive vice president in history, Dick Cheney was principally responsible for developing the torture policy and for designing the military commissions that the Supreme Court declared illegal in 2006. Cheney advocated operating on "the dark side" and laughed dismissively when a former CIA director dubbed him "the vice president for torture." Nearly drowning suspects to make them talk, he told an interviewer, was "a no brainer." —AP/Charles Dharapak

Guantánamo by the Bay. "Just for the sake of the listening world," Secretary Rumsfeld assured reporters in January 2002, "to be in an 8-by-8 cell in beautiful, sunny Guantánamo Bay, Cuba, is not inhumane treatment." The cells to which he referred were dog pens surrounded by banana rats. The toilets were buckets. The conditions were so harsh and hopeless that more than 40 prisoners attempted suicide; 4 succeeded. By July 2003, 120 of approximately 625 prisoners were on antidepressant drugs. An entire cell block was set aside for prisoners who, according to their U.S. Army chaplain, had regressed to the point that they were drawing with crayons and babbling "complete nonsense." —AP/J. Scott Applewhite

Cheney's Cheney. David S. Addington, Vice President Cheney's lawyer and chief of staff, was often referred to as the "most powerful man you have never heard of." He was a driving force behind the torture policy, military commissions, and "legal black holes," and excluded military lawyers and State Department officials from the decision-making process. He also advocated unlimited executive power in peace and war, employed presidential "signing statements" to flout the will of Congress, and invoked secrecy to nullify the constitutional system of checks and balances. A ruthless bureaucratic infighter, Addington once declared, "We're going to push and push and push until some larger force makes us stop."

The enhancer. Secretary of Defense Rumsfeld issued memos authorizing the use of "enhanced interrogation techniques" that violated established laws, treaties, and regulations. He specifically approved and then monitored the brutal interrogation of Muhammed al-Qahtani, who was questioned for twenty hours a day for at least fifty days at Guantánamo, threatened by a snarling dog while chained to the floor, and subjected to such extreme cold that he had to be hospitalized twice when his heart nearly stopped. Al-Qahtani was stripped naked in front of female soldiers, led around on a leash, and forced to do dog tricks. Interrogators also made him write his will, strongly implying that he was about to be executed. —AP/STF

The consigliere. As White House counsel, Alberto Gonzales presided over the "war council" that developed the torture policy and approved the infamous torture memo of August 1, 2002. In January 2002, he specifically advised President Bush that the interrogation techniques they were planning would constitute war crimes, but that prosecution might be avoided if the president declared the Geneva Conventions inapplicable to suspected terrorists. As attorney general, Gonzales advised a Senate committee that no one has a constitutional right to habeas corpus. The Supreme Court rejected the first advice in 2006 and the second in 2008. —AP

Freedom fighters. Under Director George Tenet, the CIA ran a network of secret prisons outside the United States, within which some suspected terrorists were waterboarded and others were made to disappear. His agents also kidnapped suspects from the United States and other countries and delivered them, via a fleet of thirty-three aircraft, to foreign intelligence agencies for interrogation under torture. Here President George W. Bush awards Tenet the Presidential Medal of Freedom, the nation's highest civilian honor, in December 2004.

The torture maven. As an attorney in the Justice Department's Office of Legal Counsel from 2001 to 2003, John Yoo secretly counseled the military and the CIA on how to avoid prosecution for war crimes. He also advised the president that, as commander in chief in wartime, he was not bound to obey the Constitution's guarantees of habeas corpus, due process, and freedom from unreasonable searches and seizures or the laws that made torture, cruelty, and warrantless wiretapping crimes. Yoo's definition of torture was so narrow that it would have absolved Saddam Hussein of many of the crimes that his interrogators inflicted at Abu Ghraib. —Karen Ballard/Redux

Honor bound? Maj. Gen. Geoffrey Miller was a gung ho artillery officer with no experience interrogating prisoners or managing prisons when Secretary Rumsfeld put him in charge of Guantánamo and later Abu Ghraib. Under Miller's command, prisoners were beaten, sexually humiliated, and subjected to life-threatening extremes of heat and cold (measured with rectal thermometers). Others were denied sleep, exercise, and human contact for such long periods that they tried to kill themselves. Miller's motto for GTMO was Honor Bound to Defend Freedom. He was awarded a Distinguished Service Medal upon his retirement at a ceremony in the Pentagon's Hall of Heroes. —AP/Khampha Bouaphanh

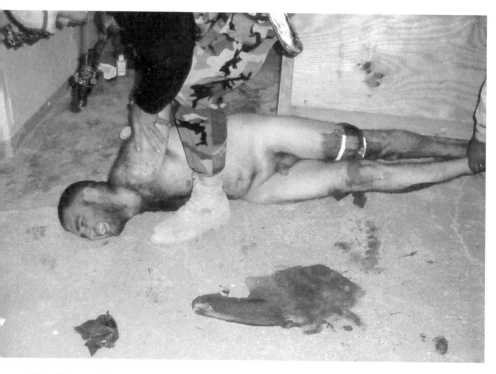

The "**doggie dance.**" In 2002 Secretary Rumsfeld authorized using dogs to terrorize prisoners, and General Miller brought the animals to Abu Ghraib in 2003. Here a naked prisoner writhes on the floor, having just been bitten on his leg by an army dog. Specialist Charles Graner, who supervised "the doggie dance" that led to this wound, admitted to a friend that "the Christian in me says it's wrong, but the corrections officer in me says, 'I love to make a grown man piss himself.'"

Mr. Frosty. Specialist Sabrina Harman poses over the ice-packed corpse of Manadel al-Jamadi, also known as "Mr. Frosty." U.S. Navy SEALS had severely beaten al-Jamadi before turning him over to CIA agents. At Abu Ghraib, agents shackled al-Jamadi's wrists to a window frame behind his back. He died about an hour later from "blunt force injuries to the torso complicated by compromised respiration." CIA agent Mark Swanner and Col. Thomas M. Pappas of Military Intelligence ordered guards to pack the body in ice while they decided how to conceal their role in his death. Although al-Jamadi's death was ruled a homicide, Swanner and Pappas were not prosecuted.

Military intelligence? Sexual humiliation was standard practice at Abu Ghraib, even though it was not likely to produce reliable information. Knowing that their Muslim prisoners were exceedingly modest about nakedness and sex, the guards often stripped them naked, made them wear bras or panties, and encouraged female American soldiers to mock their private parts. In this photograph, prisoners have been ordered to simulate oral sex. On other occasions, they were ordered to simulate masturbation. Imams, or prayer leaders, were most likely to be subjected to sexual humiliation because they were the most devout.

Profile in courage. Lt. Cdr. Charles Swift, like many military lawyers, challenged the legality of Bush's military commissions. As counsel to Salim Ahmed Hamdan, Osama bin Laden's driver, Swift helped persuade the Supreme Court to strike down the president's order creating these commissions as illegal under the Geneva Conventions and the Uniform Code of Military Justice. Although Swift was voted one of the most influential lawyers in the United States, the navy denied him a promotion, thereby ending his military career. —AP/Keven P. Casey

Amnesty for torture. On October 17, 2006, Republican legislators applauded as President George W. Bush signed a bill granting him and his subordinates amnesty for acts of torture. From left to right: Representative Chris Cannon (Utah), Representative Steve Buyer (Indiana), Representative Jim Sensenbrenner (Wisconsin), Senator Lindsey Graham (South Carolina), Representative Duncan Hunter (California), and Senator John Warner (Virginia). Gen. Peter Pace, chairman of the Joint Chiefs of Staff, and Attorney General Alberto Gonzales are in the background.

My lawyer said I could. Attorney General Michael Mukasey refused to prosecute Bush administration officials for torture and cruelty because Justice Department lawyers had said they could do it. According to this novel assertion, which is a cousin to the "Eichmann defense" of following orders and has no basis in law, government officials may obtain pre-pardons for crimes they plan to commit by seeking favorable legal advice from attorneys they (or their co-conspirators) have appointed. —Getty Images

8

CONGRESS: THE ENABLERS

What has distinguished our ancestors? That they would not admit
of tortures, or cruel and barbarous punishment. But Congress may
introduce the practice . . . and they will tell you that there is such a
necessity of strengthening the arm of government that they must . . .
extort confession by torture. . . . We are then lost and undone.
—PATRICK HENRY[1]

That intelligence agencies of any country would torture suspected terrorists is not surprising. People who are freed from legal constraints usually feel
free from moral constraints as well. That a president of the United States would
initiate a policy of torture is appalling, but more dismaying still is why members
of Congress have not mustered the courage to end the practice.

Prior Scandals

During the 1970s a Democratic-led Congress, supported by a Republican judge,
John Sirica, exercised enough oversight to drive a Republican president from
office. Richard M. Nixon, like George W. Bush, thought he was above the law.
"When the president does it, that means it is not illegal," Nixon once told an
interviewer.[2] The most notorious aspect of the Watergate scandal involved a
White House plumbers unit (of ex-CIA agents) that was caught burglarizing the
opposition party's offices for partisan purposes. The same group also searched a
psychiatrist's office for material with which to discredit Daniel Ellsberg, who had
leaked the Pentagon Papers—a secret study of how the use of military advisers
escalated into a disastrous war in Vietnam.

However, the burglaries were but a small part of covert intelligence operations directed at monitoring and suppressing dissent within the United States. Between 1970 and 1976, committees of the House and Senate exposed massive illegal spying on American citizens by the military, the FBI, the National Security Agency, and the CIA. They also uncovered unsuccessful CIA plots to assassinate the peacetime leaders of foreign nations. Most of those operations ended by 1976 only to be revived, covertly and on a more extensive scale by President Bush in the wake of 9/11.

During the 1980s, Democrats in Congress exposed the Reagan administration's covert operations involving the illegal sale of arms to Iran, a state sponsor of terrorism, to spring hostages from Lebanon and simultaneously fund a secret war against Nicaragua that Congress had forbidden. In both decades, it fell to Democrats to investigate the criminal activities of these Republican administrations. Whether a Republican majority would have investigated a Democratic administration as vigorously for similar abuses of power is an open question. A few congressmen might have, but in both scandals it was not in their party's interest to do so, and that partisan interest has for the last three decades made them defenders of executive lawbreaking.

But this is not to suggest that curbing abuses of executive power and defending civil liberties are priorities to most Democrats. So long as the hearings embarrassed the Republican Party, most Democrats supported them, but when the initiative shifted from committee chairmen to the House and Senate leadership, efforts at reform faltered. In 1976, the House of Representatives voted not to release the report of its select intelligence committee headed by Representative Otis Pike (D-NY), and when the committee's report was leaked to a reporter, the House voted to conduct an even more extensive investigation into the leak, reflecting a bipartisan majority's belief that secrecy was more important than accountability and regulation. Once the House and Senate hearings were over, the massive record of intelligence agency abuses compiled by the two committees was ignored, and the effort to write charters for the FBI and CIA collapsed. The best Congress could do was erase some emergency powers legislation and pass the highly compromised Foreign Intelligence Surveillance Act (FISA) of 1978. Both houses also created permanent intelligence committees, but under conservative leadership both panels succumbed to excessive demands for secrecy.

Instead of restraining abuses of power, they became uncritical advocates of secret government. As a result, they failed to interdict the Iran-contra scandal or advance reform legislation afterward.

Indeed, Republicans on the joint Iran-Contra Committee, led by Representative Dick Cheney (R-WY), managed to persuade the committee to grant immunity from prosecution to two key lawbreakers—Lt. Col. Oliver North and Adm. John Poindexter—for anything they might admit in open hearings. North then acknowledged illegally shredding documents, lying to Congress, and falsifying official records. Both men were subsequently convicted on information gathered prior to the hearings, but their convictions were overturned by the Court of Appeals for the District of Columbia. Conservative, Republican-appointed judges who had never overturned a conviction because of pretrial publicity freed the White House aides because the witnesses against them might have been influenced by what they saw the defendants admit on television.[3]

During the Iran-contra investigation Congressman Dick Cheney learned how to protect executive officials from accountability for their crimes. He and his fellow Republicans on the committee argued then, as they have argued recently in defense of torture, that what the Democratic majority called crimes were, in effect, mere "mistakes," because the president has sweeping constitutional powers to authorize covert action. This argument was the thrust of a short minority report that Cheney and fellow Republicans attached to the committee's extensive analysis. Eight Reagan Republicans were convicted for these mistakes, but the administration of George W. Bush hired many of them and used its control over the declassification of documents to make records of Vice President George H. W. Bush's involvement in the scandal disappear.[4]

Now the pattern is repeating itself. As in the 1960s, the executive branch has again drawn the nation into war on the basis of faulty and deceitful intelligence. As in the scandals of the 1970s and 1980s, intelligence agencies have been caught violating laws meant to restrain them, including laws against warrantless wiretapping, and again Congress has failed to restrain them.

Today, however, the situation is worse than Watergate and worse than the Iran-contra affair. From 2001 to 2007, a Republican-controlled Congress blocked most efforts to investigate the torture of prisoners by the military and the CIA. Among the strategically placed Republicans who failed to hold the torturers and their superiors accountable at that time were Senator John Warner (R-VA), chair of the Senate Armed Services Committee; Representative Duncan Hunter (R-CA), chair of the House Armed Services Committee; former representative Porter Goss (R-FL) and Representative Peter Hoekstra (R-MI), chairs of the House Permanent Committee on Intelligence; and Representative James Sensenbrenner, Jr. (R-WI), chair of the House Judiciary Committee.

In 2005 and 2006 a majority of Republicans, with the support of a group of conservative Democrats, passed laws denying prisoners the right to challenge their detentions and mistreatment in court. In 2007, when the Democrats resumed control of both houses, some oversight was attempted but was effectively stonewalled by the Bush administration, the intelligence agencies, and conservatives of both parties.

The Detainee Treatment Act of 2005

The first of these new laws was the Detainee Treatment Act of 2005. In the fall of that year, several Senate Republicans, led by pro-war senator John McCain, sought legislation purporting to reaffirm the military's rules against the abuse of prisoners.[5] McCain said he was prompted to act by a letter from Ian Fishback, an infantry officer with the 82nd Airborne Division. After witnessing "a wide range of abuses" in both Afghanistan and Iraq, Captain Fishback tried without success for seventeen months to

> determine what specific standards governed the treatment of detainees by consulting my chain of command through [the] battalion commander, multiple JAG lawyers, multiple Democrat and Republican Congressmen and their aides, the Ft. Bragg Inspector General's office, multiple government reports, the Secretary of the Army and multiple general officers, a professional interrogator at Guantanamo Bay, the deputy head of the department at West Point responsible for teaching Just War Theory and [the] Law of Land Warfare, and numerous peers who I regard as honorable and intelligent men.

Finally, the captain wrote to Senator McCain on September 16, 2005. "When," he asked, "did al Qaeda become any kind of standard by which we measure the morality of the United States?"[6]

The senator responded by proposing an amendment to the defense appropriations bill that would reaffirm the ban on cruel, inhumane, and degrading treatment of prisoners. He did so, however, by incorporating into law the U.S. Army's neglected field manual on interrogations. That move was disingenuous, to say the least, because the administration could rewrite the manual at any time without congressional approval. Indeed, even as McCain's amendment was being debated, the Defense Department produced a new draft. Unlike the previous edition, which could be read in its entirety on the Internet, this manual concealed ten pages of classified interrogations techniques.[7]

McCain initially sought to prohibit military commissions from admitting any "confession or admission that was procured by torture."[8] This prohibition was supported by Deputy Secretary of Defense Gordon R. England; Maj. Gen. John D. Altenburg (Ret.), head of the military tribunals; the vice chiefs of the military services; the judge advocate generals of the services; and State Department counselor Philip D. Zelikow. But Vice President Cheney and his counsel, David Addington, opposed it. So, too, did Rumsfeld's general counsel, Jim Haynes, and the undersecretary for intelligence, Stephen Cambone. The opponents won, and the prohibition was struck from the bill.

Senator Lindsey Graham, a former military lawyer and onetime military judge, worked both sides of the issue. While publicly supporting McCain's bill, he did everything to gut it and turn it into the opposite of what McCain had sought to do. Graham not only helped to remove the ban on coerced confessions, he won an amendment that expressly allowed the commissions to admit evidence obtained by torture.[9]

Graham was not prepared, however, to expressly repeal prisoners' rights under the Geneva Conventions. That revocation would have raised an international red flag. Instead, he persuaded the Republican leadership to include an amendment stripping all federal courts of jurisdiction to hear habeas petitions from Guantánamo prisoners. The amendment would erect a second line of defense against such suits in case the justices rejected the administration's claim that Guantánamo was not under the jurisdiction of any federal courts.

Graham knew denying all habeas relief would violate Article I, Section 9 of the Constitution. It clearly says that Congress may not suspend "the Privilege of the Writ of Habeas Corpus unless in Cases of Rebellion or Invasion the public

Safety may require it." So he offered an arguable substitute for habeas. His amendment permitted GTMO's prisoners to complain about their detention and treatment but only by *appealing their conviction* by a military commission. Unless and until they were tried and convicted, the prisoners would have no right to challenge their mistreatment in a federal court, which the habeas procedure does permit. To rig the outcome still further, Graham's amendment allowed convicted prisoners to appeal their mistreatment to only one court—the U.S. Court of Appeals for the District of Columbia, which had been packed with conservative Republican judges who were hostile to such claims.

The senator's shell game was clever enough to escape public scrutiny because most journalists (and their readers) are untutored in matters of law. Most journalists did not appreciate how directing all cases of a given kind to a particular court allows presidents to determine outcomes by packing that court with judges of their persuasion. Moreover, sending all cases of a given kind to just one court undermines Supreme Court review, which is normally granted only if two or more lower courts disagree.[10]

President Bush threatened to veto the entire military appropriations bill if McCain's toothless prohibitions remained in it, but on October 5, 2005, ninety senators (including forty-five Republicans) passed it anyway, along with Senator Graham's evisceration.[11] The vote gave Republicans a chance to distance themselves from a politically embarrassing practice without limiting the president and his secret government. It also gave interrogators at GTMO all the legal protection they needed to go on abusing prisoners at will while denying prisoners any meaningful opportunity to challenge their potentially lifelong incarceration without trial.

But Vice President Cheney was still not satisfied. He and CIA director Porter Goss argued vociferously for an amendment that would exempt from prosecution any CIA agent involved in "clandestine counterterrorism operations conducted abroad."[12] Adm. Stansfield Turner (Ret.), who had led the CIA during the 1970s, was one of many former officials who condemned Cheney's efforts. Speaking on a British television program, Turner said, "We have crossed the line into dangerous territory. I am embarrassed that the USA has a vice president for torture. I think it is just reprehensible."[13]

McCain refused to go as far as Cheney did, but he allowed administration supporters to insert a provision granting any government agent charged with abusing prisoners an unprecedented legal defense: good faith reliance on the advice of counsel. He also went along with Graham's provision that stripped Guantánamo's prisoners of the right to challenge their detentions in federal court.[14] Thus, what was supposed to be an anti-torture law became an immunity-from-prosecution law.

The final bill declared that the Defense Department would have to follow a new version of the army's field manual on interrogations, which, again, the administration could write any way it wished. CIA interrogators could not use cruel or inhumane tactics, but that directive meant only that they could not do anything that would be "cruel or unusual" as defined by the Eighth Amendment to the federal Constitution. Cheney had insisted on this provision, which gave administration lawyers two more issues to litigate. First, they could insist, as the Supreme Court had held, that the Eighth Amendment applies only to cruelties inflicted after conviction. If that maneuver did not work, they could argue that the reference to that amendment would trigger a judicial "shocks the conscience" test. Cheney was confident that the conservative judges in Northern Virginia and the District of Columbia, where these cases would probably be heard, would not be easily shocked. Interviewed on ABC's *Nightline,* the vice president observed, with some understatement, that "what shocks the conscience" is usually "in the eye of the beholder."[15]

Presidential Signing Statements: Defying Congress

But that was not the end of it. Hours before the president was to sign the bill, which had a veto-proof majority in Congress, David Addington intercepted a draft of the president's signing statement and added a single sentence: the president would interpret the new law "in a manner consistent with the constitutional authority of the president to supervise the unitary executive branch as Commander in Chief and consistent with the constitutional limitations on the judicial power."[16] Addington's addition effectively denied Congress's power to pass war crimes legislation and asserted the president's authority, as commander in chief, to ignore adverse court decisions and to authorize cruel, inhumane, or degrading treatment if he wished.[17] Top executives at the CIA and the Departments of State, Justice, and Defense opposed the addition, but White House counsel Harriet E. Miers deferred to the vice president. She sent Addington's draft to the president, and he signed it.[18] The statement was quietly released on the Friday before the New Year's weekend, when the White House press corps and the public were not paying attention.

This signing statement, together with many others Addington drafted and the president signed, marked, in effect, a reversion to the seventeenth-century monarchy of King James I. Like Bush, James had asserted the authority to set aside any law he wished and denied the authority of the House of Commons to "meddle with anything concerning our government or deep matters of State."[19] When Charles I attempted to act upon his father's claims to unlimited power, Parliament launched a civil war in 1642, executed Charles in 1649, and proved for all time that the king could not be a law unto himself. When James II succeeded to the throne in 1688 and tried to rule arbitrarily, Parliament revolted again, deposed the king, and invited William and Mary to assume the throne on the condition, among other things, that they sign a Declaration of Rights. One of its provisions declared that "the pretended power of suspending the laws, or the execution of the laws, by regal authority, without the consent of Parliament, is illegal."[20] That document became a major source of inspiration for both the Declaration of Independence and the Constitution.

The *Hamdan* Decision:
Restoring the Geneva Conventions

The Bush administration's policy of torture was based on two extraordinary but now familiar assertions. First, wartime presidents are above the law. Second, human rights treaties, like the Geneva Conventions, are not the supreme law of the land; they are mere political agreements among princes to be enforced or ignored by princes only. Both assertions were rejected by a 5-3 majority of the Supreme Court on June 29, 2006.[21]

Salim Ahmed Hamdan was not a sympathetic plaintiff; he had been Osama bin Laden's driver and bodyguard. Knowing that, most people assumed that the military had enough evidence to convict him in a regular military or civilian court, but the military did not bring him before a regular court. It did not even convene a commission to try him at Guantánamo until a federal district court in Washington, D.C., forced the issue by agreeing to hear a habeas petition challenging his detention without trial. Then the administration reluctantly scheduled Hamdan and nine other prisoners for trial before military commissions.

Lt. Cmdr. Charles Swift was chosen to defend Hamdan. A career naval officer, he had been the navigator on a guided missile frigate before attending Puget Sound (now Seattle University) Law School. Like other defense counsel, Swift was chosen in part because he was not easily intimidated by military brass. This quality turned out to be important because the chief prosecutor soon informed him that he would be granted access to his client only in order to negotiate a guilty plea. If Swift intended to mount a defense, he might not be allowed to visit his client.[22] The threat was not just a violation of Hamdan's right to counsel, it also flouted the commission's own rules and was soon withdrawn. Swift's boss, U.S. Air Force Col. Will Gunn, ran interference for the prisoners' lawyers and, in the process, gave up a good chance to become the first African American judge advocate general of the air force.[23]

Two of the five officers appointed to decide Hamdan's fate had served in Afghanistan. One was an intelligence officer; the other had supervised the brutal transportation of prisoners to Guantánamo. When Commander Swift asked what these officers had done in Afghanistan, the military judge refused to allow that information to be disclosed in open court. He then decreed that the two officers could be trusted to be fair.

Swift would later ask, "Why would [the military] put guys who were involved in the operation on the court in the first place? Surely there are enough people in the United States military who were not involved in the operations in Afghanistan to have an unbiased panel." Opposing counsel supplied the answer. Three of the prosecutors resigned, one of them wrote, because they refused to participate "in a process that appears to be rigged." U.S. Air Force Capt. John Carr explained his decision to Col. Frederick L. Borch, the senior prosecutor: "You have repeatedly said to the office that the military panel will be hand-picked and will not acquit these detainees, and we only needed to worry about building a record for the review panel."[24]

Swift appealed, and the two officers were removed from the panel. The military then decided not to replace them, which made the prosecution's task of winning a two-thirds verdict against Hamdan even easier.[25] It was a gambit worthy of Joseph Heller's *Catch-22*.

The injustices heaped upon GTMO detainees like Hamdan did not escape the notice of the organized bar. More than a thousand lawyers volunteered to represent the detainees without pay. More than a thousand worked on Hamdan's case, in one capacity or another, as it moved through the system, even though it was clear he had been one of bin Laden's bodyguards.[26]

When *Hamdan* arrived at the Supreme Court, the justices could have ruled that only Congress, not the president, has the constitutional authority to create a new legal system, and Congress had not yet exercised that power. Instead, it decided that Congress, in what is now section 21 of the Uniform Code of Military Justice, had limited whatever authority the president might have to create commissions to the standards of justice required of courts-martial, unless he could justify a deviation. For those standards of justice, the five-member majority looked to Common Article 3 of the Geneva Conventions, which Congress had incorporated into American law through the UCMJ. Article 3 forbids criminal trials outside of a "regularly constituted court affording all the judicial guarantees which are recognized as indispensable by civilized peoples."[27] The justices also agreed with career military lawyers that no military necessity justified deviating from those standards.[28]

The Justice Department argued that article 3 did not protect Hamdan because the president had decreed that the conventions protected neither al Qaeda operatives nor Taliban soldiers. The Supreme Court did not bother to address this argument. It simply treated the conventions as law and assumed, as Justice John Marshall had observed in *Marbury v. Madison,*[29] that it is the function of the courts to say what the law is in cases properly before them.[30]

The Justice Department insisted that a treaty, being an agreement among political entities, could not give prisoners like Hamdan a personal right to challenge the legality of a commission specially created to try them. But the justices sidestepped this assertion by ruling that Hamdan's right to challenge the commission came from the habeas corpus statute and not the Geneva Conventions. The conventions simply set the standard for what a lawful commission is.

While Hamdan's case was pending before the Supreme Court, the Republican majority in Congress tried to prevent the decision by passing Senator Graham's court-stripping amendment. A majority of the justices would have none of that either. They found a technical inconsistency in the Detainee Treatment

Act, planted there by Senator Dick Durbin (D-IL), which permitted judges to retain jurisdiction over *pending* cases. As a result, the justices did not have to consider whether Graham's court-stripping provision was an unconstitutional infringement of due process of law or whether the writ of habeas corpus is really a constitutional guarantee, not alterable by legislation, in order to hear a challenge. Those issues could be left to another time.

By not declaring the commissions unconstitutional, the majority gave the president a way to back off from his claims to unlimited authority and still get what he wanted. Justice Stephen Breyer was blunt about it: "Nothing prevents the president from returning to Congress to seek the authority he believes necessary."[31]

Throughout the litigation, administration lawyers insisted that the president, as commander in chief, enjoys exclusive authority to decide how to engage the enemy in time of war. The justices ignored this claim too, following their well-established rule not to address constitutional questions unless there is no alternative. By not reaching this ultimate question, the court allowed the executive to continue to keep Hamdan and his fellow prisoners behind bars indefinitely.

The court's decision dealt only with commissions, but its reasoning also applied to interrogations. As Justice Breyer observed, "By Act of Congress . . . violations of Common Article 3 are considered 'war crimes,' punishable as federal offenses."[32] This holding threw the administration into a panic because it meant that everyone who helped devise and execute the torture policy and practice was, legally speaking, a war criminal.

The military lawyers representing the prisoners understood this ruling immediately. One of the first things they did upon reading the *Hamdan* decision was to request a stay of all commission proceedings because further participation in a proceeding that violated Common Article 3 would, in and of itself, constitute a war crime.

Deputy Secretary of Defense Gordon England also got the message. He promptly instructed all military commanders to make sure that their treatment of prisoners comported with Common Article 3. While insisting that the military had always treated its prisoners humanely, he implicitly revoked practices that Rumsfeld and his general counsel had authorized, including stripping prisoners naked, dressing them in women's underwear, terrorizing them with dogs, putting them on leashes and making them bark, and subjecting them to painful stress positions, mock executions, and waterboarding.

England issued this order without consulting the attorney general, White House counsel Harriet Miers, or David Addington, who had become the vice president's chief of staff. Addington's predecessor, I. Lewis "Scooter" Libby, had been indicted for lying to a special prosecutor about circumstances surrounding a leak of classified information concerning an Iraq War critic's wife. Maj. Gen. Jack L. Rives, the U.S. Air Force's judge advocate general, informed the Senate Armed Services Committee on July 13 that "some of the techniques that have been authorized and used in the past have violated Common Article 3" of the Geneva Conventions. Seated next to him, the chief military lawyers of the other three services agreed.[33] On September 6, 2006, the Pentagon issued a revised interrogations manual that expressly banned forced nakedness, hooding, and stress positions.[34]

For a moment, it looked as if the torture policy might be shut down, but only at the Defense Department. In July 2006, while the Pentagon was publicly complying with the *Hamdan* decision, President Bush signed a secret new executive order authorizing the CIA to use enhanced interrogation techniques at its black sites overseas.[35]

Amnesty for Torturers

Faced with the *Hamdan* decision, most presidents probably would have retreated. Not George W. Bush. Even as he announced on September 6 that the CIA's prisons had been emptied, he insisted that they would remain an option.[36] Then he sponsored the Military Commissions Act (MCA) of 2006 to overturn the *Hamdan* decision.[37] One of his reasons for sponsoring this legislation, Bush said, was to protect innocent soldiers from unjust prosecutions. But that was a ruse because the bill would not have repealed those provisions of the Uniform Code of Military Justice under which military war criminals are traditionally charged. Actually, he was trying to protect everyone involved in the torture policy and its implementation from prosecution by a subsequent administration.[38] When he said on September 15 that CIA agents "don't want to be tried as war criminals,"[39] he was also speaking for himself.

Indeed, the president was so fearful that he might be prosecuted after leaving office that he personally visited Capitol Hill to lobby for the bill. He did not expressly call for the repeal of article 3. That would have been too obvious, and Senator John McCain and others had declared that option unacceptable. Rather, like Jay Bybee, Bush sought to narrow the definition of war crimes by claiming that most interrogation techniques do not constitute torture or even cruel, inhumane, and degrading treatment. Nonlethal practices, including forced nakedness, leashing, the stacking of prisoners, painful positions, dog attacks, sensory deprivation, loud music, hypothermia, and waterboarding, would no longer be war crimes, individually or in the aggregate. His bill would make them legal, even though they could cause severe psychological damage. This goal was accomplished by listing as war crimes only the most egregious abuses, like murder and rape, and by leaving the definition of what constitutes cruel, inhumane, and degrading treatment under Common Article 3 up to the president, even though foreign and international courts might disagree.

On September 28 and 29, Congress passed the Military Commissions Act with strong majorities in both houses. It gave the president nearly everything he had sought and made the United States the first nation in the world to legislatively break with the international community on what constitutes war crimes.[40]

The Military Commissions Act did not just allow these war crimes in the future; it absolved all who ordered, encouraged, carried out, and concealed their commission in the past.[41] Legally speaking, this action was equivalent to excusing Lt. William Calley of responsibility for the 1968 My Lai massacre in Vietnam. Richard Nixon and Ronald Reagan pardoned their own subordinates for crimes committed on the job. Gerald Ford pardoned President Nixon for any crimes for which he might be prosecuted in the future. George H. W. Bush pardoned Iran-contra figures, including former secretary of defense Caspar Weinberger. George W. Bush was the first American president to pre-pardon himself by persuading Congress to grant blanket amnesty for war crimes committed under his authority. In so doing, he took his place in legal history alongside Gen. Augusto Pinochet of Chile, who obtained legislative amnesty for his murderous dirty war against alleged terrorists during the 1980s.

Ironically, by granting administration officials amnesty for their war crimes, Congress may have exposed them to greater risk of prosecution abroad, because the International Criminal Court and foreign courts could no longer decline jurisdiction on the theory that the torture team could and should be tried in the

United States. Like Henry Kissinger, members of Bush's War Council might have to restrict their foreign travel in retirement.

Authorizing Torture in the Future

While administration officials tried to avoid liability for their war crimes, JAG lawyers briefly resumed their watchdog role at the Pentagon. Congress had always supported their independence, and that support prevailed during the summer of 2006. Gordon England's order to obey article 3's ban on cruel, inhumane, and degrading treatment of prisoners was the first adjustment to the *Hamdan* decision.[42] The second was a revised interrogations manual, which, among other things, bans stress positions, stripping detainees, forcing them to perform sex acts, hooding prisoners, taping their eyes, threatening them with dogs, shocking them with electricity, burning them, staging mock executions, and waterboarding.[43] "No good intelligence is going to come from abusive practices," Lt. Gen. John "Jeff" Kimmons, the deputy chief of staff for intelligence, explained during a Pentagon briefing on September 6, 2006, adding, "I think the empirical evidence of the last five years, hard years, tells us that."[44] Kimmon's statement flatly contradicted President Bush's claim, just an hour later, that the brutal interrogation of Abu Zubaydah "helped stop a terrorist attack being planned for inside the United States."[45]

But neither England's order nor the new manual restrained CIA interrogators in any way. The agency remained a law unto itself. While the Pentagon backed away from its harshest measures, President Bush secretly signed a new (and still secret) order authorizing the CIA to use enhanced interrogation techniques. This order, too, bore the legal blessing of the new head of the Office of Legal Counsel, Stephen G. Bradbury.[46] As a "senior administration official" explained to the *Los Angeles Times,* the CIA would still be able to use the harshest interrogation techniques on the most notorious prisoners. "The president made clear," he added, "that this is a small program targeting a certain category of high-level al-Qaeda members."[47] In other words, a war crime is not a crime if it is part of a small program run by a secret civilian agency.

The new law did not specifically authorize any interrogation techniques. It left that task up to the president. It repealed neither the Geneva Conventions nor the War Crimes Act, but the MCA gave the president exclusive authority to define what techniques, if any, constituted cruel, inhumane, or degrading treatment under Common Article 3. Contrary to the separation of powers mandated by the Constitution, the Republican Congress delegated to the president the authority to decide what is criminal.

Bush administration officials had previously insisted that stress positions, sleep deprivation, sexual humiliation, and even waterboarding were not so inhumane as to violate Common Article 3 of the Geneva Conventions. Following passage of the Military Commissions Act, they refused to say whether waterboarding would be allowed under the new law, but there was little doubt as to where the vice president stood. Asked by a North Dakota talk show host, "Would you agree a dunk in the water is a no-brainer if it can save lives?" Cheney replied, "Well, it's a no-brainer to me, but for a while there I was criticized as being the vice president for torture."[48]

In July 2007, when the president finally issued his executive order defining cruel, inhumane, and degrading treatment under the new law, he declared that CIA prisoners should "receive the basic necessities of life" but did not list sleep as one of those necessities. Nor did he ban waterboarding, forced feeding, extremes of hot and cold, deafening noise, sensory deprivation, or long-term isolation.[49] On the contrary, he threatened to veto any legislation banning waterboarding,[50] even as administration officials claimed that they had not waterboarded anyone since 2003[51] and that the practice was no longer, at least for the moment, agency policy.[52]

Admitting Evidence Obtained by Coercion

To build support for his bill, the president had announced on September 6, 2006, that he had ordered fourteen top al Qaeda suspects transferred to Guantánamo, where he intended to try them for war crimes as soon as Congress authorized military commissions under his proposed legislation. The transfer of these ghost detainees was meant to imply that the CIA's detention program was small and had been shut down, and was so read by some journalists.[53] But Bush never said that all the agency's secret prisons had been shut down or that no new ones would be established. Nor did he account for many of the prisoners who had been made to disappear within them.[54] John Bellinger, the State Department's legal adviser, even questioned the International Red Cross's right to visit the CIA's prisoners, presumably on the ground that the Geneva Conventions apply only to the Defense Department.[55]

The new Military Commissions Act authorized the president to create special courts, staffed by military men, to prosecute civilians who were not citizens of the United States for supposed war crimes. The irony, of course, was that these new courts answered to an administration of war criminals. When David Hicks, the former kangaroo skinner from Australia, became the first kangaroo court defendant in March 2007, it became instantly clear that the government's evidence against him was very thin. The indictment merely alleged that he had trained at an al Qaeda camp, translated some manuals, and served, without fighting, in the same Taliban unit that John Walker Lindh did.

The administration then avoided the embarrassment of a trial by inviting Hicks to plead guilty to a new crime under the MCA of 2006, namely, "providing material support" to terrorists. The offer was not made by military prosecutors; it came directly from Susan J. Crawford, the politically appointed convening authority and Vice President Cheney's protégée. As his part of the plea bargain, Hicks agreed to serve a nine-month sentence in Australia, to swear that he had not been illegally mistreated, and to promise not to talk to the press for a year.[56] His deal was far less than the twenty-year sentence and lifetime gag order that John Walker Lindh was forced to accept, but then Lindh did not have the Australian government lobbying on his behalf.[57]

The new commissions, which Congress authorized, did not come close to satisfying American or international standards for a fair trial, starting with the failure to require prompt notice of the reasons for the detention.[58] The act rejected the right to a speedy trial,[59] permitted trials to be closed to the public,[60] and allowed proceedings to occur in the absence of the accused.[61] It denied prisoners the right to be tried by an independent and impartial court,[62] allowed prosecutions for offenses not previously classified as war crimes,[63] limited the right to cross-examine prosecution witnesses and to have witnesses testify on their behalf,[64] and restricted access to exculpatory evidence.[65]

Evidence obtained by coercion prior to the passage of the Detainee Treatment Act of December 30, 2005, would still be admissible.[66] Coercive tactics used to obtain information after that date could be concealed by two provisions of the MCA. The first allows military commissions to admit hearsay,[67] which means that government witnesses could claim ignorance of the coercion used to obtain the allegations from other prisoners. A second provision denies defendants the right to see all the evidence presented against them. If the accusers are undisclosed, defense attorneys would have no way to learn how they were interrogated.[68]

Denying Habeas

The Military Commissions Act of 2006 went beyond the Detainee Treatment Act of 2005 to deny habeas relief not just to prisoners at Guantánamo but to all aliens (including college students and long-term resident aliens) "who have been determined by the United States [i.e., the president] to have been properly detained as enemy combatants," even if they have already been acquitted by a civilian court.[69] This provision, too, ran counter to the principle that where there is a right, there must be a remedy.[70] It also contradicted well-established law, under which aliens have had the right to challenge the legality of their detentions since the Habeas Corpus Act of 1640.[71] U.S. courts have expressly recognized this right since at least 1813, when Chief Justice John Marshall, sitting as a circuit judge, ordered the release of Thomas Williams, an Englishman, because he had been wrongly dubbed an "enemy alien."[72] The Supreme Court reaffirmed the principle in *Rasul v. Bush* (2004), *Hamdan v. Rumsfeld* (2006), and *Boumediene v. Bush* (2008), when it held that the president cannot strip aliens of their habeas rights simply by moving them to a U.S. military prison in Cuba.[73]

Nor are "the United States" and the president synonymous. Any act of Congress purporting to grant the president exclusive authority to strip anyone protected by the Constitution of his liberty by a mere act of labeling would violate not only the habeas clause but the Fourth Amendment's ban on the unreasonable seizure of persons, the Fifth Amendment guarantee of due process, and the Sixth Amendment right to a jury trial.

The privilege of the writ of habeas corpus is even more basic than the First Amendment right to free expression. The right to be free from indefinite detention dates back to the Magna Carta (1215), if not earlier, and was refined by Parliament during the seventeenth century.[74] The framers considered it important enough to write it into the U.S. Constitution in 1787, four years before they added a bill of rights.

Historically, there was some dispute as to whether the privilege is a constitutional or statutory right. On the one hand, if it were a constitutional right, then Congress may not abolish it by legislation. It may suspend the privilege, according to Article I, Section 9, only when "in Cases of Rebellion or Invasion the public Safety may require it." These conditions did not exist in 2006 when the Military Commissions Act was passed; nor did Congress claim that they did. On the other hand, were habeas just a statutory right, then Congress may modify or repeal it, as it attempted to do in both the Detainee Treatment Act of 2005 and the Military Commissions Act of 2006.

Most scholars considered habeas to be a constitutional right, for the obvious reason that constitutions do not incorporate by reference laws that may be repealed at any time. If they did, Congress could amend the Constitution merely by passing a law, which is not how the federal Constitution is changed. Moreover, no federal habeas statute existed in 1789 when the Constitution was ratified, so there was nothing for Article I, Section 9 to incorporate into the Constitution. There was no federal habeas statute for the obvious reason that no federal courts existed under the Articles of Confederation.

Nor was the British common law respecting habeas petitions (or anything else) incorporated into *federal* law under the Articles of Confederation. The common law was adopted only by state governments because they were the governments of general jurisdiction.

The better interpretation of the Constitution was that the authors of the habeas clause intended to acknowledge the most fundamental of all rights, which they further enhanced two years later with a Bill of Rights that guaranteed personal liberty, due process of law, a speedy trial, and trial by jury. None of these rights would have meant anything if a right to challenge arbitrary detentions in court did not already exist.

This conventional understanding of the habeas clause was well grounded in the history of the "Great Writ," the text of the Constitution, and constitutional history. Even so, Attorney General Gonzales told the Senate Judiciary Committee on January 17, 2007, that "there is no express grant of habeas [corpus] in the Constitution"; he claimed there was only "a provision against taking it away."[75] By this reasoning, freedom from detention without trial is not a fundamental right; it is just another privilege that politicians may grant or repeal at their discretion. If Gonzales was right, then politicians could also revoke the right of white men to vote, because it is not expressly granted in the Constitution either.[76]

Up to that time, the Supreme Court had never expressly declared that the privilege of the writ of habeas corpus was a constitutional right. It had also permitted Congress to pass laws altering the process by which the purposes of the habeas statute may be accomplished. For example, the court has allowed Congress to substitute appellate procedures for habeas procedures but only if the alternatives were "adequate and effective."[77] But even this ruling implied that the underlying right must be constitutionally protected; otherwise, the court would have no authority to approve or disapprove legislative substitutions.

The Military Commissions Act purported to strip the courts of jurisdiction to decide *pending*, as well as future, applications for habeas relief. Legislative interference with pending cases would seem to violate due process of law.[78] It is true that the Supreme Court once allowed itself to be stripped of jurisdiction in a pending habeas case. The year was 1868, the case was *Ex parte McCardle,* and the law at issue revoked the court's appellate jurisdiction over a pending habeas petition that challenged the legality of the U.S. Army's postwar occupation of Mississippi.[79] The stakes were huge, and the case is often cited as an instance in which politically prudent court chose to avoid a confrontation with Congress. But all Congress had really done in that instance was deny the Supreme Court's jurisdiction to hear a habeas petition *on appeal.* The right to file habeas petitions with any lower federal court, or directly with the Supreme Court, remained intact.[80] So, contrary to popular belief, the Supreme Court did not allow Congress to suspend the privilege of the writ of habeas corpus in its entirety by stripping all courts of jurisdiction to hear such petitions.

Like Senator Graham, the Bush administration claimed that the MCA did not violate Article I, Section 9, because it still allowed alleged terrorists to *appeal* a Combat Status Review Tribunal's detention decision to the U.S. Court of Appeals for the District of Columbia. But even this alternative would be an inadequate substitute for the broad investigative powers of a genuine habeas proceeding in a federal district court because the court of appeals would be forbidden to conduct an evidentiary hearing of its own. Nor would it be able to send the case down to a district court that could. Its review would be limited to those facts that a far-from-independent CSRT had chosen to gather. The court of appeals would have to assume that information contained in intelligence files is true, even if it appeared to come from patently dubious sources. Under the MCA, the CSRTs would remain free to admit evidence obtained by torture, and prevent the accused from calling witnesses who might discredit the allegations. Nor did the act allow prisoners to be represented by counsel at CSRT hearings or learn from whom the accusations against them came.

At a habeas hearing, the government would have to justify the prisoner's detention, and he would be entitled to a presumption of innocence. On appeal from a CSRT proceeding, however, he would be presumed guilty and prevented from effectively proving his innocence.

Military Necessity?

In *Hamdan,* the Supreme Court ruled that the Bush administration had failed to show a sufficient degree of military necessity to justify the "irregular tribunals" (commissions) that the president had authorized. The new commissions authorized in the 2006 act were similarly irregular when measured against the standards prescribed by the Uniform Code of Military Justice, which Congress did not repeal and which effectuates both the Geneva Conventions and constitutional guarantees. The UCMJ, unlike the Military Commissions Act, does not permit the admission of hearsay. It does not permit military prosecutors, as opposed to military judges, to decide what is too secret to be revealed in court or deny defense counsel the right to investigate how the prosecution got its evidence. Nor does the UCMJ permit a lower standard of justice for aliens or allow military judges to ignore established legal precedents. To hold that the new commissions are militarily necessary, a military judge would have to accept an argument that the Supreme Court in *Hamdan* did not—that is, justice in the war against terrorism cannot be regular and impartial but must be rigged to maximize convictions.

The Delaying Game

Truth be told, the new commissions, like the old, did not need to try anyone. Indeed, as the Bush administration understood, it would be better if they did not. Trials would focus unwanted attention on how the prisoners were interrogated and on how little hard evidence the military had for holding most of the prisoners. The chief reason for the commissions was to legitimate the detentions by creating the illusion that trials were on the way or to coerce prisoners like David Hicks to plea bargain, in which case they could be convicted without trial.[81]

A secondary function of the Military Commissions Act was to delay legal challenges to the detentions by interminable litigation. For example, after the act was passed, the Justice Department moved to dismiss all pending habeas petitions from GTMO prisoners, insisting that the court-stripping provisions of the law deprived those prisoners of the right to legal counsel. Prosecutors also forbade prisoners like José Padilla to tell their attorneys how they were interrogated because interrogation techniques are, per se, state secrets.[82] The department also claimed that prosecutors could extend the detentions by resisting everything defense counsel would normally seek, including the identities of secret accusers and pre-trial discovery to determine if coercion was used on those accusers.

The act also said that "no person may invoke" international humanitarian law "as a source of rights"[83] and that no foreign or international law shall provide a rule of decision for any court. Taken literally, this direction could mean that American judges cannot refer to the decisions of British judges in order to understand their common legal heritage, something American judges have done for centuries. It also invaded the Constitution's separation of powers. Congress can no more tell a judge how to engage in legal reasoning than a court can tell Congress how to make political calculations. Americans have always known, even before Marshall said it in *Marbury v. Madison,* that it is manifestly the duty of judges to say what the law is in cases properly before them.[84]

Congressional Abdications of Power

So how could such legislation pass? The short answer is that most members of Congress care little for the integrity of the legislative process, the primacy of Congress in the making of public policy, or constructive, bipartisan oversight. The Republican Party's leaders, and most of its members, have found it especially advantageous to support executive power and trash any institution, including Congress and the courts, that has the temerity to limit that power.

Moderate Republicans, who once dominated in the party, are nearly extinct. Their decline began with the so-called Goldwater Revolution of 1964, when their party moved to the right and began to capitalize on white resentment and fear of "black power," not just in the South, but among working-class white ethnic groups in the North.

All of this history is familiar. Less familiar may be the extent to which conservative Republicans have come to ground their party in the South, with its military bases, and in the high-tech, aerospace communities in Southern California, the Rocky Mountains, and the desert West. As a result of these strategies, today's right-leaning Republican Party receives substantial financing by corporations dependent on the military-industrial complex that President Eisenhower warned the citizenry against. These campaign donors have much to gain from the privatization of formerly military-run functions in Afghanistan and Iraq, including the interrogation of prisoners. Few Americans appreciate the extent to which traditional military duties, including interrogations, have been contracted out to corporations. By 2007, almost as many civilian contractors were serving in Iraq as there were soldiers and in most cases at higher salaries.[85]

Power by Assertion

Less well known still may be the extent to which the Republican leadership of the House and Senate was induced to abdicate legislative prerogatives to the Bush-Cheney presidency. By the 1960s it was becoming painfully clear, in Professor Aaron Wildavsky's words, that two presidencies had emerged out of the Cold War: a domestic presidency in which bargaining with Congress is still necessary and a foreign affairs presidency in which bargaining plays, at best, a small role, especially in the short term.[86] The name of the new game is *power by assertion*, played by assertive presidents who know that the leaders of both parties have become too dependent on executive largesse to fight for congressional or judicial prerogatives.

Central to the exercise of power by assertion is secrecy. Since World War II, if not before, presidents and their secret agencies have broken the law, lied with impunity, and defied Congress to do anything about it. During the 1970s, congressional investigations tried to establish bipartisan legislative oversight in the form of House and Senate intelligence committees, but the agencies and their allies in the White House were able to neuter their congressional critics by giving them classified briefings and then insisting that no notes be taken, no staff be consulted, and no other members of Congress be informed of what transpired.[87] During the 1980s, confident that Congress would not hold them in contempt, the agencies also withheld crucial information from the oversight committees and gave false testimony about the Iran-contra affair.

In 2001, Vice President Cheney succeeded in persuading the intelligence committees of the two houses to do a joint investigation of the failure to anticipate the attacks of 9/11. Joint committees are typically less assertive than competing House and Senate committees and are more easily undermined by members of the president's party. Representative Goss, then the highly partisan House cochair (and former CIA officer), saw to it that the committee's report did not mention that President Bush had received a briefing on August 6, 2001, expressly warning him that bin Laden was "determined to strike in US."[88] Goss and his Senate cochair, Lindsey Graham, also encouraged the FBI to investigate members of Congress for a possible leak, thereby diverting attention from intelligence failures. Goss was so helpful at blocking meaningful oversight that the president appointed him director of the Central Intelligence Agency in 2004.

During the Bush-Cheney years, the Republican leadership of the House and Senate abdicated its responsibility for defending their branch's independence from the executive. The Senate's Republican leaders capitulated to the vice president's demand that he sit in on their Tuesday strategy meetings, even as Democrats had refused to do this in 1961 when their majority leader, Lyndon Johnson, assumed the vice presidency. Shortly before President Bush's first inaugural in 2001, Speaker Dennis Hastert (R-IL) quietly gave the vice president a second Capitol Hill office, on the House side. As a result, Cheney did not need to approach House members on their turf; he could summon them to his.[89]

Conservative Republicans also showed considerable contempt for fair legislative proceedings. For example, Republican leaders of both houses drove most of their counterterrorism bills through Congress without bothering to hold hearings. When moderates held hearings and voted out of committee bills that the leadership and president opposed, the Republican leadership was not above substituting a bill drafted by the executive, restricting floor debate, and keeping voting open whenever it needed to round up more votes to prevail. With ruthless efficiency they shut Democrats out of the conferences where differences between House and Senate bills are ironed out, sometimes producing for floor votes bills that no Democrats had seen. Republican managers were even known to alter the content of bills after all the conferees had signed off on them.[90]

Supplicants

The Republican leadership's capitulation to an irresponsible Republican president is only part of the story because Democratic leaders did little in opposition or after they took control of Congress in 2007. To understand their failure, and perhaps why Congress as a whole had worse poll ratings than the Bush presidency, one must understand the rewards system for most of its members. The harsh truth is that most members of Congress work part time on legislative business and full time on getting reelected, which is why the effective workday on Capitol Hill for most members begins on Tuesday and ends on Thursday.

To the extent that members do work on legislation, they strive mainly to serve the interests of constituents, donors, lobbyists, or the administration in power. Little in the culture or process rewards politicians who stand up for the rights of hated minorities, the constitutional prerogatives of Congress, or the independence of the judiciary. To members of Congress, focused as they are on the spoils of domestic politics, law is not fixed. It is merely fixable for a price. Much law is not meant to be predictable. It is just an invitation to negotiations, if not in the halls of Congress, then later in the bowels of bureaucracy.[91]

As perpetual campaigners, members tend to favor position taking and credit taking over legislating and investigating, which require more thankless attention to detail.[92] If possible, members prefer to cast two votes on every issue, so that they can claim to be for or against the bill and thereby justify their record to opposing groups.[93] Thus, when members confront Constitution-stripping bills, such as the Detainee Treatment Act, the Military Commissions Act, the PATRIOT Act, or the Protect America [wiretap immunity] Act of 2007, they do not ask what the bills contain and how they might harm liberty, equality, or justice. All most members really want to know is how voting for or against the laws will affect their prospects for reelection. Following 9/11, members did not demand that emergency powers legislation go through public hearings in both houses so that its defects could be exposed. They were willing to vote for the bills without reading their text, consulting experts, or considering their long-term implications because they were desperate to deflect charges that they were "soft on terrorism."

The same is true of oversight, especially in the intelligence committees. Oversight tends to be episodic, reflecting the interests of committee chairmen rather than any systematic attention to the people's interests. Most committee members attend hearings to obtain face time on television. Since 9/11 some members, such as Randy "Duke" Cunningham (R-CA), came to appreciate the opportunity to steer contracts for intelligence and paramilitary work to supporters.

According to Bruce Fein, a former Reagan administration lawyer who has dealt with Congress for thirty years, most members "know nothing about the Constitution, have never read a Federalist Paper, and are mostly concerned with currying favor with the White House and getting reelected."[94] Constitutional law has little to do with the practice of interest-group politics or the unending search for campaign contributions.[95] To win reelection, members must service constituents, especially major donors, who care most passionately about the economic interests of their companies, states, or districts. So most members tend to focus on domestic politics, as they curry favor with executive branch officials who disburse contracts and grants.[96] Few members can afford to alienate the president by holding public hearings into his abuses of power, especially in the realm of foreign relations, for which there is little constituency interest. Prevarication was common during the era called Watergate, and it is even more widespread today. Good legislation has little to do with being a member of Congress.[97] As Senator James Reed (D-MO), an irascible curmudgeon, observed back in 1924,

> [The pending measure] will be voted for by cowards who would rather hang on to their present offices than serve their country or defend its Constitution. It would not receive a vote in this body were there not many individuals looking over their shoulders toward the ballot-boxes in November, their poltroon souls aquiver with apprehension lest they may pay the price of courageous duty by the loss of the votes of some bloc, clique, or coterie backing this infamous proposal. My language may seem brutal. If so, it is because it lays on the blistering truth.[98]

The Supreme Irony

The great irony of the torture policy, as in so much else, is that the Bush administration did not have to go it alone. As the Iraq War Resolution, the Detainee Treatment Act, the Military Commissions Act, the PATRIOT Act and its amendments, and the Protect America Act all demonstrate, Bush did not have to usurp authority to get what he wanted. With the right combination of bluster and stroking, the president can usually persuade Congress to give him what he wants, even at the cost of its own prerogatives.

9

JUDICIAL COMPLICITY

No one will question that [the war] power is the most dangerous one to free government in the whole catalogue of powers. It usually is invoked in haste and excitement when calm legislative consideration of constitutional limitation is difficult. It is executed in a time of patriotic fervor that makes moderation unpopular. And, worst of all, it is interpreted by the judges under the influence of the same passions and pressures.

—Justice Robert H. Jackson[1]

When Professor Alan Dershowitz proposed that Congress empower judges to issue warrants authorizing the torture of individual suspects, he assumed that judges can be expected, more often than not, to do what is morally right.[2] There is little evidence to support that assumption.

For most of American history, according to political scientist Robert A. Dahl, most judges, including most members of the Supreme Court, have gone along with whatever the dominant political coalition of their times demanded.[3] They supported slavery and enforced the fugitive slave laws. After slavery was abolished, they upheld racially discriminatory laws for nearly a century. They enforced laws curbing the free speech of antiwar protesters during World War I and the mass detention, without evidence, of persons of Japanese ancestry during World War II.

True, for a brief moment in the 1950s and 1960s, the Supreme Court led conventional moral, legal, and political thought. It struck down Jim Crow laws. It expanded freedom of expression, the rights of criminal defendants, and rights of privacy. Many Americans came to believe that judges might have the independence and integrity to defend the Constitution and laws against overreaching politicians and bureaucrats. But that moment passed, and post-9/11 judges returned to behaving like bishops, blessing, or at least tolerating, the latest assertions of political power.

Judges in Wartime

In the realm of war powers, in particular, courts have only rarely curbed over-reaching presidents. In times of war, fear overcomes distrust of power. Americans rally around the flag. The president wraps himself in the flag and the United States becomes very close to what Arthur M. Schlesinger, Jr., called a plebiscitary dictatorship.[4] Civil liberties are curbed. Politicians defer to the president, and judges hesitate to rule against them until the crisis has passed.

There have been exceptions to this pattern, but for the most part, judges have been only marginally more protective of the Constitution during wartime than politicians have. Some observers praise this "judicial self-restraint" as necessary to protect the politically fragile institution of judicial review. Conservative Republicans have gone further, loudly campaigning against "judicial activism" on such hot button issues as affirmative action, abortion, and gay rights, while quietly supporting judicial activism in support of more executive power, fewer civil liberties, limited access to judicial remedies, and less regulation of the economy. Conservatives did not complain when Republican activism on the Supreme Court stopped the recounting of votes in Florida in 2002 and gave the presidency to George W. Bush. Indeed, conservatives lobbied furiously through the Federalist Society to pack the courts—especially the courts most likely to decide questions of presidential power—with authoritarian Republicans.

But even nonpartisan judges of both parties have been reluctant to overturn wartime assertions of unconstitutional power until the crisis has passed. This was true during the Civil War, when the Supreme Court chose not to rule against the prosecution of civilians before military commissions until the fighting was over. It was also true during World War II, when the justices allowed legal challenges to the Japanese internment and military rule in the Hawaiian Islands to languish until President Roosevelt had been safely reelected. But the greatest act of judicial deference probably occurred in *Ex parte Quirin* (1942) when the justices, eager to give the public a small victory in their darkest hour, upheld the hasty trial and swift execution of "Nazi saboteurs" without explaining why.[5]

I do not mean to suggest that judges are any worse than other mortals; it's just that they are not, for all their training and status, reliably better. Maj. Gen. Michael Dunlavey, the reservist who initiated the abuse of prisoners at GTMO, was a judge of the Court of Common Pleas in Erie, Pennsylvania, in civilian life. Alberto Gonzales, who presided over the torture policy's development, was once a member of the Texas Supreme Court. Former district court judge Michael Mukasey, who succeeded Gonzales as attorney general, refused to admit that waterboarding is a crime, and Jay Bybee, as head of the Office of Legal Counsel, won his position on the U.S. Court of Appeals for the Ninth Circuit after issuing the most infamous of all torture memos.

The "Shocks the Conscience" Test

Judges drawn from both parties have supported, and sometimes opposed, abuses of executive power. In recent years, however, conservative Republican judges have accepted the kidnapping of suspects in the war against illegal drugs. They would not go so far as to authorize abductions in advance, but they are willing to wink at them afterward.

Liberal judges have been more hesitant. In 1974, for example, a liberal panel of the U.S. Court of Appeals for the Second Circuit refused to accept a criminal case against Francisco Toscanino after he was kidnapped in Montevideo by Uruguayan policemen in the pay of the United States and tortured while being delivered to the United States. "This is conduct that shocks the conscience," the court said.[6]

But then Congress and successive presidents declared war on crime, and when drug enforcement agents bribed foreign policemen to kidnap three suspects in the 1980s, courts winked. Typical of these cases was *United States v. Cordero.*[7] The U.S. Court of Appeals for the First Circuit held that a suspected cocaine smuggler, Josephine Cordero, lacked standing to challenge her abduction, which was at the behest of American agents and in circumvention of the U.S. extradition treaty with Panama. "[E]xtradition treaties," Judge (and future justice) Stephen Breyer declared, are not human rights laws. They "are made [only] for the benefit of the governments concerned." Besides, American officials did not personally kidnap her; they just asked a friendly dictatorship to do that for them.[8] One has to wonder whether Breyer would have been equally accepting had the U.S. government arranged for the kidnappers to torture her along the way.

Breyer apparently did not know that modern extradition treaties were developed during the Napoleonic era not just to facilitate the recovery of fugitive criminals. They were also meant to stop illegal abductions by covert foreign agents and to protect such patriotic revolutionaries as Giuseppe Mazzini of Italy and Louis Kossuth of Hungary from being surrendered as criminals to the regimes they fought to overthrow.

At no time during the first century and a half of American extradition law did the executive assert or reserve a power to kidnap fugitives, even when extradition was not possible. On the contrary, the United States refused even to negotiate extradition treaties with most Muslim nations and the Soviet bloc because it was loath to surrender anyone to an unjust regime.

This attitude changed gradually with the proliferation of airplane hijackings in the 1960s and the growth of terrorist atrocities in the 1970s. By the time the Reagan administration came along, the U.S. government had lost its historic scruples about sending political fugitives back to the regimes they had fought to overthrow. Probable cause hearings before independent judges were considered cumbersome while the exigencies of international cooperation between law enforcement and intelligence agencies led to administrative exchanges—first, by targeted deportation; and later, by kidnapping.

As a result, New Deal liberals like Stephen Breyer could warm to the idea that extradition treaties do not confer rights on individuals; they simply grant options to the executive. Alberto Gonzales could not have said it better. A duty to obey international law does not arise, no matter what a treaty says or customary international law provides. If U.S. agents corrupt foreign policemen, that conduct is not our judiciary's concern because American judges have no obligation to defend the rule of law beyond our borders or to police what our law enforcement or intelligence agencies do. That position is the essence of Judge Breyer's opinion in *Cordero,* which laid the foundation for the Supreme Court's endorsement of abduction a few years later.

The amorality of this approach is far from the ethic that led Washington, Jefferson, and Webster to refuse to engage in extradition with corrupt and unjust regimes. But American law enforcement was in its infancy then. As law enforcement agencies grew and as the pursuit of fugitives became easier, the demand for swapping fugitives became greater and more bureaucratized. By the 1970s, "disguised extradition" of the sort used in *Cordero* was probably more common than lawful extradition.[9] From there it was a short step to rationalizing kidnapping and torture.

Juan Ramon Matta-Ballesteros was one of several drug lords to be tortured during the 1980s as part of an American-organized abduction from Honduras. He had numerous stun-gun burns to prove it.[10] Matta-Ballesteros was considered one of the worst of his kind, so the trial judge was pleased to rule that his "allegations of torture do not meet the required level of outrageousness."[11] The judge also reasoned that zapping a prisoner repeatedly with high-voltage electricity did not shock the judicial conscience because Matta-Ballesteros had escaped from an American prison prior to his abduction.[12]

Nor was the Supreme Court shocked to learn that the Drug Enforcement Administration (DEA) had ordered the abduction of Humberto Alvarez-Machaín, a Mexican doctor, from Guadalajara to the United States. Chief Justice Rehnquist ruled for a largely conservative majority that the doctor's kidnapping did not violate the Fourth Amendment, even though like Matta-Ballesteros's and Cordero's, it was plotted by American officials in Washington, D.C., and carried out, in part, on American soil. Nor did the justices see anything wrong with accepting jurisdiction over people who had been stolen by government agents while simultaneously enforcing laws against private kidnappings or the receiving of stolen goods.[13] The justices did not even consider whether they should decline jurisdiction in order to protect the integrity of American courts, the rule of law in Mexico, or the rule of law in the United States. The sole issue to the majority was whether the U.S.-Mexican extradition treaty expressly forbade the abduction. It did not, so, as Breyer had done, they ruled that the kidnapping was not illegal.

The "critical flaw" in this "monstrous opinion," Justice Stevens wrote in a dissent, was its failure to recognize that Dr. Alvarez-Machaín had been the victim of an *official* kidnapping.[14] But Stevens, joined by Justices Harry Blackmun and Sandra Day O'Connor, did not argue, as he could have, that official kidnappings violate the principle of limited government that the liberty and due process clauses of the Fifth Amendment help to guarantee. Their dissent focused wholly on the treaty, implying that all nine justices agreed that American officials can kidnap foreigners in foreign lands with impunity because such people have no federal constitutional right, once in the United States, to challenge the illegality of their abduction by either a habeas petition or in defense against a criminal prosecution.

Another disturbing case involved the admissibility of evidence obtained through U.S. drug agents conducting a warrantless search of the Mexican home of René Martin Verdugo-Urquidez. The trial and appellate courts ruled that the search was unconstitutional,[15] but the Supreme Court reversed, 6-3, with an opinion that would lay the groundwork for allowing abductions.[16] Writing for the majority, Chief Justice Rehnquist reasoned that the Fourth Amendment was like an overcoat: U.S. agents could remove it when conducting searches abroad. The suspect had no reasonable expectation of privacy or freedom from judicially unauthorized searches by American agents because he was a Mexican living in Mexico. To have U.S. constitutional rights, Rehnquist reasoned, the accused would have to have developed a "voluntary connection with the country" that would place him "among the 'people' of the United States."[17]

The holding is not only bad law; it is bad political theory. The U.S. Constitution was not meant to be another medieval, commercial, or colonial contract between the rulers and the ruled. Madison's Bill of Rights did not limit the freedom from unreasonable seizures, including abductions and indefinite detentions, to citizens or resident aliens. The Bill of Rights speaks of the rights of the people and of persons and says, "Congress shall make no law . . . ," precisely because the framers saw limited government and personal liberty as two sides of the same coin.

The founders also thought largely in terms of the Protestant theory of natural rights based on what we would today call personhood or human rights. So far as they were concerned, fundamental rights were not just political rights. They were natural rights that accrued at birth and belonged to all people equally. As the Declaration of Independence asserted, they were endowed by their Creator directly to each person without the intercession of princes or politicians.

Like many conservative Republicans, including the authors of the torture memos, Chief Justice Rehnquist looked upon the Fourth Amendment as a statement of personal rights only, unconnected to the concept of limited government. The framers, however, emphasized limited government as the chief guarantee of liberty. They did not include a Bill of Rights in the original Constitution not because they didn't favor rights but because they feared that the enumeration of rights would be read as denying *any* rights not listed. They agreed to add the Bill of Rights when the anti-Federalists proposed the Ninth Amendment, which instructs judges to read the rights of the people broadly, so as to prevent the government from overreaching. In the late 1700s, limited government and guaranteed liberties were seen as twin pillars of freedom, with each necessary to the other.

Logically speaking, Rehnquist's opinion in *Verdugo-Urquidez* eliminated all constitutional deterrents to abduction, torture, and assassination by U.S. agents overseas. It also rejected the major premise of *Toscanino*, which was that foreign nationals could challenge deprivations of their liberty by American agents both within the United States and abroad because the Bill of Rights both protects people and bars institutional lawlessness. But most of this reasoning was swept aside in the abduction cases.

Similarly, a federal court in Florida was willing to accept jurisdiction over former Panamanian strongman Manuel Noriega, even though he was kidnapped pursuant to an invasion that Congress had not authorized.[18] The Noriega abduction in many ways is a forerunner of the more recent program of extraordinary rendition, although his kidnapping was not for the purpose of torture by foreign agents. It also provides some insight into the world of covert operations.

As Panama's de facto head of state, General Noriega had allowed Panama's banks to launder illegal drug money on a grand scale. He also permitted the processing and international shipment of cocaine and became rich from payoffs. The U.S. government had known about these activities since the early 1970s but looked the other way because he helped the DEA capture rival smugglers[19] and aided the Reagan administration in its secret war in Nicaragua. So long as anticommunism was the U.S. government's top priority, Noriega was not only protected, the CIA paid him a stipend that in some years rivaled President Reagan's salary.[20]

By the late 1980s, however, Noriega's chief protectors, CIA director William Casey and White House aide Oliver North, could no longer shield him from federal prosecutors in Miami. Casey was dying of cancer; North was facing prosecution for his role in the Iran-contra scandal. In 1989, Noriega nullified free elections and became the world's first narco-dictator, provoking senators as different from each other as John Kerry (D-MA) and Jesse Helms (R-NC) to call for his ouster.

Extradition was legally, as well as politically, impossible. Assassination was discussed but rejected; a post-Watergate executive order forbade it. So abduction was proposed. Reagan's secretary of state, George Shultz, was all for it, and the president ordered snatch plans to be drawn up.

To create a patina of legal authority for the abduction, Reagan's successor, George H. W. Bush, commissioned a series of legal opinions favorable to the plan. In June 1989, Assistant Attorney General Douglas Kmiec, head of the Office of Legal Counsel, quietly reversed a nine-year-old Carter administration legal opinion that opposed using FBI agents to seize fugitives abroad in violation of international law.[21] In October 1989, when a second coup against Noriega failed, Senator Helms proposed legislation authorizing the U.S. Army to go into Panama and kidnap him.[22] The administration of George H. W. Bush opposed the bill, but in November it produced a legal opinion declaring that the Posse Comitatus Act, which forbids the military enforcement of civilian law within the United States, did not forbid the military from facilitating prosecutions in the United States by seizing wanted persons abroad.[23] Another memo advised that the executive order forbidding assassinations, adopted in the wake of congressional investigations in the 1970s, did not bar U.S. support for coups d'état so long as the death of a foreign leader during the coup was not the administration's explicit goal.[24] Fearful of what scholars and human rights advocates might say about these opinions, the Justice Department tried to keep them secret, even from Congress. When their existence was leaked, the department refused to disclose their text, thus endorsing the idea of secret law.[25] On December 20, 1989, the United States undertook the most ambitious kidnapping operation in its history. More than twenty-four thousand troops attacked Panama, with thirteen thousand inside the Canal Zone. Twenty-six Americans and more than seven hundred Panamanians, mostly civilians, died as a result, and property damage exceeded $1.5 billion.[26]

Abductions tend to occur most frequently when the abducting government's respect for international law, human rights, and the sovereignty of other nations is low. This description was true of Nazi Germany, which conducted a number of kidnappings in the 1930s, and of the Soviet Union and East Germany in the late 1940s. It became true of the United States in the last quarter of the twentieth century when metaphorical wars on different kinds of crime, such as the war on drugs, became popular.

Ironically, conservative jurists who approve such practices often claim to be bound by the founders' original intent. But transnational kidnapping was not something the founders endorsed. When the Jacobin faction in revolutionary France asked President Washington if he would wink at the abduction of France's former ambassador, Citizen Genêt (a Girondist), the president refused. Washington detested Edmond-Charles Genêt, but he did not believe that his administration could—or should—allow kidnapping on American soil.[27] One reason for Washington's refusal was obvious. Since its founding, the United States adamantly opposed the British navy's abduction of sailors from American ships.

When the HMS *Leopard* attacked the USS *Chesapeake* in 1807 and abducted sailors from its crew, President Thomas Jefferson ordered an embargo on trade with Great Britain and armed American coastal forts. When the British abductions did not end, they became a major cause of the War of 1812. But what our forefathers would not tolerate when used against the United States, our current judges seem disposed to accept when practiced by the United States abroad.

Ignoring the Consequences

In deciding individual cases, judges have an obligation not just to follow precedent but to look beyond immediate outcomes and consider how a doctrinal change might work out over time.[28] Unfortunately, nothing in the opinions of Judge Breyer or Justice Rehnquist showed much concern for the political, legal, or human consequences of allowing government agencies to engage in kidnapping.

They did not have to look further than their newspapers to understand what those consequences could be. By sending warplanes to intercept an Egyptian airliner in 1985, the Reagan administration succeeded in capturing terrorists who had hijacked the cruise ship *Achille Lauro*. Unfortunately, diverting the plane to Italy caused the most pro-American administration in that country in forty years to collapse.[29] The diversion also humiliated President Hosni Mubarak of Egypt and provoked attacks on his pro-American policies.[30] The *Matta-*

Ballesteros, Alvarez-Machaín, and *Verdugo-Urquidez* decisions sent a message to drug traffickers, but they also damaged U.S. relations with Latin America.[31] Mexico curbed DEA operations within the country, demanded extradition of the abductors, and insisted on renegotiating the extradition treaty to ban kidnapping. It also lodged criminal charges against the DEA agents who authorized the abduction.[32] To restore DEA operations in Mexico, both President George H. W. Bush and President Clinton had to promise in writing that they would not authorize any kidnappings in Mexico during their administrations. Clinton also had to agree to a new extradition treaty that would bar abductions in perpetuity.[33] Meanwhile, Canada warned the United States that any government-sanctioned abduction from its soil would be regarded as a crime and a violation of the United States–Canada extradition treaty.[34] More recently, Germany has brought criminal charges against CIA personnel for kidnapping Khaled el-Masri from Macedonia. Italy has initiated proceedings against CIA agents for abducting Abu Omar from Milan, and the United Kingdom is considering criminal charges against British and CIA agents for the torture of Binyam Mohamed in Morocco.

These actions were the peaceful responses. On November 12, 1997, four U.S. oil executives and their taxi driver were shot to death in Karachi, Pakistan, apparently in retaliation for the U.S. abduction and conviction of Mir Aimal Kasi for machine-gunning CIA employees in 1993.[35] Matta-Ballesteros's abduction set off anti-American riots in Honduras. On April 8, 1988, more than a thousand protesters sacked the U.S. embassy, set fire to its annex, and destroyed the consulate. In Iran, the Parliament retaliated against the OLC's decision to allow FBI agents to arrest people abroad by giving Iran's executive the authority to arrest Americans anywhere on earth for offenses against Iranian interests and bring them to Iran for trial by Islamic courts.[36] The first target for abduction, an Iranian newspaper declared, should be the captain of the USS *Vincennes,* which mistakenly shot down an Iranian airliner over the Persian Gulf in July 1988.[37] Death threats followed, and the following March the captain's wife was nearly killed in San Diego when a bomb attached to her van exploded.[38]

Abduction, whether it is for torture or not, is the political equivalent of crack cocaine. Judges need to recognize, as Breyer, Rehnquist, and their colleagues did not, that allowing the kidnapping of a bad guy may give some Americans immediate gratification, but that high will also do long-term damage to foreign relations, to the persons involved, to the innocent victims of retaliations, and to others' respect for the law. Judges also need to understand that a nation that feels so strongly about its own sovereignty and purports to believe in the rule of law cannot go around violently breaching the sovereignty of other nations. Such hypocrisy only provokes more reprisals against Americans, both at home and abroad, because terrorism is mainly about reprisals.

Judges also need to understand that permitting warlike measures to replace traditional legal practices really allows the executive to wage war upon law. This jurisprudence is not wise. As Thomas Paine warned two centuries ago, "An avidity to punish is always dangerous to liberty [because] it leads men to stretch, to misinterpret, and to misapply even the best of laws. He that would make his own liberty secure must guard even his enemy from oppression, for if he violates this duty, he establishes a precedent that will reach to himself."[39]

The Federalist Society

It might be reassuring to view the current judiciary's deference to executive overreaching as a mere swing of the proverbial pendulum that will correct itself when the crisis has passed. That is the message of pro-executive conservatives like the late chief justice Rehnquist.[40] It is also the metaphor of those who assume that the United States has multiple constitutions—that is, one for war and one for peace, or one for overt and one for covert government—during episodic or perpetual crises.

Either way, the metaphor is misleading. Legal doctrines don't just swing back and forth with the times. They accumulate and change based on evolving legal precedents. For example, the Fourth Amendment's guarantee against the unreasonable seizure of persons meant a great deal to the framers of the Constitution. Now it means little when citizens as well as aliens can be held, incommunicado and without charges; tormented; and brutalized for years. It means even less when judges deny alleged terrorists, against whom little reliable evidence exists, access to legal remedies. Justice Robert Jackson warned of the lasting power of legal precedents in his dissent to one of the Japanese internment cases: "Once a judicial opinion rationalizes such an order, [t]he principle then lies about like a loaded weapon, ready for the hand of any authority that can bring forward a plausible claim of an urgent need. Every repetition imbeds that principle more deeply in our law and thinking and expands it to new purposes."[41]

But this power is precisely what "movement conservatives" have been seeking since the 1970s. They came together in defense of President Nixon, who, among other things, authorized a host of federal agencies—including the FBI, the Justice Department, the U.S. Army, the NSA, and the CIA—as well as White House staffers to spy on, harass, and discredit political opponents. Nixon even ordered his subordinates to have their covert operatives break into the Brookings Institution, a liberal think tank, to steal some documents.

Back then, former OLC head Justice Antonin Scalia, former solicitor general Robert Bork, and former assistant attorney general and now judge Laurence Silberman all worked for Attorney General John Mitchell, who went to prison for ordering the White House plumbers to burglarize the Democratic Party's headquarters at the Watergate apartment complex and the offices of Daniel Ellsberg's psychiatrist. Dick Cheney worked for Donald Rumsfeld, then secretary of defense. Rumsfeld was also the titular defendant in a lawsuit that successfully challenged the military's harassment of the Democratic Party's club in Germany and cost taxpayers $200,000 in damages.[42]

Since then, these movement conservatives have worked to weaken the federal judiciary, undermine congressional oversight, enhance executive power, and expand government secrecy. They fought the few reforms to come out of the post-Watergate investigations and defeated congressional and judicial efforts to hold the Reagan administration accountable for the Iran-contra scandal.

In 1987, after his nomination to the Supreme Court was rejected in a bitter fight, Robert Bork predicted that a new tide of conservative jurists, "often associated with the Federalist Society," would "sweep the elegant, erudite, pretentious, and toxic detritus of liberal jurisprudence out to sea."[43] Founded in 1982 to give conservative students a way to challenge liberal orthodoxy within most law schools and generously funded by the John M. Olin, Scaife, and Coors foundations, the Federalist Society now claims forty thousand members.[44] It expends some of its energies and much of its five-million-dollar annual budget on academic conferences.

Most of the society's influence, however, comes from the informal networks it has developed to promote the partisan causes and judicial aspirations of conservative attorneys. Members played a major role in the campaign to discredit President Clinton and remove him from office. They also helped conservatives on the Supreme Court make George W. Bush president by forcibly delaying the recounting of votes in Broward County, Florida, during the 2000 presidential election. For all its claims to being a debating society, the society's chief objectives have been to obtain judgeships for movement conservatives, not to promote the evenhanded administration of law, but to expand executive power, curb civil liberties, and restrict the access of the poor, minorities, victims of medical malpractice, criminal suspects, and immigrants to judicial relief.

The society has been remarkably successful. More than a third of the judges that President Bush appointed to U.S. courts of appeal are Federalist Society members.[45] Four of its members now serve on the U.S. Supreme Court: Scalia, Thomas, Samuel Alito, and John Roberts. Forty-two have been appointed to U.S. courts of appeals, including Laurence H. Silberman (of the D.C. Circuit), J. Michael Luttig (Fourth Circuit), and Jay Bybee (Ninth Circuit).[46] More often than not, these judges have hired Federalist Society members as their law clerks and recommended them for judicial and administration positions. In 1986, all twelve assistant attorneys general in the Reagan administration were society members. Other members, including Samuel Alito, worked for the Office of Legal Counsel, where they developed the idea of a unitary executive and championed presidential signing statements. By 1989, membership in the society was "a prerequisite for law students seeking clerkships with many Reagan judicial appointees, as well as for employment in the Justice Department and the White House."[47] From these positions the faithful have gone on to become U.S. attorneys and, eventually, judges.

For all its gestures toward academic impartiality, the society's chief objective is to turn American law in a more authoritarian direction by packing the federal courts with like-minded judges. Liberals are invited to its conferences. Some of its members are libertarians, but their careers are not promoted by the organization. Thus, when President Bush nominated a nonmember, Harriet Miers, to the Supreme Court, society leaders campaigned against her. When Bush replaced her with a Federalist Society member, Samuel Alito, the society hired Creative Response Concepts, the public relations firm that managed the "swift-boating" of Senator John Kerry's war record in 2004, to train movement conservatives to speak for Alito on radio and television.[48]

Federal civil service law forbids the selection of career lawyers in the Department of Justice on the basis of partisanship, but between 2003 and 2006, the civil rights, voting rights, and appellate divisions hired a total of eleven lawyers who admitted membership in the Federalist Society. Their job was not to promote civil rights and liberties but to undermine them, as Donald Rumsfeld and Dick Cheney had done during the Nixon administration when they decapitated legal services for the poor in 1970. Seven lawyers within the three sections have been members of the Republican National Lawyers Association, including two who were Bush-Cheney campaign workers. Several formerly worked for Whitewater prosecutor Kenneth Starr, former attorney general Edwin Meese, Senator Trent Lott (R-MS), and the conservative Mississippi judge Charles Pickering.[49]

Most of the Bush administration lawyers who contributed to the torture policy were also members of the Federalist Society. They include Attorney General John Ashcroft, Deputy Attorney General Larry Thompson (who signed the order deporting Maher Arar to Syria), Homeland Security Secretary Michael Chertoff (who coerced the hapless John Walker Lindh into twenty years behind bars), and OLC lawyers Jay Bybee and John Yoo, who issued the torture memos. Other torture policy attorneys active in the society include Bradford Berenson, Brett Kavanaugh, and Timothy Flanigan, all of the White House Counsel's Office; Undersecretary of State and U.S. Ambassador to the United Nations John Bolton; and Defense Department General Counsel Jim Haynes. Former attorney general William P. Barr, who headed the Office of Legal Counsel in 1989 and suggested the use of military commissions to Bush-Cheney lawyers in 2001, is also a Federalist Society member.[50] So, too, is Judge Richard J. Leon, who refused to consolidate his few habeas cases to Judge Joyce Green and subsequently denied those petitioners their day in court.[51]

On the Senate Judiciary Committee, which must consent to all judicial nominations, the Federalist Society has been represented by Senator Hatch. During the years he chaired that committee, Hatch went so far as to exclude the American Bar Association from advising on the qualifications of judicial nominees.

The symbol of the Federalist Society is James Madison, but nothing could be more misleading. Madison's chief contribution to American jurisprudence was the constitutional system of checks and balances, which the society seeks to tear down by concentrating power in the executive branch, weakening congressional oversight, undermining judicial review, and expanding secrecy. Madison would be particularly appalled at the society's support for unchecked war powers. "A delegation of [war] powers" to the president, he wrote "would [strike], not only at the fabric of our Constitution, but at the foundation of all well organized and well checked governments."[52] He added,

> Of all the enemies to public liberty, war . . . is the most to be dreaded, because it comprises and develops the germ of every other. War is the parent of armies; from these proceed debts and taxes; and armies, debts, and taxes are the known instruments for bringing the many under the domination of the few. In war, . . . the discretionary power of the Executive is extended; its influence in dealing out offices, honors, and emoluments is multiplied; and all the means of seducing the minds are added to those of subduing the force of the people. . . . No nation could preserve its freedom in the midst of continual warfare.[53]

Society members are also vociferous in their attacks on judicial activism, by which they mean liberal activism in the tradition of the Chief Justice Earl Warren's court and not the overruling and undermining of innovative precedents by conservatives. They claim to believe that judges should follow the framers' intentions, but as the legal opinions of society supporters like Antonin Scalia and Laurence Silberman make clear, they are as manipulative of history as any liberal. They call themselves conservatives, but it is not the original Constitution, the framers' jurisprudence, or settled precedent that they seek to conserve. In truth, they are conservative only to the extent that they wish to preserve the status, privilege, and power that conservative Republicans enjoy while shielding Republican presidents from legislative oversight, judicial review, and press scrutiny. They advocate judicial checks on excessive legislative delegations of authority to federal regulatory agencies, but they oppose judicial checks on alleged delegations of war-making power. Where presidential war powers are concerned, they are not Madisonian or even Hamiltonian. They are monarchists. Had they lived in Boston in 1776, they would have been tarred and feathered and put on a boat to Halifax.

Federalist Society members are particularly eager to concentrate power in the presidency, at least when that office is occupied by Republicans. Justice Alito, when he was a Federalist Society lawyer with the Justice Department during the Reagan administration, was a strong advocate of the so-called unitary executive and presidential signing statements. Laurence Silberman, now a senior judge on the U.S. Court of Appeals for the District of Columbia Circuit, has been a staunch Federalist Society activist and assiduous promoter of executive secrecy. In 1978, Silberman opposed the weak Foreign Intelligence Surveillance Act because he thought Congress had no authority to restrain executive power in the realm of national security. As a member of the Court of Appeals, he voted to overturn Col. Oliver North's conviction for obstructing Congress's inquiry into the Iran-contra affair, destroying documents, and accepting an illegal gratuity.[54] In 2002, as a member of the Foreign Intelligence Surveillance Court of Review, Silberman ruled that the FISA statute was intended to allow the FBI to collect evidence for use in court without bothering to meet the probable cause standards of the Fourth Amendment and Title III of the Omnibus Crime Control and Safe Streets Act of 1968.[55] Having worked for the Select Committee on Intelligence under chairman Senator Frank Church (D-ID), which wrote the statute, I know the opposite was true. That law was intended to create a wall of separation between law enforcement and intelligence operations precisely so that intelligence work would not have to meet constitutional standards. Back then, conservative Republicans were arguing that the Fourth Amendment's standard of probable cause to believe that a crime had been committed was no longer necessary. Probable cause to believe that the target of the surveillance was an agent of a foreign power was enough, they said, because the purpose of national security wiretaps was not to obtain evidence for prosecutions. As a practical matter, the Justice Department almost never prosecuted foreign agents because open trials would reveal too much about the FBI's sources and methods.

FISA was also enacted because conservative judges were beginning to read the Fourth Amendment as having one clause, not two. They emphasized the first clause, which bans unreasonable searches and seizures, and ignored the second, which requires probable cause warrants and therefore judicial supervision of executive branch searches. Liberal negotiators settled for the wall of separation in order to preserve what they could of judicial supervision over national security wiretaps. The liberals feared a ruling from conservative judges that warrantless wiretaps, bugs, searches, and seizures (even of persons) are constitutionally permissible, despite what the Fourth Amendment says, if they seem "reasonable."

The secret FISA court, staffed by judges appointed by the conservative Chief Justice Rehnquist, rarely turned down a warrant request, but it did require enough paperwork to impose some restraint within the FBI. The requirements were not onerous, but they made it at least theoretically possible that someone might be punished, or at least embarrassed, if the power to wiretap was misused and a scandal followed. That actually happened in 2001 when FISA's chief judge, the maverick conservative Royce Lamberth, discovered that FBI agent Michael Resnick had misrepresented the facts in more than seventy-five applications. The judge banned Resnick from appearing before him again.[56]

In November 2002, conservative judges on the FISA Court of Review demolished the wall of separation between law enforcement and intelligence searches. To do this, they rewrote history, claiming that FISA's sponsors never intended to bar law enforcement officials from using in court information that had been obtained through less-than-probable-cause warrants. The decision surprised judges of the FISA court, FBI officials, and Justice Department lawyers, who had maintained the wall for twenty-eight years.

The court then added, quite gratuitously, that "we take for granted that the president does have [the] authority [to collect foreign intelligence information without a warrant] and, assuming that is so, FISA [i.e., Congress plus President Jimmy Carter] could not encroach on the president's constitutional power."[57] In other words, FISA might be unconstitutional. The statement was not essential to the court's decision, so it set no precedent and left FISA standing, but it is by such pronouncements that activist judges gradually change the meaning of a law.

One of the three conservatives on the panel was Laurence H. Silberman. Judge Silberman did not just strike at one of the few reforms of the post-Watergate era. He also helped bring along a new generation of conservative law clerks who would advance the executive power movement. Eight of Silberman's clerks went on to work for Justice Scalia; Justice Thomas hired nine others. More members of the torture team clerked for Judge Silberman, a personal friend of the vice president's, than any other appellate court judge.[58] They include John Yoo, author of torture memos; Patrick Philbin, who helped design the military commissions; Bradford Berenson, who worked for the White House counsel's office on both the torture policy and the commissions; and Paul Clement, the deputy solicitor general who assured Justice Ginsberg in April 2004 that the United States doesn't torture people.

Three torture team members—Yoo, Philbin, and Bradbury—also clerked for Justice Thomas at the Supreme Court. Paul Clement clerked for Justice Scalia.

Federalist Society judges do not make up the entire federal judiciary, but they are well positioned, especially in the Court of Appeals for the District of Columbia Circuit and the Fourth Circuit, to advance the society's preference for unaccountable executive power. They are also linked to other movement conservatives through their work in the Reagan administration, as law clerks, and as judges who mentor law clerks. For example, two White House lawyers who worked on the torture policy and the military commissions order, Bradford Berenson and Brett Kavanaugh, clerked for Supreme Court justice Anthony Kennedy. Kavanaugh now sits on the Court of Appeals for the District of Columbia. Michael Chertoff worked for Samuel Alito in the U.S. attorney's office in New Jersey before joining the Court of Appeals for the District of Columbia and then becoming secretary of the Homeland Security Department. During the Reagan years, Justice Roberts was mentored by Fred Fielding, who served as counsel to President Bush. J. Michael Luttig, who as a Fourth Circuit judge twice voted against granting legal rights to Guantánamo detainees, clerked for Justice Scalia and succeeded William Barr as head of the OLC before being appointed to the Court of Appeals for the Fourth Circuit. One of Luttig's clerks became chief of staff to Attorney General Gonzales, fourteen went on to work for Justice Scalia, and eighteen were hired by Justice Thomas.[59]

Thus when Hillary Rodham Clinton complained that she and her husband were victims of "a vast, right-wing conspiracy," she was really referring to a smaller but geographically dispersed group of Federalist Society attorneys who pushed the Paula Jones scandal, not to protest an abuse of power, but to drive her husband from office by exposing his marital infidelities. Some society members helped organize the "Brooks Brothers riot" that stopped the recount of presidential votes in Florida's Broward County in 2000. Federalist Society staffers working for Attorney General Gonzales also carried out the replacement of nonpartisan career attorneys at the Department of Justice with partisan Republicans. One of those staffers, Bradley Schlozman, counseled conservative job applicants to remove mention of their Federalist Society membership from their résumés, presumably because he knew that it is illegal for the department to consider political affiliations when hiring career attorneys. Whether the society qualifies as a conspiracy is beside the point. It has worked successfully to staff the federal judiciary and the Justice Department with partisan attorneys who would strengthen executive power and secrecy, undermine civil liberties, weaken legislative oversight and judicial review, and allow interrogators to torture suspected terrorists with impunity.

Republican Jurisprudence

Richard A. Posner, a Federalist Society supporter on the U.S. Court of Appeals for the Seventh Circuit, is the most prominent spokesman for the new Republican jurisprudence of secret executive power. In *Not a Suicide Pact: The Constitution in a Time of Emergency,* Posner argues that we need illegal government actions in order to prevent the Constitution from becoming a "suicide pact."[60] He would not grant alleged terrorists the protections of the Geneva Conventions because their actions are not acts of war in the conventional sense. Nor would he grant them full constitutional rights because their actions are not criminal in the ordinary sense. Like the Bush administration, he claims that new circumstances demand new law or, more precisely, law-less-ness.

A self-styled pragmatist, Posner would turn traditional jurisprudence on its head. It is not the job of judges, he says, to second-guess executive or congressional claims of necessity,[61] but it is within their discretion to place a "heavy burden on the detainee to prove that he is not a terrorist."[62] The Constitution must bend in times of crisis, he argues, so that the president will not have to violate it in order to obey some higher law of necessity.[63] Law must give way to politics in times of crisis, real or imagined, but it can be restored later, when officials have no reason to break it.

Like the Bush administration, Posner does not believe in the rule of law in times of actual or alleged crisis. He believes in the rule of politics, where law is reduced to mere guidelines or a set of preferences that judges and politicians may indulge in safe moments.

Alternatively, he would have us believe that the torture of suspected terrorists by government officials is morally comparable to the peaceful civil disobedience of the Rev. Martin Luther King, Jr. He ignores the fact that King violated patently unconstitutional laws openly, with advance notice, and was willing to go to jail to challenge those laws.[64]

Implicit in Posner's argument is the belief that the Constitution will always spring back to its original shape once the crisis has passed. Being "practical," Posner doesn't worry much about the long-term effect of legal precedents that subordinate liberty to power in an Orwellian war without end.

Judge Posner would have us believe that constitutional interpretation is simply a matter of balancing liberty against security. But the balancing he advocates is rigged against the evenhanded application of rules of evidence. On his scales of justice, the security interests of the entire society will usually outweigh the interests of a few presumptively guilty individuals, because he expects judges to defer to the judgment of secret agencies as to what those security interests are and to grant those agencies immunity from prosecution and civil suit whenever their crimes seem justified by some secret "national security necessity."

Deferring to the judgment of politicians and intelligence agencies may be a practical solution for timid jurists, but it is not pragmatic. A pragmatist tests the value of an idea by how well it is likely to work out in practice; he does not defer to the judgment of others, especially not politicians. But Posner is not interested in questioning the government's allegations of emergency; nor does he doubt the practicality of its security measures. He will question the government vigorously in ordinary criminal cases, but when national security is at stake, he becomes studiously incurious. Like all authoritarians, he simply assumes that the politicians and their secret agencies know what they are doing and will not permanently damage the rights of most people, even if they detain, torture, and kill some of them.

When national security is at stake, Posner does not believe in equal justice under law as enforced by our ancient system of legal precedent. The balance he advocates must be "readjust[ed] from time to time as the weights of the respective interests change." The weights of the respective interests, as he would adjust them, have less to do with the weight of the evidence than with our feelings.[65] "The safer we feel," he says, "the more weight we place on the interest in personal liberty; the more endangered we feel, the more weight we place on the interest of safety."[66] Whether the accused is innocent or guilty has little to do with it.

For Posner, the Constitution does not state broad moral principles; it is a collection of technicalities that can be interpreted narrowly. Thus, the Fourth Amendment's rule against unreasonable searches, the Fifth Amendment's due process guarantee and its rule against compelling a person "in any criminal case to be a witness against himself,"[67] and the Eighth Amendment's ban on cruel and unusual punishments do not ban the kidnapping of Maher Arar from American soil or the harsh prison conditions inflicted on citizens like José Padilla and John Walker Lindh in advance of trial.[68] The Constitution prohibits only the introduction of evidence obtained by torture at criminal trials[69] and forbids torture and cruelty only when administered following a conviction.[70] Read this way, the Bill of Rights has nothing to do with keeping officials from abusing their power. It is not part of the system of checks and balances. It is not about human rights. It is just a grab bag of technicalities to be interpreted without any presumption in favor of liberty, equality, justice, or accountability.

Judge Posner's approach as an author also gives lesser weight to the personal liberty of noncitizens because liberty and justice are mainly for us. Like most result-oriented officials, he has little empathy for the individuals who may be tortured or detained until they go mad. Nor does he care what happens to their families. Being practical, he would rather side with a panicked public, risk-averse officials, and secret agencies, especially if only noncitizens are hurt in the process.

Posner is not ready to declare all torture legal. As a judge in 1997, he ruled that torture by the Chicago police is illegal.[71] In his books, however, he is clearly sympathetic to those who torture suspects to keep us safe from them, that is, suspected terrorists. Accordingly, he would allow judges to invoke national security to give military and CIA torturers qualified immunity from prosecution when their crimes cannot be kept secret, a misguided Justice Department decides to prosecute them, and the president cannot be trusted to grant them pardons.[72] He would also obstruct justice by allowing the executive to classify as secret all evidence of the torturers' crimes and he would increase the penalties if he could, for leaking classified information to the press.[73]

Supreme Court justice Scalia agrees with Posner. In June 2007, at an international judicial conference in Ottawa, Scalia took issue with a Canadian judge who declared, a bit hopefully, that "thankfully, security agencies in all our countries do not subscribe to the mantra, 'What would Jack Bauer do?'" Scalia shot right back: the hero of the popular television series *24* was right to torture terrorists in order to locate ticking bombs, he said. "Jack Bauer saved

Los Angeles. He saved hundreds of thousands of lives. Are you going to convict Jack Bauer?"[74]

Scalia was particularly impressed by the fictional agent's threat to kill a suspect's family, although that kind of intimidation violates the Geneva Conventions. He also added, in casual conversation later in the conference, "I don't care about holding [innocent] people. I really don't." All that matters is that "in Los Angeles everyone is safe."[75]

Scalia returned to the same theme in an interview with BBC Radio 4 in February 2008, declaring that it was extraordinary to assume that the Constitution's ban on cruel and unusual punishment also applies to "so-called torture." "It would be absurd," he said, "to determine that smacking someone in the face to determine where he has hidden the bomb that is about to blow up Los Angeles is prohibited by the Constitution."[76]

For Posner and Scalia and thousands of people like them, the absence of an actual ticking-bomb situation does not matter. The hypothetical is just a rhetorical trick to knock down their adversary's moral principles. Nor do they care that presidents and their intelligence agencies lie, cheat, and hyperventilate. All that matters is how "they" feel at the moment.

These theories are not the opinions of crackpots. They are the views of judges and lawyers as well as politicians—men and women in nice suits who have received expensive educations at the nation's most prestigious universities. Like the torture memos, these opinions are the product of some deliberation, even if they lack the founders' "respect for the opinions of mankind." There is a special horror in this fact.

Torture at Home

In 2003, the Supreme Court had the occasion to wrestle with the concept of torture in the context of a police interrogation in Los Angeles and came up with six separate opinions. Taken together, they cast doubt on whether there is an enforceable constitutional right not to be tortured, if the coerced statements are not used at trial.

Oliverio Martinez was riding his bicycle when two police officers ordered him to dismount and frisked him, finding a knife. A struggle ensued, and Martinez was shot five times. In the ambulance and at the hospital, one of the officers interrogated Martinez incessantly, ignoring the fact that he was screaming in pain, pleading for medical treatment, and passing in and out of consciousness.

Rendered permanently blind and paralyzed from the waist down, Martinez eventually sued the officer for damages, but a fractured majority of the Supreme Court found no constitutional violation because he was never prosecuted.[77] In other words, the privilege against self-incrimination is a mere evidentiary rule and not a ban on torture, despite its historic origins. If that interpretation is true, then it will not be long before our secret government argues that no one has a constitutional right not to be tortured by intelligence agents.[78]

Fellow Travelers

Since 9/11, the federal courts have largely allowed the Bush administration to curtail civil liberties by deciding legal challenges on narrower than necessary legal grounds. The Supreme Court could have put an end to the torture policy in the *Rasul, Hamdi,* and *Hamdan* cases simply by acknowledging that the privilege of habeas corpus is squarely grounded in the Constitution. Instead, the justices chose to focus only on the prisoners' statutory right, which invited Congress to abolish the right by legislation. The justices could have specified, in *Hamdi,* what standards of justice screening tribunals would have to meet, but they chose not to. They could have held that GTMO's prisoners are entitled to a level of due process that is virtually indistinguishable from that afforded by the UCMJ and regular courts-martial, but they didn't do that either. Instead, they invited a Republican Congress to spawn years of additional litigation by passing the Military Commissions Act.

Whatever their reasons, and the split in voting was clearly partisan, the justices chose not to end the torture and abuse. When they decided in *Hamdi* that prisoners had a right to challenge the reasons for their detention before screening panels and by filing habeas petitions in federal courts, the incarcerations continued unchanged. When they ruled two years later in *Hamdan* that the statutory right to habeas corpus had survived the Detainee Treatment Act, at least in pending cases, Congress was still free to pass another habeas-stripping law. That provision was declared unconstitutional in 2008 (see chapter 9), but other provisions will take years to litigate. Meanwhile, prisoners try to kill themselves rather than face a life without hope.

One can always praise the courts for careful deliberations, but given the glacial pace of their proceedings and the narrowness of their rulings, it is difficult to believe that wartime courts administer the law without fear or favor. During World War II, when the justices wanted to speed Nazi saboteurs to their deaths, they had no difficulty expediting the proceedings. The war on terrorism has now lasted longer than that war, but the justices have shown little urgency in restraining the executive or in vindicating the rights of detainees.

Tolerating the Intolerable: Padilla

José Padilla's ordeal is a case on point. His long detention without trial was tolerated by judges who allowed themselves to be manipulated in unconscionable ways. Padilla was arrested at Chicago's O'Hare International Airport on May 8, 2002, after consorting with al Qaeda leaders in Afghanistan and Iraq. At first he was held as a material witness to unspecified crimes for which no grand jury had been (or ever would be) impaneled. Then, on June 10, Attorney General John Ashcroft interrupted a trip to Moscow to announce that "we have disrupted an unfolding terrorist plot to attack the United States by exploding a radioactive dirty bomb."[79] The key plotter, he declared, was Padilla, a former street gang member, an American citizen, and a banquet waiter from Chicago.

The urgent announcement occurred more than a month after Padilla had been arrested. It was ordered by the White House and timed to drown out an FBI agent's criticisms of the bureau for not acting more swiftly to investigate Zacarias Moussaoui, then thought to be the twentieth highjacker.[80] Other officials quickly downplayed Ashcroft's alarming claims, because while Padilla may have discussed the idea of a dirty bomb with al Qaeda members, he had not actually done anything to effectuate the plan. Indeed, so far as the administration knew, there was no clear plan—just some loose talk about how plutonium might be separated from other nuclear materials by putting it in a bucket and swinging it rapidly overhead.[81] The attorney general did not disclose the source of his allegations or the methods used to extract the accusation.[82]

Two nights before administration lawyers were to appear in court to justify Padilla's detention, they realized that the allegations against him would not hold up in court because they had been obtained by torturing Khalid Sheikh

Mohammed, Abu Zubaydah, and Binyam Mohamed. So the administration withdrew the warrant under which Padilla had been arrested, relabeled him an enemy combatant, and secretly transported him in the middle of the night to a navy brig in South Carolina.

Padilla's court-appointed attorney, Donna Newman, immediately filed a habeas petition with Michael B. Mukasey, the judge (and Reagan appointee) who had signed the arrest warrant. Mukasey had earned a reputation for fairness in presiding over the trial of Sheikh Omar Abdul Rahman and others for plotting to blow up the United Nations and other New York City landmarks. According to Yale law school professor Bruce Ackerman, "Padilla's case was a legal no-brainer. His lawyer had every reason to expect any federal judge—conservative or liberal—to require the government to charge Padilla with a crime or release him immediately from military prison."[83]

But Mukasey, who was under twenty-four-hour protection as a result of the Rahman case, saw no problem with this surreptitious transfer, even though it effectively stripped an American citizen of his "liberty . . . without due process of law, 'his right' to be informed of the nature and cause of the accusation" against him, and his "right to a speedy and public trial, by an impartial jury." While holding that the military could not deny Padilla's right to consult with his attorney, the judge ruled that that in order to wage war on terrorism, President Bush could seize any American civilian anywhere, label him an enemy combatant, and lock him up indefinitely in a military prison.[84]

Six months later, a divided panel of the U.S. Court of Appeals for the Second Circuit overturned Mukasey's opinion, ruling that the government lacked authority, constitutional or otherwise, to detain a citizen on his native soil, outside a zone of combat, unless it charged him with a crime.[85] The effect of this decision was stayed pending appeal, and in June 2004, a 5-4 majority of the Supreme Court vacated it. Padilla's habeas petition, the conservative majority ruled, should have been filed against his new jailer in South Carolina rather than his old one in New York.[86] There was no reason to insist on this technicality; a citizen's liberty was at stake and the legal issues were ripe for adjudication. But the justices voted to give the administration more time with him, even though the prisoner already had been held in solitary confinement for two years.

Eight months later, the district court in South Carolina ruled in Padilla's favor,[87] but in December 2005, the conservative Court of Appeals for the Fourth

Circuit reversed.[88] Disregarding the Second Circuit's holding, the Fourth Circuit, in an opinion by Federalist Society member J. Michael Luttig, decided that the plurality's opinion approving battlefield detentions in *Hamdi* would also allow military detentions of civilians in Illinois, far from any battlefield, while the civilian courts remained open. This finding was not what the Supreme Court had held in *Hamdi* or *Quirin*,[89] or the old Civil War case of *Ex parte Milligan*. But Luttig was being interviewed by the Bush administration at the time for a position on the Supreme Court.

Knowing that Luttig's ruling was almost certain to be reversed by the Supreme Court, the administration changed tactics again. Days before its brief was due in the high court, the Justice Department dropped its hard-fought claim that Padilla could be detained indefinitely by the military as an enemy combatant. It asked the Fourth Circuit to allow it to try him in a civilian court in Florida and on yet a different set of charges, which were unrelated to the first two.[90]

This time the Fourth Circuit refused to permit the transfer, the purpose of which was clearly to evade an adverse ruling by the Supreme Court. Luttig, who had been passed over for the Supreme Court, was now furious at the legal gamesmanship. He had given the administration what it wanted and was now being told that all his work was unnecessary because there was enough evidence to try Padilla in a federal court after all. The administration's "shifting tactics," Luttig fumed, had the appearance of a shell game that "threatens [its] credibility with the courts."[91]

He was right, but the Supreme Court was not offended. It allowed the transfer, noting disingenuously that Padilla was finally getting what he had always wanted—a trial.[92] This observation, too, was a fraud because the Justice Department continued to insist that the president could relabel as an enemy combatant anyone the courts acquitted and detain him again, indefinitely and without charges.[93] But the justices didn't care. They were determined to duck the larger issue, which was whether the president could seize an American citizen within the United States, label him an enemy combatant (even though he is not part of any armed force), and detain him indefinitely without charges while the civilian courts remain open.

By leaving Luttig's opinion standing, the Supreme Court effectively said yes, although a more liberal panel of the Fourth Circuit briefly held otherwise in the case of Ali al-Marri, a citizen of Qatar. While a graduate student with a wife and children, he was arrested by the FBI in Peoria in December 2001 on suspicion of being a sleeper agent for al Qaeda. When all the government could charge al-Marri with was credit card fraud, the administration decided to label him an enemy combatant and sequester him in the same navy brig that held Padilla. Six years later, two Clinton appointees on the Fourth Circuit ordered the government to try or release al-Marri.[94] The Bush administration appealed their ruling to the predominantly Republican Fourth Circuit, which, in a straight party-line vote, ruled that in passing the Authorization to Use Military Force in 2001, Congress had authorized military detentions not just in Afghanistan but in Illinois as well.

Nothing in the legislative history of the AUMF supported this extraordinary claim. On the contrary, the Senate expressly rejected a last-minute White House bid to amend the law to give President Bush broad military powers within the United States, but the Republican judges ignored this history.[95]

Padilla and al-Marri had both been seized by the FBI and were only later turned over to the military, but the Fourth Circuit's logic suggested that pursuant to the AUMF, the president could someday dispatch U.S. soldiers to round up and detain thousands of Muslim citizens within the United States following a suspicious bombing. As Judge Diana Gribbon Motz, one of the dissenting Democrats, observed, "Our colleagues hold that the president can order the military to seize from his home and indefinitely detain anyone in this country— including an American citizen—even though he has never affiliated with an enemy nation, fought alongside any nation's armed forces, or borne arms against the United States anywhere in the world."[96]

But the majority's interpretation of the AUMF may not be necessary. In a FY2007 appropriations bill Bush Republicans in Congress quietly eliminated the statutory requirement that governors must first approve the presidential use of federal troops in their states. Now, in response to an alleged terrorist attack or incident like Timothy McVeigh's or to some "other condition,"[97] the president may, on his own, order the U.S. Northern Command to invade an American city, push local law enforcement aside, and round up as many suspected terrorists as he wishes.

Whether the Fourth Circuit's sweeping interpretation of the AUMF will survive Supreme Court review remains to be seen, but the fact is that a presumptively innocent American and a presumptively innocent resident alien were both imprisoned for years without trial and under punitive conditions in a military prison in apparent violation of the Fourth, Fifth, and Sixth amendments. Padilla, for example, was not just detained; he was held in total isolation for two years without a watch or calendar in a cell with its windows blacked out, so that he could not tell night from day. According to his lawyers, he was fed his meals through a slot in his cell's door, denied both a mattress and pillow for his steel pallet, forced to stand or sit for long periods in stressful positions, subjected to extremes of hot and cold, denied reading materials, and chained to the floor at times in a fetal position. He was denied contact with family, friends, and lawyers; subjected to bright lights (or total darkness) for days on end; and disrupted with bright lights and loud noises when he tried to sleep. When his attorneys finally gained access to him, they found him fearful and passive, suffering from tics and spasms. He was unwilling to discuss his interrogations, examine videotapes, or review transcripts and thereby did not assist in his defense. Administration lawyers insisted that Padilla had been treated humanely but refused to dispute any specific allegations to the contrary. Some government officials thought it might be better if Padilla were not tried at all but instead committed to a psychiatric prison. Justice had never been the goal, one said; instead, "the objective of the government always has been to incapacitate this person."[98]

The federal district court in Florida finally convicted Padilla on the allegation that his application to attend an al Qaeda training camp in Afghanistan constituted proof beyond a reasonable doubt that he had conspired to murder and kidnap persons unknown. His lawyers sought dismissal on the basis of outrageous government misconduct, but the judicial conscience of Judge Marcia G. Cooke, a George W. Bush appointee, was not that shocked by what the government had done to either Padilla or the Constitution. On January 22, 2008, she sentenced him to seventeen years and four months, which he is now serving, pending appeals, at the Supermax prison in Florence, Colorado.

Mukasey eventually retired from the federal bench, and on August 22, 2007, he published an article in the *Wall Street Journal* arguing that the *Padilla* case proved that federal courts were ill suited to trying terrorists. The ordinary rules of evidence and the ordinary rights of citizens, he wrote, should not be applied to people who, according to the government, "have cosmic goals that they are intent on achieving by cataclysmic means." The evidence against Padilla "may have been . . . inadmissible," he speculated, possibly because of "hearsay" or because "to disclose [the source] in a criminal case could harm the government's overall effort."[99] Nowhere in the article did the former judge acknowledge the real and by then well-documented reason why the evidence was inadmissible: it had been obtained by coercion.

Three weeks later, when President Bush nominated Mukasey to replace Alberto Gonzales as attorney general, he referred to the judge's article as proof of his fitness for that office.[100]

Conservatives Uphold the Court Strippers

The Military Commissions Act survived its first legal challenge in *Boumediene v. Bush*, a case that consolidated the habeas petitions of sixty-three Guantánamo prisoners that were pending when the act was passed. Judges A. Raymond Randolph (a Federalist Society supporter) and David B. Sentelle of the Court of Appeals for the D.C. Circuit (a Jesse Helms protégé) held that Article I, Section 9 of the Constitution does grant a constitutional right to habeas relief but only to citizens and aliens with "property or presence within the United States."[101] Bosnian Lakhdar Boumediene and his fellow prisoners had no property or presence within the United States, Randolph ruled; therefore, they had no right to challenge their detention or torture, despite what the Supreme Court seemed to say in *Rasul*.[102]

Nothing in the text of the Constitution or the writings of the framers supported this conclusion. The judge could not find a single British, colonial, or American case denying habeas rights to aliens held "beyond seas." Nor, for that matter, could he find any cases granting them the right. The judicial record was simply silent. So he decided that *the lack of any such cases* in British or American courts before and after the Constitution's ratification meant that the framers of the Constitution did not intend for prisoners held offshore to challenge what the government was doing to them. Of course, the absence of any cases, pro or con, can easily be explained by the difficulty of bringing them in the age of sail or by the fact that the American colonies didn't detain prisoners offshore. But Randolph did not consider that possibility.

Had the judge consulted the text of the British Habeas Corpus Act of 1640 and 1679, he would have discovered that our legal forebears sought to extend the privilege of the writ to all persons and not just to British subjects who happened to be on British soil.[103] Had he read the preamble to the 1679 act he would have discovered yet another purpose: to prevent "imprisonments beyond the seas."[104] During the 1660s, Lord Clarendon had hidden political prisoners of Charles II in remote locations, including the Isle of Jersey, so that they (or their families) would find it difficult to file habeas petitions. It was a high crime and misdemeanor, Parliament decided in the course of impeaching Clarendon in 1667, to procure "divers of his majesty's subjects to be imprisoned against the law, in remote islands, garrisons, and other places, thereby to prevent them from the benefit of the law, and to produce precedents for the imprisoning [of] any other of his majesty's subjects in like manner."[105]

The second Habeas Corpus Act was enacted in 1679 to prevent similar detentions by James II, who was about to assume the throne and who was expected to rule autocratically. The act's detailed procedures were thus intended, according to the historian A. V. Dicey, "to meet all the devices by which the effect of the writ can be evaded"[106] and to restore to all prisoners the right to a speedy trial.[107] This act also became the model on which the American colonies' habeas statutes were based.[108]

Nothing in Judge Randolph's opinion acknowledged this history, which would have been fresh in the framers' minds. Neither he nor Sentelle admitted that the framers of the U.S. Constitution were the intellectual and moral descendants of the parliamentary republicans who enacted the two habeas acts, ended torture by abolishing the Star Chamber (in the Habeas Corpus Act of 1640), and passed the Declaration of Rights of 1689, thus paving the way for judicial independence, checks and balances, and guaranteed liberties. On the contrary, Randolph treated the framers as closet monarchists who installed a loophole in the Constitution so that future Congresses could authorize presidents to detain, torture, and even kill nonresident aliens without restraint, so long as they did so on foreign soil.[109]

Had Randolph been less eager to aid the administration, he might have noted that neither the founders nor their British forebears were fans of military rule. On the contrary, they revolted against it: the British during the Puritan Revolution in the 1640s and the Americans in 1776, when Washington's troops drove the Redcoats out of Boston.

The members of the American founding generation, like their British ancestors, viewed military commissions as the hated instruments of martial rule. That is why the text of the Constitution, federal practice under the Articles of Confederation, and state practice under state constitutions did not assign the trial of civilians—like participants in Shay's Rebellion—to the military units that might capture them. The founders also charged civilian juries, rather than military commissions, with determining whether civilians had committed crimes.

The Bush administration claimed that terrorism presents a new challenge, one that Americans had never before experienced. Gen. Wesley K. Clark, the former NATO commander who faced terrorists in the former Yugoslavia, did not agree. Al Qaeda's terrorists, he argued, "are more like modern-day pirates than warriors."[110] Pirates were the terrorists of the seventeenth and eighteenth centuries and well known to the founders of the United States. They raided American seaports until the 1830s with paramilitary forces that were better armed than al Qaeda's hijackers. The infamous Blackbeard (also known as Edward Teach) did not just seize a few ships with cutlasses. In 1718 he blockaded Charlestown, South Carolina, with a forty-four-gun warship.[111]

John Yoo agreed with Clark that today's terrorists are like the pirates of colonial times, but Yoo claimed that pirates were not "covered by the legal system" because they "weren't fighting on behalf of any nation."[112] In fact, pirates—of all nationalities—were subject to trial by the civilian common-law courts in Great Britain and its American colonies.[113]

Under the Articles of Confederation, Congress had no authority to create courts—except "for the trial of piracies or felonies committed on the high seas."[114] In 1785, Congress asked John Jay, then secretary for foreign affairs, to propose legislation to implement the power. Jay's bill would have granted alleged pirates the right to counsel, a grand jury indictment, a copy of the indictment, and a jury trial.[115] Unlike George W. Bush, Jay did not suggest that the government create military tribunals to try pirates at sea. He proposed trying them as civilians in civilian courts within the United States.

The new Constitution was ratified before Jay's proposal could be acted upon. Without abrogating the authority of state courts to punish piratical attacks on their soil, the Constitution granted Congress exclusive authority to "define and punish Piracies and Felonies committed on the high seas, and Offences against the law of Nations."[116] When Congress exercised this power on April 30, 1790, Jay's view prevailed. Authority to try piracies and felonies on the high seas was given to federal civilian courts, not military tribunals.[117] Nothing in the act suggested that pirates, because they are alleged to be illegal combatants fighting a metaphorical war, should have fewer rights than other defendants have.

No one during the constitutional debates tried to restrict the privilege of the writ of habeas corpus to a limited class of persons. In recommending the federal Constitution's habeas provision to the people of New York in 1788, Alexander Hamilton quoted William Blackstone's *Commentaries on the Laws of England*: "To bereave a man of life . . . without accusation or trial would be [a] gross and notorious act of despotism, . . . but confinement of the person, by secretly hurrying him to jail, where his sufferings are unknown and forgotten is a less public, less striking, and therefore *a more dangerous engine* of arbitrary government."[118]

New York's ratifying convention made its understanding of the Constitution's habeas provision even more explicit. "[E]very *person* restrained of his liberty," it declared, "is *entitled to an inquiry* into the lawfulness of such restraint, and to a removal thereof if unlawful, and that such inquiry or removal ought not to be denied or delayed, except when, on account of public danger, the *Congress* shall suspend the privilege of the writ of habeas corpus."[119] (Emphasis added.)

As mentioned earlier, during the American Civil War military commissions sent a number of Dakota Indians and members of the conspiracy to assassinate President Lincoln to the gallows. But in *Ex parte Milligan* (1866) the Supreme Court reaffirmed the principle that civilians are to be tried by civilians, so long as the regular civilian courts are open.[120] The fact that Lambdin P. Milligan, a Southern sympathizer living in Indiana, was charged with being a rebel—easily the equivalent of a pirate or terrorist—made no difference.

The principle of civilian trials for civilians was not altered by *Ex parte Quirin* (1942), which upheld the use of a military commission because the defendants were German Marines, not civilians, who had buried their uniforms in the sand after invading the United States in time of declared war.[121] The civilians who sheltered these military personnel, however, were tried in civilian courts, not military commissions.[122] This distinction was reiterated in *Duncan v. Kahanamotu* (1946) when the Supreme Court overturned military convictions of civilians in the territory of Hawaii because martial rule had lasted longer there than was militarily necessary.[123]

When Randolph's decision was appealed to the Supreme Court in 2007 the justices refused to hear it. Boumediene's attorneys requested a rehearing, which the Supreme Court almost never grants. This time, however, they had something new: a sworn statement from Lt. Col. Stephen E. Abraham describing the evidentiary inadequacies of the Combat Status Review Tribunals. The colonel's belated affidavit apparently persuaded Justices Kennedy and Stevens. They voted to hear challenges to the Military Commissions Act, including Boumediene's.

When those cases were argued before the justices on December 5, 2007, administration lawyers conceded that the Constitution does have extraterritorial reach, if American citizens (or aliens with property in the United States) are seized by American agents abroad and detained outside the United States. But they continued to argue that the Constitution's habeas procedure would not permit independent courts to question U.S. agents who deny liberty and justice to nonaffiliated foreigners in foreign lands. Alternatively, the administration argued that the Detainee Treatment Act, which stripped foreigners held outside the United States of all habeas rights, was constitutional because it replaced them with an adequate substitute—Combat Status Review Tribunals—with appeals to the U.S. Court of Appeals for the District of Columbia.

A Duty to Torture Nonpersons

In January 2008, while the *Boumediene* cases were pending before the Supreme Court, three judges of the District of Columbia Circuit dismissed a lawsuit by four former prisoners who sought monetary damages for torture suffered while incarcerated at Guantánamo Bay. Among other things, the plaintiffs in *Rasul v. Myers* alleged that they had a been repeatedly "beaten, shackled in painful stress positions, threatened by dogs, subjected to extreme temperatures and deprived of adequate sleep, food, sanitation, medical care and communication." They also swore that they had been "harassed practicing their religion, including forced shaving of their beards, banning or interrupting their prayers, denying them copies of the Koran and prayer mats and throwing a copy of the Koran in a toilet bucket."[124]

Accepting these allegations as true, Judge Karen LeCraft Henderson ruled that the prisoners could not sue under the Alien Tort Statute because Attorney

General Gonzales had certified to the court that mistreating prisoners was within "the scope of [the interrogators'] employment" and "incidental to their duties." Indeed, he assured the court, "torture is a foreseeable consequence of the military's detention of suspected enemy combatants."[125] The panel accepted his assurance and ruled, in effect, that a military interrogator's superiors could be lawfully ordered to torture prisoners and then be judicially granted qualified immunity for their crimes.

Two of the judges then went on to rule that the prisoners could not sue government officials under the Religious Freedom Restoration Act for "substantially burdening their exercise of religion" because "*aliens* . . . located outside sovereign United States territory *are not 'persons'* within the meaning of that Act."[126] (Emphasis added.) This finding was too much for Judge Janice Rogers Brown, one of George W. Bush's most conservative appointees. "There is little mystery," she wrote, "that a 'person' is a human being."[127] But she still voted to dismiss the suit.

In February 2008, the full Court of Appeals for the District of Columbia surprised nearly everyone by deciding, in *Gates v. Bismullah,* that whenever a prisoner appealed a CSRT decision to one of its panels, the government had to provide the court with "all the information" that the tribunal was "authorized to obtain and consider" and not just the information that it chose to put on the record.[128] This 5-5 ruling posed a special challenge to the Bush administration because it forced the government finally to admit that the military and CIA had destroyed most of their interrogation tapes. The Justice Department promptly appealed, claiming that the CSRTs should be able to control what evidence prisoners could challenge on appeal.[129] The stage was finally set for the Supreme Court's review of the habeas-stripping provision of the Military Commissions Act.

The Supremes Strike Back: *Boumediene*

On June 12, 2008, the Supreme Court's patience ran out. By the narrowest of margins, the justices decided that Boumediene and his fellow prisoners had a constitutional right to have their habeas petitions heard by federal civilian courts. The alternative procedure created by the Military Commissions Act was not "a constitutionally adequate substitute" for that right.[130]

Justice Anthony Kennedy, the court's sole libertarian, supplied the swing vote, to the dismay of its four authoritarians: Roberts, Scalia, Alito, and Thomas. Kennedy's vote was not unexpected; he had signaled as much when he decided to hear the case. His opinion for the majority, however, was a body blow to the administration and gave the petitioners (and civil libertarians) as much as they could have hoped for.

Rather than quibble over the state of British case law circa 1789, Kennedy declared it inconclusive and turned to "[t]he broad historical narrative of the writ and its function,"[131] which he characterized as a central element in the Anglo American system of limited government, checks and balances, and the rule of law. Rather than allow much abused theories of sovereignty to create legal black holes, he focused on what allowing the administration's claims would do to permit "the political branches to govern without legal constraint."[132]

"Our basic charter," Kennedy declared, "cannot be contracted away" by a treaty that created a coaling station for navy ships on the island of Cuba.[133]

Even when the United States acts outside its borders, its powers are not "absolute and unlimited," but are subject "to such restrictions as are expressed in the Constitution." Abstaining from questions involving formal sovereignty and territorial governance is one thing. To hold the political branches have the power to switch the Constitution on or off at will is quite another.[134]

Senator Graham, in amending McCain's Detainee Treatment Act on behalf of the administration, had tried to preserve the use of evidence obtained by torture by making the little kangaroo courts, or CSRTs, subject to limited review by the predominantly conservative Court of Appeals for the District of Columbia. This substitute, the Court held, was inadequate for the *constitutional* right to habeas review, which guaranteed rights not provided by the CSRTs. They included the assistance of counsel, the right to confront witnesses, and the right to present exculpatory evidence—everything that Lieutenant Colonel Abraham, the whistleblowing insider, had said was lacking.

For the first time in history, the court clearly decided that the writ of habeas corpus was grounded in the Constitution and could not be modified by legislation.

The majority did not have to decide this question. It could have returned the case to the Court of Appeals and let it evaluate the substitute's adequacy, but they knew what the outcome would be. They had already given the political branches six years to come up with a constitutionally adequate system of review. The politicians had failed while evidence of torture, degrading treatment, and a basic lack of common decency mounted. As Justice David Souter emphasized in his concurrence, the time for wartime deference to assertions of military necessity had come to an end.

That ruling did not mean that the prisoners would be released immediately, only that the district courts would have to find a way to expedite the hearing of some two hundred habeas petitions. As a practical matter, the administration would have to admit that its grounds for holding nearly a hundred prisoners were inadequate.[135] The Defense Department had already come to that conclusion, but it could not find foreign countries willing to take the detainees. Thus, the department refused to release any into the United States—at least until a court could be blamed.

The administration would still try to go forward with prosecutions before the military commissions, until habeas courts released the defendants or defense lawyers established that the kangaroo commissions were no more just than the CSRTs. The current detentions were legally doomed. All that remained was for the Bush administration, and Republican candidates, to do everything they could to shift the blame to activist judges.

The opening salvo began with Chief Justice Roberts's dissent, which the three other authoritarians joined. The "procedural protections" afforded by the Detainee Treatment Act were "the most generous . . . ever afforded aliens detained by this country as enemy combatants,"[136] Roberts wrote, as if he were totally ignorant of how those protections had failed to protect innocent prisoners from systematic torture, cruelty, and degradation.

Roberts then stood precedent on its head by calling for judicial deference to the political branches in the interpretation of constitutional rights. The legislation deserved deference, he said, because it had been "crafted after much careful investigation and thorough debate."[137] In fact, the Republican leadership had been careful not to allow their court-stripping measures to be subject to legislative hearings, which is the usual forum for careful investigation and debate.

"The critical threshold question in these cases," the chief justice argued, was not whether aliens at GTMO had a constitutional right to habeas review but whether Congress's *statutory* substitute was adequate for the yet-to-be defined *constitutional* right. This question, he said, should be decided "prior to any inquiry about the writ's [constitutional] scope."[138]

"The CSRTs," Roberts added, "operate much as habeas courts would if hearing the detainee's collateral challenge for the first time: They gather evidence, call witnesses, take testimony, and render a decision on the legality of the government's decision."[139] Roberts was trying to say, despite massive evidence to the contrary, that these wallaby courts operate pretty much like real ones. Because the tribunals were adequate, he argued, prisoners should be required to exhaust all their administrative remedies without the assistance of counsel before being allowed to question the constitutional adequacy of that body's procedure to the court of appeals. Under the substitute procedure, the appeals court lacked the power of a habeas court to order their release.

Nothing in the chief justice's opinion revealed the slightest urgency for the liberty of possibly innocent prisoners or concern for the fragile mental state of many prisoners. Nor did he acknowledge, as the majority finally did, that justice delayed is justice denied. The entire thrust of his opinion was to justify more delay, allow the political branches to prescribe additional procedures, and thereby spawn still more time-consuming litigation.

According to Roberts, the *Boumediene* case was "not really about the detainees at all, but about control of federal policy regarding enemy combatants. . . . All that [majority's] opinion has done is shift responsibility for those sensitive national security decisions from the elected branches to the Federal Judiciary."[140] It had nothing to do with liberty, justice, or the rule of law; it was just a "particularly egregious" example of judicial "overreaching" that left the court open to "charges of judicial activism."[141] By implication, there would have been nothing egregious or overreaching about permitting the president to create a legal black hole in which prisoners would have no rights and could be tortured and degraded without risk of judicial review.

Justice Scalia began his dissent by blaming the majority for making "the war harder on us." The decision would have "disastrous consequences," he predicted, and "will almost certainly cause more Americans to be killed."[142] To support this dire warning, he noted that "[a]t least 30 prisoners . . . whom the military had concluded were not enemy combatants [and released] . . . have returned to [combat]."[143]

Scalia drew his statistics from a minority report of the Senate Armed Services Committee, issued in the spring of 2007, not knowing that the Defense Department had disowned those numbers by May 2008. The first retreat occurred in July 2007, when the Pentagon admitted that it could identify only fifteen of the thirty former prisoners as recidivists. Of the fifteen, according to a study by the Seton Hall Law Center for Policy and Research, five were Chinese Uighurs whose "return to the fight" consisted of publishing an article about their mistreatment from the Albanian refugee camp to which they had been sent. Three other ex-prisoners re-offended from their homes in Tipton, England, by describing their Guantánamo experiences to a documentary filmmaker. Evidence against the other seven was inconclusive. Some had been killed. Others had been arrested but under circumstances that were far from clear and, in any case, did not involve attacks on Americans. The Seton Hall study was able to confirm that only one former prisoner—ISN 220—had returned to the fight by blowing himself up in Iraq.

Justice Scalia offered these statistics as proof that the judiciary was less qualified than the executive branch to decide who could be released safely. But none of the alleged recidivists had been released by a federal judge. All had been cleared by the executive branch. The most dangerous of them, ISN 220, had actually been let go by Bush administration officials over well-founded objections from the military.[144]

Scalia also ignored the fact that hundreds of other prisoners had not returned to the fight, despite abundant grounds for bitterness. Like Vice President Cheney, Scalia and his fellow dissenters preferred to imprison hundreds of harmless people indefinitely, under brutal conditions, than risk releasing any prisoners who might retaliate.

Then Scalia addressed the question of how best to read the Constitution. According to Scalia, the only way to ascertain what the framers meant when they adopted the habeas provision was to analyze British legal precedents in the late eighteenth century. The purpose of habeas statutes, as reported by Blackstone or Hamilton, did not need to be examined, he insisted, because "[i]t is nonsensical to interpret [provisions like the habeas clause] in light of some general 'separation-of-powers principles' dreamed up by the Court." The general intentions of the framers, as evidenced by the Constitution's purposes, principles, and design, or the history out of which the habeas clause arose, are irrelevant to its meaning, he argued. All that counts is "what [the right was] understood to mean [by remote British judges] when the [American] people ratified [the Constitution],"[145] and that can be determined only by examining "the common law writ at the time of the founding."[146]

Curiously, Scalia quoted a contrary opinion by Chief Justice Joseph Story. "The common law of England," Story wrote in 1819, "is not to be taken in all respects to be that of America. Our ancestors brought with them its general principles, and claimed it as their birthright; but they brought with them and adopted only that portion which was applicable to their situation."[147] But when Scalia interpreted the habeas clause, he assumed that the founders had no larger purpose than to embalm the common law. It is not "a Constitution we are expounding," as Chief Justice Marshall once said,[148] but some arcane bit of legal history, like whether the British writ happened to extend to Berwick-upon-Tweed in 1789.[149]

Finally, Scalia thought that the prisoners should be denied relief simply because they "have failed to identify a single case in the history of Anglo-American law that supports their claim."[150] Of course, the administration had also failed to identify a single case in which the executive was allowed to create a place where prisoners could be hidden away, but that fact did not trouble Scalia because "surely such a case would have been reported" if it existed. In fact, two such instances did exist and they supported the prisoners' claims: the impeachment of Lord Clarendon for making political prisoners disappear and the Habeas Corpus Act of 1679. In both instances, Parliament rejected the practice of hiding prisoners in remote places where no courts could challenge their detention. Scalia, like Judge Randolph, ignored this history.

On December 15, 2008, the Supreme Court vacated the decision in *Rasul v. Myers*, and told the court of appeals to rethink it in light of the decision in *Boumediene*, clearly signaling that prisoners at GTMO were persons after all.[151]

One might argue that, in the end, the majority got it right and reasserted the Constitution, as the Court did in three cases after the Civil War[152] and World War II.[153] But the fact remains that in all three instances, the justices deferred to the arbitrary assertion of executive powers until the crisis, or the sense of crisis, abated. Had another terrorist attack occurred in 2007, the Supreme Court's decision might well have been different. Meanwhile, the most fundamental of all freedoms—the eight-hundred-year-old right to habeas corpus—continues to hang by a one-vote margin.

But that was enough. When the bundle of cases was returned to the district judges who had first heard them, the administration's evidence was found wanting. Judge Ricardo M. Urbina was the first to rule, in the case of seventeen Uighurs from southwestern China. The government was finally forced to admit it had no evidence at all to justify their detention, and on October 7, 2008, Urbina ordered that the prisoners be brought to his courtroom so that he could release them into the custody of supporters in the Washington, D.C., area.[154] But the government's lawyers appealed yet again, and the Court of Appeals for the District of Columbia stayed his decision.

Meanwhile, Judge Richard Leon reviewed the government's evidence against Lakhdar Boumediene and five Algerians. Three years earlier, he had ruled these prisoners had no right to have the evidence against them examined in a habeas proceeding, and he bridled at the Supreme Court's decision "to superimpose the habeas process into the world of intelligence gathering." But now he had to examine the government's evidence against the prisoners, who had been seized in Bosnia on allegations that they planned to go to Afghanistan and fight Americans. Leon quickly discovered that most of the evidence consisted of a single document containing allegations from one unnamed source. Reluctantly, he ordered the government to release Boumediene and four of the Algerians forthwith and urged its lawyers not to bother with an appeal, observing, "Seven years of waiting for our legal system to give them an answer to a question so important is, in my judgment, more than plenty."[155]

Secrecy Triumphant

While the Supreme Court rejected the idea of Guantánamo as a law-free zone, it did not strike down the MCA's grant of immunity from prosecution to torturers. Some accountability and redress might still be possible, if the victims could sue their kidnappers and torturers for monetary damages. However, judges have been dismissing such cases because they might embarrass secret agencies or reveal state secrets.

The Embarrassment Defense: *Arar*

The first civil suit challenging extraordinary rendition was brought in the U.S. District Court in Brooklyn, New York, by the Center for Constitutional Rights on behalf of Maher Arar, the Canadian seized at Kennedy International Airport and shipped to Syria for interrogation under torture. The issue was simple: where does the president get the authority to order the FBI and CIA to abduct anybody for indefinite detention or torture? No act of Congress authorizes abduction, torture, or torture by proxy. No provision of the Constitution gives the president such powers. On the contrary, the Constitution protects all persons in the United States, not just citizens, from unreasonable detention and interrogation under torture. The laws and treaties do as well. So where does the president get the authority to instruct his subordinates to dispense with the laws against kidnapping people within the United States?

During the early seventeenth century, James I claimed the authority not only to set aside laws he disliked but to exempt specific officials from having to obey those laws. In the English Declaration of Rights of 1689, the British Parliament rejected this "dispensing power," as he called it, along with its twin, his alleged power to suspend the operation of specific laws.[156] Supreme Court justice William Paterson, sitting as a circuit judge, in 1806[157] and the U.S. Supreme Court in 1838[158] also rejected the dispensing power.

In the *Arar* case, District Judge David Trager never addressed these claims or holdings.[159] He simply assumed that the president must have the authority to exempt the FBI and CIA from the criminal law and, further, that judges may not pierce the veil of secrecy that conceals such crimes. Trager did not begin his analysis with a presumption of liberty. He assumed that the president's power to secretly authorize crimes is unquestionable, similar to a royal prerogative under the Stuart kings.

Why did Trager refuse to question the legality of the government's plot to kidnap and torture Arar? Because the administration said it was secret. Trager did not expressly rule that the case had to be dismissed because it might have disclosed a state secret. Rather, he dismissed Arar's suit because a trial might have embarrassed American officials in the conduct of foreign relations.[160]

A trial also could not be held, he ruled, because it might have revealed the Canadian government's complicity in Arar's ordeal. Why that should matter, especially after the Canadian government admitted its mistake in a huge report, was not explained. The issue, after all, was not whether the Canadian government was complicit but whether U.S. officials violated Arar's rights. That concern could have been addressed without considering the source of the erroneous allegations on which American officials relied.

A trial might also have revealed the CIA's secret arrangements with Syrian torturers, but the judge could have kept the details of that arrangement secret while still providing a civil remedy for the crime. Or the government could have settled the case. The judge did not explain why the victims of extraordinary rendition should have to suffer twice while the people who kidnapped them for purposes of torture would not have to be held accountable at all.

Judge Trager, a former dean of Brooklyn Law School and a Clinton appointee, conceded that persons in the United States have rights, but he decided, like Senator Lindsey Graham, that those rights are without remedies when they are violated by secret agencies. The Constitution, laws, and treaties forbid what was done to Arar, but he cannot sue the officials who harmed him because secrecy—secrecy about illegal kidnappings and torture—is more important than liberty, justice, the rule of law, or accountability.

In July 2008, a panel of the U.S. Court of Appeals for the Second Circuit affirmed Trager's decision.[161] José A. Cabranes, a Clinton appointee, joined by Joseph M. McLaughlin, a Reagan appointee whom George H. W. Bush promoted, ruled that Arar could not sue under the Torture Victims Protection Act because U.S. officials did not act under color of foreign law when they conspired with Syrian intelligence to have Arar interrogated under torture using American questions.

Nor could Arar sue for tortuous violations of his Fifth Amendment due process rights because the majority was reluctant to create such rights where special factors involving foreign relations were at stake. Had the judges' consciences been shocked by what the government had done to Arar, a right might have been recognized, but they were not moved. "Whatever the emotive force of . . . the complaint," Cabranes wrote, "we cannot disfigure the judicial function to satisfy personal indignation."[162] However, nothing in his opinion betrayed the slightest indignation over Arar's mistreatment or the misuse of deportation to permit torture by proxy.[163] Nor did Cabranes acknowledge that a precedent shielding government kidnappers from civil suits would permanently disfigure the U.S. Constitution.

The majority also refused to recognize a new civil penalty for this kind of constitutional violation because Congress had created an alternative procedure by which immigrants could challenge sudden deportations, and Arar had not used it. He had not used it, of course, because the government, while lying to his attorney and misleading the Canadian government in the process, had spirited him out of the country before he could. But that factor did not bother the majority either. The law is the law, even if government kidnappers deny their victims access to it.[164] To make an exception and allow Arar to circumvent a separate appeals procedure Congress had established would exceed the court's authority, Cabranes wrote.[165]

Like Judge Trager, Cabranes treated Arar as if he were an illegal immigrant trying to sneak into the country. But as Judge Robert D. Sack stressed in his dissent, Arar wasn't trying to immigrate. He was just changing planes on his way home. If immigration officials didn't want him in the United States, they could have put him on his flight to Montreal. The FBI did not question Arar about possible immigration law violations; instead, its agents treated him as a terrorist. Contrary to what the majority said, he wasn't trying to circumvent immigration law. His lawsuit had nothing to do with immigration. As Sack insisted, Arar's case was "about forbidden tactics allegedly employed by United States law enforcement officers in a terrorism inquiry."[166]

The State Secrets Privilege: *El-Masri*

The second civil suit to challenge extraordinary rendition was brought by the American Civil Liberties Union on behalf of Khaled el-Masri, the German citizen who was kidnapped in Macedonia, drugged, beaten, and detained in Afghanistan for nearly five months. As in Arar's case, the government claimed that a trial would reveal state secrets, and secrecy had to trump justice. The district court agreed and dismissed the case. The U.S. Court of Appeals for the Fourth Circuit affirmed the dismissal,[167] applying the state secrets privilege, as defined by the Supreme Court in *United States v. Reynolds* (1953).[168]

Robert Reynolds and two other civilians had been killed in the crash of an Air Force B-29 bomber in 1948. Their widows sued, expecting to prove negligence, but when the government insisted that a trial would expose military secrets, their case was dismissed before trial. Years later, documents that had been wrongly classified were declassified and proved that the government had lied; there were no secrets on the plane, just a negligently maintained engine.[169] In 2003, family members sought to reopen the decision, but the Court of Appeals for the Third Circuit, with a vote from Judge Samuel Alito, refused.[170] Moreover, the panel ruled, judges should always defer to official claims of secrecy because the president and his subordinates know best what needs to be concealed.

Implicit in this ruling was the assumption that the decision to designate certain information as secret belongs to the executive only. The framers would never have gone so far because the idea of checks and balances permeated their thinking about government. As spiritual descendants of John Calvin, they had a Whiggish distrust of human nature. "[W]hat is government itself," Madison asked in *The Federalist,*

> but the greatest of all reflections on human nature? If men were angels, no government would be necessary. If angels were to govern men, neither external nor internal controls on government would be necessary. In framing a government which is to be administered by men over men, the greatest difficulty lies in this: You must first enable the government to control the governed; and in the next place, oblige it to control itself. A dependence on the people is no doubt the primary control on the government; but experience has taught mankind the necessity of auxiliary precautions.[171]

In *Reynolds,* and again in *El-Masri* and *Arar,* the judges overlooked this aspect of the framers' intent. They left Congress, the public, and nearly everyone else vulnerable to deception by the executive. They also overlooked the indiscriminate use of security classifications to protect officials from embarrassment. By allowing secrecy to trump openness, the judges released the executive from what Madison called "a dependence upon the people."

Of course, the framers would have conceded the need for diplomatic and military secrets, including some espionage, but they would not have endorsed the nature and scale of the government's secrecy today. They most certainly would not have allowed government officials to label something a state secret in order to conceal official crimes any more than they would have agreed that officials are entitled to civil immunity for such crimes as kidnapping and torture. Nor would they have accepted the double standard that individuals may sue private persons for kidnapping and torturing them, but they may not sue government officials who do the same. As a matter of neutral legal principles, the framers would have agreed: terrorists should be treated as terrorists whether they work for al Qaeda or the CIA.

The Fourth Circuit's opinion in *El-Masri* acknowledged that the plaintiff did not challenge the need to protect genuine state secrets from disclosure; it argued only that there had to be a check on "egregious executive misconduct."[172] But its response was full of double-talk. The judiciary can't "possess a roving writ to ferret out and strike down executive excess," the judges declared. Courts have a "more modest role," they said. "We simply decide cases and controversies."[173] Is that all we expect of them? Of course, they cannot reach out and decide issues that are not properly before them. The case or controversy requirement forbids that. But don't they have some obligation to decide cases in ways that preserve the system of checks and balances, the rule of law, and fundamental fairness?

The judges in *El-Masri* didn't fulfill even the modest role they set for themselves. They let CIA officials walk free and did not make them explain where they got the authority to practice extraordinary rendition. On October 9, 2007, the Supreme Court rejected el-Masri's appeal without comment, thereby refusing even to consider whether it is constitutional to elevate secrecy over all other values, including the rights not to be kidnapped and tortured.[174]

The judiciary's application of the state secrets privilege in this case makes little sense. The rendition program was no secret; the president himself had acknowledged it. A trial would not need to disclose intelligence sources and methods in order to examine where CIA officials got the authority to kidnap, detain, and torture anyone. The defendants did not have to admit specific actions in order to answer that basic question. If they could not persuade the court that their actions were legal, then they could have been expected to swear, subject to a secret trial for perjury, that el-Masri's allegations were not substantially true. If they were not willing to deny his allegations in a civil suit, when offered immunity from criminal prosecution, then the court could have interpreted their refusal as an admission of wrongdoing and directed a verdict for the plaintiff without revealing a scrap of classified information.

But the judges were not willing to be creative. Like Justice Scalia, they did not attempt to resolve ambiguities in the law with reference to our nation's promise of liberty, equality, or justice. They believe in deciding cases much as children draw pictures, by connecting the numbered dots of precedent. As a result, the larger vision of the Constitution suffers while torturers, and the officials who authorize their crimes, escape accountability.

Unlike the framers, many judges today are willing to trust secret agencies to do the right thing. Or if they don't trust the agencies, they trust Congress or the media to provide effective checks. This trust is misplaced. Congress did not legislate effective checks on the intelligence agencies during the Watergate era, when the president's political power was at its lowest ebb. Congress failed again during the Iran-contra affair, when it became known that the Reagan administration had funded a secret war by selling American arms to a terrorist regime in Iran, and it certainly has not curbed the intelligence agencies during the current war on terrorism. Since 9/11, the media's capacity to expose official crimes has been seriously degraded by the secret government's illegal access to telephone and e-mail communications between reporters and potential sources inside the government.

In *El-Masri,* the court of appeals declared that the claim of a single person "is subject to the collective interest in national security."[175] Framed that way, the individual always loses. In a constitutional republic like ours, society has interests on both sides of the judicial scales. Indeed, it can be argued that "we, the people" have a greater interest in preserving the rule of law, checks and balances, liberty, and justice than in shielding official criminals from civil suit, especially where legitimate secrets don't have to be disclosed.

Immunity from Civil Suits by Victims

The state secrets privilege is a powerful barrier against civil suits brought against government torturers by their victims, but it is not the only one. Courts have also ruled that foreigners tortured abroad have no standing to sue their tormenters in U.S. courts for what are known as constitutional torts—that is, personal injuries inflicted on them in violation of the Constitution. They have no standing, judges say, because nonresident aliens can claim no rights under the U.S. Constitution or the Geneva Conventions.[176] In addition, if they did have the right to sue, the officials responsible for ordering the torture could claim immunity from civil liability so long as their superiors were willing to certify, as Gonzales did, that the injuries they inflicted were done in the conduct of their duties. One might argue that torture is not one of their duties, but interrogation and detention are, and the latter was enough for Thomas F. Hogan, chief judge of the U.S. District Court for the District of Columbia, where most such suits would be brought. American military commanders and interrogators should not have to worry, he ruled in 2007, in *Ali v. Rumsfeld*, that they could be sued for allowing what a judge may later decide was an inappropriate interrogation technique.[177]

Similarly, should a president be sued in connection with the torture policy, he could invoke either executive privilege to prevent his advisers from testifying against him[178] or sovereign immunity to avoid all lawsuits not authorized by Congress under the Federal Tort Claims Act of 1946. That law waives sovereign immunity for personal injuries, including assaults carried out by federal interrogators or prison guards. Thus the U.S. government can be held liable for such injuries, including the negligence of supervisors. However, in 2004, in *Sosa v. Alvarez-Machaín,* the Supreme Court ruled that the statutory waiver of immunity applies only to injuries inflicted by federal agents within the United States. If the injuries are inflicted abroad, the United States is still shielded by the old British doctrine of sovereign immunity, although it is not mentioned anywhere in the U.S. Constitution. This immunity from civil suit has been held to apply even in cases where the officials plotted a kidnapping abroad from their offices in Washington, D.C., and the conspiracy and kidnapping continued on U.S. soil until the victim was formally arrested by federal agents. Thus, a Mexican doctor who was kidnapped in Mexico, brought to the United States, tried, and acquitted could not sue the U.S. government for the injuries he sustained.[179]

The old adage that "no man is above the law" is no longer valid. American courts, supported by three Republican attorneys general, have made it abundantly clear: high government officials who secretly authorize the kidnapping, torture, or murder of foreigners abroad cannot be prosecuted for the crimes the officials commit or sued for injuries they cause.

Murder Warrants?

For all these reasons and more, Professor Dershowitz's faith in judges is misplaced. But for the sake of argument, let us assume that judges could be trusted to decide when circumstances would justify torture. What would then prevent Congress or the president from trusting judges to decide when individual suspects might be killed?

A version of that power exists in Israel. Israeli judges don't issue warrants for the killing of specific individuals, but they do legitimate the practice by setting the standards for when targeted killings may be authorized by the executive. According to a 2005 decision of the Israeli Supreme Court, the government may mark a suspected Palestinian terrorist for elimination if he is taking a "direct part in hostilities." Taking a direct part in hostilities isn't limited to personal participation in an armed attack. Helping to decide that an attack should occur, planning that attack, or sending attackers on their way—all are sufficient to make one a marked man. Nor is the time frame during which a suspect may be killed limited to meetings in which decisions or plans are made or from which the attackers are dispatched. A suspected terrorist can be targeted for elimination if his terrorist organization "has become his home." Active membership in a terrorist organization is proof enough of direct participation to justify an assassination, and the Israeli government is under no obligation to consider less drastic alternatives, such as arrests.[180]

How such judicial blessings enhance the rule of law is not clear, but then Israel does not have a constitution. In this it more closely resembles the England of James Bond, where secret agents are licensed to kill and are presumed always to get the right man. At the moment, the United States resembles the United Kingdom under Margaret Thatcher, where squads of Special Forces murdered IRA suspects without a judicial blessing. The United Kingdom does not have a constitution either.

If a president wants his secret agents to kidnap, torture, or kill suspects, it would help not to have a constitution. But thanks to American judges, the U.S. Constitution is rarely an impediment.

10

WHY DO THEY HATE OUR FREEDOMS?

[I]f we should perish, the ruthlessness of the foe would be only the
secondary cause of the disaster. The primary cause would be that the
strength of a giant nation was directed by eyes too blind to see all the
hazards of the struggle; and the blindness would be induced not by some
accident of nature or history, but by hatred and vainglory.

—REINHOLD NIEBUHR[1]

Shortly after the attacks of 9/11, President Bush went before Congress
and the nation to address the haunting question: "Why do they hate us?" His
answer: "They hate our freedoms."[2]

Of course, freedom had nothing to do with it. As Michael Scheuer, the
former head of the rendition program, has explained, "[W]e are being attacked
for what we do in the Islamic world, not for who we are or what we believe in, or
how we live."[3] In 1998 Osama bin Laden called on Muslims "to kill Americans
everywhere" in reprisal for three American policies: the Clinton administration's
sanctions against Iraq, which Iraqis blamed for the deaths of thousands of
children; the stationing of American troops in Saudi Arabia, Islam's most holy
land; and America's one-sided policy toward Palestine.[4]

Like most Americans, Bush was not interested in what the terrorists had to
say or what might motivate Muslims to support or oppose al Qaeda. "They" had
attacked "us." As in 1898 and 1941, that was enough. We would retaliate.

One of the president's reprisals, we now know, was a policy of torture, often of
innocent persons. It produced little useful information, provoked an insurgency,

and disgraced the United States throughout the world. To undertake this policy, the Bush administration had to override the U.S. military's long-term opposition to torture as well as the domestic and international laws forbidding it.

Bush's torture policy was developed by a small group of bureaucratic infighters, led by Vice President Cheney and Secretary of Defense Rumsfeld, with the active assistance of Federalist Society lawyers who should have known better. By well-established legal standards, the policy's makers were guilty of war crimes—crimes similar to those for which the United States and the Allies prosecuted Nazi and Japanese officials following World War II.

The decision to torture suspects was almost instantaneous. There is no evidence that the president or his aides gave any thought to the morality or utility of the practice, the consequences of what they were unleashing, or what they would do with the battered prisoners once the war on terrorism was over.

The torture policy began on September 17, 2001, when the president secretly ordered the CIA to kidnap suspects and deliver them for interrogation to regimes well known for torture. It was expanded by the November 13 order creating military commissions, which were needed only if the objective was to admit unreliable evidence, including evidence obtained by torture. On January 11, 2002, the administration began delivering suspects—most of whom turned out to be innocent—to hastily erected dog pens at the U.S. Naval Base at Guantánamo Bay, Cuba. The location was deliberately chosen to prevent any legal challenges to or press coverage of the prisoners' detention and mistreatment.

On February 7, 2002, President Bush unleashed the military and the CIA from the anti-torture provisions of the Geneva Conventions. By that one stroke, opposed by most military personnel, Bush made the abuse, torture, and even murder of prisoners inevitable. He and his aides knew they were inviting the commission of war crimes. They knew they were exposing themselves to prosecution as war criminals. Their lawyers acknowledged that fact in a series of legal memos that admitted liability, but then they proposed ways to evade prosecution. They wrote other memorandums that twisted law, history, and morality to give the torturers and themselves a get-out-of-jail-free card should they get caught.

By the early spring of 2002, it was painfully clear to the CIA and the military that they had little or no evidence to justify detaining many of the prisoners at Guantánamo or elsewhere. But rather than set up screening tribunals to review that evidence and release the innocent, as the Geneva Conventions and standard military practice require, the Bush administration strove through cruel, inhumane, and degrading treatment to force prisoners to say something, true or not, that would justify their incarceration or someone else's. It refused to admit any mistakes, and it fought fiercely to prevent courts of law and the court of public opinion to learn what it had done to the prisoners.

The administration assumed that if prisoners are terrorized by interrogators and guards, they will divulge "actionable intelligence." When little useful information was obtained, the secretary of defense and, in at least one case, the president himself urged the interrogators to escalate their tactics. Some prisoners were tortured to death; others went mad. Still others committed suicide.

Then when CBS television broadcast photographic evidence of the torture policy on April 28, 2004, the torture makers ran for cover. They claimed that the abuse was the work of a few bad apples, when they knew it was widespread and had been carried out pursuant to their signals. They rigged investigations to minimize disclosures, but there were just too many photographs and too many reports of battered corpses, sexual humiliation, and even rape to maintain deniability.

Thus the American people came to realize that there were other reasons for them to despise us. As accounts of the torture spread throughout the Middle East, al Qaeda acquired thousands of imitators, and world opinion, which had been massively sympathetic to the victims of 9/11, came to see the United States as arrogant, brutal, and breathtakingly hypocritical.

So the cover-up began. Generals, lawyers, judges, and politicians who would claim every possible legal right on behalf of themselves strove mightily to deny all legal rights to alleged terrorists, including the right to challenge their detentions before impartial decision makers. In 2006, Republicans in Congress, with some Democratic support, did something unprecedented in American law: they granted the torturers amnesty from prosecution. They gave the president the power to imprison *any person,* citizen or alien, he chose to label as an enemy combatant, and they denied those persons the right to challenge their incarceration at a full evidentiary hearing in federal district court. Government lawyers did everything they could to interfere with the right of prisoners to bring habeas petitions and the right of lawyers to meet with their clients. Meanwhile, federal judges, who should have been more skeptical, gave the administration years in which to carry out its illegal and inhumane policies while they denied innocent victims of kidnapping and torture the right to sue for monetary damages.

So, we must ask, Why do these *officials* hate our freedoms? One answer, of course, may be that they know little about those freedoms, and how much they depend on limited government. Another is that their hatred of terrorists has blinded them to the consequences of the torture policy. A third explanation may lie in the fact that hatred, and the incitement of it, has been an electoral strategy of the Republican Party for the past forty years. It is the glue that has held the party together through one metaphorical war after another.

Fear, Revenge, and the Power They Bring

The torture policy grew out of two impulses—fear and revenge. Both were understandable in the wake of 9/11. Both helped Republicans (and Blue Dog Democrats) win subsequent elections, but neither served the nation well. Both led to existential decision making, driven by passion and unhinged from reality. That was true of the decisions to invade Afghanistan and Iraq, and it was true of the decision to torture.

September 11 was not the first time that the United States had suffered a sneak attack. Japan's bombing of Pearl Harbor in 1941 engendered just as much, if not more, hatred. But cooler heads eventually prevailed, and the war in the Pacific was delayed until the war against Germany was well launched. In 2001, however, cooler heads did not prevail. The pragmatic Republicans who had worked for George H. W. Bush were excluded from the administration of his son.

George W. Bush was as impulsive in his first year in office as John F. Kennedy was in his. But unlike Kennedy, the younger Bush did not learn from his mistakes. He surrounded himself with sycophants and relied on neoconservative advisers who believed that military power could sweep away all obstacles.

Unlike Kennedy, Bush was remarkably uncurious. He knew almost nothing about the Middle East beyond the location of its oil, and he did not foresee how the linguistic and cultural ignorance of American troops would lead them to alienate the very people they were ordered to detain and question. Indeed, the president and his aides believed that the Iraqis would forgive the United States for the aerial bombardments, the Gulf War, and the twelve-year embargo that had killed their children and welcome the conquerors with open arms. Like President Kennedy's staff, which entertained similar delusions prior to the 1961 Bay of Pigs disaster, Bush's staff did not prepare for the predictable aftermath, including the occupation, the insurgency, and the abuse of prisoners.

The Bush administration also appears to have learned nothing from other armies of occupation, including the Germans in World War II Europe, the French in Algeria, the British in Northern Ireland, or the United States in Vietnam. The ideologues who urged Bush on seem to have had a Texas-size belief that they could create any reality they wanted simply by wedding military force to propaganda. They seem to have been oblivious to the fact that wars against terrorism are less about firepower than about public opinion and that nothing alienates an occupied society faster than the humiliation of its people and the desecration of their religion and culture. Like anyone who has been too long on the campaign trail and surrounds himself with sycophants, George W. Bush had a little boy's faith in his ability to shoot unerringly from the hip.

Bush understood the political consequences of another sneak attack on the United States. He had ignored Bill Clinton's warning that terrorism would be the greatest challenge of his presidency and failed to heed the CIA's warning, a month before the attacks, that bin Laden planned to attack the United States. After taking fifty days of vacation in his first six months at the helm, Bush could not afford to be caught napping again.

Like most politicians, Bush was a short-term thinker, poised to exploit every crisis for his own partisan ends. So, too, were Rumsfeld and Cheney. The public's hatred of al Qaeda gave them a golden opportunity to exploit the shift of political power to the presidency that happens whenever the public is frightened. Action was demanded, and the ends of safety and vengeance were allowed to overcome whatever qualms anyone had about the means to achieve them. But while the president might have been jejune at first, his aides were experienced calculators. They used the crisis to inflate executive power.

By 2001, the United States was spending more on its military and intelligence establishment than all the nations of the world combined, despite the absence of a comparable rival. Al Qaeda, by contrast, was a tiny organization capable of no more than an occasional, albeit lethal, suicide attack. On 9/11, however, terrorists did not just seize four airliners and kill thousands of people; they struck the Pentagon itself, shattering the nation's belief that a large military can keep America safe. To restore that belief, the public was more than willing to allow their unproven president to unleash all of America's destructive power on anyone who resembled or might be associated with the terrorists. As former secretary of state Henry Kissinger declared, "they" had humiliated us, so "we need to humiliate them."[5]

The Party of Fear and Resentment

Exploiting insecurities and preaching vengeance was nothing new to the right wing of the Republican Party. For decades its campaign managers had understood, far better than Democrats did, that voting is more an expression of sentiments—like fear, prejudice, and insecurity—than it is making an informed choice. While the Democrats offered programs, the Republicans fanned resentments.

From the 1940s to the 1970s, anti-Communists like Senator Joseph McCarthy (R-WI) offered security from an exaggerated Communist menace and accused the Democrats, despite their leadership in World War II, of being unpatriotically soft on Communism. In the 1960s, Republicans used similar us versus them politics to win over white segregationists in the South and white ethnic groups in the North. That tactic wasn't just a strategy; McCarthyites and segregationists believed that those who questioned their policies must be Communists. Of course, Republican candidates had to be more subtle, so they couched their appeals to the fears of Wallace Democrats in the South and Reagan Democrats in the North in coded language and symbolic gestures. But their purpose was unmistakable: they wanted to win over voters who felt threatened by the civil rights and black power movements, antiwar protesters, feminists, hippies, and gays.

The strategy worked so well that conservative Republicans rebuilt the Grand Old Party around a string of wedge issues. Their war on crime and drugs was largely a coded attack on blacks, Hispanics, and the poor—groups that had voted for Democrats since the Great Depression. As a result, the United States now incarcerates more than 2.2 million of "them," or more prisoners per capita than any other nation on earth.[6] Welfare cheating by the poor (again, code for blacks) also became a successful us versus them issue for Republicans in the 1980s and 1990s, tapping the resentments of working-class whites countrywide, to the benefit of wealthy, tax averse whites.

Republicans also appealed to Christian and Jewish fundamentalists who were outraged by abortion, contemptuous of gays, and hostile to Islam. During the 1980s, the Reagan administration used a deliberate disinformation campaign to exaggerate the real, but limited, threat Libyan terrorists posed. Since then, Republicans have substituted Muslim terrorists for Communists and added poor immigrants to blacks to enlarge the pool of domestic "others." During the election of 2008, predominant Republican conservatives even persuaded majorities of blacks and Hispanics to help them pass an anti-gay marriage ballot question in California over the opposition of a majority of white voters.[7] Whatever out-groups the Republicans choose to demonize, the strategy remains the same—draw support from voters who are driven less by hopes than fear, real or imagined, that somewhere, somehow, some undeserving group is conspiring to deprive them of their status, safety, or privileges.[8]

Resentful voters, as a rule, do not care much for the rights of others. Nor do they fear power or believe that hated others ought to be presumed innocent until proven guilty. Like the German masses, whom Hitler persuaded to view Jews, Communists, homosexuals, and gypsies as enemies of the Reich, a significant segment of the American electorate can be frightened into supporting anyone who promises to keep them safe from others.

Resentful voters tend to favor authoritarian government, military solutions, and secrecy. Because they are ruled mainly by impulses, they are more likely to believe that urgent ends, like fighting terrorism, can justify illegal and immoral means, including torture, assassination, and preventive warfare. Republicans, as well as cable news channels and talk radio hosts, encouraged resentful voters to deplore "moral decay" and think of themselves as morally superior to "them," whomever they happen to be.

In the 1980s, conservative Republicans denounced "bleeding heart liberals" so effectively that Democrats switched to calling themselves progressives. Then conservatives began scapegoating government itself. "Government isn't the solution to our problem," Ronald Reagan proclaimed. "It is the problem."[9] The programs that Republicans sought to discredit and sabotaged when in power supplied social services that New Deal Democrats had won with working-class support. The judicial activism that Republicans regularly denounced had redeemed the promise of equality and justice for them too.

The cutting edge of Republican politics thus became the politics of tabloid journalism.[10] Its primary appeal has been to backlash voters[11] who, like President George W. Bush, are "dead certain"[12] that their most primitive instincts are right. It is the antithesis of deliberative, programmatic politics—that is, the politics of planning, or the rethinking of such failed policies as imprisonment without rehabilitation.[13]

Success with the politics of resentment has led right-wing Republicans, including lawyers and judges, to reject the most fundamental premise of the American legal system—that is, anyone seized by the government must be presumed innocent until proven guilty and guaranteed fair hearings. Indeed, authoritarian conservatives tend to assume that "they" are so guilty that there is no point in requiring the government to prove each of them guilty beyond a reasonable doubt. Authoritarians do not care that the criminal justice system often convicts blacks on the basis of less evidence than they would accept to convict whites. They insist on longer prison sentences for the kinds of crimes that poor blacks are most likely to commit, for example, using crack cocaine. They also champion the death penalty, serene in the knowledge that it will be used mainly against blacks, and they tolerate evidence of police perjury that they would not ignore if used against middle-class whites. Given these resentments, authoritarian Republicans had no objection to military commissions for alleged terrorists.

The politics of resentment does not just mobilize voters' passions in a way that policy proposals cannot. It also distracts swing voters from the Republicans' unwillingness to solve social problems through social services or from their zeal for granting tax cuts to wealthy donors through long-term borrowing.[14] The Republicans prefer to answer violence with violence both because they believe, falsely, that it is cheaper to punish than rehabilitate and because retribution is more satisfying to the tabloid-loving crowd that often provides the party's margin of victory.

Scapegoating for votes is a nasty business and, like torture, tends to escalate. As a result, partisan politics has become so vicious that well-meaning moderates have often dropped out of electoral politics in despair, convinced that nothing can be done.[15] The greatest losses have been suffered by the moderate wing of the Republican Party, which was once represented by such pragmatists as Dwight D. Eisenhower and Nelson Rockefeller. So far these defections have worked to the benefit of hard-line conservatives; they are freer to inflame resentful voters when they have fewer moderates in their own party to restrain them.

When scapegoating for votes, authoritarian Republicans exaggerate foreign threats. Without foreigners to demonize, their party would not be able to win funding for the defense and intelligence contracts on which its more affluent donors and constituents depend. To keep the defense contractors' support, corporate Republicans have encouraged xenophobic sentiments in the South and West. Their successes in these geographic areas make their party not only the chief sponsor of defense and intelligence industries but also the party of people most likely to favor military solutions to international problems.

The Republican Party's us versus them approach also encourages short-term, reactive thinking. The Bush administration's scary talk, endlessly repeated without regard for the truth, misled a majority of Americans into believing that Iraq was responsible for the attacks of 9/11 and therefore a proper object of retaliation.[16]

Us versus them thinking reduces morality to a set of self-serving rationalizations. It is the sort of thinking that led al Qaeda to demonize the United States and the United States to respond with torture. Unfortunately, whenever power lies with demonizers, diplomacy, morality, and the rule of law fail. Lawlessness, cruelty, and depravity take over, much as they did in Hitler's Germany and during the religious wars of the seventeenth century.

A Crisis Mentality

It takes a crisis mentality for ordinary people to endorse torture, and a crisis mentality most certainly seized the Bush administration, its right-wing base, and most Americans in the days following September 11, 2001. Administration officials repeatedly declared that this was a war unlike all other wars and that the United States had reached a turning point in history when evil might finally overwhelm good. There was no time for the deliberate processes of law enforcement or the niceties of due process. Extreme measures were called for. Liberty would have to be sacrificed for security. We were told, "They hate our freedoms" and will attack again unless we attack them first.

These new enemies could not be understood, reasoned with, or isolated politically. They were mad dogs, infected with a political disease called Islamofascism, for which military defeat was the only known cure. Like the Communists before them, this enemy's operatives were not ordinary mortals with limited resentments, resources, and ambitions; they were superhuman, globe-trotting killers like Carlos the Jackal. There was only one way to defeat such "evil doers," the administration reasoned, and that was to use their weapons, as well as ours, against them in a war to the finish. Such thinking especially appealed to the Republican Party's new core, the fundamentalist Christians who prayed for yet another morality play in which our angels would defeat their devils in overtime.

Secret Government

Since 1974, three major political-military scandals have disgraced the nation: Watergate and the associated scandals of the intelligence agencies, the Iran-contra affair, and the war on terrorism. Each of these abuses involved secret agencies and was undertaken by Republicans. Watergate and its associated scandals involved the misuse of intelligence capabilities against Americans at home; the Iran-contra affair involved their abuse abroad. The war on terrorism involves abuses by the intelligence agencies at home and abroad, mainly at the behest of the Bush administration.

Of course, both parties helped build the secret agencies that modern presidents have exploited. Much of the apparatus was in place before Nixon took office. As Senator Church's Senate Select Committee on Intelligence concluded in 1976,

> For decades Congress and the courts as well as the press and the public have accepted the notion that the control of intelligence activities was the exclusive prerogative of the Chief Executive and his surrogates. The exercise of this power was not questioned or even inquired into by outsiders. Indeed, at times the power was seen as flowing not from the law, but as inherent in the Presidency. Whatever the theory, the fact was that intelligence activities were essentially exempted from the normal system of checks and balances. Such Executive power, not founded in law or checked by Congress or the courts, contained the seeds of abuse.[17]

While a few Democrats—including Senators Sam J. Ervin, Jr., of North Carolina, Frank Church of Idaho, and Patrick Leahy of Vermont, and Representatives Otis Pike of New York and John Conyers of Michigan—took political risks to expose these abuses of authority, they could never count on a reliable majority of either house to support them. More often than not, conservative Republicans supported by a few Blue Dog Democrats from the more militaristic South torpedoed the Democrats' best efforts. Moderate Republicans, who once helped liberal Democrats pass reform legislation, no longer have much influence.

It would be a mistake to think of the torture policy as the work of one misguided administration and therefore easy to end with an election. Torture is a repertoire that the CIA has researched, advocated, and practiced, off and on, under both Republican and Democratic administrations since the late 1940s. Military intelligence has tried to develop the torturer's art too, administering mind-altering drugs to unsuspecting servicemen during the Eisenhower years.[18] Abductions were undertaken under the Reagan, George H. W. Bush, and Clinton administrations. The illegal wiretapping, burglaries, kidnapping, torture, and secret prisons of recent years are as much the consequence of secret bureaucracies as they are the work of political leaders. What is new is the presidential abrogation of the laws of war in order to use kidnappings, indefinite detentions, and torture against suspects—often innocent suspects—in the war on terrorism and the widespread dissemination of photographic evidence.

Today, secret agencies are as much a part of American government as Congress or the State Department. The military-industrial complex that won World War II never dissipated, but it has been supplemented by an ever-growing intelligence apparatus with its own corporate base. Like the Republican Party, those intelligence agencies need new enemies from time to time to escape irrelevance. As a result, the United States is now engaged in what the historian Charles A. Beard warned would become "a perpetual war for perpetual peace."[19]

This legacy of the Cold War has also given the United States a second government. In addition to the open government that children learn about in school, we have another secret, lawless, brutal, and deceitful government, with an annual budget of more than $50 billion, that commits crimes with impunity and threatens the constitutional and legal foundations of our republic. The turning point came in 1947, when the Central Intelligence Agency was created (from the remains of the World War II–era Office of Strategic Services) to combat Soviet covert action in the "back alleys of the world." At that time, Senator Arthur H. Vandenberg (R-MI) advised President Harry S. Truman that if he wished to develop covert capabilities he would have to "scare hell out of the American people."[20] Truman did. Other presidents followed suit, once they realized that scaring people is the most efficient way to expand executive power.

Americans are now so accustomed to secret government that it is difficult to imagine conducting foreign policy without it. What they have yet to do is ask whether so much secret government is worth the harm it has caused.

In hindsight, it is difficult to justify most covert operations since World War II. For example, one of the CIA's first adventures was to insert hundreds of spies, mostly displaced persons, behind the Iron Curtain. Nearly all were captured, killed, or doubled back against their handlers, putting friends and foes alike on notice that the agency was incompetent. In 1958, the CIA backed a rebellion against the Sukarno regime in Indonesia, flying bombing runs until an American pilot was captured and convicted. The coup failed, but Indonesians were not deceived. While Americans slept, the world's largest Muslim nation came to distrust the United States.

Reconnaissance flights over the Soviet Union were a success until U-2 pilot Gary Powers was shot down in 1960 and President Eisenhower was caught lying about it. The National Security Agency's electronic intercepts were also useful during the Cold War, but the invasion of Cuba that the CIA organized in 1961 was an unmitigated disaster.

Americans have all but forgotten, but the war in Vietnam and the ancillary operations in Cambodia and Laos were outgrowths of covert military and paramilitary assistance. So, too, were the disastrous "pacification" programs that led to the detention, torture, and murder of thousands of suspected Viet Cong by Special Forces and CIA units working alone or in conjunction with South Vietnamese troops.

The agency's overthrow of Mohammed Mossadegh's regime in Iran in 1953 might be counted a short-term success, but the shah it installed became a brutal dictator. He was overthrown by a popular uprising in 1979 (that the CIA did not anticipate), after which an even worse regime of ayatollahs took control.

Revolutionary students took fifty-three members of the American embassy staff hostage for more than a year. That staff's failure to obtain early warning and possibly avoid capture may be attributed, in no small part, to the inability of most of them to speak the local languages. This lack of basic competency persists to this day. The hostage crisis eventually led President Jimmy Carter, who should have known better, to authorize a rescue attempt by a paramilitary force from the Defense Department. This operation was as ill conceived as the Bay of Pigs invasion was and quickly crashed and burned in the desert. During the Reagan years, the CIA and military intelligence failed to anticipate and prevent the bombing of U.S. Marine barracks and the U.S. embassy in Lebanon. Reagan's CIA supported Saddam Hussein in his war against Iran and emboldened him to seize Kuwait. George H. W. Bush then launched the Gulf War, which President Clinton followed by bombing Iraq, off and on, for nearly a decade to enforce a no-fly zone. Is it any wonder, then, that Iranians, North Koreans, and even Syrians believe they would be more secure from the overt and covert military operations of the United States if they had their own atomic bombs?

Over the years, the CIA has helped a number of dictators seize or hold power from Guatemala to the Philippines. Some of these operations may have prevented Communists from taking over, but none advanced democracy or human rights. In 1963, the CIA helped install the Ba'ath Party in power in Iraq, which led, in due course, to Saddam Hussein's dictatorship. In the early 1980s, the agency armed the mujahideen, who ousted Soviet troops from Afghanistan. In the process, however, it jump-started the careers of Osama bin Laden, the Taliban, and their terrorist friends. In 2001, the CIA joined a cabal of Afghan warlords to defeat the Taliban, but as of this writing that militant sect is still a force to be reckoned with.[21]

In 1953, the CIA supported a right-wing coup in Guatemala, which led to thirty-six years of civil war. During that time, military death squads tortured, raped, and slaughtered tens of thousands of Mayan peasants. Today Guatemala is one of the most violent countries in the Western hemisphere, run largely by drug lords.[22]

During the 1970s, the CIA and the Republican secretary of state Henry Kissinger winked at the assassination, kidnapping, torture, and murder of thousands of Marxist dissidents by military juntas in Chile, Argentina, Brazil,

Paraguay, and Uruguay.[23] In the 1980s, the Republicans financed death squads in Guatemala, El Salvador, and Honduras and bankrolled a clandestine, futile war by the contras to depose a Marxist regime in Nicaragua, in part by selling arms to a terrorist regime in Iran. The Reagan administration then stood by while Saddam Hussein gassed thousands of his own people in Iraq. Where democratic regimes have emerged from dictatorships in the past forty years—in Spain, Portugal, central Europe, the Baltic, and Latin America—the transition was accomplished without the CIA's help.

The agency's intelligence work has been equally unimpressive. CIA analysts did not foresee the Soviet Union's acquisition of the atom bomb in 1949, the invasion of South Korea in 1950, anti-Communist uprisings during the 1950s and 1960s, the installation of Soviet missiles in Cuba in 1962, Egypt's invasion of Israel in 1973, the Iranian revolution of 1979, the Soviet invasion of Afghanistan that same year, the collapse of the Soviet Union in 1991, Iraq's invasion of Kuwait in 1990, and the acquisition of nuclear bombs by India, Pakistan, and North Korea. They also miscalled the presence of chemical, biological, or radiological weapons in Iraq in 2003. In his prize-winning history of the CIA, Tim Weiner compared the agency's record to Edward Gibbon's description of the Roman Empire as "little more than the register of crimes, follies, and misfortunes of mankind."[24] President Eisenhower was equally unsparing. The CIA's covert operations during his administration, he said, constituted "a legacy of ashes."[25]

The CIA's greatest successes have always been at home, in the realm of public relations. Despite its many failures, the agency has repeatedly persuaded gullible presidents, legislators, and journalists—people who have watched too many spy movies—to embrace the fantasy of no-cost covert operations, including those that escalated into disastrous wars in Vietnam, Laos, and Cambodia.

Of course, the CIA was not the only agency advocating covert action. The military competed for assignments and co-opted presidents and members of Congress with the can-do optimism of the Special Forces. Because bureaucracies are always in search of new ways to use their skills, few people within the precincts of secret government were willing to risk their careers by arguing that "nothing ventured" can also mean "nothing lost" and that the soft power of diplomacy and foreign aid might, in the long run, be less expensive and more rewarding. Despite the disasters of the past sixty years, little has changed.

Making Matters Worse

One of the great myths of paramilitary and covert operations is that they are risk-free extensions of diplomacy. Our operatives won't talk. Reports of their crimes can be ignored until the news cycle turns and the public is distracted by something else. Collateral damage will be slight because our agents resemble the actors who play them and because no enemy would dare strike back at the world's only superpower.

Of course, none of these myths hold true. Covert operations do not stay secret very long, and military strikes are rarely surgical. When President Reagan tried to kill Col. Muammar Qadhafi in April 1986, in retaliation for the bombing of a disco in Germany, the bombs missed the colonel, but hit the French embassy in Tripoli. Scores of people died, including the colonel's fifteen-month-old adopted daughter Hannah. Numerous reprisals followed. The Abu Nidal Organization hanged three hostages, two British and one American, and murdered an American tourist in Jerusalem. Libya sponsored the hijacking of Pan American Flight 73 on September 5, 1986; increased arms shipments to terrorist groups (including the Provisional IRA) in 1987; and on December 21, 1988, blew up Pan American Flight 103 over Lockerbie, Scotland, killing 270 people, including 189 Americans.

When such atrocities occur, as they periodically do, few Americans pause to consider that perhaps American actions, especially by clandestine and military services, were at least partially responsible for the specific crimes or for the resentments that fueled them. Instead of reviewing the back story, which is often secret, we react with the outrage of presumptively innocent victims and demand retaliation. In the face of such popular passion, anyone who proposes the soft power of diplomacy will be excoriated for not hating "them" nearly enough. In this behavior, our nation's instincts are almost as primitive as those of al Qaeda leader Dr. Ayman al-Zawahiri, who justified his organization's atrocities as "retribution for . . . the souls of the tortured people throughout the land of Islam."[26] If the conflict in Northern Ireland offers any instruction, it will take a long time, much tragedy, and much courage on both sides to break the cycle of revenge.

The Limited Repertoire

It is tempting to believe that changing presidents will stop the kidnappings, torture, and secret prisons, but those practices are too much a part of secret government to end them easily. American presidents, for all their vaunted power, actually have few options. More often than not, they must assign a new problem to an old bureaucracy that was created for different purposes. Rarely can they create a new agency with tools specifically designed to solve a new problem. Even if they could, creating it would take too long. Secretary Rumsfeld was right: "You have to go to war with the Army you have, not the Army you want."[27] The hard truth is that despite the victory of Democrat Barack Obama in the November 2008 presidential election, Congress and the public will not invest in a war-avoiding, peace-promoting bureaucracy with sufficient resources to defuse hostilities. The prideful old slogan from the XYZ affair still holds: "Millions for defense, but not one cent for tribute."

Congress won't pay for such a bureaucracy, even in the form of an expanded State Department, because the subtle arts of peace promotion cannot quench the public's thirst for revenge. Nor would such a department promise enough new jobs in enough congressional districts to compete with the military and intelligence agencies and their suppliers.

Even if Congress could, defusing conflicts and laying foundations for peace have no drama. War, like sex, stirs emotions. It mobilizes voters and keeps the military and intelligence agencies well financed through increasingly rare intervals of peace. And therein lies a tragedy. On balance, the United States would have been better off during the decades following World War II had presidents been forced to conduct foreign relations without the clandestine, paramilitary services of the Defense Department and CIA. The torture of prisoners is just the latest manifestation of how secret criminality undermines responsibility and leads to disaster.

An Elected Monarchy?

Despite the long record of disasters, penetrating even into domestic politics, the addiction to covert operations remains as strong as ever. So long as that addiction persists, the United States is doomed to fight Orwellian wars, with all the outrages that go with them, to no good end. But that is only the half of it. Secret government—and the accommodation of judges and legislators to it—has presented the United States today with the most serious crisis in its constitutional history, at least since the Civil War. The war against terrorism, combined with computer technology, has given our government all the necessary apparatus of a police state. Torture is just one manifestation of a more general rise of lawless, unaccountable government.

The push for unaccountable government dates back to the Watergate scandal, if not before. When Boston attorney James St. Clair appeared before the Supreme Court in 1974, he defended secret government by opposing the surrender of President Nixon's Oval Office tapes. But St. Clair also warned the justices, in no uncertain terms, "The president wants me to argue that he is as powerful a monarch as Louis XIV, only four years at a time, and is not subject to the processes of any court in the land except the court of impeachment."[28]

According to historian Arthur M. Schlesinger, Jr., Nixon sought an elected monarchy modeled on "the France of Louis Napoleon and Charles de Gaulle." This "imperial presidency," Schlesinger warned, "would not require a new Constitution; presidential acts, confirmed by a Supreme Court of his own appointment, could put a new gloss on the old one." It would be, in effect, a "personal dictatorship conferred by the people in accordance with constitutional rules."[29] Nixon confirmed this ambition in 1977 when he told British interviewer David Frost that "there are certain inherently governmental activities which, if undertaken by the sovereign in protection of the interests of the nation's security are lawful, but which undertaken by private persons, are not."[30] Like John Yoo, Nixon actually thought of the president as the sovereign. "Instead of placating Congress," Schlesinger observed, Nixon "confronted it with executive *faits accomplis* taken without explanation." Like George W. Bush, Nixon tried to lead his office

> toward its ultimate form in the plebiscitary Presidency—with the President accountable only once every four years, shielded . . . between elections from congressional and public harassment, empowered by his [alleged] mandate to make war or to make peace, . . . to give out information or hold it back, superseding congressional legislation by executive order, all in the name of a majority whose choice must prevail [unless Congress] wished to embark on the drastic and improbable course of impeachment.[31]

In Nixon's case, these assertions were beaten back by the Senate Watergate Committee, the House Judiciary Committee, and John Sirica, a courageous federal judge who refused to allow the White House to hide proof of its crimes from an independent counsel. When Nixon fired the special prosecutor, he sealed his own doom.

But his vision has lived on within the conservative wing of the Republican Party. In 1987, President Reagan successfully escaped accountability for the Iran-contra affair, which, like Watergate, also involved the use of clandestine government to commit criminal acts. To shield their boss from impeachment, Reagan's lawyers threw numerous legal roadblocks in front of the independent counsel and then, during the 1990s, persuaded Clinton Democrats to dispense with such inquiries altogether. Preventing effective legal challenges to a monarchical presidency became a primary goal of the Federalist Society, urged on by Robert Bork and Antonin Scalia, who, as Justice Department lawyers in 1974, had tried to shield Richard Nixon from accountability. Bork did so by firing Archibald Cox, the special prosecutor, when his superiors refused to do so. Scalia, as head of the OLC, advocated broad interpretations of executive privilege to prevent Nixon's aides from testifying against him. Bork and Scalia were both dismayed when their boss, Attorney General John Mitchell, went to jail for his crimes, and both resolved that their party would henceforth only appoint judges who promised to exercise judicial self-restraint, which meant, among many other things, not holding Republican officials accountable for illegal covert operations at home or abroad. A decade later these two conservative lawyers were joined by a third, Samuel Alito, who, as a Justice Department attorney in 1985, crafted arrogant assertions of "unitary executive power" and presidential signing statements. All three would be nominated to the Supreme Court; only Bork would fail to receive Senate confirmation.

By the time the Abu Ghraib scandal broke in 2004, the Republicans had largely succeeded in packing the federal judiciary with judges who would hold that the Constitution does not restrain U.S. officials operating abroad. They would have us believe that rights derive from the exclusionary politics of citizenship (or residency) rather than the inclusive, egalitarian status of personhood or human rights. In matters of immigration and the detention of alleged terrorists, authoritarian Republicans insist that aliens have few, if any, constitutional rights. Moreover, because they insist that rights are mere political claims, rights can be taken away, even from citizens, by political processes.

Consistent with this agenda, authoritarian conservatives have sought to separate the system of checks and balances from constitutional rights. It does not occur to them, as it does to libertarian conservatives, that an American intelligence agency would ever classify people like themselves as persons without rights.

Finally, as the Supreme Court's Republican majority made infamously clear in *Bush v. Gore* (2000),[32] law itself is political. It derives from power, not principle, which explains why self-styled supporters of states rights had no difficulty ignoring the well-established principle that the manner of recounting votes in presidential elections is for the state courts to decide and that it is the job of state judges to decide what state election laws provide. To most lawyers active in lobbying today, judicial interpretations of the Constitution do not have to be neutral.[33] The interpretations can serve the electoral interests of political parties and the financial interests of their corporate clients, because in our interest-driven political culture, law has little to do with justice and less to do with morality.[34] Democracy, to the moneyed men, is little more than a Darwinian competition for power.

———•◦•———

Kidnapping, indefinite detention, torture, and murder are the foreseeable results of unlimited executive power, which in turn is a consequence of secrecy and the negation of checks and balances. This is the situation we face today; it is not a warning of things to come. CIA gulags can be recreated at any time. The military prison at Bagram Air Base in Afghanistan now holds six hundred prisoners and is being expanded to contain a thousand, or four times those currently held at Guantánamo.[35] Congress authorized the president to define what is cruel, inhumane, or degrading treatment under the Geneva Conventions, and failed to specifically outlaw waterboarding. The courts have shielded the torture policy (and illegal surveillance of Americans) from legal challenge by invoking the so-called state secrets privilege.

Americans are reluctant to admit it, but the president is no longer a public servant. He is an elected warlord in charge of an unaccountable government with a secret army of CIA operatives and military commandos who can kidnap, detain, torture, and murder with impunity.

Nor is it still clear that the rights guaranteed by the U.S. Constitution are universal rights of personhood in the Enlightenment tradition. Since the early 1980s, Republican officials and judges have sought to reduce them to mere political rights, derived from power and revocable in secret.

People say, "It can't happen here." But it has happened here. To reverse much of the damage may require a series of two-thirds votes of both houses of Congress to override vetoes by the current or future presidents. It will also necessitate a change in the composition of the three most important federal courts: the Supreme Court, the Court of Appeals for the District of Columbia, and the Court of Appeals for the Fourth Circuit. This tall order is more, perhaps, than a docile Congress, a distracted president, and a fearful electorate are likely to accomplish. One more terrorist attack like 9/11 and the will to remain free may be extinguished for years to come.

11

RESTORING THE RULE OF LAW

To ignore evil is to become an accomplice to it.
—MARTIN LUTHER KING, JR.[1]

In *A Man for All Seasons,* Robert Bolt's brilliant play about a lawyer's resistance to the lawlessness of his king, the suitor of Sir Thomas More's daughter declares that that he would gladly "cut down every law in England" to get at the Devil. "Oh?" Sir Thomas replies, "and when the last law was down, and the Devil turned round on you—where would you hide, Roper, the laws being flat? . . . [I]f you cut them down—and you are just the man to do it—d'you think you could stand upright in the winds that would blow then?"[2]

We Americans face that situation today. The forest of checks and balances and guaranteed liberties that has shielded us from authoritarian government for more than two hundred years has been laid low. What few protections remain could easily be sacrificed in response to another terrorist attack.

Unfortunately, there is little reason to believe that Barack Obama, who swept into office on a tsunami of hope, will restore that forest. In April 2008, he promised, if elected, to have his new attorney general "immediately review the information that's already there" to see "whether crimes have been committed" as opposed to "really bad policies."[3] Then he backpedaled, declaring that he would not want "my first term consumed by what was perceived on the part of the Republicans as a partisan witch hunt, because I think we've got too many problems to solve."[4] And the criminalization of policy differences is precisely what the Republicans would allege. That would be a lie, of course. The prohibitions against torture were not just policy; they were *laws*—long-established, well-understood criminal laws with severe penalties.

Bush administration officials did not just bend a few regulations; they authorized interrogators to inflict excruciating torment on helpless prisoners, and that torment in some instances resulted in their deaths. The administration also spied on political protesters, secretly intercepted the most intimate phone calls of servicemen and their wives, conducted dragnet intercepts of billions of e-mail communications in violation of the Fourth Amendment and the Foreign Intelligence Surveillance Act, and fired U.S. attorneys when they refused to misuse their prosecutorial powers to disenfranchise Democratic voters. These officials led the nation into a disastrous war in Iraq and made outrageous assertions of unlimited executive power. They did not just commit felonies. They waged war upon the rule of law itself.

President Obama understands that most presidents accomplish little without the support of at least some members of the opposition party in Congress. Prosecuting former President Bush and his coconspirators for war crimes would infuriate an already hyper-partisan Republican establishment on Capitol Hill. But failing to prosecute Bush officials for at least some of their crimes would send a seductive message to future presidents: they may violate the criminal law with impunity, cloak their crimes in secrecy, and evade accountability in the courts, Congress, and the press for at least four years and probably longer.

Moreover, the damage done by the torture policy was not just to American laws and institutions; it destroyed the moral standing of the United States throughout the world. Despite all the hopeful talk of "change," that moral standing will not be restored until the new president directs the Justice Department to hold the Bush administration responsible for its crimes. Failure to do so would discredit the former law professor's campaign and mark him as just another hypocritical politician.

Unfortunately, hypocrisy rarely bothers politicians. It is the lubricant of their trade. Like the voters they represent, most politicians are shortsighted. Unless they see immediate political gain to be had from prosecuting war criminals, they would prefer to move on, disbursing billions of dollars on routine and emergency appropriations. Moving on is certainly the view of their campaign managers, and it is one reason why torture was not an issue in the elections of 2004, 2006, or 2008. It is also why Obama and his congressional Democrats may very well let Bush's team get away with torture.

Closing GTMO

Of course, allowing politicians to get away with crimes is what divided Congresses do best. When Nancy Pelosi (D-CA) became speaker of the House of Representatives in 2007, she insisted that there would be no effort to impeach Cheney or Bush. Many observers saw her refusal to entertain impeachment charges as a sign of her party's fear that the Democrats would be accused of being soft on terrorism. And that is true; Democrats have been terrified of similar accusations since the McCarthy era. But removing the president (and his vice president first) would have required the support of at least fifteen to twenty Republican senators. The votes weren't there, from either side of the aisle, in no small part because if Bush and Cheney were impeached, Pelosi stood next in line to occupy the presidency.

As one of his first acts in office, President Obama issued an executive order directing the Defense Department to close its prison at Guantánamo within a year. But that is much easier said than done. Robert M. Gates, Rumsfeld's successor as secretary of defense, would have liked to have closed the prison in 2008, but, as he explained to a Senate committee that May, "We're stuck" with Guantánamo "in several ways." First, "we have a serious 'not in my backyard problem.' I haven't found anybody [in Congress] who wants these terrorists to be placed in a prison in their home state."[5]

Second, as Justice Scalia argued in *Boumediene*, GTMO contains prisoners who, were they to be returned home, probably would be released and would perhaps fight again.[6] About ninety are from Yemen, which lacks the facilities to keep them locked up. The United States runs a large prison at Puli-Charki outside of Kabul, Afghanistan, and is building a sixty-million-dollar facility at Bagram Air Base,[7] but the Afghan government may not want to be stuck with hundreds of non-Afghan prisoners when the Americans leave.

Third, GTMO contains some prisoners who could safely be released, but as Gates explained, their "home government won't accept them." These prisoners come from Uzbekistan, Tunisia, Libya, and Algeria.[8]

Finally, a few admittedly innocent prisoners, like the Uighurs from China, cannot be sent home to a government that might torture them. Some of these prisoners could be released into communities of Uighurs in the United States, as Judge Ricardo Urbina has ruled,[9] but few politicians are willing to take the political risk. They remember how unscrupulous Republicans used Willie Horton's recidivism to destroy Michael Dukakis's bid for the presidency.

Habeas proceedings in federal courts may eventually force the executive branch to release more prisoners. Congress, or the new administration, might help to release still more by raising the evidentiary standards of the review tribunals, but military screeners are not likely to take that risk either. That said, the Obama administration will not persuade many other countries to accept GTMO prisoners until the United States is willing to take some too.

Rethinking Detention Practices

Even if GTMO could be closed, the United States will still have to detain some suspected terrorists somewhere. Unfortunately, federal courts have yet to confront the question of who should be detained and why. They have also not addressed the most salient element of our nation's disgrace: the mistreatment of prisoners.

Some will argue that the courts cannot address that disgrace and that writs of habeas corpus can be used to challenge only the grounds for detentions, not the abuse of prisoners. If so, then torture and cruelty can continue for as long as presidents refuse to prosecute war criminals.

The Supreme Court chose not to address the mistreatment of prisoners in *Boumediene v. Bush,* but it did declare auspiciously that the writ is capable of expansion.[10] Congress could expand it, of course, by legislation. So, too, could judges, but lower court judges are not likely to take the lead in expanding the writ. In August 2008, Judge Urbina declined to initiate that expansion when he refused hear a challenge to the prisoners' solitary confinement brought by the Chinese Uighurs he later ordered released. "[N]o court," Urbina explained, "has ever ruled that detainees, designated enemy combatants, have a right to challenge the conditions of their confinement pursuant to the constitutional writ of habeas corpus."[11] Eventually the Supreme Court may reaffirm, in the detainee context, that coerced confessions may not be used at trial, but that finding will not stop the abuse of prisoners who are never tried. To halt their abuse will require a clear expansion of what the writ of habeas corpus is meant to do. Congress could and should amend the federal code so there is no doubt that torture and cruelty in U.S. prisons can be challenged with one fast-track procedure or another.

Meanwhile, the Obama administration should commit itself to treating suspected terrorists humanely, granting them justice, and paying compensation to those who have been wrongly detained (as the Canadian government did for Maher Arar). Obama should do so not just because it is the right thing to do but because it is the most effective means we have to defuse hatred, produce *reliable* intelligence, and reduce recidivism.

Politically, doing the right thing will not be easy. Many Americans still want revenge for 9/11 and do not care if innocent Muslims are mistreated. Even citizens who oppose outright torture do not necessarily want "them" treated well. Indeed, most voters are not disposed to treat any alleged terrorists well, even if they happen to be American citizens. It is no accident that soldiers with corrections experience in the United States committed some of the worst outrages at Abu Ghraib. For forty years, the politics of fear and resentment have persuaded a majority of Americans to favor cruelty to prisoners over rehabilitation, which is one reason why recidivism among American convicts is so high.

Treating prisoners humanely requires a kind of courage not found in vengeful people. It takes no courage to torture a helpless prisoner; that is the work of cowards. But it does take courage to be decent to prisoners who hate you—prisoners whom you have good reason to hate and fear, even in their captivity. It also takes some knowledge of history to understand that in a war against terrorism, as in counterinsurgencies, the best weapons don't shoot.

It would also help if President Obama would refuse to treat the entire world as a zone of active combat and repudiate the hysterical claim that an elderly Swiss lady who gives to an Islamic charity is as much an "enemy combatant" as a mujahid captured in Afghanistan. Civilian bombers operating covertly outside zones of active combat should be treated as criminals;[12] civilians captured in combat should be treated as soldiers, even if they don't wear uniforms. The distinction between civilian criminals and paramilitary combatants is far from perfect, but it does allow civilians to deal with civilians and soldiers to deal with soldiers. It also acknowledges that no military force is capable of prosecuting all participants in a guerrilla war.

Some kind of preventive detention will be necessary to keep enemy fighters from returning to combat. The Geneva Convention on Prisoners of War anticipates this need, and nothing in *Boumediene* bars Congress from authorizing the same treatment of insurgents actually captured in an active war zone. The Geneva Conventions provide that POWs shall be permitted to challenge the legality of their detention and treatment. That right can be extended to irregular combatants too, whether or not there is any legal duty to do so. The POW Convention also provides that detainees must be housed and fed as well as the soldiers assigned to guard them. That standard can be extended to guerrillas too.

Guerrillas charged with committing war crimes within a combat zone such as Afghanistan should be tried by military courts-martial, whether the other side reciprocates or not. Civilians charged with plotting terrorist attacks on civilian populations ought to be prosecuted in civilian courts under domestic law, as Italy has done by charging CIA agents in absentia for kidnapping suspects from their soil.

Jack Goldsmith of Harvard and Neal Katyal of Georgetown (now deputy solicitor general) would replace military commissions with a national security court empowered to oversee "a comprehensive system of preventive detention" and to prosecute enemy war criminals.[13] The two professors—one conservative, the other liberal—claim this new tribunal would "reduce the burden on ordinary civilian courts." That assertion seems unlikely because they would staff the new court with judges borrowed from those courts. They say that fairness would be ensured by selecting the defendants' counsel from among the court's own "permanent staff of elite defense lawyers with special security clearances." Why elite lawyers would want to work for such a court is unclear.

Goldsmith and Katyal seem to believe that there can be different kinds of due process of law, depending on the allegations the administration chooses to bring. They would allow the executive to deny suspects access to attorneys for as long as it takes for interrogators to work their magic. Their court, like the Star Chamber under the Stuart kings, would be free to try suspects in secret and convict them on the basis of nonstandard evidence. In other words, hated suspects, most of them foreigners and Muslims, would be deliberately accorded an inferior brand of justice.

Creating a special court for alleged terrorists would also set a bad example. If Congress can create a new court to "get" one set of pariahs, it will soon want to create other special courts to get alleged drug lords, gang members, or sex offenders.[14] This proposal would not accord equal justice under law.

Like the Foreign Intelligence Surveillance Court, which has rarely encountered a wiretap request it could not bless, a national security court would soon be packed with judges who value security (or vengeance) more than liberty, equality, or justice under the law. Like the military commissions, the proposed court would not satisfy the Geneva Conventions' requirement, in Common Article 3, that captured enemies be tried in "regularly constituted courts."[15] A regularly constituted court cannot single out a disfavored class of defendants for substandard treatment. It must adhere to the precedents and procedures applicable in all criminal cases. Indeed, under the Geneva Conventions, it must also afford defendants "all the judicial guarantees which are recognized as indispensable by civilized peoples."[16] Moreover, giving a national security court a monopoly over cases involving terrorism, torture, and detention would also exempt most of its decisions from Supreme Court review, which the high court grants mainly when disputes among circuits need to be resolved.

Goldsmith and Katyal did get one thing right: the detention centers should not be run by secret agencies. President Obama was right to immediately revoke Bush's Executive Order 13440,[17] which authorized the CIA to operate secret prisons; now Congress should join him in providing that all prisoners seized in active combat or turned over to U.S. agencies by foreign governments on suspicion of terrorist connections be tranferred promptly to the regularly constituted prison systems of the armed forces or the Justice Department. Those prisons should be subject to frequent inspections by the International Committee of the Red Cross, the UN Committee Against Torture, and the relevant agencies' inspectors general. At present, ICRC reports are confidential and go only to the Defense Department, which has ignored them at will. Legislation could limit this confidentiality to a reasonable period of time and then make those reports publicly available.

Congress and the president should also prohibit forced disappearances, which occur not only during renditions but whenever the CIA, the military, or the Justice Department fails to register its captives with the ICRC. Allowing any agency to hold ghost prisoners (such as the murdered "Mr. Frosty") is an invitation to abuse. One way to avert this abuse is to require the creation of a national electronic registry of prisoners, with exceptions only for those prisoners who have been transferred to a witness (or informant) protection program and under a regimen that grants them judicially enforced rights. Similarly, guards, interrogators, and translators should be liable, both criminally and civilly, if they obstruct access to prisoners by their attorneys, families, or the ICRC.

To curb forced disappearances, President Obama was also correct to require that the ICRC receive timely notification and access to all detainees held by any

American agency.[18] The same access should be extended to the UN Committee Against Torture and authorized by Congress by ratifying the International Convention for the Protection of All Persons from Enforced Disappearances[19] and the Optional Protocol to the Convention Against Torture.[20]

Prohibitions against assassinations or any targeted killings that are not part of congressionally authorized military combat should be strengthened. Opponents will argue, How can you possibly object to killing Hitler (or bin Laden)? But that is the wrong question. Life does not imitate the movies, where the good guys are always right, competent, and successful, and assassinations have no harmful consequences. In truth, most covert military operations since the late 1940s have failed, and some have produced disastrous consequences. Attempts by the Kennedy administration to kill Fidel Castro may have led to Kennedy's assassination. We will never know, but we should not encourage international gang warfare when our own leaders are so vulnerable and our covert operatives so inept.

Instead of asking what's wrong with killing Hitler, one should ask, Given what we now know of George W. Bush's decision making, should Congress grant future presidents the authority to kill anyone they suspect of terrorist activities? Are the benefits that might accrue from such killings likely to outweigh the harm that would be done by their almost inevitable disclosure?

And just how would such a license to kill for God and country be granted? By secret legislation? By a court decision upholding the president's unbuttoned claims to unlimited power? By a secret legal opinion issued by partisan sycophants in the Office of Legal Counsel?

No agency of the federal government should be permitted to kidnap prisoners from one country and fly them to another for interrogation under torture. Accordingly, President Obama should revoke Bush's still-secret September 17, 2001, order authorizing this practice and make its contents public. The United States has extradition treaties with most European and common-law countries so that impartial judges, rather than law enforcement bureaucrats, decide whether there is probable cause to surrender alleged criminals to a foreign government for trial. The United States does not have extradition treaties with most Middle Eastern (and formerly Soviet) dictatorships because their criminal justice systems are unlikely to act justly. Under most extradition treaties, the United States refuses to surrender political offenders because the State Department has, until recently, recognized that one country's terrorist may well be another's freedom fighter. It is time to reaffirm these principles, which George Washington and Daniel Webster pioneered.[21]

Then there is the question of what to do with unwanted prisoners held by the U.S. armed forces in Afghanistan, Iraq, and elsewhere. Dozens of Afghan men have been transferred to the Karzai government, only to be convicted, mainly on American allegations, in secret proceedings lasting less than an hour and given sentences of up to twenty years in prison.[22] Under a new, vaguely worded status of forces agreement, more than twenty-one thousand prisoners are scheduled for transfer to Iraqi officials' custody, amid anguished protests, especially from minority Sunnis.[23] Two hundred and fourteen suspected militants held by the United States in Iraq have been delivered to the Egyptian, Saudi Arabian, and other *intelligence* services.[24] There is a serious moral question whether the United States should deliver anyone to such agencies against his will.

In *Munaf v. Geren,* decided the same day as *Boumediene,* the Supreme Court ruled that two *American citizens* held by the U.S. military in Iraq had the right to file a habeas petition in federal district court to challenge a decision to transfer them to an Iraqi court for trial. However, the justices did not extend (or deny) that habeas right to *foreigners* whom the U.S. military planned to deliver to Iraq or other countries.[25] Nor would it be practical, in most instances, for foreigners to pursue habeas relief in U.S. civilian courts. Some kind of independent, in-country review of the military's rendition plans needs to be legislated by Congress so that prisoners are not delivered to foreign intelligence agencies for probable torture or death at a reopened Abu Ghraib.

Ending Torture, Cruelty, and Degradation

To restore the Geneva Conventions, Congress should begin by repealing the Military Commissions Act of 2006. In that law, Congress purported to grant the president the exclusive authority to define what constitutes the war crime of "cruel, inhumane, and degrading treatment." Defining what constitutes a crime is the legislature's job and should not be delegated to the president. Congress must give everyone, including prosecutors, clear notice of what is forbidden and leave the courts to resolve marginal ambiguities in ways that respect foreign as well as American interpretations of mutual treaties. Repealing the entire MCA would not only get rid of its habeas-stripping provisions in the case of aliens (which the Supreme Court struck down in *Boumediene*), but it would also repeal an ancillary provision barring civil actions brought on behalf of alien victims of American abuse.[26]

Congress should also repeal the Detainee Treatment Act of 2005. What constitutes torture and cruelty should not be delegated to the military or its manual writers as President Obama has done with his first executive order. By repealing the entire act, Congress would get rid of the "my lawyer said I could" defense and an excessively broad definition of what constitutes an enemy combatant.

Equally important, Congress should extend the statute of limitations for federal conspiracies to ten or fifteen years. Then Obama's attorney general could not put off prosecuting the torture team until Obama's second term, by which time the five-year statute of limitations on conspiracy will have run out. Otherwise, there is little chance that Americans will ever learn the full story of how the torture policy came to be.

To avoid the secret pettifogging that marked the Bush administration's torture policy, all interrogators and guards should be publicly instructed to apply the "golden rule" of the Geneva Conventions: "If you would be outraged to learn that the interrogation techniques you are contemplating have been *inflicted on your family*, then it is forbidden by law."

More important, Congress should build on what Barack Obama accomplished in the Illinois legislature[27] and require all intelligence, military, and law enforcement agencies and their civilian contractors to *videotape all custodial interrogations.* Copies of the tapes, identifying all participants, dates, time, and location, should be delivered electronically to an impartial archive, because the prospect of accountability is the best deterrent to cruelty.[28]

In addition, all intelligence agencies and their civilian contractors should be legally required to follow the same rules of interrogation that bind the military, and those rules should be made public. To the extent that intelligence agencies are allowed to detain prisoners, the detentions should be brief and subjected to inspections by independent inspectors general.

Much of the recent prisoner abuse did not occur during interrogations. Some of it was to "prepare" prisoners for interrogations. Most of it was gratuitous because the administration signaled its indifference to abuse. Failure to set clear standards and respond to complaints should be punished for what it is—a dereliction of duty.

A Truth Commission or Congressional Hearings?

Prosecuting the torture team would constitute a major political commitment by the new administration for which there is little, if any, electoral payoff. The last time Democrats were in a position to prosecute Republicans—for secretly selling arms to a nation that sponsored terrorism—they fumbled the ball, and major principals in the Iran-contra scandal went unpunished (or were given immunity from criminal prosecution in return for an afternoon of "I don't remember" answers on Capitol Hill). After Kenneth Starr abused his powers while going after President Clinton as a congressionally mandated prosecutor independent of the Justice Department, Congress repealed the law under which he was appointed.

Some commentators have argued that elections, informed by investigations, are the best way to hold presidents accountable for their crimes. But George W. Bush was reelected in 2004 despite widespread knowledge of his torture policy, proving yet again that elections are no guarantee of government under the law.

Harvard law professor Alan Dershowitz, writing in the *Wall Street Journal,* concedes that "no one is above the law," but he advances a "countervailing principle that is equally important: the results of an election should not determine who is to be prosecuted. [E]ven if the winners [of the election of 2008] honestly believe that the losers committed 'genuine crimes' rather than having pursued 'bad policies,'" he argues, echoing Obama, they should not be prosecuted because that effort would almost certainly be seen as "a partisan witch hunt."[29]

There are several flaws in this argument. First, the issue is not that the Bush administration pursued bad policy; it engaged in criminal activity. Second, if the criminals will not prosecute themselves, why shouldn't the people elect an administration that will? Third, if appearances are to trump justice, then shouldn't al Qaeda's terrorists be exempt from prosecution, so as to avoid the appearance of "victors' justice"? Fourth, why should we assume that succeeding administrations—and federal judges—are incapable of enforcing the law fairly? Will all succeeding administrations be incapable of fairness or only those administrations dominated by an opposing political party? Taken literally, the professor's remarks would seem to suggest that President Bush lost the election of 2008, when he was not up for reelection, but the argument is far from clear.

Dershowitz apparently believes that the invention of political parties, which was extra-constitutional, had the effect of repealing the constitutional principle that no man is above the law. Or to paraphrase George Orwell, the framers intended for all men to stand equal before the law, except when the Justice Department is controlled by their political opponents.[30] Then fairness requires that they not be prosecuted.

Presidents and their aides, Dershowitz insists, must be immune from all prosecutions, no matter how heinous their crimes, because no succeeding attorney general can be trusted to be nonpartisan. Moreover, he adds, it is better to let the torture team go free than to inhibit "creative policy making and implementation" by bloody-minded presidents in the future.

Other commentators, including Stuart Taylor of *Newsweek* [31] and Nicolas Kristof of the *New York Times*,[32] have argued for an independent truth commission with subpoena power instead of congressional hearings or prosecutions. Only if Obama's Justice Department foreswears prosecutions, they say, will Bush administration officials be persuaded to confess their sins. But if there is no threat of punishment and therefore no prospect of a plea bargain, why would anyone— for example, David Addington—admit anything?

Some legislators have argued that only a truth commission, unaccompanied by any form of prosecution, can avoid renewal of the crippling animosities that accompanied Bill Clinton's impeachment. What Washington really needs, they argued, is "reconciliation," not more partisanship. These arguments typically come from members of Congress whose priorities lie more in getting additional appropriations for their districts than in upholding the rule of law or in preventing the royal prerogatives asserted by recent presidents from becoming permanent.

Truth and reconciliation commissions are for countries such as South Africa and East Timor that have suffered a total breakdown in law and order and must therefore settle for symbolic accountability. That is not our current predicament. The American legal system can easily try another dozen or so criminals—even high-profile criminals.

It is also worth remembering that commissions are rarely given the time or money to get to the bottom of a scandal, and they encounter all sorts of obstacles to acquiring information. Unlike congressional committees, commissions cannot push reforms on Capitol Hill. To prevaricating politicians, the chief function of most commissions is to run out the political clock (and the statute of limitations) while fostering an illusion that reform is on the way.

If the threatened political party cannot protect itself from congressional hearings by appointing a docile commission, its members in Congress will typically advocate creating a *joint* committee of the House and Senate. Joint committees are easier to disrupt because the natural rivalries of the House and Senate members can be exploited by the opponents of reform, much as Representative Cheney confounded the joint Iran-contra committee. Should committee members actually agree on some proposals, they still will lack the authority to push them to the floor.

Congressional hearings are not essential to establishing the Bush administration's crimes. The chief function of hearings should be to amplify what is known and push for major reforms. But who should hold them? Within Barack Obama's legal team, some support has been expressed for something similar to the Church Committee, a temporary body that effectively investigated wrongdoing by intelligence agencies working for both Democratic and Republican administrations.[33] But the Church Committee was created before Congress established permanent standing committees of both houses to oversee intelligence matters. Those committees are now well entrenched. They will not look kindly on the creation of an ad hoc committee to do their work, especially since the current predicament is, in no small part, owing to their failures at oversight.

Another alternative is to assign the task to the judiciary committees of the House and Senate. They have already held some useful hearings, but they have been disrupted by partisan conflict. One key to the Church Committee's success was its relative lack of partisanship, which was made possible by the appointment of relatively nonpartisan senators and a nonpartisan staff. Of course, there were greater numbers of moderate Republicans back then. Even so, ad hoc committees of each house, made up of the least partisan members of the intelligence, judiciary, and armed services committees, might be the better solution. Such hybrids would not only have subpoena power and the power to promote some of the reforms recommended above, but they could also complete the Church Committee's work on comprehensive charters for the CIA, FBI, and military intelligence agencies.

Some advocates of an independent commission would prefer that it focus on the Bush administration's crimes, but neither commissions nor congressional committees should focus on the crimes of specific individuals. Prosecutions are best left to nonpartisan professionals. The chief function of legislative oversight is not to expose individuals but to study the larger picture and restore checks and balances, guaranteed liberties, and the rule of law.

Prosecution and Its Obstacles

That said, prosecution is essential and should begin as soon as the amnesty provisions of the Military Commissions Act can be repealed and the statute of limitations extended. The prosecutors would presumably target underlings first and use plea bargains to obtain evidence against their superiors, including Cheney, Rumsfeld, and Gonzales. Whether George W. Bush is indicted is probably less important than sending a clear signal to future cabinet-level officials that the United States still has a government under law and that they had better obey the criminal law, no matter what their president orders or what his legal lackeys say.

Should we discover that Bush secretly pardoned himself and his subordinates, that claim must be rejected. The conventional wisdom is that pardons trump prosecutions, but that contention is a gross exaggeration. Presidents may refuse to charge their subordinates, but that exercise of prosecutorial discretion does not bind their successors. Pardons are forever; so if presidents are allowed to pardon themselves and their henchmen in advance of prosecution, then the pardon power becomes a license to commit crimes with impunity. Under such reasoning, the constitutional system of checks and balances, guaranteed liberties, and the rule of law would cease to exist.

It is one thing for a president to grant mass amnesties, as Andrew Johnson did for Confederate soldiers or Jimmy Carter did for Vietnam-era draft dodgers, but when a president pre-pardons himself and his subordinates in order to prevent prosecution for their own crimes, he is obstructing justice. Properly viewed, President Ford's pardon of Nixon in advance of a trial was mislabeled. It was really an exercise of prosecutorial discretion, which need not have bound succeeding administrations. To be eligible for a pardon, a member of Bush's torture team should, at the very least, have to go before a court and present an acceptable admission of guilt to a specific crime. Then the guilty party should be pardoned for that crime only. This essential clarity could be provided by legislation that expressly states that presidents may only *pardon* convicts.[34]

Yet another obstacle to prosecution is the claim that making interrogation policy to obtain actionable intelligence was, as Gonzales certified, within the scope of the torture team's employment. Congress could also repudiate that claim.

Finally there is the question of who should do the prosecuting. Ideally the Justice Department should be in charge, if only to restore its integrity. But that ideal does not preclude the appointment of a nonpartisan prosecutor with considerable independence, as Attorney General Elliot Richardson did when he chose Archibald Cox to lead the Watergate team. The attorney general could choose a special prosecutor from among any number of U.S. attorneys who happen to be Republicans.

If the Justice Department is unable to prosecute the torture team because of an amnesty law or statute of limitations, then the way is open for foreign trials, where congressional grants of immunity and presidential "pardons" have no legal force. The president and the two-thirds of the Senate are not likely to submit to the jurisdiction of the International Criminal Court by ratifying the Rome Statute, but President Obama could revoke the non-extradition agreements that John Bolton extorted from foreign governments and allow the Justice Department to facilitate extradition proceedings on behalf of any European prosecutor seeking to bring the torture team's members to justice under the principle of universal jurisdiction for war crimes.

The legal obstacles to prosecuting the torture team are substantial, but they are no more daunting than what Argentina and Chile encountered after their dirty wars. Whether the United States will take as long as those countries did to bring its torturers to justice remains to be seen, but a failure to prosecute now will almost certainly lead to demands for prosecution later. This issue is not likely to go away.

Curbing Secrecy

At the moment, civil suits by the victims of torture are blocked by the state secrets privilege, but that rule, too, can be changed. American judges need to start taking notice that secrecy has been massively abused for more than half a century, as the Watergate, Iran-contra, and torture scandals attest. Judges also must acknowledge that currently officials who invoke the privilege cannot explain the difference between what needs to be kept secret from foreign enemies and what is merely embarrassing to persons in power. Instead of deferring to overbroad claims to secrecy, judges should return to one of the founders' core insights—that nothing makes public officials more untrustworthy than the absence of accountability.

Congress need not wait for judges to narrow the state secrets privilege. It is not grounded in the Constitution. It was invented by judges and can be changed by them. Or Congress, which passed the Classified Information Procedures Act of 1980 to prescribe how state secrets should be handled in criminal trials,[35] can extend that law to civil suits as well. Contrary to the Bush administration's claims, it is not the function of the executive to decide what evidence may be withheld or which cases and controversies involving state secrets can be heard. Rule 501 of the Federal Rules of Evidence already empowers judges to decide what information may be withheld from trial on grounds of national security.[36] Thus if they wished, courts could extend the basic principles of the Classified Information Procedures Act to civil suits. Congress and judges can also let government lawyers know that if they do not wish to submit allegedly secret evidence for judicial inspection, in camera; consent to the documents' use at trial; or negotiate a sanitized version that the parties can agree on, then they must settle or forfeit the case.

Not so long ago it was possible to distinguish between American and British approaches to public information. In the United Kingdom, administrators assumed that the government papers were akin to the sovereign's household effects, to be kept from the prying eyes of her subjects, unless her ministers deigned to disclose them as an act of sovereign grace. In the United States, by contrast, the people were meant to be sovereign. The preamble to the Constitution says so. Public officials are supposed to be the people's *servants*. Government documents are not their private possessions but are entrusted to their stewardship. Secrets were supposed to be rare and temporary because government was supposed to be open to public scrutiny. Otherwise, the Constitution's provisions for periodic elections and checks and balances would make no sense. That original understanding has now been lost.

It is long past time for Congress to revamp the system of security classifications, which harms the proper functioning of government far more than it disadvantages possible enemies. Today, millions of executive branch employees have access to information that is routinely denied to Congress, the courts, and the press. Those employees can be punished for disclosing improperly classified documents but not for improperly classifying them in the first place.

The number of executive branch personnel with classifying authority needs to be reduced substantially. The number of security classifications and pseudo-classifications should be slashed, and both Congress and the courts need to have their own means for declassifying and/or creating sanitized versions of allegedly secret documents. The declassification process must be accelerated because the chief function of classifying or misclassifying information is not to prevent its eventual disclosure but to deprive the political process of timely access. Another way to address the same problem is to provide that all secrecy markings identify who classified the document, who can declassify it, and when the classification expires. Extensions should be made difficult, and the reclassification of documents already in the public domain should be forbidden with very rare exceptions.[37]

Timely access to unclassified documents under the Freedom of Information Act also needs to be enhanced.[38] President Obama has begun by reversing the presumption in favor of secrecy that the Reagan and Bush-Cheney administrations initiated. Congress could follow by adequately funding declassification staffs and countermanding Cheney's claim that he was not bound by the Presidential Records Act[39] because his paycheck happened to come from the Senate.[40]

Executive branch officials should not be allowed to evade accountability by discussing official business over unofficial e-mail accounts and should be subject to fines or other punishments for destroying those records. Procedures also need to be established for the routine filing of White House and cabinet-level e-mails with the National Archives.

Congress could also make it clear that changing published executive orders in secret constitutes fraud upon the government and grounds for impeachment. It could also bar OLC lawyers from issuing classified legal opinions, especially when doing so would conceal arguably criminal activity. Some delay in disclosing confidential legal advice may be countenanced under the doctrine of executive privilege, but when OLC opinions are meant to bind executive branch agencies, they should be available for public scrutiny.

Signing Statements

Congress cannot tell the president what he can say when signing a bill into law. Nor may it prevent his lawyers from testing the meaning or constitutionality of a statutory provision in open court. The president's job is to "take care that the laws be faithfully executed," and that sometimes includes openly clarifying their meaning and resolving apparent conflicts with other laws or the Constitution. The problem comes when the president signals an intent, while signing a bill or afterward, not to faithfully execute the law's manifest purposes.

Of course, a law's purpose may not be clear. Many laws are written ambiguously precisely to conceal divisions that would otherwise be fatal to their passage. Sometimes Congress's purpose is to allow crucial policy choices to be made later, within the cozy triangle of executive agencies, legislative committees, and interest groups. In such situations, a signing statement may help move negotiations along.

However, George W. Bush used some in a very different way—to flout the will of Congress. Rather than veto entire bills, which was his constitutional prerogative, he used some signing statements to assert a line-item veto that the Constitution does not give him. In so doing, he essentially asserted what James I called an indefeasible prerogative to suspend the operation of any law he did not like. He also signaled his intention not to allow his subordinates to render reports to Congress, which he clearly had no authority to do.

The proper remedy for such action is not prosecution but impeachment, because the illegality is not so much a crime as it is a failure to "take care that the laws be faithfully executed." The time for impeaching President Bush has passed, but Congress could pass concurrent resolutions laying out what actions might constitute impeachable offenses. The list need not cover everything; no one can anticipate all of the abuses of power that might justify removing a president from office. The resolutions would not be legally binding either, but they would give future presidents fair warning that denying effect to acts of Congress can be grounds for removing them from office.

The foregoing list of remedies for executive lawlessness is not exhaustive. It does not address the abuse of domestic surveillance powers, which deserve a book of their own. Nor does it examine why American citizens are largely oblivious to the most serious constitutional crisis in modern history. That issue, too, merits a separate examination. But the most urgent questions remain: Will the Obama administration take care to enforce the criminal law, or will the new president allow Bush and his torture team to get away with torture? The answer is far from clear.

notes

Epigraph

1. George Orwell, "Notes on Nationalism," *Polemic*, May 1945.

Preface

1. Various polls are summarized by Patrick Flavin and David W. Nickerson of Notre Dame University in a working paper titled "Reciprocity and Public Opinion on Torture," available at http://www.nd.edu/~dnickers/working/Nickerson.torture.pdf (accessed November 25, 2008). Six out of ten white Southern evangelicals—the base of the Republican Party—supported torture in a poll conducted in 2008. Adelle M. Banks, "Poll Shows Support for Torture among Southern Evangelicals," Religion News Service, September 11, 2008, available at http://www.pewforum.org.news/rss.php?NewsID.16465 (accessed November 25, 2008). See also Patrick Worsnip, "Sizeable Minority of Americans Condone Torture—Poll," Reuters, June 25, 2008, available at http://www.alertnet.org/thenews/newsdesk/N25481397.htm (accessed November 25, 2008).
2. See, e.g., Peter Liberman and Linda Skitla, "Just Deserts in Iraq: American Vengeance for 9/11," paper presented at meetings of the American Political Science Association, Boston, August 28, 2008.
3. Arthur M. Schlesinger, Jr., *The Imperial Presidency* (Boston: Houghton Mifflin, 1973), ix.

1. A Policy of Torture

1. Overheard by Ken Auletta, Annals of Communications column, *New Yorker*, January 11, 2004.
2. Transcript of oral arguments in *Rumsfeld v. Padilla,* U.S. Supreme Court, April 28, 2004, pp. 22–23, available at http://www.supremecourtus.gov/oral_arguments/argument_transcripts/03-1027.pdf (accessed August 2, 2008).
3. *60 Minutes II*, CBS Television, April 28, 2004.
4. Quoted in Thomas E. Ricks, *Fiasco: The American Military Adventure in Iraq* (New York: Penguin, 2006), 290.
5. Ibid., 291.
6. U.S. Department of Defense News Transcript, May 4, 2004, available at http://www.defenselink.mil/transcripts/transcript.aspx?transcriptid=2973 (accessed December 15, 2008).
7. "Pentagon Press Briefing," May 4, 2004, available at http://www.transcripts.cnn.com/TRANSCRIPTS/0405/04/se.02.html (Rumsfeld) (accessed August 4, 2008);

"President Outlines Steps to Help Iraq Achieve Democracy and Freedom," Remarks by the President on Iraq and the War on Terror, U.S. Army War College, Carlisle, PA, May 2004, available at http://www.whitehouse.gov/news/releases/2004/05/20040524-10.html (Bush) (accessed August 4, 2008).

8. David Cole, "The Disappeared," in *Enemy Aliens: Double Standards and Constitutional Freedoms in the War on Terrorism* (New York: New Press, 2003), chap. 2.

9. Jordan J. Paust, "Executive Plans and Authorization to Violate International Law Concerning Treatment and Interrogation of Detainees," *Columbia Journal of Transnational Law* 43, no. 3 (2005): 811, 850.

10. John Barry, Michael Hirsh, and Michael Isikoff, "The Roots of Torture," *Newsweek,* May 24, 2004. See also Human Rights First, "Twenty-Seven Detainee Homicides in U.S. Custody," October 19, 2005, available at http://www.humanrightsfirst.org/media/2005_alerts/etn_1019_dic.htm (accessed August 4, 2008).

11. "Final Report of the Independent Panel to Review DoD Detention Operations" (The Schlesinger Report), August 2004, in Karen J. Greenberg and Joshua L. Dratel, eds., *The Torture Papers: The Road to Abu Ghraib* (New York: Cambridge University Press, 2005), 909.

12. They can be found at http://www.aclu.org/safefree/torture/torturefoia.html (accessed January 27, 2009).

13. Human Rights Watch et al., *By the Numbers* (April 2006), available at http://www.hrw.org/en/reports/2006/04/25/numbers-0 (accessed January 27, 2009).

14. Patrick Quinn, "U.S. War Prisons Legal Vacuum for 14,000," Associated Press, September 17, 2006 (citing a report to the United Nations in May 2006). See also Robert Burns, "Army Dropped Abuse Probe, Records Show," Associated Press, January 13, 2006.

15. "Article 15-6 Investigation of the 800th Military Police Brigade" (the Taguba Report), March 2004, in Greenberg and Dratel, *The Torture Papers,* 416.

16. Hina Shamsi, "Command's Responsibility: Detainee Deaths in U.S. Custody in Iraq and Afghanistan" (New York: Human Rights First, February 22, 2006), 34, available at http://www.humanrightsfirst.info/pdf/06221-etn-hrf-dic-rep-web.pdf (accessed August 4, 2008).

17. Lolita C. Baldor, "21 Detainees Killed in U.S. Custody, ACLU Finds," *Boston Globe,* October 25, 2005, A19.

18. Mark Benjamin, "The Abu Ghraib Files," *Salon.com,* February 16, 2006. In addition to the photographs of prisoner abuse released in the spring of 2004, the Defense Department has eighty-seven other photos and four videotapes of Abu Ghraib abuses that have not been made public. Kate Zernike, "Government Defies an Order to Release Iraqi Abuse Photos," *New York Times,* July 25, 2005, A11.

19. U.S. Army/Marine Corps, *Counterinsurgency Field Manual* (Chicago: University of Chicago Press, 2007), passim.

20. Quoted by Richard A. Clarke, who was present, in *Against All Enemies: Inside America's War on Terror* (New York: Free Press, 2004), 24.

21. Paraphrased by Bob Woodward, *Bush at War* (New York: Simon & Schuster, 2002), 42.

22. "Guard and Reserves 'Define Spirit of America,'" Remarks by the President to Employees at the Pentagon, September 17, 2001, available at http://www.whitehouse.gov/news/releases/2001/09/20010917-3.html (accessed August 4, 2008).

23. Cheney's remarks, made on *Meet the Press with Tim Russert,* September 16, 2001, available at http://www.whitehouse.gov/vicepresident/news-speeches/speeches/vp20010916.html (accessed August 4, 2008).

24. Sean Wilentz, "Mr. Cheney's Minority Report," *New York Times,* July 9, 2007, A21.
25. "Reports of the Iran-Contra Committees: Excerpts from the Minority View," *New York Times,* November 17, 1987.
26. Barton Gellman and Jo Becker, "Part I: A Different Understanding with the President," *Washington Post,* June 24, 2007.
27. Jeffrey Rosen, "Conscience of a Conservative," *New York Times Magazine,* September 9, 2007. See also Jack L. Goldsmith, *The Terror Presidency: Law and Judgment Inside the Bush Administration* (New York: W. W. Norton, 2007).
28. Robert Dreyfuss, "Vice Squad," *American Prospect,* May 2006, 33.
29. This assumption also explains their decision to order warrantless wiretapping in violation of the Foreign Intelligence Surveillance Act (FISA) of 1978.
30. Lou Dubose and Jake Bernstein, *Vice: Dick Cheney and the Hijacking of the American Presidency* (New York: Random House, 2006), 178, quoting Col. Lawrence Wilkerson, Colin Powell's chief of staff.
31. Stephen Holmes, review of *Cobra II,* by Michael Gordon and Bernard Trainor, *American Prospect,* June 2006, 63. Holmes notes, in particular, Gordon and Trainor's quote (p. 117, note 16) from a paper by Gen. Charles Horner, U.S. Air Force (Ret.).
32. Ron Suskind, "Faith, Certainty, and the Presidency of George W. Bush," *New York Times Sunday Magazine,* October 17, 2004.
33. Video of speech at Rochester, NY, May 24, 2005, available at http://www.prisonplanet.com/articles/May2005/260505newbushism.htm (accessed January 27, 2009).
34. Woodward, *Bush at War,* 145–46.
35. Joint hearing of the House and Senate Intelligence Committees, "Hearings on Pre-9/11 Intelligence Failures," 107th Cong., 2nd sess., September 26, 2002, available at http://www.fas.org/irp/congress/2002_hr/092602black.html (accessed August 4, 2008).
36. Cofer Black, as quoted by Mark Bowden, "The Dark Art of Interrogation," *Atlantic Monthly,* October 1, 2003, 56. The same terminology was used in an e-mail that officials in Baghdad sent to U.S. troops on August 14, 2003. It was after that e-mail that the bulk of Abu Ghraib abuses occurred. In an interview with *Frontline,* Gen. Janis Karpinski used the same words to describe what happened when Gen. Geoffrey Miller pushed her aside. According to a military intelligence agent at Abu Ghraib, Lt. Col. Steven Jordan, the prison's supervisor, said the same thing after Miller's arrival: "We're taking the gloves off." *Frontline,* WGBH Boston, PBS, October 18, 2005, available at http://www.pbs.org/wgbh/pages/frontline/torture/interviews/Karpinski.html (accessed August 4, 2008).
37. "Wilkerson Points Finger at Cheney on Torture," Associated Press, November 4, 2005, quoting Col. Lawrence Wilkerson.
38. Stanley Milgram, "The Perils of Obedience," *Harper's Magazine,* December 1973, adapted from *Obedience to Authority: An Experimental View* (New York: Harper Collins, 1974) and available at http://home.swbell.net/revscat/perilsOfObedience.html (accessed August 4, 2008).
39. James Risen and David Johnston, "Bush Has Widened Authority of C.I.A. to Kill Terrorists," *New York Times,* December 15, 2002; and Jane Mayer, "Outsourcing Torture," *New Yorker,* February 14, 2005. The CIA acknowledged this order's existence on November 23, 2006, but its precise contents have yet to be disclosed. David Johnston, "C.I.A. Tells of Bush's Directive on the Handling of Detainees," *New York Times,* November 15, 2006, A11. According to Michael F. Scheuer, who ran the program, extraordinary rendition was begun in 1995 by President Clinton and two of his aides, Sandy Berger and Richard Clarke. However, the pre-9/11 program Scheuer

has described in various interviews appears to involve a broker's role, in which American intelligence persuaded foreign regimes to arrest suspects on their soil and deliver them to other regimes (usually their countries of origin) for questioning and prosecution. Only after 9/11 did CIA agents kidnap suspects for delivery to foreign regimes or imprison suspects themselves.

40. Woodward, *Bush at War,* 76–77.
41. Seymour M. Hersh, *Chain of Command: The Road from 9/11 to Abu Ghraib* (New York: HarperCollins, 2004), 16.
42. Joint Resolution Authorization for Use of Military Force, Public Law 107-40, 107th Cong., 2nd sess., 115 Stat. 224 (S.J. Res. 23), September 18, 2001. Deputy White House Counsel Timothy E. Flanigan, with advice from John Yoo, drafted the authorization. Gellman and Becker, "Part I: A Different Understanding with the President."
43. President George W. Bush, "Address to a Joint Session of Congress and the American People," September 20, 2001, available at http://www.whitehouse.gov/news/releases/2001/09/20010920-8.html (accessed August 4, 2008).
44. John Yoo, Memorandum Opinion for Timothy E. Flanigan, the Deputy Counsel to the President, "The President's Constitutional Authority to Conduct Military Operations against Terrorists and Nations Supporting Them," September 25, 2001, available at http://www.usdoj.gov/olc/warpowers925.htm (accessed August 4, 2008).
45. Ibid.
46. "Authority for Use of Military Force to Combat Terrorist Activities Within the United States," October 17, 2001 (undisclosed), described in a Memorandum for William J. Haynes II, from John C. Yoo, "Re: Military Interrogation of Alien Unlawful Combatants Held Outside the United States," March 14, 2003, available at http://www.aclu.org/pdfs/safefree/yoo_army_torture_memo.pdf (accessed August 4, 2008).
47. Ibid.; and Peter Slevin, "Scholar Stands by Post-9/11 Writings on Torture, Domestic Eavesdropping," *Washington Post,* December 26, 2005.
48. Laura K. Donohue, *The Cost of Counterterrorism: Power, Politics, and Liberty* (New York: Cambridge University Press, 2008), 1.
49. FY2007 National Defense Authorization Act, Public Law 109-364, sec. 1076, amending the Insurrection Act of 1807, 10 U.S.C. sec. 331–334, and weakening the Posse Comitatus Act of 1878, 18 U.S.C. sec. 1385.
50. Ibid.
51. Gellman and Becker, "Part I: A Different Understanding with the President."
52. James Madison, *Writings of James Madison,* ed. G. Hunt (New York: Putnam, 1900–1910), 6:312.
53. "The President shall be Commander in Chief of the Army and Navy of the United States, and of the Militia of the several States, when called into the actual Service of the United States."
54. Yoo, Memorandum Opinion, 7, 24.
55. *Youngstown Sheet and Tube Co. v. Sawyer,* 343 U.S. 579 (1952), 646, 653.
56. 6 U.S. (2 Cranch) 170 (1804).
57. See John Yoo, *The Powers of War and Peace: The Constitution and Foreign Affairs after 9/11* (Chicago: University of Chicago Press, 2005), and the law review articles cited therein.
58. "The 9/11 Constitution," *The New Republic,* January 16, 2006.
59. Scott Shane, David Johnston, and James Risen, "Secret U.S. Endorsement of Severe Interrogations," *New York Times,* October 4, 2007, A22.
60. "U.S. Military Lawyers Felt 'Shut Out' of Prison Policy," *Los Angeles Times,* May 14, 2004.

61. Gellman and Becker, "Part I: A Different Understanding with the President."
62. "Detention, Treatment, and Trial of Certain Non-Citizens in the War Against Terrorism," Military Order of November 13, 2001, 66 Fed. Reg. No. 2, 57831-36, in Greenberg and Dratel, *The Torture Papers*, 25. In March 2006, after oral arguments in *Hamdan v. Rumsfeld*, 548 U.S. 557, 126 S. Ct. 2749 (2006), the Pentagon changed the order to bar evidence obtained by torture but not lesser forms of coercion. Military Commission Instruction (MCI) No. 10, sec. 3(A), March 24, 2006, available at http://www.defenselink.mil/news/Mar2006/d20060327MCI10.pdf (accessed August 4, 2008).
63. Gellman and Becker, "Part I: A Different Understanding with the President."
64. Vice President Addresses U.S. Chamber of Commerce, Washington, DC, November 14, 2001, available at http://www.whitehouse.gov/news/releases/2001/11/20011114-6.html (accessed August 4, 2008).
65. William Safire, "Seizing Dictatorial Power," *New York Times,* November 15, 2001.
66. The source of this quotation was an FBI agent, according to Michael Hirsh, John Barry, and Daniel K. Caidman, "A Tortured Debate," *Newsweek,* June 21, 2004, 50. See also Mayer, "Outsourcing Torture," 112, 114–16; and Jason Vest, "Pray and Tell," *American Prospect,* July 2005, 49–50.
67. Michael Isikoff and Mark Hosenball, "Al-Libi's Tall Tales," *Newsweek,* November 10, 2005.
68. Mayer, "Outsourcing Torture."
69. Anthony Romero, *In Defense of Our America* (New York: HarperCollins, 2007), 20.
70. Lindh had surrendered on November 24, 2001, to the forces of Gen. Abdul Rashid Dostum who drove him by truck to the Qala-i-Jangi fortress near Mazar-i-Sharif. Dostum's troops were known for their brutality; they had crushed prisoners under tank treads and left more than a hundred prisoners captured with Lindh to die in sealed shipping containers. On November 25, Lindh was sitting in a prison yard when a grenade exploded. He tried to run but was shot in the thigh and lay on the ground for several hours until other prisoners helped him into the prison basement. There he remained until December 1, with no food and little drinking water. At some point, Dostum's troops poured oil into the crowded basement and lit it. They also fired rockets down a ventilation shaft and later flooded the basement with cold water. Of the more than three thousand prisoners who had surrendered with Lindh the week before, fewer than eighty-five survived. When Lindh limped out of the basement on December 1, he was "wounded, starved, frozen and exhausted." "A Nation Challenged: Excerpt from Lawyers' Filing for Lindh—'Threatened Him with Death,'" *New York Times,* February 6, 2002, A12. See also Katharine Q. Seelye, "Lawyers Portray Lindh as Vulnerable and Delirious Prisoner," *New York Times,* June 15, 2002, A12; and Jane Mayer, "Lost in the Jihad," *New Yorker,* March 10, 2003.
71. "A Nation Challenged: Excerpt from Lawyers' Filing for Lindh," A12.
72. Hersh, *Chain of Command,* 4. A navy medic later testified that the lead interrogator told him that "sleep deprivation, cold, and hunger" could be used to make Lindh talk. Richard Serrano, "Prison Interrogators' Gloves Came Off before Abu Ghraib," *Los Angeles Times,* June 9, 2004.
73. CNN.com, "War Against Terror—Transcript of John Walker Interview, July 4, 2002," available at http://www.cnn.com/2001/WORLD/asiapcf/central/12/20/ret.walker.transcript (accessed August 4, 2008).
74. Hersh, *Chain of Command,* 37.
75. Katharine Q. Seelye, "Bush Nears a Decision on American Taliban Member," *New York Times,* December 20, 2001, B5.

76. Seelye, "Lawyers Portray Lindh as Vulnerable and Delirious Prisoner." On January 15, 2002, Attorney General Ashcroft insisted that the FBI's interrogation of Lindh was legal because, while he was entitled to a lawyer, he had not hired one. Further, the lawyer his family retained did not count because Lindh had not personally retained him. Jane Mayer, "Lost in the Jihad," *New Yorker,* March 10, 2003, 58.

77. Ibid., 58–59.

78. Eric Lichtblau, "Adviser in Lindh Case Sues Justice Dept.," *New York Times,* October 29, 2004, A10.

79. Ibid.

80. Seelye, "Bush Near a Decision on American Taliban Member."

81. Quotation from Gwen Ifill, "American Taliban," *NewsHour,* PBS, December 12, 2001, available at http://www.pbs.org/newshour/bb/military/july-dec01/walker_12-12.html (accessed August 4, 2008).

82. The prosecutors denied that U.S. Army Special Forces had kept Lindh in "tortuous conditions" when he made his incriminating statements. They insisted that he was "meticulously attended to" by doctors, given food and a safe place to sleep, and "ultimately returned unharmed, healthy, and strong to the country he had forsaken." Neil A. Lewis, "Prosecutors Deny Lindh Was in Poor State When He Spoke," *New York Times,* July 2, 2002, A12.

83. Marjorie Cohn, "A Double Standard on Torture: The U.S. Should Practice What We Preach," *Jurist,* February 6, 2003.

84. This was the start of a general practice in which federal prosecutors would overcharge alleged terrorists to force a plea bargain and thus avoid judicial scrutiny of their evidence and how it was obtained.

85. Prepared Remarks of Attorney General Alberto R. Gonzales on Zacarias Moussaoui, Friday, April 22, 2005, Washington, DC, available at http://www.usdoj.gov/archive/ag/speeches/2005/prepared_remarks_042205.htm (accessed August 4, 2008).

86. *Dred Scott v. Sandford,* 60 U.S. (19 How.) 393 (1857).

87. Brant Goldstein, *Storming the Court: How a Band of Yale Law Students Sued the President and Won* (New York: Scribner, 2005), 20.

88. Lieber, "Instructions for the Government of Armies of the United States in the Field."

89. *The Armed Forces Officer* (Washington, DC: Department of Defense, 1950) (written by historian-journalist H. L. A. Marshall, at Gen. George C. Marshall's direction).

90. Geneva Convention Relative to the Protection of Civilian Persons in Time of War, *opened for signature* August 12, 1949, 6 U.S.T. 3516, 75 U.N.T.S. 287, *ratified by the United States* in 1955.

91. Convention Against Torture and Other Cruel, Inhuman or Degrading Treatment or Punishment, 1465 U.N.T.S. 85, 23 I.L.M. 1027, article 2, sec. 2.

92. George Orwell, *1984* (New York: Signet, 1964).

93. Quoted in Jeffrey St. Clair, *Grand Theft Pentagon: Tales of Corruption and Profiteering in the War on Terror* (Monroe, ME: Common Courage Press, 2005), 49.

94. David Frum and Richard Perle, *An End to Evil: How to Win the War on Terror* (New York: Random House, 2003), 229.

95. Sir Frederick Pollock, "Anglo-Saxon Law," *English Historical Review* 8, no. 30 (April 1893): 239–71.

96. G. R. C. Davis, trans., *Magna Carta,* rev. ed. (British Library, 1989). William S. Holdsworth, *A History of English Law* (London: Methuen, 1926), 9:112–14.

97. William Goodell, *The American Slave Codes in Theory and Practice* (New York: American and Foreign Anti-Slavery Society, 1853), part I, chapter 18.

98. Herbert L. Osgood, "England and the American Colonies in the Seventeenth Century," *Political Science Quarterly* 17, no. 2 (June 1902): 206–22.
99. Telford Taylor, *Anatomy of the Nuremberg Trials: A Personal Memoir* (Boston: Little, Brown, 1992), 28–33.
100. "Final Report of the Independent Panel to Review DoD Detention Operations" (the Schlesinger Report), August 2004, 80. See also Department of the Army, Field Manual 27-10, *Law of Land Warfare* (Washington, DC, 1956), para. 73. If a person is not considered a POW, he or she is still a "protected person" under the Fourth Geneva Convention, which protects civilians. According to long-standing U.S. Army doctrine, there was no such thing as a "legally unprotected person."
101. Chris Mackey with Greg Miller, *The Interrogators: Task Force 500 and America's Secret War against al Qaeda* (New York: Little, Brown, 2004). Mackey (a pseudonym) was an interrogator at Kandahar and Bagram between October 2001 and August 2002. The Defense Department censored the authors' account of interrogation procedures. Application of the Geneva Conventions was mandated by Department of the Army Regulation 190-8, "Enemy Prisoners of War, Retained Personnel, Civilian Internees and Other Detainees," October 1, 1997, secs. 1 through 6. See also *Operational Law Handbook*, ed., W. O'Brien (Charlottesville, VA: Judge Advocate General's School, 2003), 10, 22.
102. Barton Gellman and Jo Becker, "Part II: Pushing the Envelope on Presidential Power," *Washington Post,* June 25, 2007.
103. Ibid.
104. "Memo 4, January 9, 2002, to William J. Haynes II, General Counsel, Department of Defense, from John Yoo, Deputy Assistant Attorney General, U.S. Department of Justice, Office of Legal Counsel, and Robert J. Delahunty, Special Counsel, U.S. Department of Justice, Re: Application of Treaties and Laws to al Qaeda and Taliban Detainees," in Greenberg and Dratel, *The Torture Papers,* 38.
105. Gellman and Becker, "Part II: Pushing the Envelope on Presidential Power."
106. Tom Lasseter, "Easing of Laws that Led to Detainee Abuse Hatched in Secret," McClatchy Newspapers, June 19, 2008.
107. Ibid.
108. "Memo 3, December 28, 2001, to William J. Haynes II, General Counsel, Department of Defense, from Patrick F. Philbin, Deputy Assistant Attorney General, and John Yoo, Deputy Assistant Attorney General, U.S. Department of Justice, Re: Possible Habeas Jurisdiction over Aliens Held in Guantánamo Bay, Cuba," in Greenberg and Dratel, *The Torture Papers,* 29.
109. "Memo 4, to Haynes from Yoo, and Delahunty, Re: Application of Treaties and Laws to al Qaeda and Taliban Detainees," in Greenberg and Dratel, *The Torture Papers.* This memo was released only in its draft form; the final form may differ.
110. Department of the Army, Field Manual 27-10, *The Law of Land Warfare,* para. 73. It provides that if a person is determined not to be a prisoner of war, he is still a "protected person" under the Fourth Geneva Convention, including its Common Article 3, which bans cruel, inhuman, and degrading treatment. See also para. 60, which states that "the enemy population is divided in war into two general categories": POWs and civilians.
111. Mayer, "Outsourcing Torture."
112. Ibid.
113. 18 U.S.C. 2441 (Supp. III 1997). "Memo 4 to Haynes from Yoo and Delahunty, Re: Application of Treaties and Laws to al Qaeda and Taliban Detainees," in Greenberg and Dratel, *The Torture Papers.*

114. "Memo 6, January 22, 2002, to Alberto R. Gonzales, Counsel to the President, and William J. Haynes, General Counsel, Department of Defense, from Jay S. Bybee, Assistant Attorney General, U.S. Department of Justice, Re: Application of Treaties and Laws to al Qaeda and Taliban Detainees," in Greenberg and Dratel, *The Torture Papers*, 81, 92.

115. Ibid., 93.

116. For persuasive arguments against this view of the treaty power, published prior to 9/11, see Carlos Manuel Vazquez, "Laughing at Treaties," *Columbia Law Review* 99, no. 8 (1999): 2154; and Martin S. Flaherty, "History Right? Historical Scholarship, Original Understanding, and Treaties as 'Supreme Law of the Land,'" *Columbia Law Review* 99, no. 8 (1999): 2095.

117. R. Jeffrey Smith, "Detainee Abuse Charges Feared: Shield Sought from '96 War Crimes Act," *Washington Post,* July 28, 2006.

118. "Memo 7, January 25, 2002, to President Bush from Alberto R. Gonzales, Counsel to the President, Re: Decision re. Application of the Geneva Convention on Prisoners of War to the Conflict with al Qaeda and the Taliban," in Greenberg and Dratel, *The Torture Papers,* 118.

119. Scott Horton, "Through a Mirror, Darkly: Applying the Geneva Conventions to a 'New Kind of Warfare,'" in *The Torture Debate,* ed. Karen J. Greenberg (New York: Cambridge University Press, 2006), 140, 148, note 7 (German text).

120. *Opened for signature,* December 10, 1984, G.A. Res. 39/46, 39 UN GAOR Supp. No. 51, U.N. Doc. A/RES/39/708 (1984); *entered into force,* June 26, 1987, 1465 U.N.T.S., 23 I.L.M. 1027 (1984); *ratified by the United States,* 1994.

121. 18 U.S.C. sec. 2340A.

122. *Youngstown Sheet and Tube Co. v. Sawyer.*

123. Gonzales's unquestioning obedience is well documented by Bill Minutaglio in a friendly biography, *The President's Counselor: The Rise to Power of Alberto Gonzales* (New York: HarperCollins, 2006).

124. That statute, he explained, "prohibits the commission of a 'war crime' by or against a U.S. person, including U.S. officials," including "any grave breach of the GPW" (such as torture), or any violation of Common Article 3, "such as 'outrages against personal dignity.'" "Memo 7, to Bush from Gonzales, Re: Decision re: Application of the Geneva Convention on Prisoners of War," in Greenberg and Dratel, *The Torture Papers,* 118. The trial judge in Lindh's case would subsequently agree that "the Taliban falls far short when measured against the four [Geneva Conventions'] criteria for determining entitlement to lawful combatant immunity." *United States v. Lindh,* 212 F. Supp. 2d 541, 558 (E.D. Va. 2002). The War Crimes Act, passed to give effect to the Geneva Conventions, can be found at 18 U.S.C. sec. 2441.

125. "Memo 7, to Bush from Gonzales, Re: Decision re: Application of the Geneva Convention on Prisoners of War," in Greenberg and Dratel, *The Torture Papers,* 119. However, article 31 of the Fourth Geneva Convention (Civilians) provides that "no physical or moral coercion shall be exercised against protected persons, in particular to obtain information from them *or from* third parties." UNHCR (http://www.unhchr.ch/html/menu3/b/92.htm) (accessed January 26, 2009).

126. Ibid., 120.

127. "Memo 8, January 26, 2002, to Counsel to the President, Assistant to the President for National Security Affairs, from Colin L. Powell, U.S. Department of State, Re: Draft Decision Memorandum for the President on the Applicability of the Geneva Convention to the Conflict in Afghanistan," in Greenberg and Dratel, *The Torture Papers,* 123.

128. "Memo 10, February 2, 2002, to Counsel to the President from William H. Taft IV, Legal Advisor, Department of State, Re: Comments on Your Paper on the Geneva Convention," in Greenberg and Dratel, *The Torture Papers,* 129.

129. "Memo 9, February 1, 2002, to President George W. Bush, from Attorney General John Ashcroft, Attorney General, Re: Justice Department's position on why the Geneva Convention did not apply to al Qaeda and Taliban Detainees," in Greenberg and Dratel, *The Torture Papers,* 126.

130. "Memo 5, January 19, 2002, to Chairman of the Joint Chiefs of Staff from Donald Rumsfeld, Secretary of Defense, Re: Status of Taliban and al Qaeda," in Greenberg and Dratel, *The Torture Papers,* 80. On January 19, Secretary Rumsfeld countermanded General Franks's order and informed military commanders that their new prisoners would have no legal rights at all. Ibid.

131. Joseph Margulies, *Guantánamo and the Abuse of Presidential Power* (New York: Simon & Schuster, 2006), 57.

132. Reproduced in Horton, "Through a Mirror, Darkly," 142.

133. Gellman and Becker, "Part II: Pushing the Envelope on Presidential Power."

134. Al Qaeda soldiers were not protected, Bush reasoned, because they did not fight for a recognized government. Taliban soldiers, his press secretary said, deprived themselves of the Third Convention's protection by failing to conduct their operations according to the laws of war as required by article 4. Statement issued on February 7, 2002, available at http://www.lawofwar.org/Bush_torture_memo.htm (accessed June 4, 2008). See also "Memo 12, February 7, 2002, to Alberto R. Gonzales, Counsel to the President, from Jay B. Bybee, Assistant Attorney General, U.S. Department of Justice, Re: Status of Taliban Forces under Article 4 of the Third Geneva Convention of 1949," at 2(c) and (d) (declassified and released in full on June 17, 2004), in Greenberg and Dratel, *The Torture Papers,* 136. Bush relied on Alberto Gonzales and John Yoo, who claimed that Taliban soldiers did not wear full uniforms (although they did wear distinctive black turbans and had a hierarchy of command). Yoo and Gonzales ignored article 142 of the Geneva Conventions, which required the United States to give a year's notice before abrogating it. Moreover, because Afghanistan and the United States were both parties to the conventions, each had the obligation not to repudiate the agreements "until peace has been concluded."

135. Frederick A. O. Schwartz, Jr., and Aziz Z. Huq, *Unchecked and Unbalanced: Presidential Power in a Time of Terror* (New York: New Press/Brennan Center for Justice, 2007), 228, note 33.

136. Robert Kirsch, unclassified attorney notes regarding what military intelligence officers told his Guantánamo client Hadj Boudella, on file with the Center for Constitutional Rights, New York.

137. Lt. Gen. Ricardo S. Sanchez with Donald T. Phillips, *Wiser in Battle: A Soldier's Story* (New York: HarperCollins, 2008), 144.

138. Ron Suskind, *The One Percent Doctrine: Deep Inside America's Pursuit of Its Enemies Since 9/11* (New York: Simon & Schuster, 2006), 150.

139. U.S. Department of Defense, "Secretary Rumsfeld Media Availability en Route to Guantanamo Bay, Cuba," January 27, 2002, available at http://www.defenselink.mil/transcripts/transcript.aspx?transcriptid=2320 (accessed August 4, 2008).

140. U.S. Defense Department, "News Briefing—Secretary Rumsfeld and Gen. Myers," January 11, 2002, available at http://www.defenselink.mil/transcripts/transcript.aspx?transcriptid=2031 (accessed August 4, 2008).

141. Tim Golden, "Administration Officials Split over Stalled Military Tribunals," *New York Times,* October 25, 2004, A1.

142. Ibid.

143. Mackey and Miller, *The Interrogators,* 221.

144. Tim Golden and Don Van Natta, Jr., "U.S. Said to Overstate Value of Guantánamo Detainees," *New York Times,* June 21, 2004, A1.

145. Greg Miller, "Many Held at Guantánamo Not Likely Terrorists," *Los Angeles Times,* December 22, 2002, A1.

146. Mackey and Miller, *The Interrogators,* 222.

147. June 17, 2005, statement, quoted by William Fisher in "A Tale of Two Gitmos: Where Was the MSM?" Truthout/Perspective, February 22, 2006.

148. Corine Hegland, "Empty Evidence," *The National Journal,* February 3, 2006.

149. Hersh, *Chain of Command,* 2.

150. Melissa A. Jamison, "Detention of Juvenile Enemy Combatants at Guantánamo Bay," (U.C. Davis School of Law) *Journal of Juvenile Law & Policy* 9 (2005): 127, 136–37.

151. "Lawyer, Families Raise Suicide Doubts over Guantánamo Deaths," ABC NewsOnline, June 12, 2006, available at http://www.abc.net.au/news/newsitems/200606/s1660495. htm (accessed August 4, 2008).

152. Peter M. Ryan, "Its Motto: 'Oops,'" *Philadelphia Inquirer,* May 5, 2008.

153. Clive Stafford Smith, *Eight O'Clock Ferry to the Windward Side: Seeking Justice in Guantánamo Bay* (New York: Nation Books, 2007), 150–51.

154. Jane Mayer, "The Hidden Power," *New Yorker,* July 3, 2006, 54.

155. Article 5.

156. Report on Guantánamo Detainees: A Profile of 517 Detainees through Analysis of Department of Defense Data, available at http://law.shu.edu/aaafinal.pdf (accessed January 26, 2009).

157. U.S. Department of Defense Transcript, "Secretary Rumsfeld Interview with Jerry Agar, KMBZ News Radio 980 Kansas City, Kansas," June 27, 2005, available at http:// www.defenselink.mil/transcripts/transcript.aspx?transcriptid=3246 (accessed August 4, 2008).

158. "West Point Study Confirms Findings of Seton Hall Law's Report Showing Few Guantánamo Detainees Were Captured on Any Battlefield," Seton Hall Law School, November 8, 2007. The West Point figure was twenty-four.

159. Pervez Musharraf, *In the Line of Fire: A Memoir* (New York: Free Press, 2006), 237.

160. Hegland, "Empty Evidence."

161. On July 25, 2007, the Pentagon released a rebuttal study by a terrorism study center at West Point that claimed that 73 percent of the detainees were a "demonstrated threat" to American or Coalition forces and that 93 percent posed a "potential threat." Lt. Col. Joseph H. Felter claimed that his center was "independent" of the Pentagon but conceded that his superiors wanted him to contest the Seton Hall study. William Glaberson, "Pentagon Study Sees Threat in Guantánamo Detainees," *New York Times,* July 26, 2007, A15.

162. Report on Guantánamo Detainees, 18.

163. *Hamdan v. Rumsfeld,* 548 U.S. 557, 601 (2006).

164. The administration also persuaded Australian David Hicks to plead guilty in return for his release to Australia, but the evidence against him was never tested at a trial. Hamdan was sentenced to sixty-six months, but he was given credit for the sixty-one months he had already spent in custody. "Guantánamo Justice," *Washington Post,* November 27, 2008, A28.

165. Shashank Bengali, "Closing Guantánamo Faces Hurdle: Yemen," *Miami Herald,* November 29, 2008.

2. Unleashing the Dogs of War

1. Quoted by Mark Danner, "Abu Ghraib: The Hidden Story," review of *Final Report of the Independent Panel to Review DoD Detention Operations (The Schlesinger Report),* by James R. Schlesinger et al., and *AR-15-6 Investigation of the Abu Ghraib Detention Facility and 205th Military Intelligence Brigade,* by Maj. Gen. George Ray, *New York Review of Books,* October 7, 2004.

2. Leonard W. Levy, *Origins of the Fifth Amendment: The Right against Self-Incrimination* (New York: Oxford, 1968).

3. See John H. Langbein, "The Privilege and Common Law Criminal Procedure: The Sixteenth to the Eighteenth Centuries," in *The Privilege against Self-Incrimination: Its Origins and Development,* ed. R. H. Helmholz et al. (Chicago: University of Chicago Press, 1997), chap. 4.

4. "Liberty 45, Massachusetts Body of Liberties," in *The Colonial Laws of Massachusetts,* ed. W. H. Whitmore (Boston: 1890), 32–61. Torture was allowed, after conviction, to obtain the names of accomplices, but it does not appear to have been ordered. Lynn Hunt, *Inventing Human Rights: A History* (New York: W. W. Norton, 2007), 77. During the Salem witch hysteria, one person was tortured for the purpose of compelling him or her to enter a plea. Upon refusal, he or she was gradually crushed to death with stones.

5. Schwartz and Huq, *Unchecked and Unbalanced,* 222, note 26.

6. Adam Liptak, "In Terrorism Cases, Administration Sets Own Rules," *New York Times,* November 27, 2005, sec. 1, 1, quoting oral argument before the U.S. Court of Appeals.

7. The Fourth Geneva Convention protects captives who are not prisoners of war or wounded and sick soldiers, but are civilian bystanders to the conflict, including civilians "definitely suspected of or engaged in activities hostile to the security of the States." Geneva Convention 4 Relative to the Protection of Civilian Persons in Time of War, art. 5, 6. U.S.T. 3516, 75 U.N.T.S. 287 (August 12, 1949).

8. Douglas Jehl and Andrea Elliott, "The Reach of War: G.I. Instructors—Cuba Base Sent Its Interrogators to Iraqi Prison," *New York Times,* May 29, 2004.

9. Human Rights Watch, *Leadership Failure: Firsthand Accounts of Torture of Iraqi Detainees by the U.S. Army's 82nd Airborne Division* 17, no. 3 (G), September 2005, account of soldier A, available at http://hrw.org/en/node/11610/section/3 (accessed August 4, 2008).

10. Ibid., 9–12.

11. Hersh, *Chain of Command,* 12–13. A senior FBI official confirmed to Hersh that bureau agents had witnessed similar activities and reported them to headquarters.

12. The CIA resolved to create its own facilities in Afghanistan in December 2001, after prisoners of the Northern Alliance were asphyxiated in unventilated shipping containers. One of the CIA's first facilities was "the Salt Pit," an old brick factory outside Kabul. Prisoners were also held in shipping containers at Bagram Air Base and in Kandahar. Its Thai facility was closed in 2003. Dana Priest, "CIA Holds Terror Suspects in Secret Prisons," *Washington Post,* November 2, 2005, A1. A November 15, 2005, fax from Egypt's Foreign Ministry to its embassy in London stated that the United States had detained twenty-three Iraqi and Afghan prisoners in Romania. The fax also referred to similar detention facilities in Bulgaria, Kosovo, Macedonia, and Ukraine. Doreen Carvajal, "Swiss Investigate Leak to Paper on C.I.A. Prisons," *New York Times,* January

12, 2006, A8. Prisons in Poland and Romania were reportedly shut down after the press reported their existence in November 2005. Brian Ross and Richard Esposito, "Sources: Top al Qaeda Figures Held in Secret CIA Prisons," ABC News, December 5, 2005.

13. Mackey and Miller, *The Interrogators.*
14. Ibid.
15. Carlotta Gall, "Rights Group Reports Afghanistan Torture," *New York Times,* December 19, 2006, A16.
16. Jane Mayer, "The Black Sites," *New Yorker,* August 13, 2007.
17. Ibid.
18. Kate Clark, "Afghans Tell of U.S. Prison Ordeals," BBC News, July 21, 2005, available at http://news.bbc.co.uk/1/hi/world/south_asia/4648959.stm (accessed August 1, 2008).
19. Will Dunham, "Pentagon Admits 8 Afghans Died in Custody," Reuters, December 13, 2004.
20. Douglas Jehl and Tim Golden, "CIA to Avoid Charges in Most Prisoner Deaths," *New York Times,* October 23, 2005, A6. Dana Priest, "The CIA Avoids Scrutiny of Detainee Treatment," *Washington Post,* March 3, 2005, A1.
21. Tim Golden, "In U.S. Report, Brutal Details of Two Afghan Inmates' Deaths," *New York Times,* May 20, 2005.
22. Douglas Jehl, "Army Details Scale of Abuse in Afghan Jail," *New York Times,* March 12, 2005, A1.
23. Ibid.
24. Steven H. Miles, *Oath Betrayed: Torture, Medical Complicity, and the War on Terror* (New York: Random House, 2007), 68–71; David Griffith, *A Good War Is Hard to Find: The Art of Violence in America* (Brooklyn, NY: Soft Skull Press, 2006), 154; Alfred W. McCoy, *A Question of Torture: CIA Interrogation from the Cold War to the War on Terror* (New York: Metropolitan Books/Henry Holt, 2006), 126; USA Amnesty International's Supplementary Brief to the UN Committee Against Torture, May 3, 2006, 2; and Tim Golden, "Years after 2 Afghans Died, Abuse Case Falters," *New York Times,* February 13, 2006.
25. Miles, *Oath Betrayed,* 68, 91.
26. Griffith, *A Good War Is Hard to Find,* 154–55.
27. Priest, "CIA Holds Terror Suspects in Secret Prisons," A1.
28. Greg Miller, "Three Were Waterboarded, CIA Chief Confirms," *Los Angeles Times,* February 6, 2008.
29. Testimony before the Senate Armed Services Committee, September 2004, cited in *George W. Bush versus the U.S. Constitution: The Downing Street Memos and Deception, Manipulation, Torture, Retribution, Coverups in the Iraq War and Illegal Spying,* comp. John Conyers and ed. Anita Miller (Chicago: Academy Chicago Publishers, 2006), 92 (or *The Conyers Report*). See also Josh White, "Abu Ghraib Guards Kept a Log of Prison Conditions, Practices," *Washington Post,* October 25, 2004, A14. See also Katherine Shrader, "CIA in Middle of Election-Year Battle," Associated Press, September 16, 2006 (reporting ninety-six prisoners). Josh White, "General Who Ran Guantánamo Bay Retires," *Washington Post,* August 1, 2006, A6. "Army Announces Maj. Gen. Miller's Retirement," U.S. Army News Release, July 31, 2006.
30. Dana Priest, "Memo Lets CIA Take Detainees Out of Iraq," *Washington Post,* October 24, 2004, A1.
31. "Article 15-6 Investigation of the 800th Military Police Brigade" (Taguba Report), in Greenberg and Dratel, *The Torture Papers,* 425, para. 33.

32. "Profile: Task Force 5," Cooperative Research, History Commons, available at http://www. cooperativeresearch.org/entity.jsp?entity=task_force_5_1 (accessed August 4, 2008).
33. "Army Announces Maj. Gen. Miller's Retirement."
34. Untangling these covert units is not easy. At the Defense Department level, they seem to have been associated with the Strategic Support Branch (SSB) of the Defense Intelligence Agency, which had traditionally run the military attaché program of "legal spies." The SSB apparently dispatches small teams of case officers, linguists, interrogators, and technical support personnel to work together with Special Forces teams from the combat arms. The U.S. Army's Special Forces teams are organized under the U.S. Army Special Operations Command, which takes them out of regular army commands and allows them to operate covertly in numerous countries, sometimes without informing the U.S. ambassadors. At least two Special Forces groups are made up of National Guard troops. An army Special Forces company typically consists of six Operational Detachments Alpha ("A Teams") and one Operational Detachment Bravo ("B Team"). The navy's comparable Special Forces units are the SEALs.
35. Jeffrey St. Clair, "The Secret World of Stephen Cambone: Rumsfeld's Enforcer," *Counterpunch,* February 7, 2006, available at http://www.counterpunch.org/stclair 02072006.html (accessed August 4, 2008).
36. Some of the interrogators at Abu Ghraib were Arabic-speaking Israelis hired by CACI International, an American corporation. Wayne Madsen, "The Israeli Torture Template," *Counterpunch,* May 10, 2004.
37. From *Ghosts of Abu Ghraib,* DVD, directed by Rory Kennedy (HBO Home Video, 2007; Brooklyn, NY: Moxie Firecracker Films Production, 2006).
38. Philip Gourevitch and Errol Morris, "Exposure: The Woman Behind the Camera at Abu Ghraib," *New Yorker,* March 24, 2008, 56.
39. Seth Hettena, "Iraqi Died While Hung from Wrists," Associated Press, February 7, 2005; Adam Zagorin, "Haunted by 'the Iceman,'" *Time,* November 14, 2005, 38; and Jane Mayer, "A Deadly Interrogation," *New Yorker,* November 14, 2005.
40. Matt Apuzzo, "FBI Details Possible Detainee Abuse," Associated Press, January 2, 2007. American Civil Liberties Union (ACLU), "FBI Inquiry Details Abuses Reported by Agents at Guantánamo," January 3, 2007 (summarizing twenty-six eyewitness reports by FBI agents at Guantánamo), available at http://www.aclu.org/safefree/torture/ 27816prs20070103.html (accessed August 4, 2008).
41. Apuzzo, "FBI Details Possible Detainee Abuse."
42. ACLU, "FBI E-mail Refers to Presidential Order Authorizing Inhumane Interrogation Techniques," December 20, 2004, available at http://www.aclu.org/safefree/general/ 18769prs20041220.html (accessed January 26, 2009).
43. Quoted by Dan Eggen and R. Jeffrey Smith, "FBI Agents Allege Abuse of Detainees at Guantánamo Bay," *Washington Post,* December 21, 2004, A1.
44. "'Too Nice' Guantánamo Chief Sacked," BBC News, October 16, 2002.
45. Neil A. Lewis, "In New Book Ex-Chaplain at Guantánamo Tells of Abuses," *New York Times,* October 3, 2005. Both army intelligence and the FBI oppose coercive interrogations in large part because they do not produce reliable information. U.S. Army Field Manual 34-52, *Intelligence Interrogation* (Washington, DC: Department of the Army, 1992). Toni Locy and Kevin Johnson, "FBI Had Warned Pentagon on Tactics," *USA Today,* December 7, 2004. See also ACLU, "FBI E-mail Refers to Presidential Order."
46. Eggen and Smith, "FBI Agents Allege Abuse of Detainees," A1.

47. ACLU, "FBI E-Mail Refers to Presidential Order."
48. Hersh, *Chain of Command*, 12.
49. Neil Lewis, "Red Cross Finds Detainee Abuse in Guantánamo," *New York Times*, November 30, 2004, A1.
50. Honor Bound to Defend Freedom is the motto of Joint Task Force Guantánamo of the U.S. Southern Command.
51. E-mail from Scott Horton, chair of the Committee on International Law of the Association of the Bar of the City of New York, to Human Rights Watch, April 5, 2005, reporting on information "a senior uniformed officer present at the briefing" provided him in the summer of 2003. See also Barry, Hirsh, and Isikoff, "The Roots of Torture"; and Andrew Cockburn, *Rumsfeld: His Rise, Fall, and Catastrophic Legacy* (New York: Scribner, 2006), 193. According to Cockburn, Rumsfeld's principal complaint was that Abu Ghraib's interrogators were not confirming what he knew—that is, the insurgency was the work of "FSLs" (former Saddam loyalists) and "dead-enders."
52. Quoted in Tara McKelvey, *Monstering: Inside America's Policy of Secret Interrogations and Torture in the Terror War* (New York: Carroll & Graff, 2007), 61.
53. Philip Gourevitch and Errol Morris, *Standard Operating Procedure* (New York: Penguin, 2008), 19.
54. Most Iraqi soldiers captured during the invasion had been released. A few were transferred to Iraqi custody to face criminal trials while the rest were reclassified "security detainees" under UN Security Council Resolution 1546, although the criteria for this category remains unclear. Deborah Pearlstein and Priti Patel, *Behind the Wire: An Update to Ending Secret Detentions* (New York: Human Rights First, March 2005), 6 and note 102.
55. Scott Wilson and Sewell Chan, "As Insurgency Grew, So Did Prison Abuse," *Washington Post*, May 10, 2004, quoting Brig. Gen. Janis L. Karpinski.
56. "Schlesinger Report," in Greenberg and Dratel, *The Torture Papers*, 912.
57. The term "tiger" itself carried a harsh legacy from the Vietnam War. The Viet Cong had tormented U.S. prisoners in bamboo tiger cages, and a Tiger Force of the 101st Airborne Division reciprocated, torturing and killing hundreds of Vietnamese farmers, women, and children for seven months in 1967. Sometimes their bodies were mutilated for ears and scalps. "Buried Secrets, Brutal Truths," *Toledo Blade*, a four-part series beginning on October 22, 2003, available at http://nl.newsbank.com/nl-search/we/Archives?p_product=TB&p_tl (accessed January 27, 2009). The Tiger Force investigation, which occurred during Donald Rumsfeld's first tour as secretary of defense, found probable cause to prosecute eighteen soldiers, but no charges were ever brought.
58. Quoted by Gourevitch and Morris in *Standard Operating Procedure*, 204.
59. "Schlesinger Report," in Greenberg and Dratel, *Torture Papers*, 915 and appendix D. On May 19, 2004, Sanchez swore that he had never ordered sleep deprivation, excessive noise, or intimidation by dogs. Bradley Graham, "No Pattern of Prisoner Abuse, General Says," *Washington Post*, May 20, 2004, A23.
60. R. Jeffrey Smith, "General Is Said to Have Urged Use of Dogs," *Washington Post*, May 26, 2004, A01.
61. The photographs can be found in Mark Danner, *Torture and Truth: America, Abu Ghraib, and the War on Terror* (New York: New York Review Books, 2004), 224.
62. Josh White and Scott Higham, "Use of Dogs to Scare Prisoners Was Authorized," *Washington Post*, June 11, 2004, A1.
63. Quoted in Hersh, *Chain of Command*, 36.

64. Ricks, *Fiasco*, 293.
65. "The Torture Question," *Frontline*, WGBH Boston, PBS, October 18, 2005.
66. "Senate Hearings Held on Prisoner Abuse Charges," Online NewsHour, PBS, July 13, 2005, available at http://www.pbs.org/newshour/bb/military/july-dec05/gitmo_7-13.html (accessed January 29, 2009).
67. Douglas Jehl and Eric Schmitt, "Army Report: Gen. Sanchez Approved Torture at Abu Ghraib," *New York Times*, August 27, 2004.
68. Eric Schmitt, "General in Prisoner Abuse Case Declines to Testify Further," *New York Times*, January 13, 2006.
69. Gourevitch and Morris, *Standard Operating Procedure*, 41.
70. Ibid., 121.
71. Ibid., 122.
72. Hersh, *Chain of Command*, 22; and the Taguba Report, in Greenberg and Dratel, *The Torture Papers*, 405, 416–17.
73. A small sample of the photographs can be found in Danner, *Torture and Truth*, 217–24.
74. According to prisoners interviewed by Jonathan H. Pyle and cocounsel in connection with their civil suit against CACI International and the Titan Corporation.
75. Darius Rejali, "A Long-standing Trick of the Torturer's Art," *Seattle Times*, May 14, 2004.
76. Hersh, *Chain of Command*, 43.
77. Seymour Hersh, "The General's Report," *New Yorker*, June 25, 2007, 60. Also available at http://www.newyorker.com/reporting/2007/06/25/070625fa_fact_hersh (accessed August 4, 2008).
78. "Abu Ghraib GI: I'm No Bad Apple," CBS News, June 2, 2005, available at http://www.cbsnews.com/stories/2005/06/02/iraq/main699154.shtml (accessed August 4, 2008).
79. Friedrich Wilhelm Nietzsche, *Beyond Good and Evil: Prelude to a Philosophy of the Future*, trans. Walter Kaufmann (1886; New York: Vintage Books, 1966), 89.
80. Kennedy, *Ghosts of Abu Ghraib* (DVD).
81. Sworn statement for the Taguba Report, January 16, 2004, available at http://media.washingtonpost.com/wp-srv/world/iraq/abughraib/151362.pdf (accessed August 4, 2008).
82. Nicholas Riccardi, "Trial Illuminates Dark Tactics of Interrogation," *Los Angeles Times*, January 20, 2006.
83. Douglas Jehl and Andréa Elliott, "Cuba Base Sent Its Interrogators to Iraqi Prison," *New York Times*, May 29, 2004.
84. Douglas Jehl and Eric Schmidt, "Army Report: Gen. Sanchez Approved Torture at Abu Ghraib," *New York Times*, August 27, 2004, A1.
85. Eric Schmitt, "Career of General in Charge during Abu Ghraib May End," *New York Times*, January 5, 2006, A3.
86. Cockburn, *Rumsfeld*, 195, citing hearsay in stipulated testimony by Santos Cardona, a dog handler who was court-martialed for abusing prisoners at Abu Ghraib. Confirmed by another hearsay statement by Steve Pescatore, a civilian interrogator employed at Abu Ghraib recalling nightly briefings. Ibid.
87. Janis Karpinski, *One Woman's Army: The Commanding General at Abu Ghraib Tells Her Story*, with Steven Strasser (New York: Miramax, 2005), 201.
88. DIA document released by the ACLU, May 2, 2006, quoted by Information Clearing House, Daily News Digest, May 2, 2006.
89. Miles, *Oath Betrayed*, 50.
90. Riccardi, "Trial Illuminates Dark Tactics of Interrogation." See also Josh White, "Documents Tell of Brutal Improvisation by GIs," *Washington Post*, August 3, 2005.

91. Miles, "Homicide," in *Oath Betrayed,* chap. 4.

92. From Sgt. Ken Davis, quoted in Philip Zimbardo, *The Lucifer Effect: Understanding How Good People Turn Evil* (New York: Random House, 2007), 362.

93. Sgt. Ken Davis in Kennedy, *Ghosts of Abu Ghraib.*

94. From Specialist Joe Darby's testimony at Graner's trial, quoted in Zimbardo, *The Lucifer Effect,* 360. See also Silja J. A. Talvi, "Torture Fatigue," *In These Times,* June 28, 2005.

95. Reproduced in Zimbardo, *The Lucifer Effect,* 518, note 48.

96. David Rose, *Guantánamo: The War on Human Rights* (New York: New Press, 2004), 44.

97. M. Gregg Bloche and Jonathan H. Marks, "Doing Unto Others as They Did Unto Us," *New York Times,* November 14, 2005.

98. Mayer, "The Black Sites." Also available at http://www.torturingdemocracy.org/documents/20021210.pdf (accessed January 2, 2009).

99. Bloche and Marks, "Doing Unto Others," A21.

100. Jane Mayer, "The Experiment," *The New Yorker,* July 11, 2005, 67.

101. "Former Army Interrogator Describes the Harsh Techniques He Used in Iraq," *Democracy Now!* November 15, 2005, available at http://democracynow.org/2005/11/15/former _u_s_army_interrogator_describes (accessed August 4, 2008).

102. Hersh, *Chain of Command,* 270. Estimates of those killed exceed twenty thousand people, but no one was actually counting.

103. Philippe Sands, *Torture Team: Rumsfeld's Memo and the Betrayal of American Values* (New York: Palgrave Macmillan, 2008), 53.

104. See generally McCoy, *A Question of Torture.*

105. Sgt. Sara Wood, "Three Guantánamo Bay Detainees Die of Apparent Suicide," American Forces Press Service, June 10, 2006, available at http://www.defenselink.mil/news/newsarticle.aspx?id=16080 (accessed August 4, 2008).

106. "Guantánamo Suicides a 'PR Move,'" BBC News, June 11, 2006, available at http://news.bbc.co.uk/1/hi/world/americas/5069230.stm (accessed August 4, 2008).

107. For a more extensive argument that "torture lite" is not torture, see Mark Bowden, "The Dark Arts of Interrogation," *Atlantic Monthly,* October 2003, 51.

108. See Physicians for Human Rights and Human Rights First, *Leave No Marks: Enhanced Interrogation Techniques and the Risk of Criminality* (Washington, DC: Human Rights First, August 2007).

109. *Blackburn v. Alabama,* 361 U.S. 199, 206 (1960).

110. "Guantánamo Suicides a 'PR Move,'" BBC News.

111. Amnesty International, "USA: Cruel and Inhuman: Conditions of Isolation for Detainees at Guantánamo Bay," April 5, 2007, available at http://www.amnestyusa.org/document.php?lang=e&id=ENGAMR510512007 (accessed January 27, 2009).

112. James Yee, *For God and Country: Faith and Patriotism under Fire,* with Aimee Molloy (New York: Public Affairs, 2005), 101–2.

113. Carol D. Leoning, "More Join Guantánamo Hunger Strike," *Washington Post,* September 13, 2005; and Tim Golden, "Tough U.S. Steps in Hunger Strike at Camp in Cuba," *New York Times,* February 9, 2006.

114. Julian E. Barnes, "Military Says Special Chair Stops Gitmo Hunger Strikes," *U.S. News & World Report,* February 22, 2006, available at http://www.usnews.com/usnews/news/articles/060222/22gitmo.htm (accessed January 27, 2009).

115. "Critics Question Use of 'Restraint Chair' in Jails," CBC News, January 31, 2003, available at http://www.cbc.ca/canada/story/2003/01/31/chair030131.html (accessed August 4, 2008).

116. Barnes, "Military Says Special Chair Stops Gitmo Hunger Strikes."

117. Smith, *Eight O'Clock Ferry to the Windward Side*, 215.

118. Carla K. Johnson, "Halt Force-feeding, Doctors Say. Guantánamo Use Called Unethical," Associated Press, August 1, 2007.

119. Aleksandr Solzhenitsyn, *The Gulag Archipelago, 1918–1956: An Experiment in Literary Investigation*, trans. Thomas P. Whitney (New York: Harper & Row, 1973), 470.

120. Golden, "Tough U.S. Steps in Hunger Strike."

121. World Medical Association, "Declaration of Tokyo: Guidelines for Physicians Concerning Torture and Other Cruel, Inhuman or Degrading Treatment or Punishment in Relation to Detention and Imprisonment," 29th World Medical Assembly, Tokyo, Japan, October 1975, available at http://www.wma.net/e/policy/c18.htm (accessed August 4, 2008).

122. Solzhenitsyn, *The Gulag Archipelago,* 466.

3. Torture by Proxy

1. Dana Priest and Barton Gellman, "U.S. Decries Abuse but Defends Interrogations," *Washington Post,* December 26, 2002.

2. Bob Woodward, *State of Denial: Bush at War, Part III* (New York: Simon & Schuster, 2006), 80.

3. Douglas Jehl and David Johnston, "Rule Change Lets CIA Freely Send Suspects Abroad to Jails," *New York Times,* March 6, 2005, A1. Dana Priest, "Covert CIA Program Withstands New Furor," *Washington Post,* December 30, 2005.

4. John Crewdson and Tom Hundley, "Jet's Travels Cloaked in Mystery," *Chicago Tribune,* March 24, 2005.

5. David Johnston, "At a Secret Interrogation, Dispute Flared over Tactics," *New York Times,* September 10, 2006, 20.

6. See generally, Christopher H. Pyle, *Extradition, Politics, and Human Rights* (Philadelphia: Temple University Press, 2001).

7. Article 3, Convention Against Torture (CAT), *opened for signature*, December 10, 1984, G.A. Res. 39/46, 39 UN GAOR Supp. No. 51, U.N. Doc. A/RES/39/708 (1984); *entered into force*, June 26, 1987, 1465 U.N.T.S., 23 I.L.M. 1027 (1984); *ratified by the United States,* 1994.

8. Article 3, CAT, G.A. Res. 39/43, Annex, 39 U.N. GAOR Supp. No. 51, U.N. Doc. A/39/51; *ratified by the United States,* October 21, 1994.

9. Pyle, *Extradition, Politics, and Human Rights.*

10. S1373, 99th Cong., 1st sess. (June 27, 1986).

11. John Wolcott and Andy Pasztor, "Reagan Ruling to Let CIA Kidnap Terrorists Overseas Disclosed," *Wall Street Journal,* February 20, 1987, 1, 11.

12. Testimony Before the Subcommittee on Security and Terrorism, Committee on the Judiciary, U.S. Senate, 99th Cong., 1st sess., 1985, 71.

13. Walcott and Pasztor, "Reagan Ruling," 11.

14. 132 Cong. Rec., S1382-87 (February 19, 1986).

15. Walcott and Pasztor, "Reagan Ruling," 11.

16. Under the National Security Act of 1947, the CIA was expressly forbidden to exercise "police, subpoena, [or] law enforcement powers." 50 U.S.C. sec. 403(d)(3). However, Reagan's Executive Order 12333, subpara. 2.6 challenged this flat prohibition by allowing the agency to assist law enforcement.

17. Wolcott and Pasztor, "Reagan Ruling," 11.

18. *United States v. Yunis,* 681 U.S. F. Supp. 909, 915 (D.D.C. 1988).
19. Michael Otterman, *American Torture: From the Cold War to Abu Ghraib and Beyond* (London: Pluto Press, 2007), 114. Testimony of Michael Scheuer on "Extraordinary Rendition in U.S. Counterterrorism Policy: The Impact on Transatlantic Relations," before a Joint Hearing of the Subcommittee on International Organizations, Human Rights, and Oversight, and the Subcommittee on Europe of the House Committee on Foreign Affairs, April 17, 2007.
20. Clarke, *Against All Enemies,* 143–45.
21. Mayer, "Outsourcing Torture."
22. See *Kasi v. Angelone,* 300 F3d 487 (4th Cir. 2002).
23. Mayer, "Outsourcing Torture."
24. Ibid.
25. Amy Goodman and David Goodman, "Syria and the U.S.: Fellow Travelers at the Crossroads for Terrorism," *Mother Jones,* September 20, 2006.
26. Mayer, "Outsourcing Torture."
27. Seth Hettena (AP), "Navy Office Contracted Planes for CIA's Terrorist 'Renditions,'" *Boston Globe,* September 25, 2005, A21.
28. Ian Fisher, "Reports of Secret U.S. Prisons in Europe Draw Ire and Otherwise Red Faces," *New York Times,* December 1, 2005, A14. Before he resigned in June 2004, CIA director George Tenet testified that his agency had carried out approximately eighty renditions during his seven-year tenure. Statement of George Tenet, "Counterterrorism Policy," Hearing before the National Commission on Terrorist Attacks upon the United States, March 24, 2004, available at http://www.govinfo.library.unt.edu/911/ hearings/hearings8/tenet_statement.pdf (accessed August 6, 2008). By March 2005 approximately thirty more were carried out, according to Crewdson and Hundley, "Jet's Travels Cloaked in Mystery." Tenet also told the 9/11 Commission that "renditions" had become a major part of the war against terrorism during President Clinton's second term and that at least seventy had taken place prior to September 11, 2001. Farah Stockman, "Terror Suspects' Torture Claims Have Mass. Link," *Boston Globe,* November 29, 2004, 6. See also Douglas Jehl, "Qaeda-Iraq Link U.S. Cited Is Tied to Coercion Claim, *New York Times,* December 9, 2005, A1 (estimating 150 prisoners secretly rendered to other countries between September 2001 and December 2005). See also Trevor Paglen and A. C. Thompson, *Torture Taxi: On the Trail of the CIA's Rendition Flights* (Hoboken, NJ: Melville House, 2006); and Stephen Grey, *Ghost Plane: The True Story of the CIA Torture Program* (New York: St. Martin's Press, 2006).
29. Dana Priest, "Wrongful Imprisonment: Anatomy of a CIA Mistake," *Washington Post,* December 4, 2005, A1, citing a CIA official.
30. Hersh, *Chain of Command,* 53–55.
31. Karen DeYoung, "Gonzales Revisits Deportation Remarks," *Washington Post,* September 22, 2006, A14. Testimony of Maher Arar to a Joint Oversight Hearing, Rendition to Torture: The Case of Maher Arar, U.S. House of Representatives, October 18, 2007.
32. Pyle, *Extradition, Politics, and Human Rights,* chap. 16.
33. Neela Banerjee, "Administration Is Rebuffed in a Ruling on Deportation," *New York Times,* January 11, 2008.
34. Mayer, "Outsourcing Torture."
35. Glenn Greenwald, *A Tragic Legacy: How a Good vs. Evil Mentality Destroyed the Bush Presidency* (New York: Crown, 2007), 251, quoting the report of a Canadian commission that conducted an eighteen-month investigation into Arar's abduction and exonerated him completely.

36. Ian Austen, "Deported Canadian Was No Threat, Report Shows," *New York Times,* August 10, 2007.

37. Mayer, "Outsourcing Torture," 106; and CBC, "Missing Ottawa Engineer Turns Up in Syria," available at http://www.cbc.ca/canada/story/2002/10/21/arar_021021.html (accessed August 4, 2008). Arar's account of his rendition has been found credible by the Canadian Commission of Inquiry into the Actions of Canadian Officials in Relation to Maher Arar, Report of Professor Stephen J. Toope, Fact Finder, October 14, 2005, available at http://www.maherarar.ca/cms/images/uploads/Opening_Submissions_OPP__June_14_2004.pdf (accessed January 26, 2009).

38. Austen, "Deported Canadian Was No Threat."

39. Plaintiff's complaint, *Arar v. Ashcroft,* No. CV-00249 (E.D.N.Y. filed January 22, 2004).

40. Douglas Struck, "Canadian Was Falsely Accused, Panel Says," *Washington Post,* September 19, 1006, A1.

41. Tim Harper, "Arar Deportation 'Within the Law,'" *Toronto Star,* November 21, 2003, A13.

42. Andrew Mayeda, "Harper Apologizes for Canada's Role in Arar's 'Terrible Ordeal,'" CanWest News Service, January 27, 2007.

43. DeYoung, "Gonzales Revisits Deportation Remarks," A14.

44. "Wilkins Says Canada Should Back Off on Arar," CTV, January 24, 2007.

45. Margaret Satterthwaite, "Dirty Secrets of the War on Terror," *Amnesty International Magazine,* Fall 2006.

46. Priest, "Wrongful Imprisonment," A1.

47. Dominique Dhombres, "The CIA's Secret Flights to Europe," *Le Monde,* September 12, 2006. Declaration of Khaled el-Masri in Support of Plaintiff's Opposition to the United States' Motion to Dismiss or, in the Alternative, for Summary Judgment, *El-Masri v. Tenet,* Civil Action No. 1:05cv1417-TSE-TRJ.

48. Priest, "Wrongful Imprisonment."

49. Mayer, "Outsourcing Torture."

50. Farah Stockman, "Firms Get Scrutiny over CIA Captures," *Boston Sunday Globe,* December 11, 2005, 44, quoting German chancellor Angela Merkel telling reporters that U.S. secretary of state Condoleezza Rice had admitted that el-Masri's abduction was "a mistake."

51. Mark Lander, "German Court Challenges C.I.A. over Abduction," *New York Times,* February 1, 2007, A1.

52. Jane Mayer, *The Dark Side: The Inside Story of How the War on Terror Turned Into a War on American Ideals* (New York: Doubleday, 2008), 334.

53. Talvi, "Torture Fatigue."

54. *Hamdi v. Rumsfeld,* 542 U.S. 507 (2004).

55. Martin Mubanga to David Rose, "How I Entered the Hellish World of Guantánamo Bay," *The Observer* (UK), February 6, 2005.

56. Craig Whitlock, "Cleric Details CIA Abduction, Torture," *Washington Post,* November 10, 2006, quoting from an eleven-page letter smuggled out of prison.

57. Crewdson and Hundley, "Jet's Travels Cloaked in Mystery," citing Italian judicial records. See also Haider Rizvi, "Terror Policies Draw Outrage at Home and Abroad," *Common Dreams,* June 28, 2005. "EU Arrest Warrant Issued for 22 CIA Operatives," Reuters, December 23, 2005.

58. Nadia Abou El-Magd, "Accuser in Case vs. CIA Agents Tells of Torture," *Boston Globe,* February 23, 2007, A3.

59. Colleen Barry, "31 to Stand Trial in CIA Kidnapping Case," Associated Press, February 16, 2007; and Human Rights Watch, "U.S./Italy: Italian Court Challenges CIA Rendition Program," April 16, 2008, available at http://www.hrw.org/english/docs/2008/04/16/usint18540.htm (accessed August 4, 2008).

60. This information appears to have been reported by his attorney, Clive Stafford Smith, legal director of Reprieve, an anti-death penalty organization, available at http://www.reprieve.org.uk/casework_binyammohammed.htm (accessed August 4, 2008).

61. Stephen Grey and Ian Cobain, "Suspect's Tale of Travel and Torture," *The Guardian* (UK), August 2, 2005. See also the diary of Binyam Mohammed al Habashi, "Diary of Terror—Part 3," *Daily MailOnline* (UK), December 11, 2005, available at http://www.dailymail.co.uk/news/article-371330/Diary-terror-Part 3.html (accessed August 4, 2008).

62. Ibid., "Diary of Terror—Part 2, Cont.," available at http://www.dailymail.co.uk/news/article-371328/Diary-terror-Part2-cont.html (accessed August 4, 2008). See also "MI6 and CIA Sent Student to Morocco to Be Tortured," *The Observer,* December 11, 1005.

63. Andy Worthington, "High Court Rules on Binyam Mohamed," ukwatch.net, September 2, 2008, available at http://www.ukwatch.net/article/high_court_rules_on_binyam_mohamed (accessed November 29, 2008).

64. Raymond Bonner, "British Court Rejects U.S. Denial of Torture Claim," *New York Times,* August 22, 2008.

65. Peter Finn, "Charges Against 5 Detainees Dropped Temporarily," *Washington Post,* October 22, 2008, A14.

66. Richard Norton-Taylor and Duncan Campbell, "Smith Orders Inquiry into MI5 and CIA Torture Claims," *The Guardian* (UK), October 30, 2008.

67. Mayer, "Outsourcing Torture."

68. Craig S. Smith and Souad Mekhennet, "Algerian Tells of Dark Term in U.S. Hands," *New York Times,* July 7, 2006, 10. "Tirat" came from mixing the English word "tire" with the Arabic plural "at."

69. Ibid.

70. Michael Scheuer, "A Fine Rendition," *New York Times,* March 11, 2005, A23.

71. Ibid.

72. "Transcript of 'File on 4' Rendition," BBC Current Affairs Group, February 8, 2005.

73. Statement by Director of Central Intelligence George J. Tenet for the Senate Select Committee on Intelligence, 106th Cong., 2nd sess., February 2, 2000.

74. George J. Tenet, *At the Center of the Storm: My Years at the CIA* (New York: HarperCollins, 2007), 353.

75. Dana Priest, "Man Was Deported after Syrian Assurances," *Washington Post,* November 20, 2003, A24.

76. R. Jeffrey Smith, "Gonzales Defends Transfer of Detainees," *New York Times,* March 8, 2005.

77. Glenn Kessler, "Rice to Admit German's Abduction Was an Error," *Washington Post,* December 7, 2005, A18.

78. "President Meets with World Health Organization Director-General," Oval Office, December 6, 2005, available at http://www.whitehouse.gov/news/releases/2005/12/20051206-1.html (accessed August 4, 2008). Egyptian prime minister Ahmed Mazif told reporters from the *Chicago Tribune* that the CIA had delivered between sixty and seventy suspected terrorists to his country. Craig Whitlock, "CIA Ruse Is Said to Have Damaged Probe in Milan," *Washington Post,* December 6, 2005, A1. Egypt's use of

torture is well documented by the Bureau of Democracy, Human Rights, and Labor, U.S. Department of State, "Egypt: Country Reports on Human Rights Practices— 2002," Human Rights Report, Washington, D.C., March 31, 2003, available at http:// www.state.gov/g/drl/rls/hrrpt/2002/18274.htm (accessed August 4, 2008).

79. E-mail by the Honorable Craig Murray, July 2004, in Miles, *Oath Betrayed,* part 1.
80. Mayer, "Outsourcing Torture."
81. E-mail to Steven H. Miles, in Miles, *Oath Betrayed.*
82. Priest, "Man Was Deported after Syrian Assurances."
83. As one Arab diplomat explained, "It would be stupid to keep track of them because then you would know what's going on. It's really more like 'Don't ask, don't tell.'" Dana Priest, "CIA's Assurances on Transferred Suspects Doubted," *Washington Post,* March 17, 2005.
84. Ibid.
85. Farah Stockman, "Rice Defends Rendition, Calls It Vital Tool against Terror," *Boston Globe,* December 6, 2005, A25. Her admission was announced in advance by a Pentagon spokesman on November 23, 2005. William J. Kole, "Austria Probes CIA's Alleged Use of Flight Space," *Boston Globe,* November 24, 2005, A38. This transparent ruse had been pioneered by the Justice Department's Nazi-hunting Office of Special Investigations in the late 1970s. It is part of a larger effort to replace judicially supervised extradition procedures with executive deportations of alleged war criminals and terrorists, even to countries likely to torture them for their political opposition to the regime in power.
86. "Exporting Prisoner Abuse," CBS News, March 6, 2005, available at http://www. cbsnews.com/stories/2005/03/06/national/main678373.shtml (accessed January 26, 2008).
87. Quoted in Stephen Gray, "America's Gulag," *New Statesman,* May 17, 2004.
88. Shannon McCaffrey, "Canadian Sent to Syrian Prison Disputes U.S. Claims against Torture," Knight-Ridder, July 29, 2004.
89. Ibid.
90. Ibid.
91. Peter Bergen, "The Body Snatchers: Inside the CIA's Extraordinary Rendition Program— and the Most Bungled Abduction that Exposed Its Secrets," *Mother Jones,* March–April 2008.
92. Cited by Mayer in *The Dark Side,* 109.
93. Ibid.

4. Signaling Permission

1. Reinhold Niebuhr, *Moral Man and Immoral Society* (1932; New York: Continuum International Publishing Group, 2005), xvi.
2. James Risen, *State of War: The Secret History of the CIA and the Bush Administration* (New York: Free Press, 2006), 24–26.
3. President Delivers "State of the Union," U.S. Capitol, January 28, 2003, available at http://www.whitehouse.gov/news/releases/2003/01/20030128-19.html (accessed August 4, 2008).
4. Military Order, November 13, 2001, 66 F.R. No. 2, pp. 57831–836, and in Greenberg and Dratel, *Torture Papers,* 25.
5. *Duncan v. Kahanamoku,* 327 U.S. 304 (1946). See also Louis Fisher, *Military Tribunals and Presidential Power: American Revolution to the War on Terrorism* (Lawrence: University Press of Kansas, 2005).

6. The court came into existence on July 1, 2002, despite long American opposition. Its jurisdiction is limited to crimes by personnel of a member state and to crimes committed on the soil of member states. Neither the United States nor Iraq were members, but the United States has troops in about a hundred countries at any given time and intends to fight al Qaeda around the world.

7. Greenberg and Dratel, *The Torture Papers,* 118.

8. *Filártiga v. Peña-Irala,* 630 F. 2d 876 (2d Cir. 1980).

9. *Regina v. Bartle. Regina v. Evans, ex Parte Pinochet,* [1998] 4 All ER 897; [1999] 2WLR 272; [1999] 2WLR 827.

10. See Goldsmith, *The Terror Presidency,* 54–64.

11. Rome Statute of the International Criminal Court, art. 8, 2187 U.N.T.S. 3, 92; *opened for signature* July 17, 1998; *entered into force,* July 1, 2002 (without the United States).

12. Pursuant to the American Servicemembers' Protection Act, 22 U.S.C. 7421, the administration has cut foreign aid to some two dozen countries, mostly poor, for refusing to sign immunity agreements. Twelve of these countries are in Latin America and the Caribbean and lost funds for a variety of social and health care programs, including AIDS education, refugee assistance, and judicial reforms. Dominica, a Caribbean island, was denied $400,000 and could not afford to operate its coast guard for a year. Peru lost $4 million, Ecuador $15 million, and Bolivia $1.5 million. Juan Forero, "Bush's Aid Cuts on Court Issue Roil Neighbors," *New York Times,* August 19, 2005.

13. Goldsmith, *The Terror Presidency,* 62–63.

14. Priest, "Memo Lets CIA Take Detainees Out of Iraq."

15. Marcella Bombardieri, "Harvard Hire's Detainee Memo Stirs Debate," *Boston Globe,* December 9, 2004.

16. Hersh, *Chain of Command,* 48–50.

17. Ibid., 16.

18. Ibid., 52.

19. Seymour Hersh, "The Gray Zone: How a Secret Pentagon Program Came to Abu Ghraib," *New Yorker,* May 24, 2004.

20. Hersh, *Chain of Command,* 47–48.

21. Report of attorney Scott Horton to the German Bundesanwaltschaft, January 28, 2005, 2, based on out-of-channels complaints by a delegation of senior uniformed military lawyers to the Association of the Bar, City of New York, in May 2003.

22. Charlie Savage, "Military Lawyers See Limits on Trial Input," *Boston Globe,* August 28, 2006, A21.

23. Johan Steyn, "Guantánamo Bay: The Legal Black Hole," Twenty-seventh F. A. Mann Lecture, London, November 25, 2003, www.statewatch.org/news/2003/nov/17Guantánamo.htm (accessed August 4, 2008).

24. Katherine Q. Seelye, "U.S. to Hold Taliban Detainees in 'the Least Worse Place,'" *New York Times,* December 28, 2001, A1.

25. Charlie Savage, *Takeover: The Return of the Imperial Presidency and the Subversion of American Democracy* (New York: Little, Brown, 2007), 144 (interview).

26. The search for a legal black hole was the subject of "Memo 3 to Haynes from Philbin and Yoo, Re: Possible Habeas Jurisdiction," in Greenberg and Dratel, *The Torture Papers.* The government's claim that GTMO prisoners could not file habeas actions challenging their detention because Guantánamo Bay was sovereign Cuban territory was rejected by the Supreme Court in *Rasul v. Bush,* 542 U.S. 466 (2004).

27. Sands, *Torture Team,* 50.

28. Ibid.

29. *Opened for signature*, December 10, 1984, G.A. Res. 39/46, 39 UN GAOR Supp. No. 51, U.N. Doc. A/RES/39/708 (1984); *entered into force*, June 26, 1987, 1465 U.N.T.S., 23 I.L.M. 1027 (1984); *ratified by the United States*, 1994.

30. David Luban, "Torture, American Style," *Washington Post*, November 27, 2005, B1.

31. Sen. Rep. 103–107 at 59 (1993).

32. Luban, "Torture, American Style," quoting Abraham Sofaer, the former legal adviser to the State Department for the Reagan administration.

33. Suskind, *The One Percent Doctrine*, 99–101.

34. Available at http://www.youtube.com/watch?v=xMvJYN5izQY (accessed August 4, 2008). See also Johnston, "At a Secret Interrogation, Dispute Flared," A1, A20.

35. Evan Thomas and Michael Hirsch, "The Debate over Torture," *Newsweek*, November 21, 2005, 26.

36. Ibid. See also R. Jeffrey Smith and Dan Eggen, "Gonzales Helped Set the Course for Detainees," *Washington Post*, January 5, 2005.

37. Miller, "Three Were Waterboarded."

38. "President Discusses Creation of Military Commissions to Try Suspected Terrorists," September 6, 2006, available at http:/www.whitehouse.gov/news/releases/2006/09/20060906-3.html (accessed November 30, 2008).

39. Savage, *Takeover*, 219–220.

40. Johnston, "At a Secret Interrogation, Dispute Flared," A20.

41. President Bush Delivers Remarks on Terrorism, CQ Transcripts, September 6, 2006, available at http://www.washingtonpost.com/wp-dyn/content/article/2006/09/06/AR2006090601425.html (accessed August 4, 2008). As of February 2007, the Justice Department was still refusing to disclose the legal memorandum authorizing these procedures.

42. Suskind, *The One Percent Doctrine*, 100.

43. Paul Kramer, "The Water Cure," *The New Yorker*, February 25, 2008, 38.

44. *United States v. Lee*, 744 F. 2d 1124 (5th Cir. 1984). See also Evan Wallach, "Drop by Drop: Forgetting the History of Water Torture in U.S. Courts," *Columbia Journal of Transnational Law* 45 (2007): 468.

45. David Johnston and James Risen, "Aides Say Memo Backed Coercion for Qaeda Cases," *New York Times*, June 24, 2004.

46. "Memo 14, August 1, 2002, to Alberto Gonzales, Counsel to the President, from Jay S. Bybee, Assistant Attorney General, U.S. Department of Justice, Re: Standards of Conduct for Interrogation under 18 U.S.C. secs. 2340–2340A," in Greenberg and Dratel, *The Torture Papers*, 172.

47. Ibid. Gonzales's request is acknowledged in a letter from Justice Department attorney John Yoo to Alberto Gonzales: "Memo 15, August 1, 2002, Re: Letter regarding 'the views of our Office concerning the legality, under international law, of interrogation methods to be used on captured al Qaeda operatives," in ibid., 218.

48. See, e.g., the Convention Against Torture, art. 1 ("whether physical or mental") and art. 2 ("no exceptions whatever").

49. "Memo 14, August 1, 2002, to Gonzales from Bybee, Re: Standards of Conduct for Interrogation," in Greenberg and Dratel, *The Torture Papers*, 172.

50. Ibid., 181.

51. Ibid., 177–78.

52. Ibid., 178.

53. Ibid., 182.

54. U.S. Army, Field Manual 34-52, *Intelligence Interrogation*.

55. Testimony, Senate Committee on the Judiciary, 109th Cong., 1st sess., January 6, 2005, 4, available at http://www.judiciary.senate.gov/hearings/testimony.cfm?id=1345&wit_id=3938 (accessed January 29, 2009).
56. Memo 14, Greenberg and Dratel, *The Torture Papers*, 175.
57. Ibid., 207.
58. 1465 U.N.T.S. 85, 23 I.L.M. 1027, art. 2, sec. 2.
59. Andrea Weigl, "Passaro Convicted of Assaulting Afghan," (Charlotte, NC) *News Observer,* August 18, 2006; and Scott Shane, "C.I.A. Contractor Guilty in Beating of Afghan Who Later Died," *New York Times,* August 18, 2006, A6.
60. Memo 14, Greenberg and Dratel, *The Torture Papers*, 207.
61. E.g. 18 U.S.C. sec. 2340A.
62. Memo 14, Greenberg and Dratel, *The Torture Papers,* 204.
63. Goldsmith, *The Terror Presidency,* 149.
64. *United States v. Rabinowitz,* 339 U.S. 56, 69 (1950).
65. Anthony Lewis, "Making Torture Legal," *New York Review of Books,* July 15, 2004.
66. Goldsmith, *The Terror Presidency,* 150.
67. Ibid., 96–97.
68. Testimony, Senate Judiciary Committee, January 6, 2005, 3, 4.
69. Dana Priest, "CIA Puts Harsh Tactics on Hold: Memo on Methods of Interrogation Had Wide Review," *Washington Post,* June 27, 2004, A1.
70. Goldsmith, *The Terror Presidency,* 144.
71. Ibid.
72. Otterman, *American Torture,* 108–9.
73. 18 U.S.C. sec. 2340.
74. Shane, Johnston, and Risen, "Secret U.S. Endorsement of Severe Interrogations."
75. Gellman and Becker, "Part II: Pushing the Envelope on Presidential Power."
76. Mayer, "The Hidden Power," 52.
77. Priest, "Covert CIA Program Withstands New Furor," A1, quoting Professor A. John Radsan of the William Mitchell College of Law in St. Paul, Minnesota.
78. Ibid.
79. Spencer Ackerman, "Roadmap to Torture," *The Washington Independent,* June 18, 2008.
80. Quoted by Sands, *Torture Team,* 61.
81. "DoD Provides Details on Interrogation Process," U.S. Department of Defense Press Release, June 22, 2004, available at http://www.defenselink.mil/releases/release.aspx?releaseid=7487 (accessed August 4, 2008). See also Ackerman, "Roadmap to Torture," quoting General Dunlavey's lawyer, Lt. Col. Diane Beaver, telling CIA attorney Jonathan Fredman in October 2002: "We will need documentation to protect us." Available at http://www.truthout.org/article/roadmap-torture (accessed January 27, 2009).
82. Warren P. Strobel, "Documents Confirm US Hid Detainees from Red Cross," McClatchy Newspapers, June 18, 2008.
83. Ibid., citing minutes of the meeting.
84. Gourevitch and Morris, *Standard Operating Procedure,* 62.
85. Ibid., 63.
86. Ibid., 64.
87. Strobel, "Documents Confirm U.S. Hid Detainees."
88. Andrew Sullivan, "Verschärfte Vernehmunbg," Atlantic.com, May 29, 2007, available at http://andrewsullivan.theatlantic.com/the_daily_dish/2007/week22/index.html

(accessed August 4, 2008). See also Michael Marrus, ed., *The Nuremberg War Crimes Trials, 1945–46: A Documentary History* (Boston: St. Martin's, 1997), 65.

89. "Memo 21, November 27, 2002 (approved by Rumsfeld, December 2, 2002), to Donald Rumsfeld, Secretary of Defense, from William J. Haynes II, General Counsel, Department of Defense, Re: Counter-Resistance Techniques," in Greenberg and Dratel, *The Torture Papers,* 237.

90. McCoy, *A Question of Torture,* 46.

91. U.S. Army, Field Manual 34-52, *Intelligence Interrogation,* 1–9, expressly cites "forcing an individual to stand, sit, or kneel in abnormal positions for prolonged periods of time" as torture.

92. E-mail from CITF commander Col. Brittain Mallow regarding "participation in discussions of interrogation strategies, techniques, etc.," December 2, 2002, in Jameel Jaffer and Amrit Singh, eds. *Administration of Torture: A Documentary Record from Washington to Abu Ghraib and Beyond* (New York: Columbia University Press, 2007), A-145.

93. FBI e-mails reprinted in ibid., A-132, 135, 143, 144.

94. Tim Golden, "Senior Lawyer at Pentagon Broke Ranks on Detainees," *New York Times,* February 20, 2006; John Shattuck, "In Search of Political Courage," *Boston Globe,* May 22, 2006, A11; and Smith, "Detainee Abuse Charges Feared,"

95. Jane Mayer, "The Memo," *New Yorker,* February 27, 2006, 35.

96. Gourevitch and Morris, *Standard Operating Procedure,* 142. "Memo 22, January 15, 2003, to [William Haynes II,] General Counsel of the Department of Defense, from Donald Rumsfeld, Secretary of Defense, Re: Detainee Interrogations," in Greenberg and Dratel, *The Torture Papers,* 239. See also "The Torture Question," *Frontline.*

97. Memorandum for Haynes from Yoo, "Re: Military Interrogation of Alien Unlawful Combatants Held Outside the United States," 21.

98. Ibid., 35.

99. Ibid., 18.

100. Ibid., 16.

101. Article I, Sec. 8, clauses 9 and 13.

102. Article I, Sec. 8, clause 18.

103. Memorandum for Haynes from Yoo, "Re: Military Interrogation of Alien Unlawful Combatants," 16.

104. Ibid., 19.

105. "'Torture Memo' Author John Yoo Responds to This Week's Revelations," *Esquire,* June 2008, available at http://www.esquire.com/print-this/qa/john-yoo-responds (accessed September 4, 2008).

106. Golden, "Senior Lawyer at Pentagon Broke Ranks on Detainees."

107. Memorandum for Haynes from Yoo, "Re: Military Interrogation of Alien Unlawful Combatants," 26–29.

108. U.S. criticism of these techniques, when practiced by other nations, is documented by Tom Malinowski, "Banned State Department Practices," in *Torture: A Human Rights Perspective,* ed. Kenneth Roth and Minky Worden (New York: New Press, 2005), chap 11.

109. "Memo 25, March 6, 2003, Draft of Working Group Report on Detainee Interrogations in the Global War on Terrorism—Assessment of Legal, Historical, Policy, and Operational Considerations," and "Memo 26, April 4, 2003, Classified Working Group Report," in Greenberg and Dratel, *The Torture Papers,* 241, 286, 334.

110. Memo 26, in ibid., 347.

111. "Memo 27, April 16, 2003, to James T. Hill, Commander, U.S. Southern Command, from Donald Rumsfeld, Secretary of Defense, Re: Counter-Resistance Techniques in the War on Terrorism," in Greenberg and Dratel, *The Torture Papers,* 360.

112. Savage, *Takeover,* 181 and note 11.

113. Shattuck, "In Search of Political Courage," A11.

114. According to Jeffrey Gordon, a Pentagon spokesman, "Al-Qahtani's interrogation was guided by a very detailed plan, conducted by trained professionals in a controlled environment, with active supervision and oversight. Nothing was done randomly." Human Rights Watch, "U.S.: Rumsfeld Potentially Liable for Torture," hrw.org, April 13, 2006, available at http://www.hrw.org/english/docs/2006/04/14/usdom13190.htm (accessed August 4, 2008).

115. Sands, *Torture Team,* 47.

116. Final Report of Lt. Gen. Randall Schmidt and Brig. Gen. John Furlow, "Investigation into FBI Allegations of Detainee Abuse at Guantánamo Bay, Cuba Facility," July 14, 2005, in Jaffer and Singh, *Administration of Torture,* A-111, 112, 114, 115, 117.

117. Sands, *Torture Team,* 6.

118. Mayer, "The Experiment," 60–71. See, also, Amnesty International, "USA: Where Is the Accountability? Health Concern as Charges against Mohamed al-Qahtani Dismissed," May 20, 2008, available at http://www.amnestyusa.org/document.php?id=ENGAMR5 10422008&lang=e (accessed August 4, 2008). The duration of this interrogation is in some dispute. The log begins on November 23, while the FBI reports complain of much earlier abuse. The unremitting interrogation, employing category 3 techniques, began on December 3.

119. Amnesty International, "USA: Where Is the Accountability?"

120. Scott Shane, "China Inspired Interrogations at Guantánamo," *New York Times,* July 2, 2008, A14.

121. Amnesty International, "USA: Where Is the Accountability?"

122. Human Rights Watch, "U.S.: Rumsfeld Potentially Liable for Torture."

123. Amnesty International, "USA: Where Is the Accountability?" See testimony to the army general counsel.

124. "President Delivers 'State of the Union.'"

125. Michael Scherer and Mark Benjamin, "What Rumsfeld Knew," *Salon,* April 14, 2006, available at http://www.salon.com/news/feature/2006/04/14/rummy/index.html (accessed August 4, 2008).

126. Interrogation Log, Detainee 063, November 23, 2002–January 11, 2003, available at http://ccrjustice.org/files/A1%20Qahtani%20Publication_alQahtaniLog.pdf (accessed August 4, 2008). The final three days of the interrogation are missing. See also "Inside the Interrogation of Detainee 063," *Time,* June 12, 2005, available at http://www.time.com/time/magazine/article/0,9171,1071284,00.html (accessed January 27, 2009).

127. Executive Order No. 12333, United States Intelligence Activities (as amended by Executive Orders 13284 [2003], 13355 [2004], and 13470 [2008]), available at http://www.fas.org/irp/offdocs/eo/eo-12333-2008.pdf (accessed August 22, 2008).

128. Steve Coll, *Ghost Wars: The Secret History of the CIA, Afghanistan, and Bin Laden, from the Soviet Invasion to September 10, 2001* (New York: Penguin, 2004), 425–26.

129. Priest, "CIA Holds Terrors Suspects in Secret Prisons," A1.

130. Woodward, *Bush at War,* 224.

131. Goldsmith, *The Terror Presidency,* 94–95.

132. "American Killed in CIA's Yemen Attack," BBC News, November 7, 2002, available at http://news.bbc.co.uk/2/hi/middle_east/2416403.stm (accessed August 4, 2008).

5. Covering Up

1. "President Bush Welcomes Prime Minister of Hungary" (statement during a photo session with the Hungarian prime minister Peter Medgyessy), June 22, 2004, available at http://www.whitehouse.gov/news/releases/2004/06/20040622-4.html (accessed August 4, 2008).

2. Goldsmith, *The Terror Presidency,* 156.

3. Eric Schmitt and Douglas Jehl, "Army Says C.I.A. Hid More Iraqis Than It Claimed," *New York Times,* September 10, 2004.

4. "Newly Released Documents Point to Agreement between Defense Department and CIA on 'Ghost' Detainees, ACLU Says," March 10, 2005, available at http://www.aclu.org/safefree/general/17597pr520050310.html (accessed January 15, 2009).

5. Edward Epstein, "'The System Is Broken,' Army Commander Tells Senate Panel," *San Francisco Chronicle,* May 20, 2004.

6. Human Rights Watch, "Getting Away with Torture? Command Responsibility for the U.S. Abuse of Detainees," quoted in Matthew Rothschild, "Rumsfeld Shouldn't Be Fired, He Should Be Indicted," *The Progressive*, April 17, 2006.

7. Department of Defense News Transcript, November 29, 2005, available at http://www.defenselink.mil/transcripts/trancript.aspx?transcriptid=1492 (accessed on August 4, 2008).

8. "Rumsfeld Bids Farewell to Defense Employees," Associated Press, December 8, 2006.

9. Quoted in Cockburn, *Rumsfeld,* 194.

10. See, generally, Robert Jackall, *Moral Mazes: The World of Corporate Managers* (New York: Oxford, 1988).

11. Hersh, "The General's Report."

12. Gourevitch and Morris, *Standard Operating Procedure,* 211.

13. Karpinski, *One Woman's Army,* 14.

14. Gourevitch and Morris, *Standard Operating Procedure,* 251–52.

15. Hersh, "The General's Report."

16. The first report, prepared by Lt. Gen. Paul Mikolashek, the army's inspector general, reviewed ninety-four confirmed cases of detainee abuse in Afghanistan and Iraq but found no policy or any responsibility on the part of senior officers. The abuses were all "unauthorized actions taken by a few individuals." Quoted by Reed Brody in "The Road to Abu Ghraib," in Roth and Worden, *Torture,* 152.

17. "Memo, January 19, 2004, to Commander, U.S. Central Command, from Ricardo S. Sanchez, Lt., Gen. USA Commanding, Re: Request for Investigating Officer," in Greenberg and Dratel, *The Torture Papers,* 469.

18. Hersh, "The General's Report," 58.

19. Ibid.

20. Vice Adm. A. T. Church III, Review of Department of Defense Detention Operations and Detainee Interrogation Techniques (March 7, 2005), 3, available at http://www.humanrights.ucdavis.edu/projects/the-guantanamo-testimonials-project/testimonies/testimonies-of-the-defense-department/review-of-department-of-defense-detention-operations-and-detaineee-interrogation-techniques-the-church-report (accessed August 4, 2008).

21. Schmidt and Furlow, "Investigation into FBI Allegations of Detainee Abuse," in Jaffer and Singh, *Administration of Torture,* A-98.

22. "August 2004, Investigation of Intelligence Activities at Abu Ghraib/Investigation of the Abu Ghraib Prison and 205th Military Intelligence Brigade, LTG Anthony R. Jones/Investigation of the Abu Ghraib Detention Facility and 205th Military Intelligence

Brigade, MG George R. Ray (The Fay-Jones Report)," in Greenberg and Dratel, *The Torture Papers,* 1105.

23. Attorney Scott Horton, quoted by McKelvey in *Monstering,* 178.
24. "August 2004, Final Report of the Independent Panel to Review DoD Detention Operations (The Schlesinger Report)," in Greenberg and Dratel, *The Torture Papers,* 917.
25. Ibid., 908.
26. Josh White, "Defendants' Lawyers Fear Loss of Potential Evidence at Guantánamo Bay," *Washington Post,* February 14, 2008. See also Mark Denbeaux et al., "Captured on Tape: Interrogation and Videotaping of Detainees in Guantánamo, Seton Hall Law Center for Policy and Research," undated, but first released in February 7, 2008.
27. Josh White, "U.S. May Have Taped Visits to Detainees," *Washington Post,* August 5, 2008.
28. Michael Melia, "Lawyer: Gitmo Interrogators Told to Trash Notes," Associated Press, June 9, 2008.
29. *Brady v. Maryland,* 373 U.S. 83 (1963).
30. *Kyles v. Whitley,* 514 U.S. 419 (1995).
31. Pamela Hess, "Hayden Knew of Interrogation Videotapes," Associated Press, December 12, 2007.
32. Justice Department lawyers would later claim that Padilla's request had no merit because he could not prove that Abu Zubaydah, who allegedly linked Padilla to al Qaeda, had been tortured. Associated Press, "Dems Want Probe of CIA Tape Destruction," *USA Today,* December 7, 2007.
33. Michael Isikoff and Mark Hosenball, "Tracking the Paper Trail," *Newsweek,* December 24, 2007.
34. "Lawmakers Investigate CIA Interrogation Tape Disposal," Online NewsHour, PBS, December 11, 2007, available at http://www.pbs.org/newshour/bb/politics/july-dec07/ciatapes_12-11.html (accessed August 4, 2008).
35. Associated Press, "Dems Want Probe of CIA Tape Destruction."
36. Scott Shane, "Prosecutor to Review Official Handling of C.I.A. Tapes," *New York Times,* February 10, 2008, 19.
37. Mark Mazzetti and Scott Shane, "Destruction of C.I.A. Tapes," *New York Times,* December 11, 2007.
38. "CIA Destroyed Tapes Despite Court Orders," Associated Press, December 12, 2007.
39. "Moussaoui Prosecutor Kept CIA Tapes," Associated Press, February 6, 2008.
40. Douglas Jehl, "Report Warned C.I.A. on Tactics in Interrogation," *New York Times,* November 9, 2005.
41. Jason Leopold, "Report May Have Motivated Destruction of Torture Tapes," Truthout, January 3, 2008.
42. Mazzetti and Shane, "Destruction of C.I.A. Tapes."
43. See also Mark Mazzetti and Scott Shane, "Tape Inquiry: Ex-Spymaster in the Middle," *New York Times,* February 20, 2008.
44. Leopold, "Report May Have Motivated Destruction of Torture Tapes."
45. Mark Mazzetti and Scott Shane, "C.I.A. Destroyed Tapes as Judge Sought Data from Them," *New York Times,* February 7, 2008, A12.
46. Ibid.
47. John Cochran, "Showdown over Destroyed CIA Tapes This Week," ABC News, January 13, 2007, available http://www.abcnews.go.com/WN/story?id=4128320 (accessed August 4, 2008).

48. Thomas H. Kean and Lee H. Hamilton, "Stonewalled by the CIA," *New York Times,* January 2, 2008.

49. Charlie Savage, "AG Won't Probe Whether CIA Broke Torture Laws," *Boston Globe,* February 8, 2008, A2.

50. The new memorandum did not expressly reject coercion and abuse; nor did it clearly state that the president may never authorize unlawful methods. Daniel Levin, Acting Assistant Attorney General, U.S. Department of Justice, Office of Legal Counsel (OLC), Memorandum for James B. Comey, Deputy Attorney General, "Re: Legal Standards Applicable Under 18 U.S.C. secs. 2340–2340A," December 30, 2004, available at http://www.humanrightsfirst.org/US_law/etn/pdf/levin-memo-123004.pdf (accessed August 4, 2008).

51. Goldsmith, *The Terror Presidency,* 146–53.

52. OLC Memorandum from Levin to Comey.

53. John Yoo, *War by Other Means: An Insider's Account of the War on Terror* (New York: Atlantic Monthly Press, 2006), 183. See also Jeffrey Rosen, "Conscience of a Conservative," *New York Times Sunday Magazine,* September 9, 2007.

54. Shane, Johnston, and Risen, "Secret U.S. Endorsement of Severe Interrogations," 23.

55. Ibid., A1, A23.

56. Ibid., A23.

57. "CIA Prisons Moved to North Africa?" CBS News, December 13, 2005.

58. "U.S. Doesn't Sign Ban on Disappearances," ANCOSO Development GmbH, press release, February 7, 2007.

59. Karen DeYoung, "Bush Approves New CIA Methods," *Washington Post,* July 21, 2007.

60. *Rasul v. Bush,* 542 U.S. 466 (2004); and *Hamdi v. Bush,* 542 U.S. 507 (2004).

61. Smith, *Eight O'Clock Ferry to the Windward Side,* 152.

62. William Glaberson, "An Unlikely Adversary Arises to Criticize Detainee Hearings," *New York Times,* July 23, 2007, A1, A16.

63. Ibid.

64. Ibid.

65. The affidavit was filed in support of a Kuwaiti prisoner's request that the court reconsider its decision not to hear a challenge to the Fourth Circuit's holding in *Boumediene v. Bush* (discussed in chapter 9) that the Military Commissions Act barred habeas challenges from Guantánamo. William Glaberson, "Reserve Officer Criticizes Process of Identifying 'Enemy Combatants' at Guantánamo," *New York Times,* June 23, 2007, A10.

66. Ibid.

67. Ibid.

68. Glaberson, "An Unlikely Adversary Arises," A1, A16.

69. Farah Stockman, "Some Cleared Guantánamo Inmates Stay in Custody," *Boston Globe,* November 19, 2007, quoting the Center for Constitutional Rights and a Pentagon website.

70. Ibid. Of fourteen Saudis sent home in 2006, only two had appeared before CSRTs.

71. "U.S. Drops Charges against '20th Hijacker,'" Associated Press, May 13, 2008.

72. See, for example, Smith, *Eight O'Clock Ferry to the Windward Side.*

73. Tim Golden, "Naming Names at GTMO," *New York Times Sunday Magazine,* October 21, 2007, 81, as overheard by Lt. Cmdr. (and lawyer) Matthew Diaz.

74. Ibid.

75. Neil A. Lewis, "Official Attacks Top Law Firms over Detainees," *New York Times,* January 13, 2007.

76. See, for example, Charles Fried, "Mr. Stimson and the American Way," *Wall Street Journal,* January 16, 2007.
77. "Feds Disavow Gitmo Lawyer Boycott Remarks," CBS News, January 13, 2007.
78. Pauline Jelinek (AP), "Defense Official Resigns over Remarks," *Washington Post,* February 2, 2007. Josh White, "Evidence from Waterboarding Could Be Used in Military Trials," *Washington Post,* December 12, 2007.
79. Julie Hirschfeld Davis, "Bush Apologizes for Abuse," *Baltimore Sun,* May 7, 2004.
80. Tim Golden, "U.S. Army Report of Torture of Afghan Detainees Notes Sadism," *Sydney* (Australia) *Morning Herald,* May 21, 2005. See also Human Rights Watch, *The Road to Abu Ghraib,* June 8, 2004, 21–23, available at http://www.hrw.org/en/reports/2004/06/08/road-abu-ghraib (accessed January 27, 2009); and Miles, *Oath Betrayed,* 68–69 and reports cited therein.
81. Miles, *Oath Betrayed,* 71.
82. Amnesty International's Supplementary Brief to the UN Committee Against Torture, 2. See also "Deaths Index," Center for Bioethics, University of Minnesota, available at http://www1.umn.edu/humanrts/OathBetrayed/deaths-index.html (accessed January 27, 2009).
83. Paul Reynolds, "Junior Ranks Take Flak for Abu Ghraib," BBC News, August 30, 2007, available at http://news.bbc.co.uk/2/hi/americas/6970212.stm (accessed August 4, 2008).
84. Jackie Spinner, "MP Captain Tells of Efforts to Hide Details of Detainee's Death," *Washington Post,* June 25, 2004, A18.
85. Gourevitch and Morris, *Standard Operating Procedure,* 211.
86. On Jordan's mental state, see Zimbardo, *The Lucifer Effect.*
87. R. Jeffrey Smith, "Abu Ghraib Officer Gets Reprimand," *Washington Post,* May 12, 2005, A16.
88. "Split Verdict for Abu Ghraib Interrogation Chief," Associated Press, August 28, 2007, available at http://www.msnbc.msn.com/id/20478391? (accessed August 4, 2008).
89. *Democracy Now* interview, October 26, 2005, available at http://democracynow.org/2005/10/26/col_janis_karpinski_the_former_head (accessed August 4, 2008).
90. Josh White, "Army Interrogator Reprimanded in Iraqi's Death," *Washington Post,* January 24, 2006, A2.
91. White, "General Who Ran Guantánamo Bay Retires," A6.
92. Justin Berton, "Stanford Students, Faculty Protest Rumsfeld's Hoover Appointment," *San Francisco Chronicle,* September 22, 2007.

6. The War Criminals

1. Instructions to Col. Benedict Arnold concerning the invasion of Canada, September 14, 1775, available at http://www.beliefnet.com/resourcelib/docs/107/Letter_from_George_Washington_to_Benedict_Arnold_1.html (accessed January 27, 2009).
2. For another assessment of legal responsibility see Michael Ratner, *The Trial of Donald Rumsfeld: A Prosecution by Book* (New York: New Press, 2008).
3. The chief federal conspiracy statute is 18 U.S.C. sec. 371. For a convenient overview of federal conspiracy law, see Anne Langer and James Parnes, "Federal Criminal Conspiracy," *American Criminal Law Review,* March 22, 2008, available at http://goliath.ecnext.com/coms2/summary_0199-7854060_ITM (accessed January 27, 2009). For the crime of conspiracy to commit torture, see 18 U.S.C. sec. 2340A (c). See also 18 U.S.C. sec. 241 for conspiracy to deprive American citizens (e.g., Padilla) of their civil rights.
4. 18 U.S.C. sec. 2 (a).

5. "Secretary Rumsfeld Interview with George Stephanopoulos," *ABC This Week,* February 6, 2005, Department of Defense, News Transcript, available at http://www.defenselink. mil/transcripts/transcript.aspx?transcriptid=1697 (accessed August 6, 2008).

6. Department of the Army, Field Manual 27-10, *The Law of Land Warfare,* para. 501.

7. Public Law 109-366, 120 Stat. 2600, 10 U.S.C. sec. 950q: "Any person is punishable as a principal under this chapter [47A] . . . who . . . should have known, that a subordinate was about to commit [war crimes] and who failed to take the necessary and reasonable measures to prevent such acts or to punish the perpetrators thereof."

8. Yamashita's conviction was upheld by the U.S. Supreme Court in *In re Yamashita,* 327 U.S. 1 (1946).

9. Human Rights Watch, "Impunity for the Architects of Illegal Policy," in *Getting Away with Torture?* April 23, 2005, 9, available at http://www.hrw.org/en/node/11765/ section/7 (accessed January 27, 2009) (citing interviews in Afghanistan).

10. Peter Slevin and Robin Wright, "Pentagon Was Warned of Abuse Months Ago," *Washington Post,* May 8, 2004, A12. See also Mark Matthews, "Powell: Bush Told of Red Cross Reports," *Baltimore Sun,* May 12, 2004.

11. Slevin and Wright, "Pentagon Was Warned of Abuse," 12.

12. Conyers, *George W. Bush versus the U.S. Constitution (The Conyers Report),* 100.

13. "Schlesinger Report," in Greenberg and Dratel, *The Torture Papers,* 908.

14. The prisoner was Hiwa Abdul Rahman Rashul, a member of Ansar al-Islam. The request came from CIA director George Tenet. General Sanchez carried out Rumsfeld's order and hid the prisoner from the Red Cross at Camp Cropper, near the Baghdad Airport. Conyers, *George W. Bush versus the Constitution (The Conyers Report),* 102 and sources cited therein.

15. Hersh, "The General's Report."

16. Gourevitch and Morris, *Standard Operating Procedure,* 169, 211.

17. Under article 134 of the UCMJ.

18. 18 U.S.C. sec. 2441.

19. 18 U.S.C. sec. 2340A: "(a) Offense.—Whoever outside the United States commits or attempts to commit torture shall be fined under this title or imprisoned not more than 20 years, or both, and if death results to any person from conduct prohibited by this subsection, shall be punished by death or imprisoned for any term of years or for life."

20. Article 93 bans cruelty. Article 128 defines "attempts." Article 81 defines "conspiracies." The Military Commissions Act of 2006, which grants immunity from prosecution to both the torturers and their superiors, did not repeal the UCMJ. See chapter 8.

21. The UCMJ is codified at 10 U.S.C. sec. 801 et seq. The relevant provisions include homicide (arts. 118–19), assault (art. 128), cruelty and maltreatment (art. 93), and maiming (art. 124).

22. 10 U.S.C. sec. 893.

23. Josh White, "U.S. Generals in Iraq Were Told of Abuse Early, Inquiry Finds," *Washington Post,* December 1, 2004, A1.

24. 10 U.S.C. sec. 892. Dereliction of duty has been the most common charge against soldiers charged with abusing prisoners in Afghanistan and Iraq. Warren's role in restricting access has been described by Brig. Gen. Janis Karpinski, the prison commander. Douglas Jehl and Eric Schmitt, "Army Tried to Limit Abu Ghraib Access," *New York Times,* May 20, 2004, A1. Blocking the Red Cross's access also violates the Geneva Conventions.

25. Lewis, "Red Cross Finds Detainee Abuse at Guantánamo," A1.

26. See Amnesty International, "USA: Guantánamo—an Icon of Lawlessness," January

6, 2005, available at http://www.amnesty.org/en/library/asset/AMR51/002/2005/en/dom-AMR510022005en.html (accessed January 27, 2009).

27. George Tenet has admitted that the CIA took part in some eighty renditions *prior to* September 11, 2001. Statement of George Tenet, "Counterterrorism Policy," Hearing before the National Commission on Terrorist Attacks upon the United States, March 24, 2004, available at http://govinfo.library.unt.edu/911/hearings/hearing8/tenet_statement.pdf (accessed August 6, 2008).

28. President Bush acknowledged it on September 6, 2006. John Donnelly and Rick Klein, "Bush Admits to CIA Jails; Top Suspects Are Relocated," *Boston Globe,* September 7, 2006, A1. Sheryl Gay Stolberg, "First White House Acknowledgement of C.I.A. Prisons," *New York Times,* September 7, 2006, A1.

29. Commission on Human Rights, United Nations (Geneva, 2004), Resolution 2004/41.

30. For international crimes, see Jordan J. Paust, *Beyond the Law: The Bush Administration's Unlawful Responses in the "War" on Terror* (New York: Cambridge University Press, 2007).

31. The federal law implementing the UN Convention Against Torture provides that "[n]othing in this chapter shall be construed as precluding the application of State or local laws on the same subject." 18 U.S.C. 2340B.

32. Walter Pincus, "Waterboarding Historically Controversial," *Washington Post,* October 5, 2006, A17.

33. Douglas Jehl and Eric Lichtblau, "Shift on Suspect Is Linked to Role of Qaeda Figures," *New York Times,* November 24, 2005.

34. U.S. Department of State, "Tunisia," Country Reports on Human Rights Practices, 2005.

35. *Hamdan v. Rumsfeld,* 548 U.S. 557, 126 S. Ct. 2749, 2799–2809 (2006).

36. E.g., 18 U.S.C. sec. 371. A five-year statute of limitations may apply.

37. "Schlesinger Report," in Greenberg and Dratel, *The Torture Papers,* 949.

38. John C. Yoo, "A Crucial Look at Torture Law," *Los Angeles Times,* July 6, 2004.

39. Goldsmith, *The Terror Presidency,* 149.

40. *Youngstown Sheet and Tube Co. v. Sawyer,* 343 U.S. 579 (1952).

41. Tim Golden, "After Terror, a Secret Rewriting of Military Law," *New York Times,* October 24, 2004, A1, A12.

42. Yoo, *War by Other Means,* 28.

43. Oliver Wendell Holmes, "The Path of the Law," *Harvard Law Review* 10 (1897): 457, 459.

44. American Bar Association (ABA), "Rule 1.12, Client-Lawyer Relationship: Former Judge, Arbitrator, Mediator or Other Third-Party Neutral," *Model Rules of Professional Conduct* (2004).

45. See 18 U.S.C. sec. 2.

46. See, e.g., Geoffrey Hazard, Jr., "How Far May a Lawyer Go in Assisting a Client in Unlawful Conduct?" *University of Miami Law Review* 35 (1981): 669.

47. 18 U.S.C. sec. 2340A. While subsection (a) provides that the acts of torture must occur outside the United States, subsection (c) does not require that the conspiracy to torture people outside the United States has to take place outside the United States.

48. 18 U.S.C. sec. 2441.

49. See Horton, "Through a Mirror, Darkly," 145.

50. *United States v. Altstoetter et al., Trials of War Criminals before the International Military Tribunal* (February 17–December 4, 1947), 3:286.

51. From Closing Argument for the Prosecution in *United States v. Altstoetter et al.,* 45.

52. Quoted in Gourevitch and Morris, *Standard Operating Procedure,* 199.
53. Paust, "Executive Plans and Authorizations to Violate International Law," 811.
54. ABA, "Rule 1.13: Organization as Client," *Model Rules of Professional Conduct.* See also Roger C. Cramton, "The Lawyer as Whistleblower: Confidentiality and the Government Lawyer," *Georgetown Journal of Legal Ethics* 5 (1991): 291–94.
55. Woodward, *Bush at War,* 96.
56. Paust, "Executive Plans and Authorizations to Violate International Law," 846–48.
57. Jan Crawford Greenburg, Howard L. Rosenberg, and Ariane de Vogue, "Bush Aware of Advisers' Interrogation Talks," ABC News, April 11, 2008, available at http://abcnews.go.com/TheLaw/LawPolitics/Story?id=4635175&page=1 (accessed August 6, 2008).
58. Ibid.
59. Ibid.
60. Philip Shenon, "Mukasey Offers View of Waterboarding," *New York Times,* January 30, 2008. See also Manu Raju, "Democrats Grill Mukasey," *The Hill,* January 30, 2008.
61. Johnston, "At Secret CIA Interrogation, Dispute Flared"; and Greg Miller, "Waterboarding Is Legal, White House Says," *Los Angeles Times,* February 7, 2008.
62. At a White House briefing in April 2002, CIA director George Tenet was asked what his agency had learned from its interrogation of Abu Zubaydah, who had nearly died from untreated bullet fragments in his abdomen and groin. Nothing yet, Tenet had replied, because pain medicine had prevented the prisoner from talking coherently. "Who authorized putting him on pain medication?" the president asked. Risen, *State of War,* 22. According to Gerald Posner in *Why America Slept: The Failure to Prevent 9/11* (New York: Random House, 2003), 185 and 187, CIA doctors put Zubaydah on a quick, on-off pain medication; deprived him of sleep; and administered sodium pentathol.

7. Torture Reconsidered

1. For an elaboration of this view, see Greenwald, *A Tragic Legacy.*
2. Charles Krauthammer, "The Truth about Torture: It's Time to Be Honest about Doing Terrible Things," *The Weekly Standard* 11, no. 12 (December 5, 2005).
3. Jeremy Bentham's unpublished essay, "Of Torture," can be found in W. L. Twining and P. J. Twining, "Bentham on Torture," *Northern Ireland Legal Quarterly* 23 (1973): 305–56. Bentham, of course, justifies the torture of a few when and if there is benefit to the many, but he does not consider what it means to institutionalize the practice.
4. Jean-Paul Sartre, *Situations II: Qu'est-ce que la Litterature?* (Paris: Gallimard, 1948); Paul Arthur Schilpp, ed., *The Philosophy of Jean-Paul Sartre* (Carbondale, IL: Southern Illinois University Press, 1981).
5. Michael Walzer, "Political Action: The Problem of Dirty Hands," *Philosophy & Public Affairs* 2, no. 2 (Winter 1973). Like Richard Posner, Walzer is willing to excuse torture upon a showing of necessity but views it as more of a field expedient than an institutional program.
6. Alan Dershowitz, *Why Terrorism Works: Understanding the Threat, Responding to the Challenge* (Chicago: R. R. Donnelley & Sons, 2002). Dershowitz's proposal for "torture warrants" is a reversion to the jurisprudence of the Middle Ages when the law courts of Europe routinely tortured suspects in capital cases. See John H. Langbein, *Torture and the Law of Proof: Europe and England in the Ancien Régime* (Chicago: University of Chicago Press, 1997), 129–31.
7. See, for example, Niebuhr, *Moral Man and Immoral Society.*
8. Sir William S. Holdsworth, *A History of English Law,* 3rd ed. (London: Methuen, 1903–1972), 5:195.

9. Tony Lagouranis and Allen Mikaelian, *Fear Up Harsh* (New York: NAL Caliber, 2007), 246.

10. Mayer, "Outsourcing Torture."

11. Ibid.

12. Krauthammer, "The Truth About Torture." Stuart Taylor, Jr., "On This Issue, Bush and Cheney Need Adult Supervision," *Atlantic Monthly,* November 15, 2005, available at http://theatlantic.com/doc/200511u/nj_taylor_2005-11-15 (accessed August 10, 2008).

13. Krauthammer, "The Truth About Torture." Alan Dershowitz, "Democrats and Waterboarding," *Wall Street Journal,* November 7, 2007.

14. Intelligence Science Board, *Educing Information—Interrogation: Science and Art* (Washington, DC: National Defense Intelligence College, December 2006). See also Scott Shane and Mark Mazzetti, "Advisers Fault Harsh Methods in Interrogation," *New York Times,* May 30, 2007.

15. Intelligence Science Board, *Educing Information,* xx.

16. Ibid.

17. Department of Defense, *Working Group Report on Detainee Interrogations in the Global War on Terrorism: Assessment of Legal, Historical, Policy, and Operational Considerations,* March 6, 2003, available at http://online.wsj.com/public/resources/documents/military_0604.pdf (accessed August 10, 2008).

18. The author was head of the legal section of the Department of Counterintelligence, U.S. Army Intelligence School, at Fort Holabird, Maryland, in 1967 and 1968.

19. Mackey and Miller, *The Interrogators,* 477.

20. Ibid.

21. Ibid., 179–80.

22. "Torture's Terrible Toll," *Newsweek,* November 21, 2005.

23. Gourevitch and Morris, *Standard Operating Procedure,* 212, 202.

24. Peter Bergen, *Washington Monthly's No More: No Torture, No Exceptions* issue, January/February/March 2008, 20–21.

25. Lagouranis and Mikaelian, *Fear Up Harsh,* 244–45.

26. Ibid., 246.

27. Ibid.

28. Kennedy, *Ghosts of Abu Ghraib.*

29. *Report of the Commission of Inquiry into the Methods of Investigation of the General Security Service Regarding Hostile Terrorist Activity* (Landau Commission), excerpted in *Israeli Law Review* 23 (1989): 146. John T. Parry and Welsh S. White, "Interrogating Suspected Terrorists: Should Torture Be an Option?" *University of Pittsburgh Law Review* 63 (2002): 743, 758.

30. Lagouranis and Mikaelian, *Fear Up Harsh,* 246.

31. Richard A. Posner, *Catastrophe: Risk and Response* (New York: Oxford University Press, 2004), 240. See also Richard A. Posner, *Not a Suicide Pact: The Constitution in a Time of National Emergency* (New York: Oxford University Press, 2006).

32. Peter Laufer and Markos Kounalakis, "The Monthly Interview: Philip Zimbardo," *Washington Monthly,* December 2007, 18.

33. Michael Balfour, *Theatre in Prison: Theory and Practice* (Portland, OR: Intellect Books, 2004), 29–30.

34. Laufer and Kounalakis, "The Monthly Interview," 18.

35. Moazzam Begg, *Enemy Combatant: My Imprisonment at Guantánamo, Bagram, and Kandahar* (New York: New Press, 2006).

36. Quoted in Ricks, *Fiasco,* 290.
37. David Sands, "Suicide Bombing Popular Terrorist Tactic," *Washington Times,* May 8, 2006. See also Warren P. Strobel, "Report Documents Major Increase in Terrorist Incidents," Knight Ridder Newspapers, April 20, 2006, available at http://www. mcclatchydc.com/154/story/13738.html (accessed December 23, 2008).
38. Thomas Powers, "Bringing 'Em On," *New York Times,* December 25, 2005.
39. Fareed Zakaria, "Psst . . . Nobody Loves a Torturer," *Newsweek,* November 14, 2005.
40. Statistics from John Shattuck, "Healing Our Self-Inflicted Wounds," *American Prospect,* January–February 2008, 36.
41. Quoted in David Hackett Fischer, *Washington's Crossing* (New York: Oxford University Press, 2004), 379. Not all Americans obeyed these instructions, of course, especially in the Carolinas, where guerrilla warfare was the norm.
42. Howard S. Levie, *Prisoners of War in International Armed Conflict* (Newport, RI: Naval War College Press, 1977), 10, note 44.
43. Evan Mawdsley, *Thunder in the East: The Nazi-Soviet War, 1941–1945* (New York: Oxford University Press, 2005), 103, 238.
44. Amnesty International, "No Return to Execution," November 29, 2001, citing Thailand, Spain, the United Kingdom, and Russia.
45. David Cole, "The Man Behind the Torture," review of *The Terror Presidency,* by Jack Goldsmith, *New York Review of Books,* December 6, 2007, 38, quoting Jack Goldsmith, former head of the OLC.
46. On Ashcroft's opposition to the military commissions, see Gellman and Becker, "Part I: A Different Understanding with the President."
47. Ackerman, "Roadmap to Torture."
48. George F. Kennan, "Where Do You Stand on Communism?" *New York Times Magazine,* May 27, 1951.
49. Commanding General David H. Petraeus, "Letter about Values," Headquarters, Multi-National Force–Iraq, Baghdad, Iraq, May 10, 2007, available at http://www.globalsecurity. org/military/library/policy/army/other/petraeus_values-msg_torture.070510.htm (accessed August 10, 2008).
50. William Fisher, "Leading GOP Candidates Surge to Embrace Torture," Truthout, May 23, 2007.
51. Hannah Arendt, *Responsibility and Judgment,* ed. Jerome Kohn (New York: Schocken Books, 2003), 159.

8. Congress: The Enablers

1. Debate in the Virginia Ratifying Convention, June 16, 1788, Jonathan Elliot, ed., *The Debates of the Several State Conventions on the Adoption of the Federal Constitution as Recommended by the General Convention at Philadelphia in 1787,* 2nd ed. (Philadelphia: Lippincott, 1896), 3:447–48.
2. Nixon-Frost interviews in the *New York Times,* May 20, 1977.
3. Lawrence E. Walsh, *Firewall: The Iran-Contra Conspiracy and Cover-Up* (New York: W. W. Norton, 1997), 310–12.
4. John W. Dean, "Vice President Cheney and the Fight over 'Inherent' Presidential Powers: His Attempt to Swing the Pendulum Back Began Long before 9/11," FindLaw. com, February 10, 2006.
5. Senator Dick Durbin (D-IL) had tried without success to move a similar amendment earlier in the session but had met with united opposition from Senate Republicans.

6. Ian Fishback, "A Matter of Honor," *Washington Post,* September 28, 2005 (text of letter).

7. Eric Schmitt, "New Army Rules May Snarl Talks with McCain on Detainee Issue," *New York Times,* December 14, 2005.

8. Eric Schmitt and Tim Golden, "Lawmakers Back Use of Evidence Coerced from Detainees," *New York Times,* December 11, 2005.

9. Ibid.

10. Conservatives used this strategy with great success in 1978, when they persuaded Congress to send all applications for national security wiretaps to a single Foreign Intelligence Surveillance Court (subject to single Court of Review). Over the years, William H. Rehnquist, the Supreme Court's conservative chief justice, selected mostly conservative judges to serve on it.

11. "Bush Moves to Block Torture Probe," Reuters, September 30, 2005. The amendment was passed on October 5, 2005.

12. Eric Schmitt, "Exception Sought in Detainee Abuse Ban," *New York Times,* October 25, 2005.

13. "Ex-CIA Boss: Cheney Is 'Vice President for Torture,'" CNN.com, November 21, 2005, available at http://www.cnn.com/2005/WORLD/europe/11/18/torture.vp/index.html (accessed August 10, 2008).

14. Michael John Garcia, "Interrogation of Detainees: Overview of the McCain Amendment," CRS Report for Congress, January 24, 2006 (updated December 11, 2007).

15. Gellman and Becker, "Part II: Pushing the Envelope on Presidential Power."

16. Ibid.

17. Charlie Savage, "3 GOP Senators Blast Bush Bid to Bypass Torture Ban," *Boston Globe,* January 5, 2006.

18. Gellman and Becker, "Part II: Pushing the Envelope on Presidential Power."

19. G. W. Prothero, *Selected Statutes and Other Constitutional Documents Illustrative of the Reigns of Elizabeth and James I* (Oxford: Clarendon Press, 1894), 310.

20. 1 Will and Mar sess. 2, ch. 2. For good measure Parliament repeated the prohibition three times.

21. *Hamdan v. Rumsfeld,* 548 U.S. 557, 126 S. Ct. 2749 (2006).

22. Eric Scigliano, "Swift Justice," *Seattle Metropolitan,* June 2007, 72.

23. Interview with Charles Swift, May 26, 2007.

24. Quoted in Smith, *Eight O'Clock Ferry to the Windward Side,* 92. See also Lt. Cmdr. Charles Swift, "The American Way of Justice," *Esquire,* March 2007, 198. Any attempt "to coerce" or "influence the action of a court-martial or any other military tribunal" is forbidden by the Uniform Code of Military Justice, 10 U.S. C. sec. 837(a).

25. Ibid.

26. Neal Kumar Katyal, "Comment: *Hamdan v. Rumsfeld*: The Legal Academy Goes to Practice," *Harvard Law Review* 120 (2006): 65.

27. See, e.g., Geneva Convention 4 (Civilians), art. 3.

28. *Hamdan v. Rumsfeld,* 548 U.S. at 633.

29. 5 U.S. (1 Cranch) 137, 167 (1803).

30. See also *Sanchez Llamas v. Oregon,* 548 U.S. 331 (2006).

31. *Hamdan v. Rumsfeld,* 548 U.S. at 636 (J. Breyer concurring).

32. Ibid., 548 U.S. at 642 (J. Breyer concurring).

33. Smith, "Detainee Abuse Charges Feared."

34. Patrick Quinn, "U.S. War Prisons Legal Vacuum for 14,000," Associated Press, September 17, 2006.
35. Shane, Johnston, and Risen, "Secret U.S. Endorsement of Severe Interrogations"; and Randall Mikkelsen, "CIA Detention Program Remains Active: U.S. Official," Reuters, October 4, 2007.
36. Ibid.
37. See, for example, Pete Yost (AP), "White House Proposes Retroactive War Crimes Protection: Moves to Shield Policy Makers," *Boston Globe*, August 10, 2006.
38. At least twenty killings have been referred to the Justice Department for prosecution as war crimes, but only one was taken to trial. David Passaro, a CIA contractor who beat an Afghan prisoner to death, was not charged with violating the War Crimes Act, which could have meant a sentence of death. Instead, he was charged and convicted under the PATRIOT Act, which allowed the administration to reduce the charges to assault.
39. Shrader, "CIA in Middle of Election-Year Battle."
40. Military Commissions Act of 2006, Public Law 109-366, 120 Stat. 2600 (October 17, 2006) (hereinafter MCA).
41. MCA, sec. 8.
42. DoD Directive 2310.01E, the Department of Defense Detainee Program, reproduced Common Article 3 of the Geneva Conventions verbatim.
43. Julian E. Barnes, "CIA Can Still Get Tough on Detainees," *Los Angeles Times,* September 8, 2006. See also Pauline Jelinek, "New Army Manual Bans Specific Torture Methods," *Boston Globe,* September 7, 2006. Under the new rules, interrogators can still exploit pre-existing fears; flatter prisoners; ply "good cop, bad cop" routines; and pretend to be non-U.S. citizens. The manual does contain one exception to the Geneva Conventions— isolation from other prisoners—however, it can be used only on al Qaeda suspects and only when authorized by a four-star general, as if that somehow cures the legal violation.
44. R. Jeffrey Smith and Michael Fletcher, "Bush Says Detainees Will Be Tried," *Washington Post,* September 7, 2006, A1. See also Kate Zernike and Neil Lewis, "Proposal for New Tribunals for Terror Suspects Would Hew to the First Series," *New York Times,* September 7, 2006.
45. Smith and Fletcher, "Bush Says Detainees Will Be Tried," A1. See also "Bush: We're Fighting for Our Way of Life," CNN.com, September 6, 2006, available at http://www.cnn.com/2006/POLITICS/09/06/bush.transcript/index.html (accessed January 27, 2009).
46. Shane, Johnston, and Risen, "Secret U.S. Endorsement of Severe Interrogations."
47. Ibid. According to an ABC News report eight months earlier, the authority to use "enhanced interrogation techniques" had been delegated to "about 14 CIA officers." Ross and Esposito, "Sources: Top al Qaeda Figures Held in Secret CIA Prisons."
48. Terence Hunt, "Cheney Embrace of Torture Denied," *Boston Globe,* October 28, 2006; Neil A. Lewis, "Furor over Cheney Remark on Tactics for Terror Suspects," *New York Times,* October 28, 2006; and Jonathan S. Landay, "Cheney Confirms that Detainees Were Subjected to Water-boarding," McClatchy Newspapers, October 25, 2006.
49. "Executive Order: Interpretation of the Geneva Conventions Common Article 3 as Applied to a Program of Detention and Interrogation Operated by the Central Intelligence Agency," July 20, 2007, sec. 3 (b)(iv), available at http://www.whitehouse.gov/news/releases/2007/07/20070720-4.html (accessed August 10, 2008).
50. "House Votes to Ban Harsh CIA Methods," Associated Press, December 13, 2007.
51. "Limits Proposed on CIA Interrogators," Associated Press, December 6, 2007.

52. Laurie Kellman (AP), "Justice: Waterboarding Is Not Legal Now," *Washington Post*, February 14, 2008.

53. Tim Golden, "Detainee Memo Created Divide in White House," *New York Times*, October 1, 2006.

54. Donnelly and Klein, "Bush Admits to CIA Jails." For a list of the "disappeared," see Grey, *Ghost Plane*, appendix A, 269–83. Among those unaccounted for are two minor children of Khalid Sheikh Mohammed, seized from a Karachi safe house. Suskind, *The One Percent Doctrine*, 229.

55. Bradley S. Klapper (AP), "Red Cross Wary of New U.S. Antiterrorism Law," *Boston Globe*, October 20, 2006.

56. "Rights Lawyers Say Hick's Plea Condition Unfair," ABC News Online, April 1, 2007.

57. Scott Horton, "The Plea Bargain of David Hicks," *Harper's Magazine*, April 2, 2007.

58. MCA, Public Law 109-366, 120 Stat. 2600, sec. 3(a)(1) amending sec. 948q(b). See also MCA, sec. 3(a)(1) amending sec. 948(s) (2006).

59. MCA, sec. 3(a)(1) amending sec. 948b(d).

60. MCA, sec. 3(a)(1) amending sec. 948d(d).

61. MCA, sec. 3(a)(1) amending sec. 949d(e).

62. MCA, sec. 3(a)(1) amending sec. 948j.

63. MCA, sec. 3(a)(1) amending secs. 950v(b), 950v(b)(25), and 950v(b)(28).

64. MCA, sec. 3(a)(1) amending sec. 949j.

65. MCA, sec. 3(a)(1) amending secs. 949c(b)(4), 949d(f), 949j(c), and 949j(d).

66. MCA, sec. 3(a)(1) amending secs. 948r and 949a(b)(2).

67. MCA, sec. 3 (a)(1), amending secs. 949a(b)(2)(A), 949a(b)(2)(B), and 949a(b)(2)(E).

68. MCA, sec. 3(a)(1), amending secs. 949d(f)(2)(B) and 949j(c)(2).

69. MCA, sec. 7.

70. *Marbury v. Madison*, 5 U.S. (1 Cranch) 137, 163 (1803).

71. 16 Car. C. 10, sec. VIII (1640).

72. See Gerald Neuman and Charles F. Hobson, "John Marshall and the Enemy Alien: A Case Missing from the Canon," *The Green Bag*, Autumn 2005 (*United States v. Thomas Williams*, unreported case, 1813), available at http://www.law.Columbia.edu/law_school/communications/reports/winter06/facforum2 (accessed August 10, 2008).

73. *Rasul v. Bush*, 542 U.S. 466 (2004), *Hamdan v. Rumsfeld*, 548 U.S. 557 (2006), *Boumediene v. Bush*, 553 U.S. (2008).

74. See, especially, the Habeas Corpus Act of 1679 (31 Car. II, c. 2).

75. Robert Parry, "Commentary: Gonzales Questions *Habeas Corpus*," *Baltimore Chronicle*, January 19, 2007. Transcript available at http://www.baltimorechronicle.com/2007/011907Parry.shtml (accessed August 10, 2008).

76. Voting rights of racial minorities, women, and those eighteen years old and older are expressly guaranteed by the Fifteenth, Nineteenth, and Twenty-sixth amendments, respectively. Gonzales's argument was rejected by a 2-1 majority in the U.S. Court of Appeals for the District of Columbia in *Boumediene v. Bush*, No. 05-5064 (D.C. Cir., February 20, 2007). It ruled that Article I, Sec. 9 does grant people protection against arbitrary detentions, but only if they are persons "with property or presence in the United States."

77. *Swain v. Pressley*, 430 U.S. 372 (1977). See also *United States v. Hayman*, 342 U.S. 205 (1952).

78. *United States v. Klein*, 80 U.S. (13 Wall.) 128 (1872).

79. 74 U.S. (7 Wall.) 506 (1869).

80. *Ex parte Yerger*, 75 U.S. (8 Wall.) 85 (1868) (petitioner released before decision); and

Felker v. Turpin, 518 U.S. 651 (1996) (stripping lower courts of habeas jurisdiction does not prevent petitions directly to the Supreme Court).

81. For Hicks's story, see Leigh Sales, *Detainee 002: The Case of David Hicks* (Melbourne, Australia: Melbourne University Press, 2007).

82. Carol D. Leonnig and Eric Rich, "U.S. Seeks Silence on CIA Prisons: Court Is Asked to Bar Detainees from Talking about Interrogations," *Washington Post,* November 4, 2006.

83. MCA, sec. 7.

84. 5 U.S. (1 Cranch) 137, 167 (1803). Thus the Supreme Court struck down the Religious Freedom Restoration Act because it purported to recognize constitutional rights not previously found by the courts in the Fourteenth Amendment. *City of Boerne v. Flores,* 521 U.S. 507 (1997).

85. Renae Merle, "Census Counts 100,000 Contractors in Iraq," *Washington Post,* December 5, 2006.

86. Aaron Wildavsky, "The Two Presidencies," *Trans-Action* 4, no. 2 (December 1966): 7–14.

87. For the failure of the intelligence committee investigations, see Kathryn S. Olmsted, *Challenging the Secret Government: The Post-Watergate Investigations of the CIA and FBI* (Chapel Hill: University of North Carolina Press, 1996).

88. A transcript of this briefing ("Bin Laden Determined to Strike in U.S.," April 10, 2004) is available at http://www.cnn.com/2004/ALLPOLITICS/04/10/august6.memo/index. html (accessed August 10, 2008).

89. See, generally, Dubose and Bernstein, *Vice: Dick Cheney and the Hijacking of the American Presidency,* 192–94.

90. E.g., see John Dean, *Broken Government: How Republican Rule Destroyed the Legislative, Executive, and Judicial Branches* (New York: Viking, 2007), 191.

91. See, for example, William Greider, *Who Will Tell the People? The Betrayal of American Democracy* (New York: Simon & Schuster, 1992).

92. David Mayhew, *Congress: The Electoral Connection,* 2nd ed. (New Haven: Yale University Press, 2004).

93. Anthony King and Giles Alston, "Good Government and the Politics of High Exposure," in *The Bush Presidency: First Appraisals,* ed. Colin Campbell and Bert A. Rockman (Chatham, NJ: Chatham House, 1991), 249–85.

94. Interview with William Fisher, "The Right Seeks to Rein in Presidential Power," Truthout, April 4, 2007, available at http://www.truthout.org/article/the-right-seeks-rein-in-presidential-power (accessed January 27, 2009).

95. Theodore J. Lowi, *The End of Liberalism: The Second Republic of the United States* (New York: W. W. Norton, 1979).

96. Richard Rose, author of *The Postmodern President: George Bush Meets the World,* 2nd ed. (Chatham, NJ: Chatham House, 1991), compares members of the House to peasants and the president to a feudal lord.

97. Mayhew, *Congress.*

98. Speech on June 2, 1924, quoted in H. L. Mencken, *Notes on Democracy* (New York: Knopf, 1926), 128.

9. Judicial Complicity

1. Justice Robert H. Jackson concurring, *Woods v. Miller,* 333 U.S. 138, 146 (1948).

2. Dershowitz, *Why Terrorism Works,* chap. 4, "Should the Ticking Bomb Terrorist Be Tortured? A Case Study in How a Democracy Should Make Tragic Choices."

3. Robert Dahl, "Decision Making in a Democracy: The Supreme Court as a National Policy Maker," *Journal of Public Law* 6 (1957): 279.
4. Schlesinger, *The Imperial Presidency,* 254–55.
5. Louis Fisher, *Nazi Saboteurs on Trial: A Military Tribunal and American Law* (Lawrence: University Press of Kansas, 2003).
6. *United States v. Toscanino,* 500 F. 2d 267, 272 (2d Cir. 1974).
7. 668 F.2d 32 (1st Cir. 1981).
8. Ibid., 37–38.
9. See, generally, Alona Evans, "Acquisition of Custody over the International Fugitive Offender—Alternatives to Extradition: A Survey of United States Practice," *British Yearbook of International Law* 40 (1966): 77.
10. *Matta-Ballesteros v. Henman,* 697 F. Supp. 1040, 1042 (S.D. Ill. 1988); *affirmed,* 896 F. 2d 255 (7th Cir. 1990); *cert. denied,* 498 U.S. 878 (1990).
11. 697 F. Supp. at 1057.
12. Ibid.
13. *United States v. Alvarez-Machaín,* 504 U.S. 655 (1992).
14. 504 U.S. at 682, 687.
15. *United States v. Verdugo-Urquidez,* CR 87-422Er (C.D. Cal., November 22, 1988); *affirmed* 856 F. 2d 1314 (9th Cir. 1988).
16. *United States v. Verdugo-Urquidez,* 494 U.S. 259 (1990).
17. Ibid., 273.
18. *United States v. Noriega,* 746 F. Supp. 1506 (S.D. Fla. 1989).
19. Elaine Shannon, *Desperados: Latin Drug Lords, U.S. Lawmen, and the War America Can't Win* (New York: Viking, 1988), 164.
20. Frederick Kempe, *Divorcing the Dictator: America's Bungled Affair with Noriega* (New York: Putnam's, 1990), 224.
21. 4B Op. Off. Legal Counsel, 543 (1980).
22. *Congressional Record* 135 S 12, 679–80 (daily ed., October 5, 1989).
23. Michael Isikoff and Patrick E. Tyler, "U.S. Military Given Foreign Arrest Powers," *Washington Post,* December 16, 1989.
24. David B. Ottaway and Don Oberdorfer, "Administration Alters Assassination Ban," *Washington Post,* November 4, 1989.
25. Ibid.
26. Ved P. Nanda, "Agora—U.S. Forces in Panama: Defenders, Aggressors, or Human Rights Activists?" *American Journal of International Law* 84 (1990): 494, 497.
27. See chapter 1 of Pyle, *Extradition, Politics, and Human Rights.*
28. Herbert Wechsler, "Toward Neutral Principles of Constitutional Law," *Harvard Law Review* 73 (1959):1. Learned Hand, *The Bill of Rights* (Cambridge, MA: Harvard University Press, 1958).
29. Loren Jenkins, "Coalition Collapses in Italy," *Washington Post,* October 17, 1985; "The Price of Success," *Time,* October 28, 1985, 22.
30. Bernard Gwertzman, "The U.S. May Pay a High Price for Its Triumph," *New York Times,* October 20, 1985, 1.
31. The presidents of Latin American countries met in Madrid and passed a resolution urging the UN General Assembly to request an advisory opinion from the International Court of Justice condemning the *Alvarez-Machaín* decision. "Conclusiones de la Il Cumbre Iberoamerica," *El National* (Mexico), July 25, 1992, 18.
32. David O. Stewart, "The Price of Vengeance," *ABA Journal,* November 1992, 50, 52.

33. Tim Golden, "Dispute Holds Up U.S. Extradition Treaty with Mexico," *New York Times,* May 15, 1994.

34. Barry E. Carter and Phillip R. Trimble, eds., *International Law,* 3rd ed. (Boston: Little, Brown, 1999), 792.

35. Brian Knowlton, "Americans Abroad Face a Rising Risk of Terrorism," *International Herald Tribune,* November 21, 1997.

36. Carter and Trimble, *International Law,* 792.

37. "Teheran Enables Arrest Abroad of Americans Harming Iran," *Washington Post,* November 2, 1989.

38. Ed Magnuson, "Bombs across the Ocean?" *Time*, March 20, 1989, 26.

39. *The Complete Writings of Thomas Paine,* ed. Philip S. Foner (New York: Citadel Press, 1945), 588. Quoted by Justice Stevens, dissenting in *United States v. Alvarez-Machaín,* 504 U.S. 655, 688.

40. William H. Rehnquist, *All the Laws but One: Civil Liberties in Wartime* (New York: Knopf, 1998).

41. *Korematsu v. United States,* 323 U.S 214, 246, 246 (1944).

42. *Berlin Democratic Club v. Rumsfeld,* 410 F. Supp. 144 (D.D.C. 1976).

43. Quoted in Gail Russell Chaddock, "A Judicial Think Tank—or a Plot?" *Christian Science Monitor,* August 4, 2005.

44. Jason DeParle, "Debating the Subtle Sway of the Federalist Society," *New York Times,* August 1, 2005. Martin Garbus, "A Hostile Takeover: How the Federalist Society Is Capturing the Federal Courts," *The American Prospect,* March 1, 2003, available at http://www.prospect.org/cs/articles?article=a_hostile_takeover (accessed January 27, 2009). The society, at its 2007 convention, claimed forty thousand members.

45. Chaddock, "A Judicial Think Tank—or a Plot?"

46. Nancy Scherer and Banks Miller, "The Federalist Society's Influence on the Federal Judiciary," unpublished paper, 26. Available through nscherer@wellesley.edu, and published online in *Political Research Quarterly,* May 1, 2008.

47. Edward Lazarus, *Closed Chambers: The Rise, Fall, and Future of the Modern Supreme Court* (New York: Penguin Books, 1999), 264.

48. Jason DeParle, "Nomination Stirs a Debate on Federalists' Sway," *New York Times,* August 1, 2005.

49. Savage, *Takeover,* 296–97.

50. Ibid., note 58.

51. *Khalid v. Bush,* 355 F. Supp. 2d 311 (D.D.C. 2005) (the *Boumediene* cases).

52. James Madison, *The Letters and Other Writings of James Madison* (Philadelphia: Lippincott, 1867), 4: 491.

53. Ibid.

54. David Johnston, "North Conviction Reversed in Part; Review Is Ordered," *New York Times,* July 21, 1990.

55. *In re Sealed Case,* 310 F.3d 717 (F.I.S.C.R. 2002).

56. Stephanie Mencimer, "Lone Star Justice," *Washington Monthly,* April 2002.

57. *In re Sealed Case,* 310 F.3d 717 (F.I.S.C.R. 2002).

58. Savage, *Takeover,* 72.

59. Source of clerkships: "List of Law Clerks of the Supreme Court of the United States," Wikipedia.

60. Posner, *Not a Suicide Pact.*

61. Ibid., 37.

62. Ibid., 61.

63. Ibid., 1.

64. Ibid., 85.

65. Ibid., 11.

66. Ibid., 148.

67. Those who believe that the Constitution merely accumulates specific provisions, with no overarching principles drawn from morality, will probably claim that the privilege against self-incrimination does not bar torturing an individual to obtain incriminating information about someone else.

68. Advocates of torture are likely to say that reading several specific provisions together to establish a broad Kantian rule against torture is similar to Justice William O. Douglas's use of "penumbras and emanations" of the First, Third, Fourth, Fifth, and Ninth amendments to invent a right to obtain and use contraceptives. *Griswold v. Connecticut,* 381 U.S. 479, 484 (1965).

69. Posner, *Not a Suicide Pact,* 152.

70. Ibid., 56, 80.

71. *Wilson v. City of Chicago,* 120 F.3d 681 (7th Cir. 1977).

72. Posner, *Not a Suicide Pact,* 155.

73. Ibid., 107.

74. Colin Freeze, "What Would Jack Bauer Do?" (Toronto) *Globe and Mail,* June 16, 2007, reporting on a judicial conference during the previous week.

75. Ibid.

76. "U.S. Judge Steps in to Torture Row," BBC News, February 12, 2008, available http://news.bbc.co.uk/2/hi/americas/7239748.stm (accessed August 10, 2008).

77. *Chavez v. Martinez,* 538 U.S. 760 (2003).

78. Alan M. Dershowitz, *Is There a Right to Remain Silent? Coercive Interrogation and the Fifth Amendment after 9/11* (New York: Oxford University Press, 2008).

79. "Dirty Bomb Suspect Captured," CNN.com/Transcripts, June 10, 2002.

80. Nina Totenberg, "U.S. Faces Major Hurdles in Prosecuting Padilla," *Morning Edition,* National Public Radio, January 3, 2007, quoting Ashcroft's spokesman, Mark Corallo.

81. "Lawyer: Dirty Bomb Suspect's Rights Violated," CNN.com, June 11, 2002, quoting Paul Wolfowitz. See also Dick Meyer, "John Ashcroft: Minister of Fear," CBS News, June 12, 2002, available at http://www.cbsnews.com/stories/2002/06/12/opinion/meyer/main512021.shtml (accessed August 10, 2008).

82. Johnston, "At a Secret Interrogation, Dispute Flared over Tactics."

83. Bruce Ackerman, *Before the Next Attack: Preserving Civil Liberties in an Age of Terrorism* (New Haven: Yale, 2006), 26.

84. *Padilla ex. rel. Newman v. Bush,* 233 F. Supp. 2d 564 (SD.N.Y, 2002).

85. *Padilla v. Rumsfeld,* 352 F.3d 695 (2d Cir. 2003).

86. *Rumsfeld v. Padilla,* 542 U.S. 426 (2004).

87. *Padilla v. Hanft,* 389 F. Supp. 2d 678 (DSC 2005).

88. *Padilla v. Hanft,* 423 F.3d 386 (4th Cir. 2005).

89. The plurality in *Hamdi* found that the Authorization for the Use of Military Force permitted the detention of anyone in Afghanistan who was "part of or supporting forces hostile to the United States" and actually engaged in armed conflict against the United States." Less than two weeks later, Deputy Secretary of Defense Paul Wolfowitz reinterpreted this definition of an "enemy combatant" to allow the detention of anyone who provided "support [for the] Taliban or al Qaeda forces" anywhere, without engaging in armed conflict. In *Ex parte Milligan,* 71 U.S. (4 Wall.) 2 (1866), the Supreme Court

struck down the use of a military commission to try a civilian Southern sympathizer during the Civil War because Indiana was too far from the conflict to be considered a "war zone." By contrast, the German marines in *Quirin* had landed from submarines on beaches close to where American ships were being torpedoed.

90. Eric Lichtblau, "The Padilla Case: In Legal Shift, U.S. Charges Detainee in Terrorism Case," *New York Times,* November 23, 2005.

91. Phil Hirschkorn, "Court Rejects Government Request to Move 'Enemy Combatant,'" CNN, December 22, 2005.

92. Linda Greenhouse, "Justices Let U.S. Transfer Padilla to Civilian Custody," *New York Times,* January 5, 2006.

93. Dan Eggen, "More Setbacks for Case against Terror Suspect," *Washington Post,* November 19, 2002. See, also, Smith, *Eight O'Clock Ferry to the Windward Side,* 91, quoting press conference by Defense Department general counsel William Haynes II, March 21, 2002.

94. Adam Liptak, "In Terror Cases, Administration Sets Own Rules," *New York Times,* November 27, 2005. *Al-Marri v. Wright,* 487 F.3d 160 (4th Cir. 2007).

95. Tom Daschle, "Power We Didn't Grant," *Washington Post,* December 22, 2005.

96. *Al-Marri v. Pucciarelli,* No. 06-7427 (4th Cir. 2008); Motz concurring, 7.

97. Public Law 109-364, amending 10 U.S.C. sec. 333.

98. Tottenberg, "U.S. Faces Major Hurdles in Prosecuting Padilla."

99. Michael Mukasey, "Jose Padilla Makes Bad Law," *Wall Street Journal,* August 22, 2007.

100. Office of the Press Secretary, "Fact Sheet: Michael Mukasey—a Strong Attorney General," September 17, 2007, available at http://www.whitehouse.gov/news/releases/2007/09/20070917.html (accessed August 10, 2008).

101. *Boumediene v. Bush,* 476 F.3d 981, 990–991 (D.C. Cir. 2007). Of course, this finding contradicts the attorney general's claim that Article I, Section 9, does not grant any such right—not even to citizens.

102. *Rasul v. Bush,* 542 U.S. 466, 485, 487 (2004).

103. The 1640 act declared that "any person imprisoned by Order of the King or Council should have habeas corpus and be brought before the court without delay with the cause of imprisonment shown." 16 Car. 1, c. 10, sec. VIII (1640). The 1679 act can be found at 31 Car. II, c. 2, sec. II. Accord, A. V. Dicey, *Introduction to the Study of the Law of the Constitution,* 5th ed. (London, Macmillan, 1897), 210.

104. 31 Car. II, c.2.

105. Henry Hallam, *The Constitutional History of England: From the Accession of Henry VII to the Death of George II* (New York: Harper & Bros., 1873), c. XI, sec. 34, 406.

106. Dicey, *Introduction to the Study of the Law of the Constitution,* 207, 217.

107. Ibid., 208.

108. Rex A. Collings, Jr., "Habeas Corpus for Convicts—Constitutional Right or Legislative Grace?" *California Law Review* 40 (1952): 335, 338–39.

109. Randolph and Sentelle also refused to regard Guantánamo Bay as under U.S. dominion, despite the Supreme Court's decisions in *Rasul* and *Hamdan.*

110. Wesley K. Clark and Kal Raustiala, "Why Terrorists Aren't Soldiers," *New York Times,* August 8, 2007.

111. See "The Trial of Stede Bonnet," *Howard State Trials* 15 (1718): 1231.

112. Mayer, "Outsourcing Torture."

113. Alfred P. Rubin, *The Law of Piracy* (Irvington-on-Hudson, NY: Transnational Publishers, 1998), chaps. 2, 3.

114. Article 9 (I).

115. *Journal of the Continental Congress,* 29:801.
116. Article 1, sec. 8.
117. 1 Stat. 112.
118. Alexander Hamilton, "Article 84," in *The Federalist,* ed. J. R. Pole (Indianapolis, IN: Hackett, 2005), 453.
119. J. Elliot, *Debates in the Several State Constitutions on the Adoption of the Federal Constitution,* 2nd. ed. (Philadelphia: J. P. Lippincott, 1859), 1:328.
120. 71 U.S. (7 Wall.) 2 (1866).
121. 317 U.S. 1 (1942).
122. E.g., *Haupt v. United States,* 330 U.S. 631 (1947).
123. 327 U.S. 304 (1946).
124. *Rasul v. Myers,* 512 F.3d 644, 648, 650 (2008).
125. Ibid., 512 F.3d at 655.
126. Ibid., 512 F.3d at 672.
127. Ibid., dissent, 512 F.3d at 674.
128. *Gates v. Bismullah,* 501 F.3d 178 (C.A.D.C., 2007); *rehearing denied,* 503 F. 3d 137 (C.A.D.C. 2007).
129. Linda Greenhouse, "Bush Appeals to Justice on Detainees Case," *New York Times,* February 15, 2008.
130. *Boumediene v. Bush,* 553 U.S. ___, 128 S. Ct. 2229, 2272; 171 L. Ed 2d 41, 92 (2008).
131. Ibid., 128 S. Ct. 2248; 171 L. Ed 2d 65.
132. Ibid., 128 S. Ct. 2252 and 2259; 171 L. Ed. 2d 70, 77.
133. Ibid.
134. Ibid., citing *Murphy v. Ramsey,* 114 U.S. 15, 44 (1885).
135. The military would release seventy prisoners if their home governments would take them, and it has twenty-five whom it would like to place in third countries but can't send home for fear of retribution. Carol Rosenberg, "Some War on Terror Detainees Can't Go Home," *Miami Herald,* June 16, 2008.
136. *Boumediene v. Bush,* 553 U.S. ___, 128 S. Ct. 2279; 171 L. Ed 2d 99 (C J. Roberts dissenting).
137. Ibid.
138. Ibid.
139. Ibid. 128 S. Ct. 2284; 171 L. Ed 2d 104.
140. Ibid., 128 S. Ct. 2279; 171 L. Ed 2d 99.
141. Ibid., 128 S. Ct. 2280; 171 L. Ed 2d 100.
142. 128 S. Ct. 2294; 171 L. Ed 2d 115 (J. Scalia dissenting). Curiously, he did not issue a similar prediction, a week later, in his majority opinion striking down the District of Columbia's gun control law.
143. 128 S. Ct. 2295; 171 L. Ed 2d 116.
144. Mark Denbeaux et al., "Justice Scalia, the Department of Defense, and the Perpetuation of an Urban Legend: The Truth about Recidivism of Released Guantánamo Detainees," Report of the Seton Hall Law Center for Policy and Research, June 2008.
145. 128 S. Ct. 2298; 171 L. Ed 2d 119.
146. 128 S. Ct. 2303; 171 L. Ed. 2d 125.
147. 128 S. Ct. 2306; L. Ed 2d 129, quoting *Van Ness v. Pacard,* 27 U.S. (2 Pet.) 137, 144 (1829).
148. 17 U.S. (4 Wheat.) 316 (1819).
149. 128 S. Ct. 2249; 171 L. Ed 2d 66.
150. 128 S. Ct. 2305; 171 L. Ed 2d 128.

151. *Rasul v. Bush,* 77 U.S.L.W. 3358 (2008).
152. *Ex parte Milligan,* 71 U.S. (4 Wall.) 2 (1866) (granting habeas to strike down use of military commissions to try civilians when civil courts are open).
153. *Ex parte Endo,* 323 U.S. 283 (1944) (holding that the continuing detention of Japanese Americans had gone on too long under the relevant legislation); *Duncan v. Kahanamoku, Sheriff,* 327 U.S. 304 (1946) (ruling that martial law in Hawaii had gone on too long under the law authorizing it).
154. William Glaberson, "Judge Orders 17 Detainees at Guantánamo Freed," *New York Times,* October 7, 2008.
155. Ibid.
156. 1 Will. and Mar. sess. 2, c. 2.
157. *United States v. Smith,* 27 F. Cas. 1192, 1229–30 (C.C.N.Y. 1806) (no. 16342).
158. *Kendall v. United States ex. rel. Stokes,* 37 U.S. (12 Pet.) 524, 638 (1838).
159. *Arar v. Ashcroft,* 414 F. Supp. 2d 250 (E.D.N.Y. 2006).
160. Ibid., 287.
161. *Arar v. Ashcroft,* Docket no. 06-4216-cv (June 30, 2008).
162. Ibid., 9.
163. Ibid.
164. Ibid., majority opinion, 18.
165. Ibid., 18–19.
166. Ibid., J. Sack dissenting, 2.
167. *El-Masri v. Tenet,* 437 F. Supp. 2d 530 (E.D. Va. 2006); *affirmed* 479 F.3d 296 (4th Cir. 2007).
168. 345 U.S. 1 (1953).
169. Louis Fisher, *In the Name of National Security: Unchecked Presidential Power and the Reynolds Case* (Lawrence: University Press of Kansas, 2006). See also Barry Siegal, *Claim of Privilege: A Mysterious Plane Crash, a Landmark Supreme Court Case, and the Rise of State Secrets* (New York: Harper, 2008).
170. Savage, *Takeover,* 171. *Herring v. United States,* 424 F.3d 384 (3d Cir. 2005); *cert. denied,* 547 U.S. 1123 (2006).
171. James Madison, "Article 51," in *The Federalist,* 281.
172. *El-Masri v. United States,* 479 F.3d 296, 312 (2007).
173. Ibid.
174. *El-Masri v. United States,* 128 S. Ct. 373 (2007). David Stout, "Supreme Court Won't Hear Torture Appeal," *New York Times,* October 9, 2007.
175. *El-Masri v. United States,* 479 F.3d at 312.
176. *In re: Iraq and Afghanistan Detainees Litigation (Ali v. Pappas et al.),* Misc. no. 06-0145 (TFH) (D.D.C. 2007).
177. Ibid., 32, 36, 37.
178. *United States v. Nixon,* 418 U.S. 683 (1974).
179. 542 U.S. 692 (2004) (opinion by J. Souter).
180. *Public Committee Against Torture in Israel v. Government of Israel,* HCJ 769/02 (December 11, 2005), available at http://elyon1.court.gov.il/Files_ENG/02/690/007/a34/02007690.a34.pdf (accessed August 10, 2008).

10. Why Do They Hate Our Freedoms?

1. Reinhold Niebuhr, *The Irony of American History* (New York: Scribner, 1952), 174.
2. Bush, "Address to a Joint Session of Congress and the American People."

3. "Lou Dobbs Tonight—London Terror Attacks," CNN, July 7, 2005, available at http://transcripts.cnn.com/TRANSCRIPTS/0507/07/ldt.01.html (accessed August 10, 2008).

4. "Al Qaeda's Fatwa," Online NewsHour, PBS, available at http://www.pbs.org/newshour/terrorism/international/fatwa_1998.html (accessed August 10, 2008).

5. Woodward, *State of Denial,* 408.

6. N. C. Aizenman, "New High in U.S. Prison Numbers," *Washington Post,* February 29, 2008.

7. Jesse McKinley and Laurie Goodstein, "Bans in 3 States on Gay Marriages," *New York Times,* November 5, 2008.

8. For more documentation, see Chip Berlet and Matthew N. Lyons, *Right-Wing Populism in America: Too Close for Comfort* (New York: Guilford Press, 2000).

9. Ronald Reagan, First Inaugural Address, January 20, 1981, available at http://avalon.law.yale.edu/20th_century/reagan1.asp (accessed December 23, 2008).

10. See, for example, François Debrix, *Tabloid Terror: War, Culture, and Geopolitics* (London: Routledge, 2007).

11. Thomas Frank, *What's the Matter with Kansas? How Conservatives Won the Heart of America* (New York: Holt, 2004).

12. See Robert Draper, *Dead Certain: The Presidency of George W. Bush* (New York: Free Press, 2007).

13. See, for example, Irving L. Janis, *Victims of Groupthink: A Psychological Study of Foreign-Policy Decisions and Fiascoes* (Boston: Houghton Mifflin, 1972).

14. See Frank, *What's the Matter with Kansas?*

15. Stephen Ansolabehere and Shanto Iyengar, *Going Negative: How Attack Ads Shrink and Polarize the Electorate* (New York: Free Press, 1995), 9.

16. Bruce Morton, "Selling an Iraq–al Qaeda connection," CNN, March 11, 2003; Dana Milbank, "Hussein Link to 9/11 Lingers in Many Minds," *Washington Post,* September 6, 2003; Associated Press, "Bush Overstated Iraq Links to al-Qaeda, Former Intelligence Officers Say," *USA Today,* July 13, 2003; "Bush Administration on Iraq Link," BBC News, September 18, 2003. See also polling data collected by Rick Shenkman in *Just How Stupid Are We? Facing the Truth about the American Voter* (New York: Basic Books, 2008), chap. 1, "The Problem."

17. Senate Select Committee to Study Governmental Operations with Respect to Intelligence Activities, *Intelligence Activities and the Rights of Americans,* book 2, *Conclusions and Recommendations* (Washington, DC: GPO, 1976), available at http://www.icdc.com/~paulwulf/cointelpro/churchfinalreportIIa.htm (accessed August 10, 2008).

18. McCoy, *A Question of Torture.*

19. See Gore Vidal, *Perpetual War for Perpetual Peace: How We Got to Be So Hated* (New York: Thunder's Mouth Press/Nation Books, 2002).

20. William H. Chafe, *The Unfinished Journey: America since World War II* (New York: Oxford University Press, 1985), 65.

21. "Taliban Control Half of Afghanistan, Report Says," *Telegraph* (UK), November 22, 2007.

22. Francisco Goldman, *The Art of Political Murder: Who Killed the Bishop* (New York: Grove, 2007).

23. Lucy Komisar, "Documented Complicity: U.S. State Department Releases Documents about U.S. Involvement with Chile during 1970's," *The Progressive,* September 1, 1999.

24. Tim Weiner, *Legacy of Ashes: The History of the CIA* (New York: Doubleday, 2007), xiii.

25. Ibid.
26. Laura Mansfield, trans., *His Own Words: A Translation of the Writings of Dr. Ayman al Zawahiri* (Old Tappan, NJ: TLG Publications, 2006), 204.
27. "Troops Put Rumsfeld in the Hot Seat," CNN, December 8, 2004, available at http://www.cnn.com/2004/US/12/08/rumsfeld.kuwait/index.html (accessed January 27, 2009).
28. Oral argument *United States v. Nixon,* 418 U.S. 683 (1974). Audio recording available at http://www.oyez.org/cases/1970-1979/1974/1974_73_1766/ (accessed August 10, 2008).
29. Schlesinger, *The Imperial Presidency,* 254.
30. Interview with David Frost, *New York Times,* May 20, 1977.
31. Schlesinger, *The Imperial Presidency,* 255.
32. 531 U.S. 98 (2000).
33. For an elaboration of this nonpartisan standard, see Wechsler, "Toward Neutral Principles of Constitutional Law."
34. See, generally, Stephen Mencimer, *Blocking the Courthouse Door: How the Republican Party and Its Corporate Allies Are Taking Away Your Right to Sue* (New York: Free Press), 2006.
35. Peter Eisler, "Pentagon to Expand Intel Ops at U.S. Prison in Afghanistan," *USA Today,* September 16, 2008.

11. Restoring the Rule of Law

1. Martin Luther King, Jr., *Where Do We Go from Here: Chaos or Community?* (New York: Bantam, 1967), 32.
2. Robert Bolt, *A Man for All Seasons* (New York: Vintage, 1962), 38.
3. Will Bunch, "Obama Would Ask His AG to 'Immediately Review' Potential of Crimes in Bush White House," (Philadelphia) *Daily News,* April 14, 2008, available at http://www.philly.com/philly/blogs/attytood/17692064.html (accessed January 27, 2009).
4. Mark Benjamin, "Would Obama Prosecute the Bush Administration for Torture?" *Salon.com,* April 4, 2008, available at http://www.salon.com/news/feature/2008/08/04/obama/ (accessed November 21, 2008).
5. "Gates: US 'Stuck' in Guantánamo," CNN, May 20, 2008, available at http://www.cnn.com/2008/US/05/20/gates.guantanamo/index.html (accessed August 4, 2008). Indeed, during the previous July the Senate voted 94-3 not to transfer any of Guantánamo's remaining prisoners—then about 270—to facilities in the United States. Senators presumably feared that some might escape or be released by judges.
6. Ibid.
7. Eric Schmitt and Tim Golden, "U.S. Planning Big New Prison in Afghanistan," *New York Times,* May 17, 2008, available at http://www.nytimes.com/2008/05/17/world/asia/17detain.html (accessed January 27, 2009).
8. Paul Reynolds, "Why US Is 'Stuck' with Guantánamo Bay," BBC News, May 21, 2008, available at http://news.bbc.co.uk/2/hi/americas/7413181.stm (accessed August 10, 2008).
9. Glaberson, "Judge Orders 17 Detainees at Guantánamo Freed."
10. *Boumediene v. Bush,* 553 U.S. ___, 128 S. Ct. 2229, 2267 (2008). See also *Munaf v. Geren,* 128 S. Ct. 2207, 2221 (2008), decided the same day as *Boumediene,* which defined habeas as "at its core a remedy for unlawful executive detention."
11. *In Re: Guantánamo Bay Detainee Litigation,* Memorandum Opinion, Misc. No.: 08-0442 (TFH) (D.D.C. August 11, 2008), 1.

12. The term "zones of active combat" comes from Philip B. Heymann and Juliette N. Kayyem's excellent analysis of possible remedies in *Protecting Liberty in an Age of Terror* (Cambridge, MA: MIT Press, 2005). It builds on the Supreme Court's opinion in *Ex parte Milligan* and rejects the broader idea of a combat zone represented by the Japanese internment cases and even the case of so-called Nazi saboteurs. If the courts are open, the area is not an active combat zone.

13. Jack L. Goldsmith and Neal Katyal, "The Terrorists' Court," *New York Times,* July 11, 2007.

14. Special courts to decide disputes involving bankruptcy, tax, and patent law are in no way analogous to special courts for despised foreigners or for citizens who are alleged to have given them material assistance.

15. Geneva Conventions, Common Article 3 (1)(d).

16. Ibid.

17. Interpretation of the Geneva Conventions Common Article 3 as Applied to a Program of Detention and Interrogation by the Central Intelligence Agency, July 20, 2007.

18. Legislation requiring this notification and access can be found in the Senate intelligence authorization bill of 2008.

19. UN Gen. Assembly, sess. 61, meeting 82, December 20, 2006.

20. Optional Protocol to the Convention Against Torture and Other Cruel, Inhuman, or Degrading Treatment or Punishment, UN Gen. Assembly, Res A/Res/57/199; *entered into force* June 22, 2006.

21. See Pyle, *Extradition, Politics, and Human Rights,* 22.

22. Tim Golden and David Rohde, "Afghans Hold Secret Trials for Men that U.S. Detained," *International Herald Tribune,* April 10, 2008.

23. Ali Gharib and Zainab Mineeia, "'Serious Risk of Torture' for Iraqi Prisoners Facing Transfer by U.S.," AlterNet, October 31, 2008, available at http://www.alternet. org/waroniraq/105564/%22serious_risk_of_torture%22_for_iraqi_prisoners_ facing_transfer_by_u.s./ (accessed December 1, 2008). For more comprehensive statistics covering Camps Bucca and Cropper, see David Enders, "Camp Bucca: Iraq's Guantánamo," *The Nation,* October 8, 2008.

24. Mark Mazzetti and Eric Schmitt, "Military Sending Foreign Fighters to Home Nations," *New York Times,* August 28, 2008.

25. *Munaf v. Geren,* 553 U.S. ___, 128 S. Ct. 2207 (2008).

26. MCA, sec. 7(e)(2).

27. Eli Saslow, "From Outsider to Politician," *Washington Post,* October 9, 2008, A01.

28. Representative Rush Holt (D-NJ), chair of the House Select Intelligence Oversight Panel, advanced a version of this proposal, limited to the military. Republicans defeated it in straight party line votes.

29. Alan Dershowitz, "Indictments Are Not the Best Revenge," *Wall Street Journal,* September 12, 2008.

30. I am indebted to Dean Lawrence Velvel of the Massachusetts School of Law for bringing this argument to my attention in a blog entitled "Re: Alan Dershowitz on Whether to Prosecute Executive Branch Officials," October 7, 2008.

31. Stuart Taylor, Jr., "The Truth about Torture," *Newsweek,* July 12, 2008.

32. Nicholas D. Kristof, "The Truth Commission," *New York Times,* July 6, 2008.

33. Tim Shorrock, "Exposing Bush's Historic Abuse of Power," *Salon,* July 23, 2008.

34. The power to pardon belongs to the president, but the power to define "all other powers vested by this Constitution in . . . any Officer" of the government belongs to Congress (Article I, Section 8, clause 18 of the Constitution). There are dicta in *Schick v. Reed,*

419 U.S. 256 (1974) to the effect that the pardon power can be modified only by constitutional amendment, but that need not limit the authority of Congress to forbid presidents from pardoning themselves and their subordinates in order to obstruct justice.

Jordan J. Paust argues that the president's pardon power is limited to pardoning "offenses against the United States, as opposed to all offenses against the laws of the United States," but it seems unlikely that any court would accept this distinction and thereby disallow pardons within the federal justice system for offenses that were also against the law of nations. *Beyond the Law,* 202, note 150.

35. 18 U.S.C. appendix III.
36. "Except as otherwise required by the Constitution . . . or . . . Act of Congress or in rules prescribed by the Supreme Court pursuant to statutory authority, the privilege of a . . . government . . . shall be governed by the principles of the common law as they may be interpreted by the courts of the United States in the light of reason and experience." Rule 501, Federal Rules of Evidence.
37. Congress got a start on this practice in 2008 when the House passed H.R. 6575, the Over-Classification Reduction Act, at the behest of the Committee on Oversight and Government Reform. It directs the nation's archivist to promulgate rules for the duration of classifications, the identification and training of classifiers, the marking of documents, and classification audits by inspectors general. However, one statute will probably not fit all agencies, which have somewhat different reasons for marking documents secret. Because the incentives to classify far outstrip the incentives to declassify, perhaps each agency should be given a quota on the number of documents that can be under classification at any given time.
38. 5 U.S.C. sec. 552.
39. 44 U.S.C. chapter 22.
40. John Dean, "The Misunderestimated Mr. Cheney: The Vice President's Record of Willfully Violating the Law, and Wrongly Claiming Authority to Do So," FindLaw. com, June 29, 2007, available at http://writ.news.findlaw.com/dean/20070629.html (accessed December 1, 2008).

a note on sources

Any author who accuses public officials of criminal wrongdoing must be candid about his sources. Hence I've included the many endnotes and this note on sources.

Documents

Remarkably, given the subject matter, the core of this book stems from an extensive documentary record, most of it pried out of the Bush administration by exhaustive litigation. The most important compendia are *The Torture Papers: The Road to Abu Ghraib* edited by Karen J. Greenberg and Joshua L. Dratel (New York: Cambridge University Press, 2005), *Torture and Truth: America, Abu Ghraib, and the War on Terror* by Mark Danner (New York: New York Review of Books, 2004), *The Administration of Torture: A Documentary Record from Washington to Abu Ghraib and Beyond* by Jameel Jaffer and Amrit Singh (New York: Columbia University Press, 2007), and *The Enemy Combatant Papers: American Justice, the Courts, and the War on Terror* (New York: Cambridge University Press, 2008), also edited by Karen Greenberg and Joshua L. Dratel. The *Torture Papers* include not only legal memorandums and orders but reports of military investigations into the abuses. Similar documents can be found on websites maintained by the American Civil Liberties Union and the Center for Constitutional Rights. Most records of CIA interrogations, secret prisons, and missing prisoners are still hidden away, if not destroyed. The same is true of thousands of videotapes of military and CIA interrogations and photographs of additional abuses at Abu Ghraib, but the broad outlines of the story can be gleaned from the more than 100,000 pages that have been disclosed.

Biographical Accounts

Biographical accounts need to be treated with some caution, as they are frequently self-serving. That is true not only of prisoner accounts, but of the memoirs of those officials who might, but for the amnesty law, be subject to prosecution. Prisoner accounts are most reliable when they confirm or illustrate standard operating procedures and are best read in conjunction with accounts by former interrogators and guards. For example, these titles—*Enemy Combatant: My Imprisonment at Guantánamo, Bagram, and Kandahar* by Moazzam Begg (New York: New Press, 2006), *Five Years of My Life: An Innocent Man in Guantánamo* by Murat Kurnaz with Helmut Kuhn and translated by Jefferson Chase (New York: Palgrave Macmillan, 2008), *Detainee 002: The Case of David Hicks* by Leigh Sales (Melbourne, Australia: Melbourne University Press, 2007), and *Monstering: Inside America's Policy of Secret Interrogations and Torture in the Terror War* by Tara McKelvey (New York: Carroll & Graff, 2007)—find considerable confirmation in *The Interrogators: Task Force 500 and America's Secret War against al Qaeda* by Chris Mackey and Gregg Miller (New York: Little, Brown, 2004), *Inside the Wire: A Military Intelligence Soldier's Eyewitness Account of Life at Guantánamo* by Erik Saar and Viveca Novak (New York: New American Library, 2007), *Fear Up Harsh: An Army Interrogator's Dark Journey through Iraq* by Tony Lagouranis and Allen Mikaelian (New York: NAL Caliber, 2007), and *Standard Operating Procedure* by Philip Gourevitch and Errol Morris (New York: Penguin, 2008). For insights into the anti-Muslim culture that drove culturally ignorant soldiers at GTMO to persecute their Muslim chaplain (and West Pointer), see *For God and Country: Faith and Patriotism under Fire* by James Yee with Aimee Molloy (New York: Public Affairs, 2005).

For a revealing account of how the torture policy was pushed through, written by an administration lawyer who approved harsh interrogations while disputing John Yoo's legal reasoning and David Addington's bullying, see *The Terror Presidency: Law and Judgment Inside the Bush Administration* by Jack Goldsmith (New York: W. W. Norton, 2007).

Defense Counsel

Some of the best-informed and most insightful accounts of what happened to prisoners at Guantánamo, Abu Ghraib, and elsewhere come from their American and British attorneys. The first path-breaking books, from the Center for Constitutional Rights, were *Secret Trials and Executions: Military Tribunals and the Threat to Democracy* by Barbara Olshansky (New York: Seven Stories Press, 2002), *America's Disappeared: Secret Imprisonment, Detainees, and the "War on Terror"* edited by Rachel Meeropol (New York: Seven Stories Press, 2005), and *Guantánamo: What the World Should Know* by Michael Ratner and Ellen Ray (White River Junction, VT: Chelsea Green, 2004). Other gems include *Enemy Aliens: Double Standards and Constitutional Freedoms in the War on Terrorism* by David Cole (New York: New Press, 2003), *Guantánamo and the Abuse of Presidential Power* by Joseph Margulies (New York: Simon & Schuster, 2006), *Eight O'Clock Ferry to the Windward Side: Seeking Justice in Guantánamo Bay* by Clive Stafford Smith (New York: Nation Books, 2007), *Torture Team: Rumsfeld's Memo and the Betrayal of American Values* by Philippe Sands (New York: Palgrave Macmillan, 2008), and *The Trial of Donald Rumsfeld: A Prosecution by Book* by Michael Ratner (New York: New Press, 2008).

Outstanding Journalists

The making of the torture policy and its cover-up have been investigated and reported by a host of talented reporters, many of whom have been acknowledged in the endnotes. Here I will mention only those who have also written books. Among the best, all by Pulitzer Prize–winning reporters, are *Chain of Command: The Road from 9/11 to Abu Ghraib* by Seymour M. Hersh (New York: HarperCollins, 2004), *Bush's Law: The Remaking of American Justice* by Eric Lichtblau (New York: Pantheon, 2008), *State of War: The Secret History of the CIA and the Bush Administration* by James Risen (New York: Free Press, 2006), *The One Percent Doctrine: Deep Inside America's Pursuit of Its Enemies since 9/11* by Ron Suskind (New York: Simon & Schuster, 2006), *Fiasco: The American Military Adventure in Iraq* by Thomas Ricks (New York: Penguin, 2006), *Legacy of Ashes: The History of the CIA* by Tim Weiner (New York: Doubleday, 2007), and *Takeover: Return of the Imperial Presidency and the Subversion of American Democracy* by Charlie Savage (New York: Little, Brown, 2007). Other books of Pulitzer quality are *A Tragic Legacy: How a Good vs. Evil Mentality Destroyed the Bush Presidency* by Glenn Greenwald (New York: Crown, 2007) and *The Dark Side: The Inside Story of How the War on Terror Turned into a War on American Ideals* by Jane Mayer (New York: Doubleday, 2008).

Legal Analysts

For legal analyses from a reformist perspective, I am deeply indebted to *Unchecked and Unbalanced: Presidential Power in a Time of Terror* by Frederick A. O. Schwarz, Jr., and Aziz Z. Huq (New York: New Press/Brennan Center for Justice, 2007), *Less Safe and Less Free: Why America Is Losing the War on Terror* by David Cole and Jules Lobel (New York: New Press, 2007), *Beyond the Law: The Bush Administration's Unlawful Responses in the "War" on Terror* by Jordan J. Paust (New York: Cambridge University Press, 2007), *Terror and Consent: The Wars for the Twenty-First Century* by Philip Bobbitt (New York: Knopf, 2008), *Protecting Liberty in an Age of Terror* by Philip B. Heymann and Juliette N. Kayyem (Cambridge, MA: MIT Press, 2005), and *Terrorism, Freedom, and Security: Winning Without War* also by Philip B. Heymann (Cambridge, MA: MIT Press, 2003). Equally indispensable, but from conservative perspectives, are *Not a Suicide Pact: The Constitution in a Time of National Emergency* by Richard A. Posner (New York: Oxford University Press, 2006); *War by Other Means: An Insider's Account of the War on Terror* (New York: Atlantic Monthly Press, 2006), and *The Powers of War and Peace: The Constitution and Foreign Affairs after 9/11* (Chicago: University of Chicago Press, 2005), both by John Yoo; and *Law and the Long War: The Future of Justice in the Age of Terror* by Benjamin Wittes (New York: Penguin, 2008).

Political Scientists

As usual, most members of the political science profession have been asleep at the switch. Two stellar exceptions are presidential scholars Richard M. Pious, author of *The War on Terrorism and the Rule of Law* (Los Angeles: Roxbury, 2006), and Louis Fisher, whose foundational works include *Presidential War Power* (Lawrence: University Press of Kansas, 2004), *Nazi Saboteurs on Trial: A Military Tribunal and American Law* (Lawrence: University Press of Kansas, 2005), *The Politics of Executive Privilege* (Durham, NC: Carolina Academic Press, 2004), *Military Tribunals and Presidential Power: American Revolution to the War on Terrorism* (Lawrence: University Press of Kansas, 2005), *In the Name of National Security: Unchecked Presidential Power and the Reynolds Case* (Lawrence: University Press of Kansas, 2006) (on state secrets privilege), *Suspected Terrorists and What to Do with Them* (with Jennifer Elsea) (New York: Novinka Books, 2006), and

The Constitution and 9/11: Recurring Threats to America's Freedoms (Lawrence: University Press of Kansas, 2008).

Historians

While it is a bit early for historians to supply a long view, two who anticipated important issues raised by the torture scandal are Marouf Hasian, Jr., *In the Name of Necessity: Military Tribunals and the Loss of American Civil Liberties* (Tuscaloosa: University of Alabama Press, 2005), and Alfred W. McCoy, *A Question of Torture: CIA Interrogation from the Cold War to the War on Terror* (New York: Metropolitan Books/Henry Holt, 2006).

acknowledgments

My many debts to authors are acknowledged in footnotes and in the note on sources. Here I wish to thank family members, friends, and colleagues who helped me along the way. First, kudos to Donal O'Shea, dean of Mount Holyoke's faculty, and Penny Gill, former chair of the Politics Department, who recognized the scale of this project and urged me to take an unscheduled leave to get it done. Second, thanks to Mount Holyoke College and its faculty grants, which facilitated the project along the way. Special thanks to all who critiqued the manuscript, including Professors Carole E. Straw and Joseph J. Ellis of Mount Holyoke's Department of History; my lawyer sons, Jeffrey Pyle and Jonathan Pyle; lawyer and editor Mickey Rathbun; and editors Don McKeon, Hilary Claggett, and Vicki Chamlee of Potomac Books. Thanks also to Steven B. Buttner, Carole Straw, and John O. Fox, who funneled a steady stream of breaking news my way; Brigid M. Davis, Kara L. Parks, and Cindy F. Pyle, who double- and triple-checked my sources; James Gehrt and Joanna Brown, who chased down photos; Mike German, who introduced me to his publisher; and Joan Davis, who compiled the index.

Finally, of course, there are the debts I can never repay to my wife, Cindy, who makes everything possible.

index

abductions: bill to legalize, 63–64; as cause of War of 1812, 189; by Clinton administration, 64–66; damage to U.S. relations in Latin America by, 189–90; by Reagan administration, 62–64, 167; of sailors, by British navy, 189; of suspects, 183–84; for torture, 61–62; as violations of international law, 65

Abizaid, General John P., 104, 106

Abraham, Lieutenant Colonel Stephen E., 114–15, 213

Abu Ghraib: abuses, 47–56; broadcast of photos of, 106; civilian interrogators at, 50; cover-up, 105; damage to U.S. reputation by, 148–49; failure to prosecute for, 117–20; files, in Defense Department, 268n18; "independent" body of investigators of, 107; interrogations "Gitmo-ized" at, 47; military investigations of, 106–107; military police lack of training at, 54–55; photographs of, x, 1–2, 231

Abu Nidal Organization, 243

accountability, avoidance of, 124, 129–30; restrictions on Taguba investigation as, 106–107; and Schlesinger Report, 51, 107. *See also* CYA doctrine

Achille Lauro affair, 63

Ackerman, Bruce, 205

action heroes, American penchant for, 80

Adams, John, 13–14, 149

Addington, David S., 5–6; addition to president's signing statement by, 161; on admissible evidence, 159; as Cheney's chief of staff, 166; at CIA, 57; criminal responsibility for torture policy, 128; as drafter of memorandums, 27, 88; on U.S. reputation abroad, 151; as GTMO visitor, 93, 99; and incriminating evidence, 109; as member of War Council, 6; meeting of with CIA, 24, 25; in military commissions planning group, 15, 91; remains unpunished, 120; as sycophant, 122

Afghanistan, 70, 74–75; CIA facilities in, 277–78n12; confirmed cases of detainee abuse in, 293n16; interrogation procedures in, 93

Agiza, Ahmed, 66

al Qaeda: lack of affiliation of with a government, 275n134; motivation to support, 229; public's hatred of, 233; training camps, attack on, 102

al-Assad, Muhammad, 69

al-Haj, Sami, 33

Al-Haramain Islamic Foundation, 69, 74

Ali v. Rumsfeld, 227

Alien Tort Claims Statute, 213

aliens, as non-persons, 214

Alito, Samuel, 193, 195–96, 198, 246

al-Jamadi, Manadel, torture to death of, 44–45, 118–19

al-Libi, Ibn al-Sheikh, mistreatment of, 17–18

al-Marri, Ali, 207

al-Nashiri, Abd al-Rahim, 87, 108

al-Qahtani, Muhammed, 49, 98–100, 116, 125, 292n114, 292n118

al-Shibh, Ramzi bin, 144

al-Shiekh, Ameen Sa'eed, 51–52

Altenburg, Major General John D. (Ret.), 159

Altstoetter, Joseph, 131

Alvarez-Macha\u00edn, Humberto, abduction of, 185

al-Zawahiri, Dr. Ayman, 101, 243

al-Zery, Muhammad, 66

American Civil Liberties Union, 223

American colonies: due process in, 37; powers of government in, 37

325

about the author

Christopher H. Pyle teaches constitutional law and civil liberties at Mount Holyoke College in South Hadley, Massachusetts. In 1970, as a former captain in army intelligence, he disclosed the military's surveillance of civilian politics and helped to end it by working for Senator Sam J. Ervin's Judiciary Subcommittee on Constitutional Rights and Senator Frank Church's Select Committee to Study Government Operations with Respect to Intelligence Activities. Pyle is the author of four books, most recently *Extradition, Politics, and Human Rights*. He lives in South Hadley.